D0945413

Religion in America

EARLY HISTORY

OF

THE DISCIPLES

IN THE

WESTERN RESERVE, OHIO

A[mos] S. Hayden

ARNO PRESS

A NEW YORK TIMES COMPANY

Reprint Edition 1972 by Arno Press Inc.

Reprinted from a copy in
The Princeton Theological Seminary Library

RELIGION IN AMERICA - Series II
ISBN for complete set: 0-405-04050-4
See last pages of this volume for titles.

Manufactured in the United States of America

Library of Congress Cataloging in Publication Data

Hayden, Amos Sutton, 1813-1880.
   Early history of the Disciples in the Western
Reserve, Ohio.

   (Religion in America, series II)
   1. Disciples of Christ--Ohio. I. Title.
BX7317.O3H3 1972   286'.6771   76-38449
ISBN 0-405-04068-7

EARLY HISTORY

OF

THE DISCIPLES

IN THE

WESTERN RESERVE, OHIO;

WITH

Biographical Sketches of the Principal Agents in their Religious Movement.

BY

A. S. HAYDEN.

CINCINNATI:

CHASE & HALL, PUBLISHERS.

1875.

PREFACE.

THE beginning of the second quarter of the nineteenth century is memorable as the period when a new and powerful religious awakening began in North-eastern Ohio. The Western Reserve was the principal theater of this benign work. In recording the history of this revival, it will be necessary to trace the origin of the movement; to describe its character, its spirit, and its aims; to note the principal events which attended its origin and progress; and, in turn, to consider this remarkable outburst of Christian zeal and activity in its relation to the future, as the direct and potent cause of succeeding developments in the kingdom of Christ.

This movement was so unexpected, so rapid, so general, and accompanied by many incidents and events so peculiar, as to stamp the phenomenon with the clearest indications of a providential visitation of great mercy to the world. Many of its first advocates were plain, unpretending men, called unexpectedly to the front, and urged forward by the resistless impulses of the work itself. Some of these men exhibited fine oratorial powers. They have left their impress durably on a wide and growing society. Brief biographical sketches of the principal early actors in the scenes to pass before the reader can not fail to be interesting to him. They will also constitute an important part of the record of the times.

Great care has been bestowed on the accuracy of every statement, both of date and incident; a branch of duty often laborious, requiring the collation of many documents, and the reconciliation of conflicting testimonies.

Many persons yet remaining of the generation herein chiefly described, will find in these pages events with which they are personally familiar. The young will discover in the same pages the planting and establishment of principles of religious reform which are now providentially committed to their trust, and which, in their faithful hands, are yet, we hope, to be developed into yet fairer symmetry and greater perfection of individual Christian character, and higher Church order and activity.

As far as possible the whole work has been brought within the following plan :

1. A sketch of the condition of religious society at the opening of the work.

2. A short account of the agencies by which it was accomplished.

3. A history of the work itself.

4. Biographical notices of the principal actors.

A. S. H.

CONTENTS.

CHAPTER V.

CHAPTER VI.

CHAPTER VII.

CHAPTER VIII.

CHAPTER IX.

CHAPTER X.

CHAPTER XI.

CHAPTER XII.

CHAPTER XIII.

CONTENTS. ix

CHAPTER XX.

CHAPTER XXI.

CHAPTER XXII.

The following resolutions, moved by Pres't. B. A. Hinsdale, were passed unanimously by the Western Reserve Christian Preachers' Association, held in Ravenna, Portage Co., Nov. 7, 8, and 9, 1871. There were twenty-two preachers present :

WHEREAS, It is greatly to be desired that the chronicles of the Western Reserve churches should be written: and
WHEREAS, Bro. A. S. Hayden is preëminently the man to write them : therefore,
Resolved, That we affectionately request Bro. Hayden to undertake this work ; and in case he consents, we urgently press upon him the desirability of its being undertaken as speedily, and prosecuted as rapidly, as his other engagements may permit.
Resolved, That we pledge to Bro. Hayden, who has for years been collecting material for such a work, our united coöperation and moral support in his undertaking.

A. B. GREEN, *Pres't. of the Association.*

H. J. WHITE, *Sec.*

THE WESTERN RESERVE:

HISTORY AND DESCRIPTION.

————————

A S we shall have frequent occasion to refer to the
Western Reserve in the course of the following
work, we give here a brief description and historic
account of it. This notice is collected from several
sources, and presented somewhat abridged.

This district of country, also called *Connecticut
Western Reserve*, and *New Connecticut*, is situated
in the north-east part of the State of Ohio. It is
bounded on the north by Lake Erie, east by Pennsylvania, south by the 41st parallel of north latitude,
and on the west by Sandusky and Seneca counties.
It extends 120 miles from east to west, and aver-
ages about 50 from north to south. Its greatest
breadth is at the east end, extending on the Pennsylvania line 68 miles. The area includes about
3,000,000 acres. It embraces the following counties,
viz.: Ashtabula, Trumbull, north part of Mahoning,
Lake, Geauga, Portage, Cuyahoga, Summit, Medina,
Lorain, Erie, and Huron.

Connecticut became possessed of the land in
question in the following manner: King Charles II.
of England, pursuing the example of other sover-
eigns, granted to the colony of Connecticut, in 1662,
a charter-right to all lands in the new world included
within certain specified limits. But as the geo-

graphical knowledge of Europeans concerning America was very limited and confused, patents for lands often interfered with each other, and many of them, by their express terms, extended to the Pacific Ocean, or mythical "South Sea," which the Pacific Ocean was thought to be. Among the rest, that for Connecticut embraced all lands contained between the 41st and 42d parallels of north latitude, and from Providence Plantations on the east to the Pacific Ocean west, with the exception of the colonies of New York and Pennsylvania; and, indeed, pretensions to these were not finally relinquished without considerable altercation. When the colonies, as the result of the Revolutionary War, became a united and independent nation, these interfering claims occasioned much collision between the Federal Government and several of the States; with no one more than Connecticut. Negotiations were pending for several years before a compromise was finally effected. In September, 1786, the State of Connecticut ceded to the United States her claim, both of soil and jurisdiction, to all her charter-lands lying west of the present western limits of the "Western Reserve." On the 30th of May, 1801, she also ceded her jurisdictional claims to all the territory called the "Western Reserve of Connecticut," when, in fulfillment of the compact then formed, the President conveyed, by patent, the *fee* of the soil to the Governor of the State of Connecticut, for the use of grantees and purchasers claiming under her. This tract, including the "Fire Lands," by a proclamation by Gov. St. Clair, September 22, 1800, was all erected into one county, and named *Trumbull*, in honor of two successive governors of Connecticut. Of this mammoth county Warren was the seat of justice.

In May, 1795, the Legislature of Connecticut appointed a commission to issue proposals and make sale of the lands she had "reserved" in the Northwest Territory, afterward Ohio. This committee sold the lands to sundry citizens of that State and of other States. In September of that year the title was confirmed to the purchasers by deeds of conveyance. The purchasers proceeded to survey into townships, of five miles square, the whole of this tract lying east of the Cuyahoga, the Indians still asserting their claims to the portion of it lying west of that river. By a treaty with them at Fort Industry, near Sandusky, in 1805, their claim was finally extinguished in favor of the grantees of Connecticut.

The State of Connecticut sold out the lands to the contractors at 40 cents per acre, receiving for the sale one million two hundred thousand dollars. This money, permanently invested, constitutes her school fund. The State gave only a quit-claim deed, transferring only such title as she possessed, and leaving all the Indian titles of the "Reserve" to be extinguished by the purchasers.

On the 4th of July, 1796, the first surveying party of the Western Reserve landed at the mouth of Conneaut Creek—the Plymouth of the Western Reserve. Patriotic sons of revolutionary sires, and some, themselves, the participants in that immortal struggle, they prepared to give "to the day its due, and to patriotism its awards." With their *tin cups* dipping from the broad lake the crystal waters with

which to pledge the national honor, with the ordnance accompanyment of a few fowling-pieces, they
discharged the national salute. They called the
place Fort Independence.

"A cabin was erected on the bank of Conneaut
Creek, and in honor of the commissary of the expe-
dition, was called 'Stowe Castle.' At this time the
whole inhabitants west of the Genesee River and
along the coasts of the lakes, were as follows: The
garrison at Niagara, two families at Lewiston, one at
Buffalo, one at Cleveland, and one at Sandusky.
There were no other families east of Detroit, and
with the exception of a few adventurers at the 'Salt
Springs' of the Mahoning, the interior of New Connecticut was an unbroken wilderness.

"The work of surveying was commenced at once.
One party went southward on the Pennsylvania line
to find the 41st parallel, and began to survey;
another, under Gen. Cleaveland, coasted along the
lake to the mouth of the Cuyahoga, which they
reached on the 22d of July, and there laid the foundation of the chief city of the Western Reserve. A
large portion of the survey was made during that
season, and the work was completed the following
year."

The surveying party numbered fifty-two persons,
among whom were two females and one child. As
these individuals were the advance of after millions
of population, their names become worthy of record,
and are therefore given, viz.: Moses Cleaveland,
agent of the company; Augustus Porter, principal
surveyor; Seth Pease, astronomer and surveyor;
Moses Warren, Amos Spafford, Milton Hawley,

Richard M. Stoddard, surveyors; Joshua Stowe, commissary; Theodore Shepard, physician; Joseph Tinker, principal boatman; Joseph McIntyre, George Proudfoot, Francis Gay, Samuel Forbes, Elijah Gunn, wife and child, Amos Sawten, Stephen Benton, Amos Barber, Samuel Hungerford, William B. Hall, Samuel Davenport, Asa Mason, Amzi Atwater, Michael Coffin, Elisha Ayres, Thomas Harris, Norman Wilcox, Timothy Dunham, George Goodwin, Shadrach Benham, Samuel Agnew, Warham Shepard, David Beard, John Bryant, Titus V. Munson, Joseph Landon, Job V. Stiles and wife, Charles Parker, Ezekiel Hawley, Nathaniel Doan, Luke Hanchet, James Hasket, James Hamilton, Olney F. Rice, John Locke, and four others whose names are not mentioned.

2

CHAPTER I.

PRELIMINARY AGENCIES.

Debates with Walker and McCalla—The Christian Baptist—The Mahoning Association—Creed and Constitution—Memorable Sermon by A. Campbell—Biographies of Elder Thomas Campbell, and of A. Campbell.

AMONG the causes operating to bring about a scriptural reform among the churches on the Western Reserve, the following chain of events claims a prominent place:

In the month of June, 1820, a discussion was held in Mt. Pleasant, Ohio, between A. Campbell, founder and principal of the Buffalo Academy, Va., and Rev. John Walker, a minister of acknowledged ability among the Seceders. The discussion, taken down and published, was a marked event of the times. Mr. Campbell had already considerable reputation for scholarship and ability, and for his advocacy of the Christian religion as unfolded in the Bible, as distinguished from its embodiment in the creeds and denominationalism of the day. Some of the more cautious of the Baptist ministers, with whom he then had a standing, were startled by the boldness and novelty of some of his views, especially in respect to the nature and claims of the Law of Moses, as propounded in his famous sermon on that subject before the Redstone Association in 1816. A large majority, however, listened to his views and reasonings with instructed approbation.

Among the more liberal in sentiment was Adamson Bentley, pastor of the Baptist church in Warren, Ohio. He had read the debate with Walker. Forming a high estimate of Mr. Campbell's powers, and rightly judging that God had raised him up for a great work, he resolved at the earliest opportunity to make his personal acquaintance.

A providential opportunity soon came for him to fulfill his purpose. Called into Kentucky on a mission for the churches, he returned by Mr. Campbell's residence. Sidney Rigdon was with him. The following is Mr. Campbell's account of their interview:

"After tea in the evening, we commenced and prolonged our discourse till the next morning. Beginning with the baptism that John preached, we went back to Adam, and forward to the judgment. The dispensations or covenants—Adamic, Abrahamic, Jewish and Christian —passed and repassed before us. Mount Sinai in Arabia, Mount Zion, Mount Calvary, Mount Tabor, the Red Sea and the Jordan, the Passovers and the Pentecosts, the Law and the Gospel—but especially the ancient order of things and the modern—occasionally commanded and engaged our attention.

"On parting the next day, Sidney Rigdon, with all apparent candor, said, if he had within the last year taught and promulgated from the pulpit one error he had a thousand. At that time he was the great orator of the Mahoning Association—though in authority with the people second always to Adamson Bentley. I found it expedient to caution them not to begin to pull down any thing they had builded, until they had reviewed, again and again, what they had heard ; nor even then rashly and without

much consideration.   Fearing that they might undo their
influence with the people, I felt constrained to restrain,
rather than urge them forward in the work of reformation.

"With many an invitation to visit the Western Reserve, and with many an assurance of a full and candid
hearing on the part of the uncommitted community, and
an immediate access to the ears of the Baptist churches
within the sphere of their influence, we took the parting
hand.   They went on their way rejoicing, and in the
course of a single year prepared the whole association to
hear us with earnestness and candor."

Investigations of Bible truth led to liberality of
views among the people, and especially in the Baptist churches.   The Mahoning Association was
founded on the Philadelphia Confession of Faith as
its organic law.   But this system of doctrine did not
receive the cordial consent of all.   Discussions were
common among the ministry and the members on
the law as a rule of life for Christians—whether it
was ever binding on Gentiles—the nature of faith—
and the necessity for any other rules of faith or
church articles besides the Holy Scriptures.   As the
light came apace, many became convinced that much
reformation was needed to bring the churches up to
the New Testament models

It is probably illogical to refer this movement
toward reform, so wide and so active, to any one
leading impulse.   As in all similar general movements which have become permanent, it is probably
more correct to assign the result to several concurrent causes.   The peculiar character of the population of the Western Reserve, mostly from New
England, with a liberal intermingling of people from

other States, resulting in comparisons, often in col-
lisions of views, was a powerful stimulus to investigation.   Yet history would not be faithful to omit,
as among the most direct evident causes and guides
in this increasing demand for a restoration of the
divinely established order of the Gospel, the writings
and personal labors of Alexander Campbell.   His debate with Rev. John Walker, published in 1821, and
that with Rev. W. L. McCalla, which appeared in
1824, distinguished by freedom from conventional
forms of belief, and by their boldness and clearness
of exposition of Scripture, served in some sort as a
warrant to others equally inclined but less bold to
burst the denominational shell in which they felt
themselves confined.

Added to these the " Christian Baptist," to which
the preface was written the 4th of July, 1823, went
forth monthly to advocate definitely and distinct-
ively the restoration of the apostolic teaching and
practice in all things ; in faith, conversion, baptism,
the office of the Holy Spirit, church order, and,
summarily, every thing authorized by Jesus Christ,
the Author and Finisher of the Christian religion.

Many were prepared to welcome the " Christian
Baptist" when it first appeared.   In the winter of
1822–3, Elder Bentley discoursed frequently on such
themes as " The Law," " The Scriptures a Sufficient
Guide," etc.   Jacob Osborne, though young, was
active and influential in promoting this search of
the word for " things new and old."   Sidney Rigdon
added the persuasions of a very commanding and
popular eloquence.   Joseph Freeman, a promising
young Baptist minister, who had spent some time in

Mr. Campbell's seminary, made a tour of preaching
in the winter of 1823-4, helping forward the tide
now setting in toward Jerusalem. His worthy father
also, the pious Elder Rufus Freeman, though never
fully committed to follow the Apostles *withersoever*
they go, yet took the liberal side in frequent discourses. Nor should the name of Edward Scofield
be omitted as one of the same class. Besides these,
many of less public note, as Deacon Rudolph, of
Garrettsville; Jesse Hall, of Hubbard; Benjamin
Ross, of Youngstown; David Hays and William
Dean, of Canfield, with many others whose names
are in the Lamb's Book of Life, were hoping and
laboring for a better day.

This was especially true of the younger class of
preachers, whose intellectual and religious activities
were more ready for the coming investigations; such
men as Marcus Bosworth, William Hayden, Darwin
Atwater, Zeb Rudolph, John Applegate, Nathan
Porter, and William Collins.

The disallegiance to creeds and confessions, and
confidence in the sufficiency of the Holy Scriptures,
gained steady advancement. The Baptist church
of Nelson, organized in 1808, by Elder Thos. G.
Jones, was composed of members scattered over the
territory of Nelson, Hiram, and a part of Mantua.
So thoroughly satisfied had many of its members
become of the detriment of the Confession of Faith
to mature Christian manhood, that at a meeting of
this church, held August 24, 1824, a resolution was
passed, nearly unanimously, "to remove the Philadelphia Confession of Faith and the Church Articles, and to take the Word of God for our Rule of

Faith and Practice." The two classes of views on
the step thus taken were on the alert to maintain
their ground. The brethren leading on this reform
were Deacon John Rudolph, his two sons John and
Zeb, and Darwin Atwater. The opposition was led
by Mrs. Garrett, whose skill in *fencing*, shrewdness,
and determination, united with piety and talent, put
her forward without an effort of hers, as the counselor and manager of the cause of the dissidents.
She was a lady of culture and intelligence, well
skilled in the "doctrines of grace" and the methods
of their defense. She was a daughter of Rev. Dr.
Jones, a Baptist minister, who held a chaplaincy
under General Washington in the Revolutionary War.
She lived to a great age. She was a prodigy of
memory, displaying to the last the most accurate re-
tention of names, dates, and events.

The meeting of the association came close after
this action of the church in Nelson. The church
appointed Elder Rufus Freeman, its pastor; James
Rudolph and Darwin Atwater as her messengers to
that body. As no counteraction could be taken by
the opposing members with any show of authority,
Mrs. Garrett wrote a letter warning the association
not to receive these messengers. No notice was
taken of her letter, and the messengers were received. The next year, 1825, the association convened in Palmyra. Both parts of the church sent
messengers, and all were received. For the reforming brethren they were: Jacob Osborne, ordained
minister, John Rudolph and John Rudolph, Jr. In
behalf of those holding the "Articles," Joshua
Maxon, Martin Manly, and Joseph Tinker.

It will be readily seen in these movements of the churches, the origin of the queries which were sent to the association at Hubbard. They were received, entered on record, but held under advisement a whole year. In the minutes of its meeting in Palmyra, 1825, the answers are given. The questions and answers are put together here. This was Mr. Campbell's first appearance in the Mahoning Association:

"*Answers to the queries from the church at Nelson.*

" *Query* 1. Will this association hold in its connection a church which acknowledges no other rule of faith and practice than the Scriptures?

"*Ans.* Yes. On satisfactory evidence that they walk according to this rule.

" *Query* 2. In what manner were members received into the churches that were set in order by the Apostles?

"*Ans.* Those who believed and were baptized were added to the church.

" *Query* 3. How were members excluded from those churches?

"*Ans.* By a vote of the brethren.

"*Answer to the query from New Lisbon.*

" *Query.* Is it scriptural to license a brother to administer the word, and not the ordinances?

"*Ans.* We have no such custom taught in the scriptures.

"*Answer to the query from Randolph*, viz.:

Can associations in their present modifications find their model in the New Testament?

"*Ans.* Not exactly."

The tendency of religious inquiry is here clearly exhibited. The source also of some of the answers

is discernible. The answer to the last one at
least is authoritatively attributed to Mr. Campbell.
The wisdom of it, admitting the need of a scriptural
reformation, yet carefully avoiding direct collision
with the tenacious elders, was commented on at the
time as evidence of his prudence in counsel.

The Mahoning Association, its Constitution and Creed.

Associations among the Baptists are voluntary
unions of churches, for mutual encouragement, for
counsel in church affairs, and for protection against
heresy and impostors. Each church is entitled to
three representative messengers, who bring with
them a written statement of its creed. If this document is orthodox, or in harmony with its accepted
standards of faith, the church is received by a plu-
rality vote, upon which the moderator gives the
right hand of fellowship to its messengers, and bids
them to a seat.

The Mahoning Association was formed on Wednesday, the 30th of August, 1820. There is something curious, if not significant, in the fact that in
those days the associations took their names from
rivers: Thus we had the Beaver Association, the
Grand River Association; one bears the name of
Huron, another is called Stillwater; and the Mahoning River is equally honored.

Another circumstance: Baptist churches were in
the habit of assuming names having a sentimental
or historical import. Thus the church of Warren
was called "Concord;" that in Nelson "Bethesda"—probably in allusion to John v: 2, and the

3

healing of the helpless by the compassionate Redeemer. The church in Youngstown took the name
"Zoar," significantly reminding its members that
when the LORD rained upon Sodom and upon Go-
morrah brimstone and fire from the LORD out of
heaven, Lot found safety by fleeing from destruction, and entering into *Zoar*. Gen. xix: 23, 24. A
church on the Sandy was known as the "Valley of
Achor," teaching us that admission into it was en-
trance into a "door of hope." Hosea ii: 15. The
church in Hubbard was "Mount Hope." "Bethel"
is met with in several associations.

These and others are found on the records of their
history. It is important to know them, not only as
showing a habit of that people, but as explanatory
of some things in the history.

The constitution of the "Mahoning Baptist Association" declares:

"It is our object to glorify God. This we would endeavor to do by urging the importance of the doctrine
and precepts of the gospel in their moral and evangelical
nature, commending ourselves to every man's conscience
in the sight of God; not pretending to have authority
over any man's [conscience,] nor over the churches,
whose representatives form this association. But we act
as an advisory counsel only, disclaiming all superiority, jurisdiction, coercive right and infallibility; and acknowledg-
ing the independence of every church ; which has received
authority from Christ to perform all duties enjoined respecting the government of his church in this world."

If ecclesiastical authority was vested in the association, it will be seen that it existed in a very mild
form. It was not constituted as a court of appeal.

It assumed no judicial nor executive powers over the churches. It existed as an "advisory council" merely, and for the custodial charge of "the doctrine" and "the precepts" of the gospel. What the association meant by "the doctrine" and "the precepts" of the gospel will be apparent a little further on when we give its "creed," for the conservation of which the framers of its constitution deemed it important to compact the churches into this union. It is safe to say that of all the forms of modern ecclesiasticism, the association was the least liable to complaint, as it contained the greatest liberty with the least "coercive" restraint upon the conscience. It is to be lamented that all bodies are liable to transcend their constitutional limits, and in some States the association has been made an engine of usurpation and tyranny, of which the "Star Chamber" in its healthiest day might have been emulous. The "Beaver Anathema," the "Appomattox and Dover Decrees" of Pennsylvania and of Virginia, are ample confirmations of the truth of this statement, as also the tortuous and vindictive policy of the Redstone Association. But those outbursts of clerical intolerance were spasmodic and unauthorized, resulting in far greater damage to the actors in those scenes of persecution, than to the disciples against whom their fulminations of power were directed.

The creed of the association is thus set forth in its constitution:

"The doctrine of this association is as follows:

"1. Three persons in the Godhead—the Father, the Word, and the Holy Ghost; and these three are one. 1 John v: 7.

" 2. Eternal and personal election to holiness, and the adoption of children by Jesus Christ the Redeemer. Eph. 1 : 4, 5.

" 3. The condemnation of all mankind in consequence of Adam's transgression. Rom. v: 16, 18.

" 4. The depravity of all mankind, in all the faculties of the soul, the understanding, will, and affections. Col. i : 18; Acts xxvi: 18; Eph. iv: 18, 23; John v: 40; Rom. viii. 7.

" 5. Particular redemption by the blood of Jesus Christ. Rom. v: 9 ; Isa. xxxv. 10; John vi: 37, 39.

" 6. Pardon of all sin through the merits of Christ's blood to all true believers. 1 John i: 7; Col. i: 14; Acts x: 43.

" 7. Free justification by the righteousness of Christ imputed to all true believers. Jer. xxxiii: 6 ; 1 Cor. i: 30 ; Rom. ix: 5, 18, 19.

" 8. The irresistible power of the Holy Ghost in re-generation. Eph. ii: 1 ; John i: 13.

" 9. The perseverance of the saints in grace, by the power of God unto eternal life. John x: 27, 28, 29 ; Col. iii: 3, 9 ; John x: 29.

" 10. Water baptism, by immersion of the whole body of the party, so as to be buried with Christ by baptism ; and not by sprinkling or pouring, as the manner of some is. Mark i: 9, 10; John iii: 23 ; Acts viii: 38, 39 ; Rom. vi: 4; Col. ii: 12; Heb. x: 22.

" 11. The subjects of baptism : those who repent of their sins and believe in Christ, and openly confess⋅ faith in the Son of God. Matt. iii: 8 ; Acts viii: 37 ; x: 47.

" 12. The everlasting punishment of the finally impen-itent in as unlimited sense as the happiness of the right-eous. Matt. xxv: 41–46 ; Mark iii: 29 ; Rev. xiv: 11.

" 13. We believe that the first day of the week is the

Lord's day, and that it ought to be held sacred to the
memory of Christ's glorious resurrection, and devoted in a
special manner to the duties of religion.

" Finally, we believe the Holy Scriptures to be the only
certain rule of faith and practice."

The Mahoning Association was formed from the
Beaver, and in this statement of its faith it copied,
without change, that of the Beaver Association.

It is remarkable that while the association declared
fully its creed in its constitution, each church was
at liberty to form its own creed, only provided its
declaration of doctrine agreed in sentiment with that
of the association.   It seemed to be much trouble to
" fix " this business.   A creed mania prevailed, and
the churches vied with each other in fencing out
heresy, and fencing in their orthodoxy with walls
broad and high, built of the " soundest " material of
Christendom.   Their Calvinism was the diamond of
" purest ray serene."   They sought to eliminate all
gaseous and volatile elements from the mixture.
They aimed to form a compound of belief so pure,
doctrinally, and so translucent, that it should resist
the action of the elements and never more be subject
to corrosion or decay!

Alas! for all human hope!   Revolution stops not
to unbuild.   It often sweeps the foundation of many
a massive structure, and with it its admired turret,
cope, and dome.   When it became apparent that
these belabored theories of divine grace and of human regeneration were not the gospel delivered
over to the Holy Twelve, it mattered little how
sound, or firm, or beautiful.   They were in the way.
They were "stumbling blocks" in the way of the

union of the Lord's people.   Remove them, saith the
prophet.   Isa. lvii : 14.

As a specimen of the orthodox belief which could
pass the gate unchallenged, I append two articles of
the creed of one of the strong churches of the association.   It is the articles of belief of the church of
Youngstown, called " Zoar."   This creed was copied
by several other churches, evidently because the
tone of its ring showed it to be pure metal.   The
whole creed of this church is elaborated in thirteen
articles of great length and precision:

" 8. We believe that the work of regeneration, conversion, sanctification, and belief is not an act of man's free
will and power, but of the mighty, efficacious, and irresistible grace of God.

" 9. We believe that all those who are chosen by the
Father, redeemed by the Son, and sanctified by the Spirit,
shall certainly and finally persevere ; so that not one of
them shall ever perish, but shall have everlasting life."

Does the reader weary under its length and pon-
derous terms ?   What think you, then, of the patience
of the saints of those days, who, four times a year,
sat uncovered and reverent to hear it all ; nay,
whose pity is not awakened for the new converts,
the lambs, who must hear it over, and profess belief in each and every item of it !   When Philip
said to the eunuch " If thou believest with all thy
heart thou mayest "—as he had never seen and mas-
tered this confession, nor any other of modern orthodoxy—it is certain he simply called for the convert's faith in Jesus Christ as alone sufficient for
obedience and all the demands of a new life.

It is cheering to know that ever since the great

Saxon sounded the note of liberty of conscience, every new body is more and more liberal, approaching gradually to the primitive order of the gospel of Christ. The Mahoning Association was no exception. It was far more tolerant than its ecclesiastical ancestors, the Redstone and the Wooster Associations. As proof, in 1824, she admitted the church of Wellsburg, Virginia, with a statement of belief containing not one hint of the "doctrines of grace," commonly known as Calvinism! In that year the church of Wellsburg was formed, the members having been dismissed for that purpose from the church of Brush Run, and it sought admission into the Mahoning Association. It appointed A. Campbell, John Brown, and George Young its messengers to carry the church letter and to ask admission.

The statement of belief which these messengers bore to the association, was written by Mr. Campbell, who himself did not attend its meeting, wishing to be present at the Redstone Association, where a coalition was forming against him on account of his published views of reformation.

The statement of belief here follows, copied from the records of the association, which met that year in Hubbard:

"A Belief of the Wellsburg Church.

"We have agreed to walk together in obedience to the authority and institution of our Lord and King, as exposed in the form of sound words delivered unto us by the apostles, evangelists, and prophets of the Savior, and recorded in the Holy Scriptures of the volume called the New Testament. Our views of this volume are briefly these:—We believe that the whole Christian religion is fully and explicitly developed in it, and that nothing is ever to be added thereto, either by any new revelations of the Spirit, or by any doctrines or commandments of men; but that it is, as presented to us, perfectly adapted to all the wise and holy ends of its all-wise and benevolent Author.

"From this volume, with the Old Testament Scripture, which we also receive as of divine inspiration and authority, we learn every thing necessary to be known of God, his works of creation, providence and redemption; and considering the Old Testament as containing the Jew's religion as fully as the New contains the Christian, we avail ourselves of both as containing every thing profitable for doctrine, for reproof, for correction and instruction in righteousness, to make the man of God perfect, thoroughly furnished unto every good work. But we adhere to the New, as containing the whole Christian religion. The New teaches us—and we solemnly declare our belief of it—that Jesus of Nazareth is the Son of God, the Savior, which was to come into the world; that died for our sins, was buried, and rose again the third day from the dead, and ascended to the right hand of the Majesty on high; that after his ascension he sent down the Holy Spirit to convince the world of sin, of righteousness, and of judgment, by giving testimony of the Savior, and by confirming the word of the apostles by signs, and miracles, and spiritual gifts; that every one that believeth by means of the demonstration of the Holy Spirit and the power of God, is born of God, and overcometh the world, and hath eternal life abiding in him; that such persons, so born of the Spirit, are to receive the washing of water as well as the renewal of the Holy Spirit in order to admission into the Church of the living God.

"And that such being the natural darkness and enmity

of the children of men, and their hearts so alienated from
the life of God through the ignorance that is in them and
by their wicked works, none can enter into this kingdom
of heaven but in consequence of the regeneration or renewal of the Holy Spirit. For it is now, as it ever was,
that only to as many as received Him, who are born not
of blood, nor the will of the flesh, but of God, does He
give power to become the sons of God, even to them that
believe in His name. For we are born again not of cor-
ruptible seed, but by the incorruptible seed of the word
of God, which abideth forever.

"Our views of the Church of God are also derived
from the same source, and from it we are taught that it is
a society of those who have believed the record that God
gave of His Son : that this record is their bond of union ;
that after a public profession of this faith, and immersion
into the name of the Father, Son, and Holy Spirit, they
are to be received and acknowledged as brethren for
whom Christ died. That such a society has a right to
appoint its own bishops and deacons, and to do all and
every thing belonging to a church of Christ, independent
of any authority under heaven."

This document is especially noticeable for—

Its manly independence ;

Its freedom from technicality and creed verbiage ;

Its comprehension of the whole matter of faith
and obedience to Christ ;

Its marked exaltation of the Holy Scriptures ;

Its assertion of their absolute sufficiency for all
Christian purposes ;

Its discrimination between the Jewish and Christian portions of the Bible ;

Its declaration of the necessity of personal regeneration ;

Its recognition of the Holy Spirit as the agent of that change;

Its affirmation of the power of the gospel as the means of faith and conversion;

Its repudiation of all human authority over the churches;

Finally, that it contains the germs of the religious reformation about being initiated, and which has since spread so wonderfully in the world.

In August, 1826, the Mahoning Baptist Association was held in Canfield, then in Trumbull County. It convened in a barn belonging to David Hays, who was a pillar in the church. Adamson Bentley was the moderator, and Joab Gaskill, clerk.

Among the ministers in attendance were A. Bentley; Thomas Campbell and Alexander Campbell, of Virginia; Walter Scott, of Pittsburgh; Sidney Rigdon, Thomas Miller, William West, Corbly Martin, and Jacob Osborne.

It was customary in the association to have preaching for the public while the messengers were transacting business. A. Campbell preached on Saturday. Disapproving of all priestly style, either in language, mien, or garb, he was dressed in a plain suit of drab. He stood up as a man—a Christian man—rather than as a "minister," to teach the Christian religion as he read it in the Scriptures. His manner impressed even youth with his superiority. He was somewhat emaciated, suffering from dyspepsia. His subject was the 7th chapter of Romans: a deep subject, but his exhibition of it was so lucid and instructive that he riveted attention to the close.

The meeting, Saturday, ended with a baptism.

The congregation retired over a lawn of velvet and green to a stream near by, flowing among rocks, and skirted by a grove. They proceeded to the water singing, and returned in the same manner.

The Congregational meeting-house, at the center of the town, was procured for Sunday. At a very early hour it was filled, and many around it endeavored to hear. Rigdon and Scott preached in the morning. Some having heard the eloquent preacher from Pittsburgh, left the meeting, supposing they had heard Mr. Campbell, whose name had already become famous. Mr. Campbell followed after a brief recess. He founded his discourse on Malachi iv: 2: "Unto you that fear my name, shall the Sun of righteousness arise with healing in his wings." He announced his theme, "The Progress of revealed Light." His discourse abounded in thoughts so fresh, he made his theme so luminous and instructive, that the most rapt attention followed him throughout the delivery.

Seizing on the evident analogy between light and knowledge, and using the former, as the Scripture every-where does, as a metaphor for the latter, the eloquent preacher exhibited the gradual and progressive unfolding of divine revelation under four successive periods of development, which he characterized as, 1st, The Starlight Age; 2d, The Moonlight Age; 3d, The Twilight Age; 4th, The Sunlight Age; and employed these respectively to explain, 1st, The Patriarchal; 2d, The Jewish Dispensation; 3d, The ministry of John the Baptist, with the personal ministry of the Lord on the earth; and, 4th, The full glory of the perfect system of salvation under the apostles when the Holy Spirit was poured out on them, after the ascension and coronation of Jesus as Lord of all.   Under his remarks, and applications of his theme, the whole Bible became luminous with a light it never before seemed to possess.   The scope of the whole book appeared clear and intelligible ; its parts were so shown to be in harmony with each other, and with the whole, that the exhibition of the subject seemed little else to many than a new revelation, like a " second sun risen on midnoon," shedding a flood of light on a book hitherto looked upon as dark and mysterious.   The style of the preacher was plain, common sense, manly.   His argumentation was sweeping, powerful, and convincing ; and above all, and better, his manner of preaching formed so pleasing and instructive a contrast with the customary style of taking a text merely, or of sermonizing, in which mystery prevailed and the " darkness " became " visible," that the assembly listened to the last of a long address scarcely conscious of the lapse of time.   At the conclusion of the sermon, after dwelling with earnest and thrilling eloquence on the glory of the gospel dispensation, the consummation of all the revelations of God, the Sun of righteousness " now risen with healing in his wings," putting an end to the moonlight and starlight ages, he proceeded :

   " The day of light, so illustrious in its beginning, became cloudy.   The Papacy arose and darkened the heavens for a long period, obscuring the brightness of the risen glory of the Sun of righteousness so that men groped in darkness.   By the reformation of the 17th century that dark cloud was broken in fragments ; and though the

heavens of gospel light are still obscured by many clouds—
the sects of various names—the promise is that 'at evening-
time it shall be light.' The primitive gospel, in its
effulgence and power, is yet to shine out in its original
splendor to regenerate the world.''

That discourse was never forgotten. It never will
be. It formed an era in respect to the gospel on the
Western Reserve. The shell of sect-sermons was
broken. The Bible was a new book; its meaning
could be comprehended; its language could be
understood.

Early in August, 1823, was issued from Buffalo
Creek, Va., (now Bethany), the first number of the
"Christian Baptist." It was edited by Alex. Campbell.
It was a monthly, devoted to the promulgation, exposition and defense of the Christian religion as it is
expressly revealed in the New Testament. Its bold
exposition of prevailing errors, and uncompromising
defense of the "faith once delivered to the saints,"
will be at once perceived by the Scripture motto
which stood at the head of every monthly number
for the whole seven years it continued to be published:

" *Style no man on earth your father; for He alone
is your father who is in heaven; and all ye are brethren. Assume not the title of Rabbi; for ye have only
one teacher: neither assume the title of leader, for ye
have only one leader, the Messiah:*" *instructions of the
Lord Messiah, in Matth. xxiii: 8, 9.*

The sentiments and positions of the "Christian
Baptist" were so fresh, so free from the shackles of
doctrinal form peculiar to any sect, so rational, manifestly so scriptural, and enforced by abilities so
varied and commanding, that the work increased its

circulation every year.   It paid no deference to reigning customs.   Following its motto, it owned no master, no leader, but Christ.   Its editor was unsparing
in his denunciations of the clergy, who, as he averred,
had usurped the thrones of the Holy Twelve.   The
exclusive right of the inspired apostles to the twelve
thrones of Christendom, was asserted and vindicated
with great power.   It was the peculiar feature of the
"Christian Baptist" that it put forth no doctrinal basis
on which to unite the disciples of Christ, except
what the apostles proclaimed at the beginning.

The boldness of its bugle-blast of reform startled
the slumbering camps of the half-sleeping Israel.
Gideon's cake, which smote the tent and laid it all
along in ruins, was not more significant nor decisive
in its portent of the issues of the coming contest.

Mr. Campbell's visits to the Western Reserve, not
only at the annual gatherings of the associations, but
at the ministers' meetings also, gave great impulse to
the views of reform propounded in his periodical, and
thus prepared the way for a mighty breaking up in
things ecclesiastic, and the revolution soon to follow.
These ministers' meetings among the Baptist preachers were much the same as the preachers' associations more recently established among the Disciples.
It seems, from best obtainable information, that
Elder Adamson Bentley was chiefly instrumental
in establishing them.   Being himself a gentleman
of culture, possessed of more than the average education and reading existing among the Baptist cler-
gymen of that day—having, with other advantages,
had the benefits of association with the celebrated
Dr. Stoughton of Philadelphia—he felt the need of

elevating the standard of ministerial qualification among his Baptist brethren. He accordingly encouraged them to meet statedly for mutual improvement.

In June, 1821, the ministers' meeting was held in Warren. Mr. Campbell attended, and this was probably his first visit to the Western Reserve. His reputation had preceded him. William Hayden and many others came to the meeting, desiring to hear him and make his acquaintance.

When Hayden entered the house, Mr. Campbell was speaking. He had never seen him, but was familiar with his name and his history. "Who is that?" he said to himself—"so tall and straight, with such piercing eyes! What a shrill, penetrating voice! That must be Campbell." So he thought and so it was. He was far in advance of the preachers present in learning, ability, and acquaintance with the Christian institution, yet he declined asserting any superiority among them, leaving them the fullest liberty of discourse and investigation.

Some one propounded the question "Whether the apostolic preaching and mode of establishing churches is an example binding on us?" "Certainly," responded Mr. Campbell, in his turn, "in all cases possible." The subject of *election*, a doctrine held by all the Baptist ministry, came up for remark, as one of the sermons was under review. Mr. Campbell affirmed "that preaching the doctrine of election never converted a single sinner to God." "Astonishing!" retorted Elder Freeman, "Astonishing!" "Where are they?" inquired Mr. Campbell. Mr. Freeman replied, "all around you!" "I very much

doubt it," responded Mr. Campbell; adding, "you
have preached election, foreordination, effectual calling and perseverance; and along with it you have
held up the love of God to lost sinners, the death of
Christ for their salvation, his resurrection for their
justification, the final judgment and eternal glory:
sinners were converted, and you have attributed it to
the Calvinistic 'doctrines of grace.'"

The right interpretation of the Scriptures; that
they were to be understood; that the same rules of
interpretation were to be applied to them, as to other
writings; that no new rules were to be coined for
their benefit; that they were not to be applied to the
building up of any sect; that the word of God,
rightly interpreted and applied, would put an end to
religious controversy, and restore the primitive union
of the church; these, and kindred themes, as novel
to many as they were convincing, came up in statement and illustration.

It is necessary in opening this history to present
a short biography of some of the men through whose
instrumentality God led his people into a clearer
knowledge of his "ancient paths." They were men
of no mean abilities, and descended from a race not
unknown in history. The Campbell clan of Scotland
and the North of Ireland was once the most numerous and among the most powerful of the races
which in feudal times disputed for the mastery of
Scotland. Inheriting the high, ambitious, and cherished traditional honors of such an ancestry, when
the heroic Knox rescued that mountain land from the
grasp of Romanism, and established there the Ge-
nevan reformation, they enlisted in the defense of

Presbyterianism with all the enthusiasm which, in former times, distinguished the tournament and the profession of arms; and even when that form of religion was shattered by the shock of religious strife, and riven into fragmentary sects, the world witnessed, on another theater, a display of the characteristic qualities of this race of noble men:

Biography of T. Campbell.

Thomas Campbell,* father of Alexander Campbell, descended from the Campbells of Argyleshire. He was born in County Down, near Newry, Ireland, February 1, 1763. He was the oldest of four sons. His father, Archibald Campbell, who served as a soldier in the British Army under General Wolfe, and who was at the capture of Quebec, gave him and his three brothers, James, Archibald, and Enos, the advantages of culture and an English education in a military academy.

Thomas Campbell began in early life to exhibit the serious and meditative dispositions of heart which in all his life were so manifest to all who knew him. The rigid formalities of the Episcopal Church, of which his father was a strict member, failed to satisfy the deeply religious feelings, which were early awakened in him. He fled to the gospels. He found more congenial, spiritual aliment among the warm-hearted and zealous Seceders. Among this people—a branch of the Presbyterian Church, a secession from the Kirk of Scotland—he became deeply anxious for his soul's salvation. He passed through mental struggles of indescribable anguish. The coveted peace at length dawned on his soul, and in the raptures of grat-

---

* For the materials of this sketch of this excellent man, I am chiefly indebted to Prof. Richardson's learned and admirable work, "Memoirs of A. Campbell;" to which the reader is referred for fuller information.

4

itude for so great a deliverance, he resolved to consecrate himself to the public service of the blessed Redeemer, to whom his soul now clung with the ardors of a most devoted love. He was soon rapidly on the road to the ministry. Being an excellent English scholar, he engaged for awhile in teaching. In the University of Glasgow he completed the usual classical studies, and also a course in medicine and lectures in law. He next completed the theological course in Divinity Hall, under Archibald Bruce, D.D., a master of profound abilities, and was commissioned, under the rigid and thorough examinations of the Scotch Seceder Church, with the full credentials of the Christian ministry.

In June, 1787, he was united in marriage to Miss Jane Corneigle, whose ancestors were of the French Huguenots, the Protestant reformers who were driven out of France by the bloody persecutions of the papacy under Louis XIV. She was a lady of equal dignity and gentleness, with mental and moral endowments fitted to be a queen. With this superior Christian woman, the faithful companion of all his cares and toils, Elder Thomas Campbell spent the greater part of his laborious and useful life. She was the mother of eight children, four sons and four daughters—one son dying young—and lived to impress her own virtues upon all.

Mr. Campbell served for some time as a pastor of a church near the city of Armagh. His habits in that capacity were ordered by the same rules of exactness, thoroughness, and affectionate kindness which marked all his course in life. He visited, conversed, taught the people privately the duties of social life, prayed with them, relieved them, in which benefaction his wife was ever his cheerful assistant, and in many ways labored for the increase of the piety and the personal improvement of the people under his charge.

He cultivated early and ever that deep reverence for

the Bible which made him so familiar with its meaning
and its language, and, which, by exalting the word of
God into such incomparable pre-eminence above all human compositions, laid the foundations for the attempt to
discard all human creeds as bonds of union, and to unite
all the true followers of Christ into the 'unity of the
spirit and the bond of peace.' His faith was equal to
any demands upon it from that infallible, divine authority.
Simple trusting reliance on the Lord, and childlike obedience to all his known requirements constituted the whole
of his religion practically viewed.

An anecdote related of him by Professor Richardson,
so strikingly illustrates this admirable trait of his religious
life, and displays so well his calm self-possession, that I do
not withhold it.

During the political agitations, embittered by the heated
antipathies of Catholics and Protestants, by which society was rent and life made insecure, "Mr. Campbell
was one day preaching to a congregation, when the house
was suddenly surrounded by a troop of Welsh Horse, no-
torious for their severities and outrages on those they conceived to be rebels. The captain, conceiving that in this
remote place he had come upon a meeting of the rebels,
dismounted, and in a threatening manner marched into
the church. It was a moment of awful suspense. The
audience were panic-stricken, expecting every moment to
be subjected to the fury of the soldiers. Just at this moment, as the captain stalked up the aisle, casting fierce
glances on all sides, a venerable elder sitting near Mr.
Campbell called to him solemnly: '*Pray, sir !*' Where-
upon, in response to the call, and in a deep, unfaltering
voice, he began in the language of the forty-sixth Psalm:
'Thou, O God, art our refuge and strength: a very present help in trouble. Therefore will we not fear though
the earth be removed, and though the mountains be carried into the depths of the sea.' No sooner was the

first verse uttered, then the captain paused, and, apparently impressed, bent his head, listened to the close, then bowed, and retracing his steps, mounted his horse and dashed away with his entire troop."

Under the united duties of the care of the church, and the work of teaching, his health was impaired. A sea voyage was resolved upon as the necessary means of recovery. Accordingly on the 8th of April, 1807, after bidding an affectionate farewell to his congregation, and leaving his school in the hands of his oldest son, Alexander, he commended his family tenderly to God, and sailed out of harbor in a vessel bound for Philadelphia, into which port he entered after a prosperous voyage of thirty-five days.

In the emigration then flowing from the old world to the shores of the United States, many of Mr. Campbell's intimate friends had preceded him to this country, and some of them, as the Hodgens and the Fosters, came soon after. Among these, Mr. Campbell found the most hospitable welcome. He began at once to urge the claims of the gospel—the undivided gospel of God upon the people. His charitable spirit, with his able expositions of Scripture, drew around him the pious of different church communions. As no reason appeared for their separation, but rather many for their union in worship and work on Bible principles, they agreed to form an association of Christians, to meet statedly for personal advancement in knowledge and duty. They soon felt the importance of diffusing for the good of others those principles which they found so congenial to the word of God, and such an enlargement of their own hearts. Thus come into being the "Christian Association," of Washington, Pa., which issued the very first document of this reformation, which now girdles the globe, and holds a membership of five or six hundred thousand souls! That document written by Elder Thomas Campbell, is a pamphlet of 56 pages, titled

"Declaration and Address of the Christian Association of Washington, Pa." It is a remarkable production—for its catholicity, its supreme exaltation of the word of God, its clear, unequivocal statement of the true and only practical ground of union, and its enunciation of all the principles of this rising religious movement. It came from the press in the autumn of 1809.

In the same fall he was joined by his family. For more than forty years he plead for the religion of Christ among men. He traveled extensively, and was everywhere listened to with marked attention for his distinguished abilities, and for the dignity and urbanity of his manners. He died at the age of ninety-one, honored of all.

BIOGRAPHY OF A. CAMPBELL.

"ALEXANDER CAMPBELL was born September 12th, 1788, in the County of Antrim, Ireland. But though born in Ireland, his ancestors were, on one side, of Scotch origin, and on the other, descended from the Huguenots, in France. Inheriting a vigorous and well-balanced physical and mental constitution, and trained from his earliest years, by his learned and accomplished father, to habits of severe application, he grew up to manhood a constant and laborious student—completing his course of education in the University of Glasgow. Blessed with an exceedingly intellectual and pious parentage, and reared in one of the strictest schools of Presbyterianism, he early formed and cultivated habits of piety, and a taste for theological studies, which gave shape to his entire life. A profound reverence for the Word of God, was a marked feature of the character alike of the boy and of the man.

"Coming to this country in 1809, and settling in Western Pennsylvania—whither his father had preceded him—

---

* This biography of Bro. Campbell was published in the first issue of the "Christian Standard," for which it was written, by the editor, Isaac Errett.

he closely scanned the condition of religious society. Both father and son became deeply impressed with a conviction of the evils and inherent sinfulness of sectarianism. Their first movement, as reformers, was the repudiation of human creeds as tests of fellowship, and a proposal to unite all the disciples of Jesus in one church, with the Bible as the only authoritative standard of faith and practice. Pursuing the study of the Scriptures, as free as possible from party bias, they, and those in association with them, were soon convinced that infant membership in the church, and sprinkling, were unauthorized of God. They were accordingly immersed, on a confession of faith in the Son of God, and united with the regular Baptists—stipulating, however, that they should not be required to subscribe to any creed or articles of faith other than the Bible. The prejudice and passion of some excitable and intolerant men who then held a leading influence in the Redstone Association, rendered it prudent for Mr. Campbell to withdraw, after a few years, from that connection. Against his own wishes, he was compelled by the force of ecclesiastical opposition, to act separately from the Baptists, seeking fellowship only with those who were willing to be governed by the Bible alone. Thus cut loose from his former connections, and with a fierce opposition stirred up against him, he gave himself supremely to the advocacy and defense of his plea for a return to primitive Christianity. For half a century he gave his strength to this work, making tributary to it all his treasures of learning and eloquence. For forty years—from 1823 to 1863—he never failed to publish, monthly, a religious magazine, laden with varied information, rich thought, keen argument, and pious sentiment. This was published, the first seven years, under the name of *The Christian Baptist*. In 1830, it appeared in enlarged form, under the title of *The Millennial Harbinger*. These publications, although enriched with contributions from many gifted pens, were principally occupied with editorial essays; and on this mainly depended their popularity and power. The earlier years of his editorial career were distinguished by lively and earnest controversy—the arguments and criticisms of his opponents being given in full on his pages, and the replies exhibiting a completeness of information on the topics discussed, ripeness of judgment, strength of argument, keenness of retort, and withering exposures of sophistry, that render them admirable models of polemical theology. Seldom is such playfulness of wit and keenness of satire joined with such gentlemanly dignity and logical power. We have always regarded the correspondence with Bishop Semple as one of the finest specimens of the epistolary style of discussion, anywhere to be found.

"Afterwards, when the heat of controversy had somewhat abated, there is traceable, in his journalism, a gentleness and mellowness which, while admitting of no compromise with error, dealt more forbearingly with opposition, and delighted more in the sweetness of piety, and in the practical aspects of Bible doctrine. Seldom, however, even in the hottest of the strife, were sentences written unworthy of the dignity and benevolence of the religion of Jesus. We doubt, in going over these forty volumes, and noting the wide range of subjects—doctrinal, critical, ethical, historical, and literary—whether the same amount and variety of writing can be found in any controversial author with less which, when dying, he would wish to erase.

"In addition to these forty volumes, Mr. Campbell published several other works: A Translation of the New Testament, by G. Campbell, Doddridge and Macknight, with Prefaces, Emendations and Critical Notes of his own; the Christian System; Infidelity refuted by Infidels; Baptism, its Antecedents and Consequents; a volume of Literary Addresses; a life of his father, Thomas Campbell, etc. He also held several public discussions, which were reported and published : A debate on baptism in 1820, with Rev. John Walker; one on the same subject in 1823, with Rev. W. L. McCalla ; one on the Evidences of Christianity in 1829, with Robert Owen ; one on Roman Catholicism in 1837, with Bishop (now Archbishop) Purcell , and one on the points in dispute between Presbyterians and Reformers, in 1843, with Rev. N. L. Rice. This last discussion occupied eighteen days.   He had also a written discussion with Dr. Skinner, on Universalism.   In all these he maintained a high reputation for learning, dignity, and logical and critical acumen.

"He was not less laborious as a speaker than as a writer.   During all these years, he traveled extensively, traversing most of the States of the Union, and visiting Great Britain and Ireland ; discoursing every-where to crowded audiences, on the great themes that occupied his heart, and coming into contact with many of the best minds of the age, from whom, whatever their difference of sentiment, he constantly challenged respect and admiration.   His discourses were extemporaneous, often exceeding two hours in length, but were so clear in statement, cogent in argument, rich in diction, and forcible in illustration, as to hold his auditors in rapt attention to the close.   His was not the highest style of oratory.   Indeed he rather despised oratory as an art, relying on the inherent attractiveness of the truths he uttered.   We have known him, in his prime, stand for two hours, leaning on a cane, and talk in true conversational style, with scarce a gesture in the entire discourse.   But to a fine personal appearance and dignity of manner, he added a clearness of statement, a force of reasoning, a purity and sometimes a pomp of diction, a wealth of learning, a splendor of imagination, and an earnestness often rising into impassioned utterance, which clothed his pulpit efforts with a high degree of oratorical excellence.   His habit of extemporaneous speaking never caused him to degenerate into slovenliness of style, but sometimes led to undue diffusiveness and discursiveness.

"In conversation, he expended, perhaps more time and strength than in pulpit discourse. Possessed of a strong social nature, and gifted with rare conversational powers, his delighted visitors hung for hours on the wisdom and eloquence of his lips. We do not compare him with Johnson or Coleridge, who, as conversationists won so great a fame. Mr. Campbell conversed on different themes, and to a widely different circle of hearers. But we doubt if any of his age excelled him in capacity to charm and instruct in the social circle. Perhaps more prejudice was dissipated, and more adherents were gained, in these daily conversations, than in his best pulpit efforts.

"It is not designed to enter here on a consideration of the peculiar features of Mr. Campbell's teaching. Briefly, they may be sketched thus :

"Christ, the only Master: involving a rejection of all human names and leaderships in religion. The Bible, the only authoritative book : necessitating a denial of the authority of all human creeds. The Church of Christ, as founded by him, and built by the apostles, for a habitation of the Spirit, the only divine institution for spiritual ends : logically leading to the repudiation of all sects in religion as unscriptural and dishonoring to the head of the church. Faith in Jesus, as the Christ, the Son of God, and repentance toward God, the only scriptural prerequisites to baptism and consequent church-membership : thus dismissing all doctrinal speculation and all theological dogmata, whether true or false, as unworthy to be urged as tests of fitness for membership in the church of Christ. Obedience to the divine commandments, and not correctness of opinion, the test of Christian standing. The gospel the essential channel of spiritual influence in conversion ; thus ignoring all reliance on abstract and immediate influence of the Holy Spirit, and calling the attention

5

of inquirers away from dreams, visions, and impressions, which are so liable to deceive, to the living and powerful truths of the gospel, which are reliable, immutable, and eternal. The *truth* of the gospel, to enlighten ; the *love* of God in the gospel, to persuade; the *ordinances* of the gospel, as tests of submission to the divine will ; the *promises* of ths gospel, as the evidence of pardon and acceptance; and the Holy Spirit, in and through all these, accomplishing his work of enlightening, convincing of sin, guiding the penitent soul to pardon, and bearing witness to the obedient believer, of his adoption into the family of God.

"He was intensely Protestant, steadily cherishing through his life the cardinal principles of what is called evangelical faith and piety—the divinity of Christ, his sacrificial death, as a sin-offering, and the indwelling of the Holy Spirit in the hearts of believers. A Trinitarian in sentiment, he repudiated the unscriptural technicalities of Trinitarian theology, as involving a mischievous strife of words. A devout believer in the atoning sacrifice of the Lamb of God, he would not teach, as gospel, any *theory* of atonement. A stout advocate of spiritual influence and special providence, he was the enemy of all theories of abstract spiritual power, as tending to ignore the word of God, and leading to a deceptive trust in psychological peculiarities as the voice of the Spirit of God. Sternly opposed to baptismal regeneration, he still insisted on the baptism of the believing penitent "for the remission of sins." Educated in Calvinism, and always inclining to that school, he was so fearful of the tendency of all speculative theology, that it is difficult to trace his own proclivities on these questions anywhere in his voluminous writings. Deeply sympathizing with evangelical Protestantism, in its grand ideas and principles, he nevertheless looked on its present divided and distracted state as evidence that Protestants are only partially rescued from the great

apostasy; regarded the enforcement of speculative doctrines and creed authority as the tap-root of sectarianism;
and insisted, through half a century, on the abandonment
of party names, leaders, and symbols, to prepare the way
for the union of all believers in one body; arguing that
thus only have we a right to expect the conversion of the
world. He suffered much unjust reproach for a plea
which, just as he was passing away, he saw rising into exceeding interest among all evangelical parties.

"As an educator, he is entitled to the honor of successfully instituting a college course, with the Bible as a text-
book, and as the basis of the entire curriculum of study.
He gave the ripest years of his life to the erection and en-
dowment of Bethany College, from which hundreds of
young men have gone forth, bearing the impress of his
spirit, and the molding influence of his noble Christian
life.

"In estimating the character of this illustrious man, it
ought not to be forgotten that he possessed eminently
practical talents. He was no recluse, shut out from sympathy with the activities of life. He was diligent in business as well as fervent in spirit, seeking to serve the Lord
in the former as religiously as in the latter. He had
splendid business capacity, and employed it to great advantage; so that, while traveling and preaching at his own
expense, entertaining generously the throngs that gathered
at Bethany, and meeting the constant demands on his
purse which every public man of generous nature is plied
with, he was still enabled to accumulate considerable
wealth. He once told us of his standing at an early day
on the site of the present city of Cleveland, when engaged
with his father-in-law in locating lands. His quick perceptions took in at a glance the advantages of this site,
and he urged the propriety of purchasing in a locality
which it was evident would one day be a great commercial

center. His father-in-law did not readily accept the prophecy, and their lands were selected in Holmes County.

" Once only did he venture on the stormy sea of politics. In 1829, at the earnest solicitation of the people of West Virginia, and with a special pledge from his friends that he should not be required to take the stump, he consented to be a candidate for a seat in the Virginia Constitutional Convention. He was elected. He bore a prominent part in the proceedings of that convention, acting on the Judiciary Committee with Chief Justice Marshall, on intimate terms with ex-President Madison, and coming into conflict with John Randolph and other leading minds of Eastern Virginia, in his advocacy of the interests of the western portion of the State. In all this, he never for a moment forfeited the dignity of his character as a Christian minister.

" His reputation was without spot. His bitterest enemies failed to find a flaw in his character for truth, integrity, and goodness. But to those who knew him well, he was most cheerful, gentle, genial, just, and devout ; and as dearly beloved for his goodness as he was venerated for his greatness. It will ever be remembered to his honor, that with an almost unbounded personal influence over a religious community numbering hundreds of thousands, he never sought the least ecclesiastical control. Although the telegram from Wheeling announcing his death spoke of him as " Bishop Campbell," it will surprise many to learn that he was merely *one* of the bishops of the congregation meeting in Bethany, and that outside of this, he never sought and never exercised, the least ecclesiastical authority.

"For many years he was possessed of the conviction that the year 1866 would exhaust many prophetic dates, and witness great changes in ecclesiastical and spiritual affairs. It is not unpleasant to think that this has become to him the year of years, and to his ransomed spirit will unseal many of the mysteries of apocalyptic visions which, here, even his piercing intellect failed to penetrate.

"He passed away on the Lord's day—the day in which he so much delighted, to the peace and bliss of an eternal Sabbath. In his later years, the personal dignity and official relations of the Son of God, was his constant theme of discourse. Who can imagine the reverence and rapture that shall fill his spirit when beholding the glory of Immanuel, whom, unseen, he loved so well, and at whose feet he laid, adoringly, the gifts of his nature, and the toils of his life!

"He fell asleep in Jesus, on the 4th of March, 1866, near midnight, at his home in Bethany, West Virginia.

"It was an event not unexpected. Coming 'in a good old age,' when his work was done, and his tired faculties craved rest from the incessant anxiety and toil of half a century; coming slowly, attended with but little suffering, allowing his last years to be spent pleasantly in the scenes he loved best, and his last hours to be cheered and soothed by the fondest ministrations of conjugal and filial affection, death appeared in a milder form, and granted a gentler descent to the tomb, than is often permitted."

CHAPTER II.

The Association in New Lisbon, 1827—An evangelist appointed—
Biography of Walter Scott—Scott among the churches.

AS at the coming of day, the light springs forth in
no one locality, but brightens alike over the whole
land ; so, in many places, with no traceable connection, the same investigations were going on, and the
same conclusions were reached from the careful study
of the New Testament. The style of speech indica-
ted the change of thought. Sect language gradually
gave place to Scripture terms and phrases, as more
appropriate and correct, and authorized by the sanction of the Holy Spirit. Instead of " relating a Christian experience," converts now began to "confess
their faith in Christ." Church records assumed the
scriptural designation of "disciples." The spirit
of research was fully set free. It peered into every
thing, to sift out what was erroneous, and to make all
things according to the pattern shown by the apostles
in the New Testament. Even from the hymns and
the prayers were eliminated objectionable terms and
forms of speech, carrying in them thoughts and peti-
tions unsanctioned by the Word of God. The dia-
lect of the Holy Spirit in the language of apostles
and prophets, it was urged, must be substituted for
the corrupt language of the great apostasy which still
pollutes the tongue of Christendom. The reformation
must be radical. From the language of the Jews, the
language of Ashdod must be expurgated. Thus,
many terms that were trite and dear from their fa-

miliar association in religious life were objected to as
improper, and rejected as misleading.

CALL FOR AN EVANGELIST.

As the Calvinistic theory of conversion began to
yield, and it was seen that sinners have something to
do in hearing the gospel, that they may believe and
be saved, and, also, that the church has in her hands
the work of preaching it, the feeling began to take
definite form that the time had come to take this responsibility which was devolved upon her by the Lord
Jesus, to convert the world through the proclamation
of the glad tidings.   It was apparent, no less in the
wants of the people than in the light of the Sacred
Scriptures, that a suitable person should be selected
to travel among the churches, to preach the gospel,
and to set things in order according to the teachings
of the primitive church.   So evident had it become
that this long neglected duty must be resumed, that a
petition to this end was sent to the Mahoning Association from the church in Braceville.   It was understood that the church in Nelson was consulted, and
that it concurred in the movement.   Mr. Campbell
came to this association with the same purpose in his
heart.   Passing through Steubenville, he called on
Walter Scott, principal of the academy in that place,
and persuaded him to come to New Lisbon, with the
intention of securing his appointment as the evangelist of the association.

On this occasion, memorable in history, the association met by regular appointment in New Lisbon,
Columbiana County, August 23, 1827.   Jacob Osborne
was moderator, and John Rudolph, Jr., clerk.

The churches and delegates composing the association, were as follows:

CHURCHES.	NAMES OF MESSENGERS.	Added by Baptism.	Added by Letter.	Dismissed.	Excluded.	Deceased.	Total.
Warren........	Adamson Bentley...						
	Jacob Smith..........	3	1	4	4	2	72
	Jacob Drake.........						
New Lisbon..	Joab Gaskill..........						
	John Campbell......			2	1		41
	Henry Beck..........						
Mantua and Hiram.......	Darwin Atwater......						
	Zeb. Rudolph..........	9					26
	John Rudolph, Jr...						
Palmyra.......	Stephen Wood.......						
	Noah Davis...........			1	3		49
	William Bacon......						
Hubbard......	Jesse Hall..........						
	Walter Clark........	1					37
	Archibald Price......						
Braceville.....	Jacob Osborne.......						
	Henry Harsh.........		3		2	1	36
Yellow Creek	William McGavern.						
	Thomas Ray..........	5		1	2		30
	Simon Kelley.......						
Val. of Achor	Arthur Wherry......						
	John Jackman.......	1		2			70
Canfield.......	David Hays...........						
	Myron Sacket........	1		1			28
Wellsburg Va	Alexander Campbell						
	John Brown..........	11	5	3	1	1	56
Salem..........	Arthur G. Hayden...						
	Aaron Hise...........	3	4				34
	David Gaskill.......						
Hartford.........	No intelligence.						
Youngstown..	Samuel Hayden......						
	Joseph Pearce.......						
Southington	No intelligence.						
Randolph.,....	Abijah Sturdevant..						
	William Churchill...						13
Sandy.............	No intelligence.						
	Total number.	34	13	14	13	4	492

Besides these accredited messengers, the following preachers were present, who, by a resolution of the association, were invited to a seat in its counsels: Walter Scott, Samuel Holmes, William West, and Sidney Rigdon.

There were present, also, J. Merrill, John Secrest, and Joseph Gaston, advocates of the gospel among the "Christian" fraternity. These brethren were, by resolution, made equally welcome to the sittings of the association.

The following petition from the church in Brace-ville, Trumbull County, sent by the hand of Bro. Osborne, was received and entertained:

" We wish that this association may take into serious consideration the peculiar situation of the churches of the association, and if it would be a possible thing for an evangelical preacher to be employed to travel and teach among the churches, we think that a blessing would follow."

The action of this convention of churches in relation to this subject, is reported as follows:

"*Voted*, That all the teachers of Christianity present, be a committee to nominate a person to travel and labor among the churches, and to suggest a plan for the support of the person so appointed."

The preachers present composing this committee, were the following: Adamson Bentley, Joab Gaskill, Jacob Osborne, A. Campbell, Abijah Sturdevant, Walter Scott, Samuel Holmes, William West, Sidney Rigdon, J. Merrill, John Secrest, Joseph Gaston— twelve; besides, Darwin Atwater, Zeb. Rudolph, and John Jackman, who soon after became prominent as teachers of the gospel. Let us now hear their unanimous report:

" The committee, to which was referred the nomination

of a person to labor among the churches, and to recommend a plan for his support, reported as follows:

" 1. That Bro. Walter Scott is a suitable person for the task, and that he is willing, provided the association concur in his appointment, to devote his whole energies to the work.

" 2. That voluntary and liberal contributions be recommended to the churches for creating a fund for his support.

"3. That at the discretion of Bro. Scott, as far as respects time and place, four quarterly meetings for public worship, be held in the bounds of the association this year; and at these meetings such contributions as have been made, in the churches in those vicinities, be handed over to Bro. Scott, and an account be kept of the same to be produced at the next association ; also, that at any time and in any church, when and where Bro. Scott may be laboring, any contributions made to him shall be accounted for to the next association.

"*Voted*, That the above report, in all its items, be adopted."

These men were devoutly in earnest in their purpose. An extract from the records is instructive on this point:

" Met Lord's day at sunrise, in the Baptist meeting-house, for prayer and praise, and continued till eight o'clock."

They were not sleepy drones. The morning sun, at his rising, found them assembled in prayer. Three hours and more they lifted to the Mercy-seat their suppliant appeals, while praises went to the third heaven from souls all dewy with the morning grace, which came plentifully upon them. Great and glorious epochs in the kingdom are the birth of great prayer.

" Met again in the Presbyterian meeting-house, Lisbon, where, after public worship, Bro. Jacob Osborne delivered a discourse, Heb. 1st chapter. He was followed by Bro. A. Campbell, who delivered a discourse on Good Works, predicated upon the last paragraph of the Sermon on the Mount, and the conclusion of Matt. 25th chapter.

" After a recess of a few minutes, and the immersion of some disciples in the creek, the brethren met at the Baptist meeting house and broke bread, after which they dispersed, much comforted and edified by the exercises of the day."

This association deserves much more than a passing notice. It was the first ecclesiastical body in modern times, which, transcending the limits of its own constitutional prerogatives, initiated a movement exactly conformed to the word of God, and utterly disentangled from all sectarian restraints. Let us pause to consider its action :

1. The association threw open its doors, and brought in, as a composite element, disciples of Christ, ministers of another ecclesiastical connection, making these ministers fully equal in its action ; thus setting aside its denominational character, and standing on the broad, firm charter of the Christian religion alone. These men were of the " Christian connection," and the most that was known of either party respecting the other was that each respectively was zealously, and conscientiously engaged in preaching the gospel as he best understood it. Here was a practical exhibition of the union of Christians for a common purpose.

2. Here was the appointment of an evangelist in the pure New Testament idea of that official minister.

by the concurrent action of the ministry of a given
district of country.   In this it took upon itself the
new duty of *establishing* and *regulating an evangelical agency, or ministry.*

3. This association, like all others, had restricted its
action to sundry ecclesiastical matters, making no provision for evangelical operations.   Its duty was mainly
the care of churches, responding to questions, and
hearing cases of appeal ; affairs which churches can
manage more successfully at home.   This association
assumed a new power, and with this higher prerogative, entered upon the discharge of a far higher and
wider responsibility.   And what was it ? Simply to revive the work laid by divine authority upon its hand at
the beginning, to "preach the gospel to every creature."
This pure, simple, most significant act was here for
the first time performed by a body of churches assembled in delegate capacity.   The selection of an evangelist to travel among the congregations of a given
district, clothing him with power to set things in order,
to preach the gospel, and by every means to promote
the work of Christ, deserves the clearest and most em-
phatic statement as a direct, practical measure in restoring the apostolic order to the world.

4. No one church assumed the grave responsibility of selecting, authorizing, and sending forth an
evangelist.   The suggestion for such an appointment,
while coming from one of the churches, at the instance
of a wise preacher among them, was, by the association, wisely and properly referred to the ministers of
the gospel for full consideration and final action.
And their action in the premises, duly taken and de-

clared, received the cordial indorsement and acquiescence of all the churches represented.

5. But, further, the association bound its evangelist by no doctrinal restrictions or limitations. No creed basis, no confession of doctrines, no articles of belief: he was simply to "preach the word."

This was a bold and untried step. It was a long step toward Mount Zion. But it was a safe step, as the Scriptures can lead no one astray; and, also, it was the only method of bringing about the restoration of original Christianity in fact, in faith, and in form, in letter, in spirit, and in practice.

BIOGRAPHY OF WALTER SCOTT.

Walter Scott was born in Moffat, Dumfriesshire, Scotland, October 31, 1796. His father, John Scott, a gentleman of fine culture, was a professor of music. His mother, Mary Innes Scott, was a person of most pure life, and eminently religious. They had ten children, five sons and five daughters; Walter was the sixth child.

A remarkable providence is related as occurring in connection with the death of his parents. His father went to the town of Annan on business of his profession, and died there suddenly. Mrs. Scott was so deeply affected by the intelligence of his demise, that she died immediately, and was buried with him in the same grave.

He had a maternal uncle in the custom-house, in the city of New York, who held his situation for thirty years under all the changes of administration. The death of this man was also remarkable. He died on his knees while in prayer.

The Scott family were all strict members of the Kirk of Scotland. Walter Scott early displayed the fine qualities of character for which he afterwards became conspicuous.

He was intellectual, sensitive, tender-hearted, and pious. He was educated in the University of Edinburgh.

A characteristic incident is related concerning him which occurred while he was pursuing his collegiate studies. When about sixteen he walked out one evening into the city, and not returning as soon as his parents expected, at a late hour they sent his older brother James in search of him. James explored the city diligently, but failed to find him till long after midnight. He found him in the midst of a crowd singing the popular Scottish airs, collecting money in this way for a poor blind beggar. When accosted by his brother, he seemed not aware of the lateness of the hour, so completely was his young and benevolent heart interested in procuring relief for the needy man.

On invitation of his uncle in New York, George Innes, Esq., he crossed the ocean. He resided awhile in his uncle's family, and also, for a time, taught a classical school on Long Island. With the spirit of adventure, common to the young, he came to Pittsburgh, crossing the mountains afoot in company with a young companion. He soon made the acquaintance of a fellow-countryman, Mr. George Forrester, in whose family he found a welcome and for considerable time a home. Mr. Forrester was a preacher of the Haldanean school, who had prepared for the ministry in the institution established in Scotland by the celebrated Robert and James Alexander Haldane, for educating young men for the preaching of the gospel. He was conducting a school, and also preaching to a small membership whom he had collected together. The friendly hearts of these men, as well as the tie of nationality, created a warm attachment between them. Mr. Scott was here invited to the examination of the claims of pedobaptism, in which he had been trained up. He had too much reverence for the authority of God's Word to resist its teaching ; so after a full search for scriptural authority for this practice of his church, and finding none, he abandoned it as a defenseless relic of the

Papacy ; and, accordingly, was immersed by his friend Mr. Forrester.

The new views which presented themselves to him by this new search of the Holy Scriptures, and the fresh interest awakened by them in a mind naturally inquisitive and greatly devoted to religious pursuits, give him a powerful impulse to farther scriptural investigations. He rapidly outstripped his teachers. He was not long in acquiring a wonderful store of knowledge of the Christian religion. He opened a classical and English high school; but the duties of that profession, a profession in which he was eminently successful, did not interfere with his assiduous prosecution of the systematic study of the Bible.

About this time, at one of Mr. Campbell's visits to the city of Pittsburgh, he and Mr. Scott became personally acquainted. By reputation they were not strangers. These men discovered in each other so many admirable and brilliant qualities of character, intellectual and social, that a lasting friendship was formed between them. This coalescence of feeling, however, was quite as much the result of the coincidence of their conclusions on great scriptural themes; their agreement in the power of the gospel to recover Christendom from its numberless sects and divisions; and to restore the unity of the " faith once delivered to the saints." From that day they were mutual co-operants in the common cause of re-proclaiming to the world the gospel as it began in Jerusalem on the first Pentecost after the Lord's ascension.

Mr. Campbell, at the time of his introduction to Scott, was about issuing a *monthly*, designed to develop the truth of the gospel, and to plead for the union of Christians on Bible grounds. Mr. Scott fell in with the proposition, and espoused the scheme. Mr. Campbell proposed the name " The Christian," as a suitable title for his new periodical. Mr. Scott thought " The Christian Baptist " would be a title more likely to win an immediate hearing. This

was agreed upon.   And in the very beginning of that masterly work, the grand triumvirate, Thomas Campbell,
Alexander Campbell, and Walter Scott appeared side by
side as contributors to its pages.   The appearance of that
periodical, August, 1823, forms a marked epoch in the public announcement of the principles of a much-needed reformation.   Mr. Scott remained yet a few years in Pittsburgh, where he became acquainted, and for a time associated, with Sidney Rigdon, then pastor of a small Baptist church in the city.   The two communions, that under
Rigdon and the company to whom Scott preached, united
together and became one body.

Early in 1827 we find him in Steubenville, established
in the academy, as already related.   He had issued a pros-
pectus, and was on the eve of commencing the publication
of the " Millennial Herald," to be devoted to the statement
and defense of the gospel, and to the publication of views of
the millennium, in which he had become much interested.

" The heart of man deviseth his way; but the Lord
directeth his steps."   A foreseeing providence was preparing a far different theater for the display of his remarkable
talents, and was at the same time preparing him for that
field.   This was the work of an evangelist opened for him
in New Lisbon; which, after some persuasion, he accepted
with all his heart.   His great powers were now plumed
for great purposes.   Here was scope and comprehension
for his gifts of oratory, of argumentation, and persuasion.
All his talents for analysis and classification were here to
find amplest scope and fullest display.   Many and glorious events were born the day that the arrangement was
completed to send Scott forth to preach the gospel; the
gospel long thought to be a mystery, but soon to come as
a revelation to the people.

The history of this extraordinary man is in the pages
that follow; rather, in the mighty revolution in religious
society in America, which, like a majestic stream, is widen-

ing and deepening in its flow; a revolution to which he has
contributed very much by his discoveries in Bible truth, and
by his powers of eloquence and argument in presenting
and defending it before the people.

His style was chaste and classical. He was a man of
great faith, and of a most lovable and gentle spirit. In
discourse he was often bold as a lion; yet he as often
played among lambs. He came before the world with a
mission on his soul; the restoration of the gospel *plea*,
the "advocacy," as he termed it. He affirmed that the
gospel contains an advocacy for converting sinners to Christ.
This appeal, with its appointed conditions of pardon, constituted Scott's special mission to the men of this generation. Long and faithfully did he conduct the high argument; and many thousands of his beloved Master's children will rise up and bless his memory.

He fell asleep, full of faith and hope, at his residence
in Mayslick, Ky., Tuesday evening, April 23, 1861, in the
sixty-fifth year of his age.

Scott among the Churches.

After his appointment Scott lost no time in preparation for his new duty. Giving up both his paper
and his academy, and leaving his family in Steubenville, he was almost immediately on the territory he
was to traverse. Great hopes were entertained of the
results of his labors. Yet no man, himself not excepted, had any adequate conception of the great and
unparalleled blessings which were in store for the
people within that year.

The first of the quarterly meetings recommended
in the report of the committee at New Lisbon, was
held in Braceville, then the residence of Jacob Osborne, the brother who moved the association to ap-

point an " evangelical preacher." Bro. Marcus Bosworth also resided in Braceville, a young preacher of warm heart and of sweet and winning speech. It was Lord's day, September 16, 1827. It was largely attended, and was prolific in important results. The principal preachers were Scott, Bentley, and Osborne. Darwin Atwater, whose clear, personal recollections avouch this record, was also present, with others from abroad. The principles of reform were making constant and sure progress in many places, though they were yet encumbered and delayed by the cautious prudence of some, and by the opposition of others. The leading steps of its march are susceptible of historic record. The first distinctive position assumed was the plea for the union of Christians on apostolic ground. This, as a consequence, directed an enfilading fire against the works in which the creed power was intrenched. Creeds, confessions of faith as terms of membership and communion, articles of church government separate from the New Testament, and distinctive of the sect, with all that pertained to them, were gradually losing ground ; while at the same time, as a correlative part of the plea, the fullness, sufficiency, plainness, and authority of the word of God for all the purposes of faith and practice, were urged with a great variety of argument, illustration, and Scripture testimony.

Closely allied to this came, secondly, the whole subject of conversion, regeneration, and evidence of pardon. The theory of metaphysical regeneration, brought into the church by St. Augustine, in the fourth century, formed into system by the equally illustrious Calvin, of the sixteenth century, and lin-

gering in most of the modern standards of orthodoxy, was put to the most rigid test of the word of
God. This involved the whole subject of spiritual
influence and illumination. And while the reformers maintained, on Scripture grounds, a firm belief
in the converting power of the Holy Spirit, and his
actual presence in the hearts of Christians, they asserted that the work of conversion was wrought
through the knowledge and belief of the gospel. As
the Holy Scriptures were the *only* guide, practices
untaught therein were repudiated as of human origin, and dangerous to the peace and purity of the
church. On this ground, infant church-membership
was delivered back to the papacy, whence it originated, with " confirmation," its consequent and com-
plement, sponsorship, and whatever depended upon
this postscript to the apostolic gospel. Conversion
without faith is impossible ; but faith comes of testimony—divine testimony, the word of God. Rom. x :
17. But this must be preached ; and so it is the
preaching of the gospel which produces faith in Jesus
Christ.

A link was yet wanting to complete the theory of
salvation. That the sufferings of Christ are the
procuring cause of pardon, was clearly asserted.
Faith, involving a personal trust in Jesus Christ, was
becoming equally clear and well established in the
widening plea. But what is the evidence of pardon ?
the " witness," the assurance of the penitent sinner's
acceptance ? " Experience ! " Yes ; but experiences
are both *variable*, as different persons " experience
a hope " at different places and by different processes,
and *fallible* as these experiences are formed according

to the models of teaching under which the convert has been trained.   Cases are numerous and painful in which after years of agonizing self-abasement, the load of conscious sins still lies on the heart.   A large number of professing Christians are subject to conflicting doubt, and harassed with distressing uncertainty of their acceptance ; very many " seek " on in silent, despairing darkness ; not a few throw themselves into the vortex of infidelity, while some lose their reason in the fruitless search for the evidence that God has spoken peace to their souls.

Has the gospel, perfect in all its provisions, complete in all its appointments for salvation, left this one point without a testimony—without a provided assurance ?   Does God in his gospel show sinners their danger, arouse them by faith to flee from "the wrath to come," lead them to repentance by the sufferings of his Son, and when they come crying for mercy, is this same gospel unfurnished with a provision special to this very need, which shall uniformly and unfailingly meet them with the needed assurance of pardon ?

The divine testimony had not been explored in vain touching this point.   In essays, in debate, in conversations, the unequivocal declaration of the new Institution had been brought out to view, that baptism in the name of Jesus Christ was ordained by him, for bringing the actual believer in him, penitent for his sins, into this new relation, and for giving him the knowledge of pardon by the promises of the new covenant.   This had been ably set forth from the commission, from Acts ii: 38, and many other New Testament authorities.

Yet who in those days, having discovered this established scriptural connection, had ventured to apply this truth to the relief of mourning sinners?

Theory before practice : yet practice is often tardy and tremulous. It is well ; let it be cautious, and walk only on solid rocks, like the priests who stood on rocks in the midst of Jordan, while Israel all passed by into the promised land. A new light was dawning, and a farther glimpse into the light of the gospel was obtained at this meeting in Braceville.

After the services of the day were over, Scott, Bentley, Osborne, and Atwater walked out together. Conversation turned on this subject. Bentley had preached on it. He urged that it was intended to bring penitent sinners to the immediate relief they sought, by bringing them into the new covenant, whose immediate and distinguishing blessing was the actual pardon of all past sins. Osborne, turning to Scott, asked him " if he had ever thought that baptism in the name of the Lord was for the remission of sins?" Holding himself somewhat in reserve, he intimated a desire for Osborne to proceed. " It is," said he, "certainly established for that purpose. It holds the same place under the gospel in relation to pardon, that the positive institution of the altar held to forgiveness under the law of Moses ; under that dispensation the sinner offered the prescribed victim on the altar and was acquitted, pardoned through the merits of the sacrifice of Christ, of which his offering was a type. So under the gospel age, the sinner comes to the death of Christ, the meritorious ground of his salvation, through baptism, which is a symbol of the death, burial, and resurrection of Jesus

Christ." "Very well," replied Scott, whose thoughts were very deeply engaged revolving the whole subject, "it is evidently so."

After a little, Mr. Osborne remarked to Elder Bentley, "you have christened baptism to-day." "How so?" "You termed it a remitting ordinance." * Bentley replied, "I do not see how we are to avoid the conclusion with the Bible in our hands."

The second chapter of Acts of Apostles, it will be seen, was under constant and close scrutiny of investigation. It contains evidence of the coronation in heaven of the King of kings, with his royal proclamation of mercy, and terms of pardon to his rebellious subjects.

These three preachers were again together soon after the events narrated above, when Bro. Osborne again introduced the design of baptism in public discourse, and remarked in the connection that the gift of the Holy Spirit is after conversion and baptism, and consequent upon them, citing the inspired words of the apostle Peter in Acts ii: 38, as proof: "Repent, and be baptized every one of you in the name of Jesus Christ for the remission of sins, and ye shall receive the gift of the Holy Spirit."

After the meeting, Scott said to Osborne, "You are the boldest man I ever saw! Don't you think so, Bro. Bentley?" "How so?" said Bentley. "Why he said in his sermon that no one had a right to expect the Holy Spirit till after baptism." Scott was a genius; often eccentric, often profoundly meditative. It may not be necessary, as perhaps it would

---

* Words were sometimes used in those days with less accuracy than in later times.

be impossible to tell, whether Mr. Scott was leading them, or they him, in those views. It is certain, however, that he had now premises sufficient for a generalization, which was soon to produce the most brilliant and unexpected results. In the powers of analysis and combination, he has rarely been equaled. Under his classification, the great elements of the gospel bearing on the conversion of sinners, assumed the following definite, rational, and scriptural order: (1) Faith; (2) Repentance; (3) Baptism; (4) Remission of sins;. (5) The Holy Spirit; (6) Eternal life, through a patient continuance in well doing.

This arrangement of these themes was so plain, so manifestly in harmony with soundest reason, and so clearly correct in a metaphysical point of view, as well as sustained by the Holy Scriptures, that Scott was transported with the discovery. The key of knowledge was now in his possession. The points which before were dark or mysterious, were now luminous. It cleared away the mist, and let in the day just where all had struggled for ages, and many had stranded. The whole Scripture sorted itself into a plain and intelligible system in illustration and proof of this elementary order of the gospel. The darkened cloud withdrew. A new era for the gospel had dawned.

So reasoned Scott. Moreover this discovery was most opportune as a preparation for his mission to which the association had called him, of preaching the gospel within its bounds.

CHAPTER III.

The plea opened in New Lisbon—Co-operating agencies.

EVENTS were rapidly culminating for the work of conversion to open under new and peculiar conditions of success._ The preachers were astir holding meetings in many places ; not "protracted meetings," for the day for such meetings had not yet come.   Many incidents of rare interest are connected with the stirring reformatory movement of the years from 1826 to 1832 ; but none, perhaps, more noteworthy than the opening of the great work in New Lisbon, in November, 1827.   Bro. Scott felt that the evangelical part of the great commission had fallen into decay, and his soul was burdened with a great weight of duty to revive the apostolic method of preaching the gospel.   After the discovery of the system of the gospel items already mentioned, he went to a community where he endeavored to impress the people with its truth ; but he failed to enlist any souls for Christ. He felt the discouragement, and went on his knees to Jesus.   He plead as did the lawgiver of Israel for his people.   He was most earnest in prayer.   He believed God.   He believed his word ; his promise of help.   No man more sincerely, humbly, pleadingly, ever lay prostrate before God in supplications.   His prayers in public, from a tender heart, melted all hearts around him.

The effort must be repeated.   It *is* the gospel—so

his meditation ran—Christ's own gospel, blessed by him at first for conversion, and to be blessed by him for that purpose to the end of time. "Lo! I am with you, world without end." Then he will be with his servants still. "This is thy word ; I am thy serv-ant." So "cast down, but not destroyed," he cried ; and, again, with the prophet, "I believed, therefore have I spoken. I am greatly afflicted. I believe his word, and I will preach it again!"

It seemed a blessed providence which permitted the first trial to be a defeat. God had him under farther discipline for a higher work. If he threw him on his back in discomfiture, it was that he might fall on his face in conscious need of Christ's own help for Christ's own work ; that his gospel might be re-announced to the world in self-abasement, in weakness, and with the consciousness of the Lord's presence to aid in his work. He had been in ecstasy with the novelty and grandeur of the newly discovered truth, and with the thought of bringing sinners once more, and at once, through faith and obedience into the joys of salva-tion ; with no less of joy in the gospel as it now flamed upon his heart, but perhaps tempered with fear and trembling, a state of feeling he often experienced, he resolved to go to New Lisbon.

The old Baptist meeting-house, in which two months before he received the appointment of the as-sociation, was honored as the place for the opening of this grand appeal ; a plea which was to shake so-ciety throughout the land. Scott was in his highest key. He realized the peril of the experiment, should it, on the one hand, not meet with an encouraging re-sponse ; and on the other, the results to follow if he

7

should be sustained in this bold advance step ; but his faith was equal to the occasion. He had examined the firmness of the ground, on which, in his new work he was to take his stand. He opened the plea with circumspection. He fortified his positions with clear and unanswerable arguments from the Word of God. As he advanced he became more inspired, forcible, and convincing. His audience were entranced. He moved on in eloquent demonstration. He was handling old themes, but he was bringing out a new and startling proposition—old as the apostles, but new in this age—that at any hour when a sinner yields and obeys the Lord Jesus, that same hour will the Lord receive him into favor and forgive his sins ; that pardon is offered in the gospel on the terms of faith and obedience, and whoever believes on him with all his heart and obeys him, shall be pardoned through his blood ; and that the promise of the gospel is his evidence and assurance of this salvation. A new era dawned when this was urged upon the people, as it was by the preacher on that occasion, for their immediate acceptance.

When the preacher was drawing toward a conclusion of this scriptural exposition of the apostolic plan of salvation, he noticed a stranger enter the door. This man was a highly respectable citizen, and a worthy member of the Presbyterian Church. He was a diligent and pious student of the gospel; and had long been convinced that the Savior's command to convert the world was not now obeyed as it was preached by the apostles. He spoke frequently to his wife on the subject, and was so engaged that he sometimes read and conversed to a late hour at night.

She said on one of these occasions, "William, you will never find any one that will agree with you on that subject." He replied, "When I find any person preaching, as did the apostle Peter in the second chapter of Acts, I shall offer myself for obedience and go with him." This man was "waiting for the consolation of Israel."

Having prepared the way by showing from the Scriptures that the Kingdom of Christ was to be opened on Pentecost, and from Matt. xvi : 18, that the apostle Peter had the keys to open the door of it, or to proclaim the terms of admission into it, Scott was bringing his subject to a conclusion. Mr. Amend, having entered from the Presbyterian prayer-meeting, heard enough to see his drift, and to appreciate him when he repeated the language of inspiration, "Repent, and be baptized every one of you in the name of Jesus Christ for remission of sins, and you shall receive the gift of the Holy Spirit." Acts ii : 38, 39. He was standing on his feet listening with fixed attention. The preacher, all alive to his subject, called out for any of his audience who believed God and would take him at his word, to come forward and confess the Lord Jesus, and be baptized in his name for the remission of sins.

"The time has come at last," said Amend ; "God has accepted my condition ; he has sent a man to preach as the New Testament reads ; shall I fail to fulfill my pledge of obedience?" All this passed through his mind with instantaneous rapidity. "My pledge is on high ; my prayer is answered ; I will not confer with flesh and blood." With a promptness which astonished both the audience and the preacher, he came to the seat assigned to converts. "Who is this man?" whispered the astonished preacher, who had seen him enter and had scanned his movement. "The best man in the community; an orderly member of the Presbyterian Church."

It was enough. Success sanctioned the appeal. Mr. Scott looked upon it as a divine attestation of the correctness of his method; the Scriptures being his warrant for the truth of the things proclaimed. Here is a case in proof that the Word of God can be understood alike by all who study it with unbiased mind. This devout Presbyterian loved the truth as it is in Jesus. The doctrine of party is nothing to such men. The testimony of the apostles will have the same effect on all candid men when the doctrines and commandments of men are laid aside. From that day, with this seal to his ministry, he was stronger than Ajax. To borrow one of his own expressions, " he rushed in upon the people like an armed man!" Within a few days seventeen souls "hearing, believed and were baptized." There was great joy in New Lisbon. The whole town was aroused; some spoke against this way, others were amazed at the new things brought to their ears. The novelty and boldness of the movement broke up entirely the monotony of the customary process of "waiting," "seeking," tarrying at the pool till an angel of grace should trouble the waters of salvation.

The contrast between the process of conversion, as generally taught, which led the soul through "much tribulation" of darkness and uncertainty, to a faint and flickering hope—and this the apostolic method—was so direct and palpable, that the conflict was immediately initiated and strongly marked. The one led the sinner up through states of mind and frames of feeling, and upon the genuineness of these was based his hope of peace. The other brings him, with the same conscious conviction of his sins, to trust the mercy of Jesus, and to rely on Christ's promise of forgiveness, which he approaches and secures through the obedience of faith.

It was singular, and indeed inexplicable to Mr. Scott, that the first person to respond to his call, and come forth to obey the gospel, should be a man who had not heard his sermon. If he had heard his premises, and had been enlightened by his argument, the case would have presented no cause of marvel. He had heard only his conclusion. He came. It was a mystery.

Mr. Scott was restless under it. Several years afterward he addressed to Mr. Amend a note of inquiry in regard to it, and received in reply the following explanation :

" I will answer your questions. I was baptized on the 18th of Nov., 1827, and will relate to you a circumstance which occurred a few days before that date. I had read the second chapter of Acts, when I expressed myself to my wife as follows: Oh, this is the gospel ; this is the thing we wish, the remission of our sins ! Oh, that I could hear the gospel in those same words as Peter preached it ! I hope I shall some day hear, and the first man I meet who will preach the gospel thus, with him will I go. So, my brother, on the day you saw me come into the meeting-house, my heart was open to receive the word of God, and when you cried, ' The Scripture shall no longer be a sealed book, God means what he says. Is there any man present who will take God at his word and be baptized for the remission of sins,'—at that moment my feelings were such, that I could have cried out, 'Glory to God ! I have found the man whom I have long sought for.' So I entered the kingdom, when I readily laid hold of the hope set before me.   WILLIAM AMEND.''

It is no easy task, now that the position then assumed by Mr. Scott has won the victory, and become a distinguishing practice of many hundred thousand Christians, to appreciate the nature or the magnitude of the difficulties which environed him. When we consider his natural timidity ; that he was not emboldened by the presence, or encouraged by the example, of any one in modern times ; that the whole land, and, indeed, the whole world had been for ages silent as the grave respecting this peculiar and special plea, the surprise grows into wonder and amazement, and the event takes on the most evident tokens of the hand of God in it.

It is true the "Christian Baptist," in the first volume, had taught the scriptural connection between baptism and remission, in an essay by the elder Campbell ; also in A. Campbell's Debate with Mr. McCalla the same truth was distinctly set forth. But it remained among the theories. Sinners still languished in despairing doubt, awaiting some light, emotion, or sensation on which they might settle as the " white stone" of elective grace, specially imparted to assure them they were of the elect for whom Christ died. Besides, all the prominent creeds of christendom contain the doctrine of baptism as a pledge of remission, as an item of dogmatic belief. But not one of the sects built upon them carries out its creed, in this particular, into practical result, and

tells the awakened sinner, as did Peter on the first
Pentecost after the ascension: "Repent, and be baptized every one of you in the name of Jesus Christ,
for the remission of sins."

This practical use and application of the gospel to
bring convicted sinners into the immediate enjoy-
ment of the forgiveness of sins, through the pardon-
ing mercy of God in Christ, constitutes an epoch of
grand significance in the return of the disciples from
the great apostasy back to Jerusalem, to its gospel
and its glory. It had been taught and accepted as a
doctrine; now it became an advocacy. It was a truth
acknowledged in theory; it was now a duty demand-
ing practice. Now restored as a practical truth, it
was destined to become, in the hands of the proclaimers of the gospel, the means of revolutionizing the
practice of the church as it relates to the reception
of converts to Christ, by restoring to the ministry
the method established by the holy apostles under
the great commission.

"The Lord gave the word, great was the company
of them that published it." This re-announcement
of the gospel was soon noised abroad. There were
many Simeons and Annas, too, as well as Josephs,
who were waiting for this consolation of Israel.
There was, besides the preachers of the Mahoning
Association, a class of preachers of ardent zeal and
great influence with the people, who had come by a
different path to the point in the process of conversion, at which the newly restored manner of presenting the gospel commended itself to them as a necessity, and as the only missing link in the chain of gospel agencies. These were known as "Christians,"

"Bible Christians," or, sometimes, "New Lights." This last appellation they steadily repudiated. James Hughes, Lewis Hamrick, Lewis Comer, and John Secrest, all from Kentucky, coadjutors with the celebrated and godly B. W. Stone, came through Belmont and Columbiana counties, converting many, and planting churches according to the light of the gospel so far as they had attained to it. They repudiated all creeds, contended for the Bible alone, were sticklers for the name "Christian," and being full of zeal and gifted in exhortation, they gained many converts. They pursued the method known as the "mourning-bench system," completing the process of conversion and reception by giving to the convert publicly the "right hand of fellowship," when he was regarded as a member of the church. One of these, John Secrest, a man of mark in person, with glossy dark hair and black eyes, grave in manner, with powerful voice and persuasive address, came to William Mitchell's, in Belmont County, whose three sons, James G., Nathan J., and David G. Mitchell, afterward became men of much note and great usefulness in the reformation. These were all youths at the visit of Secrest.

In conversation, Secrest said:

"Bro. Mitchell, I have just been at Bethany, Va., to see Alexander Campbell. He edits a monthly called the 'Christian Baptist.' He is a man of great talent, a scholar, and he has got forty years ahead of this generation, and whether they ever catch up I have my doubts. He has waged war with the clergy, and he will bring them all down on his head, the Baptists in particular; and if he carries the thing through as he has commenced, he will

revolutionize the whole Protestant world, for his foundation can never be shaken.   He has with him a man by the
name of Scott, to whom I was introduced.   He asked me
these questions: ' Bro. Secrest, do you baptize a good
many persons?'   I told him I baptized quite a number.
' Then,' said he, ' into what do you baptize them ?'   This
was a new thought, and it perplexed me.   I tell you, Bro.
Mitchell, the apostles baptized persons into Christ; not
into the Baptist Church, or any other, but into Christ;
and baptism is more than a mere outward ordinance; it
has a greater significance than most people are aware of.
In it we become related to Christ.''

The " Christian Baptist" became a regular guest in
that family.

Of this wing of the reformation came such men as
John Whitacre, of Minerva; William Schooley, of
Salem, both having birthright in the Quaker frater-
nity; John Flick also, and Joseph Gaston, with
others of reputation among the churches.   It was
John Secrest and Joseph Gaston who appeared, and
were welcomed among the Baptist ministry in the
New Lisbon Association.

All these men, upon examination, accepted the
order of the gospel as presented by Scott, adopted
it, and spent their lives in its defense.   Thus was afforded another case illustrating the manner in which
the union of Christians is to be effected ; by the
knowledge, belief, and practice of the apostolic teaching ; not by orders in council, not by conventional
decrees, nor by some ethereal liberalism of sentiment without basis or bounds.

Scott and Joseph Gaston became greatly devoted
to each other, traveling and laboring much together.

They were as David and Jonathan. Gaston was charmed and instructed by the manly, intellectual eloquence of Scott, who, in turn, equally admired and loved the piety, simplicity, and pathos of Gaston. This brother hath a history—brief, sad, and lovely. He was the son of James and Mary Gaston, born on Peter's Creek, Washington County, Pa., March 25, 1801. When he was twenty years of age, his mother, then a widow, moved to Augusta, Carroll County, Ohio. Attending a prayer meeting, and showing some levity inconsistent in such a place, a Miss Walton, a member of the family where the meeting was held, fell upon her knees, and so earnestly commended his soul to Jesus, as to plant impressions there never to be effaced. Soon after, at a meeting held in Minerva by John Secrest, he confessed the Lord and was baptized. In the exercises of prayer and of exhortation, public and private, his heart and mouth were immediately opened. Many felt the power of religion under his earnest and impassioned appeals. Falling in with Bro. Scott, and learning more perfectly of "this way," he was carried up to new heights of wonder at the perfection of the knowledge of God, and of enthusiasm in pleading for sinners to be reconciled to God. The oil of Joseph's lamp burned brightly, but it was destined soon to burn out. He was afflicted with hemorrhage of the lungs. The violence of his labors brought on a crisis ; and on the 6th of December, 1834, closed his most triumphant course. For twenty minutes immediately before his death, he exhorted those about him with great strength of voice, and almost angelic fervor ; then he fell asleep as peacefully as when an infant is hushed to its gentle slumbers.

He was led to clearer views of the gospel in the following manner, as related by Bro. Scott:

"I had appointed a certain day in which to break bread with the Baptist Church at Salem. Bro. Gaston was a resident of Columbiana County, and was at that time in the vicinity of Salem. The Baptist brethren regarded him as a good man and a true disciple; but he was a Christian or New Light, and contended for open communion—things which they greatly disliked. Before meeting, the principal brethren requested me to converse with him on the subject, saying they were sure I could convert him.

"Accordingly I took him out in presence of them all; but he gave me no time, being as impatient and undoubting on open communion as they were on close communion. I told him, however, that the brethren had commissioned me to convert him to their opinions, and smiled. He said he had come to convert me to his.

"I then set before him the terms of the ancient gospel as I had arranged them, and told him that their dispute about communion was silly and unprofitable. He heard me with delight. I appealed to the Scriptures, and he smiled; and soon, with a laugh, he exclaimed, 'It is all true! and I believe every word of it, and I will take you to a Christian brother who will receive it in a moment.'

"After meeting, I accompanied him to the house of said brother, living a mile and a half from the village; and the man and his wife hearing it, and examining the Scriptures, received it with all readiness that same night, so that on that day were brought over to the side of the gospel two excellent men, both laborers among the 'Christians.'"

The "Christian brother" alluded to above, was William Schooley, a very useful and exemplary man. He was a pioneer of great independence; manly, and long a pillar in the cause of primitive Christianity.

He was born in Bedford County, Va., August 5, 1792. In 1802, when Ohio was yet a territory, he settled, with his parents, near the spot where the town of Salem now stands. In 1839, he removed to Maysville, Clay County, Ill. This, with the exception of a few years in Fulton County, Ill., was his continued residence till his death, which occurred Jan. 31, 1873, in the eighty-first year of his age.

He was educated amcng the Friends, or Quakers, and imbibed their doctrines. But maturing in mind, as in years, and seeing Christendom all given up to the idolatry of partisan faiths, he became skeptical. Yet his reverence for the Bible held him fast. He read the gospel. In it his sincere and candid heart saw beauty and truth. "I thought," he says, "if there is any thing in religion, it is as much to me as any one else." In this state of mind he went several miles to hear one Robert Hocking, a "New Light" or Bible Christian. He claimed the Bible to be sufficient, opposed creeds as foundations of religious parties, and assumed the term Christian as the distinctive name of the followers of Christ. This gained his ready assent. Soon after, Thomas Whitacre came, and held a meeting in Schooley's house. Following up his convictions, he and many others confessed the Lord, and, after the manner of that people, were received into church relation by the "right hand of fellowship."

Population was sparse, and preachers few. Bro. Schooley was soon called forth to exhort the members, and to defend the "new religion," as these simple and elementary views of the gospel began to be called. The people spoke of him as a preacher; and from that time, November, 1822, till he was past eighty, he ceased not to labor in the gospel. He was ordained March 16, 1823, by Elders John Secrest and Thomas Whitacre. His labors were mostly in Columbiana County, though he preached in one or two counties adjoining, and traveled some in Pennsylvania and Virginia. He says: "I went to the warfare at my own expense. I do not reccollect that I received more than one dollar for my labors, as it was thought among the brethren that it was wrong to pay for preaching the gospel. This idea came from the Quakers. However, it was very convenient; it cost them nothing. Yet it was a heavy burden to those that preached. I have never thought it right to sell the gospel, or to make it a matter of merchandise; but I think the members of the church ought to know their duty, and to be prudently liberal towards the laborers of the gospel." So writes this good and sound man at an advanced age.

Schooley was a large, heavy man, remarkably firm and unyielding in his conscientious convictions. He was more distinguished for sound sense, prudence in counsel, and for his clear teaching of the gospel, than for eloquence or power of appeal. Hence he was less a revivalist than many; but he yielded a far more steady and permanent support to the churches. He was a leading man in the community, profoundly respected for his thorough honesty and benevolence.

The souls of Gaston and Scott became "knit together in love." They labored together with great zeal and overwhelming success; whole churches of the "New Lights" and of the Baptists, in Salem, New Lisbon, East Fairfield, Green, New Garden, Hanover, and Minerva, unloading the ship of the cantraband wares of human tradition, became one people in the Lord and in his word. Conversions followed their labors in all places.

Bro. Gaston was ordained among the "Bible Christians." His fervid soul knew no bounds in his efforts to save sinners. A plaintive strain of tenderness mingled with his impassioned persuasiveness. In tears he begged the people to turn from sin and come to Christ. In the ardor of his soul he has been known to fall upon his knees that he might plead more effectively, and win the lost soul to the Savior. Once when Scott's own powers of exhortation—a gift in which he was a great master—failed to bring the people to repentance, he turned suddenly around, exclaiming, " Bro. Joseph, you get at these people !"

As he found his lungs giving away he exclaimed, " Oh ! if I had only understood the gospel when I made my start in religion ! How much suffering I might have escaped, and how much more good I might have done ! But now I must go down to an untimely grave, and leave this good and glorious work of publishing the gospel to others !" After some six years of a most active, laborious, self-denying and very successful ministry, this pure, devoted man gathered up his feet upon his couch and was with Jesus. He expired, in Steubenville, at the residence of his brother-in-law, Mr. Manful. His brother James leaned over his sainted brother in his departure. His breathing became heavy, his eyes closed, and while all waited the last pulse, he suddenly revived, and addressed to all about him an exhortation of wonderful power. It was delivered in a full sonorous voice, accompanied by the free use of his hands. Then the farewell to his wife and children followed, and in a few moments he entered the chariot.

It was noted that every one in the room at the time of his death, who was not already a Christian, turned to the Lord.

The bright jewel of the " Ancient Gospel," as the newly discovered arrangement of its fundamental items began now to be designated, attracted universal attention. So simple, so novel, so convincingly clear, and so evidently supported by the reading of the Acts, it won friends and wrought victories wherever it was proclaimed. It spread rapidly and became the topic of excited investigation from New Lisbon to the Lakes. Mr. Scott's success in Columbiana County had so completely demonstrated the correctness of his method of the direct application of the gospel for the salvation of sinners, that his zeal knew no bounds. He was a rapid rider. Mantled in his cloak, with a small polyglot Bible in the minion type, which he constantly studied, he hurried from place to place to tell the news ; to preach the things concerning the kingdom of God and the name of Jesus Christ.

BIOGRAPHY OF JOHN WHITACRE.

In Columbiana and adjoining counties, no man had greater influence than John Whitacre. He was born to be a leader. Though unambitious, he possessed varied abilities of a higher order which naturally gave him eminence. He was frequently solicited to stand the *poll* for the legislature, and for congress, but he steadily refused. He was elected to the office of County Surveyor for Stark County by a handsome majority, when the voters on the opposing ticket counted nine hundred of a majority.

He was born in Loudon County, Va., February 14, 1790. His father and mother, Edward and Martha Whitacre, were strict members of the Friends' Society ; consequently, their children had a birthright among that people. They moved into Columbiana County when the Indians, and the game which they chased, abounded in the forests. Chances for education were scanty, but he drank with avidity from all springs of knowledge, taught in the schools, became master of the art of surveying, and served as the surveyor of the county about thirty-four years. In his surveying tours he often preached the gospel with great effect. He joined the movement which originated about the beginning of this century under the labors of Stone, Hughes, O'Kane, and others; and was baptized by Robert Hawkins, of Pennsylvania. When the advocates of the *newer* light, or, rather, the older light of the original gospel, came to him, he met them book in hand. After a careful consideration of this plea, and a candid examination of the Scriptures, he said, "It is true; and as I have set out to follow the Bible, I can not reject it." He never wavered, but held on till the day of his death preaching the glad tidings wherever an opportunity offered. He was very zealous, and sought in every way to teach the people. He was popular as a preacher, convincing in proof, warm and persuasive in exhortation, and brought many souls to Christ. He abounded in anecdote, was ready and apt in figures, pointed and witty in retort. These qualities, with a benevolent disposition, and a manly, noble form, singled him out as a man first in society, and first before great assemblies. He was not only hospitable, but "given to hospitality." His business talents—the owner and successful conductor of the mills at Minerva—enabled him to gratify his generous and social dispositions, by entertaining, with great liberality, the many guests who for many years were welcome in his family mansion.

Staying over night at a hotel where were other guests, strangers to him, in the evening the conversation arose among them in regard to Christianity. A young man who had imbibed skeptical sentiments spoke up pertly: "I would not believe those old Bible stories eighteen hundred years old, nor any thing for which I had not the evidence of my senses." Whitacre, who, till now had been silent, spoke: "Young man, I perceive you have no mind." He replied, with warmth: "Sir, I claim to have as much mind as you, or any other man." "Let me ask you a question," said Whitacre: "Did you ever *see* your mind, or *hear* it? or did you ever *feel*, taste, or smell your mind?" "No, sir," said the youth. "Then, according to your own assertion, you have no mind!" This "brought the house down," and the young man was afterward wiser and more modest. On another occasion, he was at a meeting where several persons were gathered at the "altar" in prayer for divine power to come down. Among them was a lady of intelligent appearance, who evidently was in deep distress. She prayed that God would "give her faith—saving faith; that he would help her to believe in Jesus." When she closed, Whitacre spoke to her: "Madam," said he, "what would you give for faith in Mahomet?" "Nothing," was her somewhat indignant reply. "Why not?" he continued. "Because," she rejoined, "I believe him to be an impostor." "But why are you so anxious for faith in Jesus Christ?" "Because," said she, "I believe he is my only Savior." "Well," said Whitacre, "why are you praying for that which you say you have? Why not go forward and obey the gospel, and be made free from sin?" On an occasion, while out surveying, he asked a young lady in the family if she was a Christian. "No, sir, I am not." "Would you like to be?" he asked. "Yes, sir; if I only knew how, I would gladly become one." He made an appointment, and 'so preached' and taught the people that not only she, but many others turned to the Lord; and a church was founded which for many years was a blessing to the people.

He was taken sick while surveying the farm of Ira M. Allen, near Canton, and died at Mr. Allen's house. The nervous system was prostrated; the brain power gave way; the 'wheel was broken at the fountain, and the silver cord was loosed.'

8

He belonged to a generation of noble men who
wrought a work which no man appreciated in their day.
For unflinching integrity, and a life-long devotion to truth
and righteousness, it is not easy to overestimate the grandeur and excellence of his life. He died the 26th day of
November, in the 77th year of his age.

CHAPTER IV.

Origin of the Church in Warren—Siege of Warren—The Church in Lordstown—Biography of Bentley—Biography of C. Bosworth —East Fairfield—Death of Mitchell.

THE Baptist Church in Warren was formed September 3, 1803, by Elder Chas. B. Smith. It consisted of the following ten persons: Isaac R. Dally, Effie Dally, Jane Dally, Saml. Burnett, Nancy Burnett, John Leavitt, Jr., Caleb Jones, Mary Jones, Saml. Fortner, and Henry Fortner. Isaac R. Dally was the deacon, and John Leavitt, Jr., clerk. No elder was appointed, as the Baptist order made no provision for "ruling elders," the preachers only being eligible to that designation. May 5, 1804, they were re-inforced by five additions—Samuel Quimby, Samuel and Sophia Hayden, residing in Youngstown, and Wm. and Martha Jackson.

From 1806 to 1810, Elder T. G. Jones preached occasionally to them. May 19, 1810, A. Bentley, then a licentiate minister, was received and ordained the same day. Some of the members residing in Youngstown, it was resolved Jan. 5, 1811, to meet alternately in that town, near Parkhurst's Mills, and in Warren. February 8, 1812, Isaac R. Dally and Saml. Hayden, after being "proved," were ordained as deacons.

This church was a parent of churches—Youngstown, Bazetta, Lordstown, and Howland, all sprang from it. January 11, 1815, thirteen members were

dismissed on application to organize in Youngstown,
viz.: Saml. and Sophia Hayden, Benj. and Elizabeth
Ross, Wm. and Parthena Dean, Caleb and Mary
Jones, Isaac R. Allee, Saml. Burnett, Lydia Cook,
Sarah Morris, and Nancy Jones; which church was,
formed Lord's day the 19th of April following—
Thos. Rigdon, J. Woodworth, and A. Bentley, officiating. They took the name of "Zoar," (Gen. xix:
20, 22,) that is, "little;" probably in allusion to the
language of Lot: "Oh, let me escape thither, and
my soul shall live."

This Thomas Rigdon was a man of much prominence as a preacher, and was worthy of the distinction conferred on him. He served with accept-
ability a term in the Ohio Legislature. There were
three brothers, Thomas, John, and Charles, all Baptist ministers. They all fully adopted the views of
the reformation, and faithfully defended them. They
were cousins of the famous Sidney Rigdon.

December 4, 1819, the church granted the petition of eight members in Bazetta to form a church in
that town. Benajah and Olive Austin were accepted
for membership, February 5, 1820, and baptized the
20th of the same month by Mr. Bentley. March 4th,
following, Sidney Rigdon was received into membership, and licensed April 1st, to preach. He married
Miss Phebe Brooks, and after two years moved to
Pittsburgh.

The Baptist people of those times were a humble,
Bible-loving brotherhood. The gospel in their hands
was plead with much simplicity and pious zeal.
Churches were increasing, and ministers multiplying.
Warren was the leading center; as it was also for

years the seat of justice for the Western Reserve. Here in 1821, and again in 1822, were held the ministerial assemblies of which Mr. Campbell thus speaks :

"Ministers' meetings once a year in different parts of that section of Ohio, for the purpose of making discourses before the people, and then for criticising them *in concione clerum*, and for propounding and answering questions on the sacred Scriptures, were about this time instituted and conducted with great harmony and much advantage. I became a regular attendant, and found in them much pleasure and profit." "These meetings were not appreciated too highly, as the sequel developed, inasmuch as they disabused the minds of the Baptist ministry of the Mahoning Association of much prejudice, and prepared the way for a great change of views and practice all over those 3,000,000 acres of the nine * counties which constitute the Western Reserve."

Changes, to be safe, must be gradual. The light of day bursts not suddenly on the earth, and the earth itself, with all things upon it, came into being by a measured progress. Great principles are slow in operation. Revolutions, to be permanent, must mature as they progress. This community of churches was discussing great subjects ; and as rapidly as was safe the people were preparing for the scenes which I proceed now to relate.

Late in the autumn of 1827, as Walter Scott was riding down Buffalo Creek from Bethany toward Wellsburg, Va., he met John Secrest and James G. Mitchell, on their way to visit Mr. Campbell. They sat on their horses a good while talking over the

---

* Eleven counties by divisions since made.

state and prospects of the cause of Christ. Scott
was soon on his favorite theme—the "ancient gospel," as he called it. He said he was sick at heart
hearing people talk about their dreams and visions,
but not one syllable about their obedience to Jesus
Christ—not a word about what blessing the ancient
gospel secured to those who submitted themselves to
the Messiah of God.

Young Mitchell was charmed with his conversation, and the brogue of his native Scotch tongue.
He had never met him before. Scott, turning to Secrest, asked if this young man had any gift in exhortation? He replied that he had, and that if he
would keep humble he might do much good. "God
bless him," said Scott. "I hope he will; he is the
man I want. You meet me at Bro. Jacob Campbell's, in New Lisbon, and we will away to Warren
and besiege the town ten days and nights: I will
preach and you will exhort, and we will make their
ears tingle with the ancient gospel."

The Mitchells were a preaching family. They were
men of firmness, promptitude, untiring zeal, and
abundant in labors. The three brothers—James,
Nathan, and David—were sons of William Mitchell,
whose ancestors emigrated from England with Lord
Baltimore, and settled in Maryland. William Mitchell removed to Washington County, Pa., where James
was born, December 5, 1805, and Nathan, March 2,
1808. Near Morristown, Belmont County, O., in 1813,
where Mr. Mitchell had moved with his family, Joseph
Hughes, of saintly memory, and Lewis Hamrick, re-
vivalists of the "Christian connection," found them,
and led them, father and sons, out of the wilderness

of religious doubt and conflict into the way of the
gospel as practiced by that order of people. Brought
forward in "exhortation," as was their custom,
James and Nathan, and eventually David also, became prominent, and they have long been in the
front rank among the most active and useful preachers of the gospel.

At the time agreed on, Bro. Mitchell went to New
Lisbon, where he found Bro. Scott waiting for him.
They arrived at Scott's residence in Canfield that
evening, and next morning they proceeded to Warren, and found a welcome in the family of Bro. Richard Brooks.

It was January, 1828. The town lay in spiritual
lethargy, profoundly ignorant of the tempest of
spiritual excitement about to sweep over the place.
Bentley had preached well and lived well; but he
held not the key to the heart, nor was he skilled to
awaken the music of the soul. A new era was at
hand in the religious history of Warren.

Scott came unheralded. His first appointment
was attended by few. There was neither expectation nor interest sufficient to collect an audience. A
group of little boys, to some of whom he had spoken
along the street in his eccentric way, were attracted
by curiosity to the meeting which was held in the
court-house. These, with a few old people, constituted his audience. In his discourse, after addressing the old with little apparent effect, he turned playfully to the boys, related to them some anecdotes,
then skillfully changing his theme and tone, he
melted them with sympathy for the sufferings of Jesus. His discourse was anecdote, pathos, wit, elo-

quence, and general remark, the whole intended for future rather than present effect. He announced another appointment, and dismissed. Mitchell was disgusted.

"We had not gone far," he writes, "before I asked him if that was the way he was going to pursue in besieging the town of Warren!—and if that was his ancient gospel! If so, I have no farther business in Warren." 'Oh!' he said, 'my dear brother, there was no one there worth preaching to, and I just threw that out for a bait. Hold still, we shall have a hearing yet, and then we will pour the great truths of the gospel red hot into their ears!' I thought possibly he was strategic in his method of gaining a hearing, and concluded to wait the issue.

"He was cheerful and social all the afternoon, anxious to get a hearing. Bro. Brooks kept silent. We could learn nothing concerning the discourse from the old folks or the boys. So passed this first day of the siege.

"At the appointed time we started to the meeting. The Baptist Church was secured, doubtless through Bro. Bentley's permission. Passing up, we found it crowded to its utmost capacity, and a number on the outside. Giving me an elbow touch, 'Do you see them nibbling at the bait?' said he. 'Yes,' I told him, 'I see plenty of people present.' We pressed our way through the dense crowd to the pulpit. We sung his favorite song—

> " Come and taste along with me
> Consolation running free
> From my Father's wealthy throne,
> Sweeter than the honey-comb."

I opened with prayer. After it, he arose and read the third and fourth chapters of Matthew. The baptism of Christ and the temptation, was his theme. He straightened himself to his full height, his great chocolate eyes glisten-ing, his whole face full of animation and earnestness. He brought his siege guns into position, and for an hour and a half the house rang with his eloquence. I shall not attempt to give an outline, for no man could do justice to that sermon. While he described the Son of God hurling the word of his Father and his God on the great adversary, and lashing his hardened soul with words that had pro-ceeded out of the mouth of God, until his brazen face shriveled, and his countenance most brazen fell, and he left, cowed, dismayed, foiled in his attempt, and the won-derful hero of redemption master of the field, victorious in the terrible conflict, while heaven's hosts came and ministered to him—he was powerful, lofty, and sublime. I had never heard such a discourse, so touching, so telling, not only on me, for the whole audience was moved.

"The siege was now fairly commenced. Up to the next Thursday an incessant fire was kept up day and night. The ancient gospel *was* poured into their ears. They were astonished, amazed. They got their Bibles, and went to reading and searching for the truth. No word fell on the floor, or hit the wall—all was eagerly caught and tried by the book. They could do nothing against it; it was the simple gospel of Christ in its facts, and commands, and promises.

"After the discourse on the temptation, he said we will sing a hymn, and see who will be on the Lord's side. We sang—

"Come and taste along with me," etc.

"Three persons came forward. He asked them if they believed with all their heart that Jesus is the Christ, the Son of God. 'These persons,' said he, 'will be baptized to-morrow after sermon, for the remission of their sins.' We baptized every day, and sometimes the same hour of the night."

9

The tide of interest was flowing high. Scott's next discourse was on Peter's confession, Matt. xvi: "Thou art the Christ, the Son of the living God," a grand theme, favorite with him, and grandly handled. Mitchell came after with a spirited and powerful exhortation to the people to come and take their stand on this durable and firm foundation which God has laid as the only hope of the world.

Baptism followed the evening meeting. Mitchell says to Scott, "Do not let the people know where we are going, and we will slip over to Bro. Jacob Harsh's and get a good night's rest, and be prepared for the labors of the next day"—for every night the places where they put up were crowded with inquiring and anxious souls. Mitchell retired and left Bro. Scott drying his clothes. It was but a few minutes before the house was filled with awakened people. Scott said, "If you follow me to learn the ancient gospel, I will pour it into your ears as long as I can wag a word off the end of my tongue." Mitchell fell asleep, leaving Mr. Scott speaking to the people. A number were deeply penitent. Scott awoke Mitchell, and told him to come and deliver one of his pathetic exhortations. "I would be in a fine mood, Bro. Walter, to exhort the people, just aroused from sleep!" "The iron is hot; one stroke when hot is worth a dozen when it is cold!" Out came Mitchell, singing as he came an old hymn, beginning:

> "Begone, unbelief! my Savior is near,
> And for my relief will surely appear."

He then began an exhortation based on the word "*lost*." The great loss, ah! the greatest, was to lose the soul; to be lost to God and Christ; and heaven and angels ; and the pure and good ; lost to eternal life and all bliss. Mr. John Tait, a Presbyterian, who had been strongly opposed, but who was now deeply moved, cried out, " Young man, for mercy's sake pray for me, for my heart is as hard and unfeeling as a stone." "Bless God !" said Scott, " Tait is a converted man." They all kneeled down, and Bro. Mitchell prayed for him. He wept aloud ; so did Scott. "We are," said he, " to weep with them that weep, and rejoice with them that rejoice." Then, addressing Tait, Scott said, " Are you willing to follow your faith ? Do you believe with all your heart in Jesus Christ the Son of God ? "Mr. Scott, I do ; but my heart is so hard ; I am as unfeeling as a stone." "Ah ! but 'we walk by faith.' 'This is the victory that overcometh the world, even our faith.' Let your feelings gush up from your faith in God's Son, effects which must follow the obedience of faith." " Mr. Scott, I am ready to obey my faith." "Bless God ! that is the path to travel."

Once more they started for the Mahoning, singing out on the midnight air as they went,

" Come and taste along with me,
Consolation running free."

Mr. Tait and several others were baptized upon the confession of their faith in the Savior of sinners ; after which, Scott, addressing them, said, "Follow your faith."

Next morning, the crowd still large, Scott asked Bro. Mitchell to proceed in the discourse ; which he did from the words of Peter concerning the "lively hope." He was only well begun, when Mr. Tait cried out, " I give glory to God ! my soul is full of

love to God and man." The effect was wonderful.
"Go on," said Scott to the preacher. "It is no use;
the feelings of the people are too high above any
effort I can make." Scott took the audience, and in
a very forcible manner gave an opportunity to obey
the glorious gospel and be filled with the fullness of
God. A number came penitently to confess their
Savior.

The next meeting closed the siege. Two such
houses would not have held the people. "Too many,"
said Scott, "for the effect we wish to produce." The
closing discourse was a recapitulation of the principal topics discoursed during the meeting. So ended
the siege of Warren, with over fifty conversions.

Bro. Mitchell adds in conclusion:

"It is due Bro. Walter Scott to give him credit as among
the first on the continent of America, if not the very first,
who took the old field-notes of the apostles and run the
original survey, beginning at Jerusalem. The first man I
ever heard preach baptism in the name of Jesus, with its
antecedents, for the remission of sins, and reduce it to
practice. And from this period, 1827, it spread like fire
on a prairie all over the country, and happy thousands have
rejoiced to learn how to become disciples of Christ according to the divine arrangement and purpose of God."

Scarce a vestige remained of the church in Warren
to oppose the establishment of the ancient order.
Additions continued to come in under the preaching
of Bentley, Osborne, and Elder Thomas Campbell,
who arrived soon afterward in the place. The fires
of a new religious life were kindled in neighboring
communities. On the 6th of March, 1830, the brethren in Howland were dismissed to form a church in

that place. In the beginning of the year 1831, Cyrus Bosworth and Benajah Austin were chosen bishops of the church, and Richard S. Brooks, James Gibson, and Moses Haskell, deacons. The members in Lordstown, whose names were chronicled in Warren, sent a petition to be set off, to unite with the church in that town, which was granted October 21st, 1832.

Bro. Bentley having located near Chagrin Falls, the church in Warren was left to supply itself with another pastor. At their call, Bro. Jonas Hartzel came; and on the 5th of April, 1835, he was installed as preacher, and associate elder with Bro. C. Bosworth. Subsequently, the church has had J. E. Gaston, Isaac Errett, John W. Errett, and others, who, with a judicious and experienced eldership, have maintained to this day the cause of Christ in Warren.

Very early a congregation sprang up in Lordstown. The new converts—fruits of Scott's meeting in Warren, with the members already there, and others gathered by Henry, Marcus Bosworth, and others—gave them such strength, that on the 20th of March, 1830, forty-one came together in the order of the Scripture models. Robert Tait and Moses Haskell were overseers, and John Tait and David Lewis, deacons. The church grew to considerable strength, and few have had a more stable brotherhood. They have participated in all the enterprises by which the cause of primitive Christianity has been sustained. The present number is about fifty. They have a good house of worship, and have been favored recently with the diligent and prudent labors, as pastor and elder, of Philander Green.

BIOGRAPHY OF ADAMSON BENTLEY.

The life of a good man is a blessing to the world. As certain waters transmute to stone the perishable wood deposited in them, so communion with God turns all the actions of a man's life to immortality. Biography has its office—its mission among men. The biographic pen, like the pencil, rightly used, works out immortal things. Its rightful use is to record, in durable permanence, a useful life which floats in transient recollections, and to extend it from the family to the world.

Adamson Bentley is beloved for his work's sake, tenderly remembered for qualities of character which mark him as a rare and noble man. He was born July 4th, 1785, in Allegheny County, Pa. While he was yet young his father moved with his numerous family to Brookfield, Trumbull County, Ohio; a country not yet rescued from the dominion of the primitive forest. Here young Bentley experienced the privations common to pioneer life. He struggled through encumbering difficulties till he obtained a suitable education for the profession in life in which he was so long distinguished.

He made public confession of his faith in Christ when he was a youth, in the Baptist order. His religious guardians discovering the bent and capacity of the young Timothy, and correctly foreseeing the usefulness to which he might attain, advised him to prepare for the ministry.

He began to preach at nineteen. Holding the system of Calvinism to be the unquestionable scheme of saving grace, he taught and urged its doctrines with the most unscrupulous fidelity. The clashing between the offers of mercy to all men, and the system which denied this salvation to any but the elect, was constantly present and constantly felt. In the honest devotion of his nature he carried the system in his head, and the love of God in his

heart. And as the heart, in this behalf, was better than
the head, he proclaimed the love of Christ so powerfully
that many conversions followed his ministry. As no man,
probably, ever believed this doctrine more sincerely, so
no one ever rejoiced more fully when its scales fell from
his eyes. Take the following testimony from his own lips,
as the writer heard him, in his own solemn style, declare his
feelings in the great yearly meeting in Hubbard, 1837:

"I used to take my little children on my knee, and
look upon them as they played in harmless innocence
about me, and wonder which of them was to be finally and
forever lost! It can not be that God has been so good
to me as to elect all my children! No, no! I am myself
a miracle of mercy, and it can not be that God has been
kinder to me than to all other parents. Some of these
must be of the non-elect, and will be finally banished from
God and all good. 'And now,' he continued, his parental heart swelling with unutterable emotions, 'if I only
knew which of my children were to dwell in everlasting
burnings, oh! how kind and tender would I be to them,
knowing that all the comfort they would ever experience
would be here in this world! But now I see the gospel admits all to salvation. Now I can have every one
for eternal happiness. Now I can pray and labor for
them in hope.'"

His prayers were heard: years before his departure, he
enjoyed that greatest bliss of a pious parent's heart—he
saw all his children walking in the truth.

He preached about five years as a licentiate. In 1810,
he settled in Warren, and on the 19th of May, that year,
he was ordained. On the 4th of May, the next year, at
the unanimous call of the church, he accepted the duties
of pastor. For a long time he was popular in that community. The bland dignity of his manners, and his social
courtesy, won him many friends. Though his talents as a
preacher were above mediocrity, and he was heard with

delight and profit by numerous auditors, to his social qualities and moral excellencies, as a man and a citizen, are to be traced the sources of that extensive power which he possessed among the people. It is our fortune to be acquainted with few persons in a life-time, who wield a personal influence so supreme. Tall, manly, graceful, with a countenance radiant with good nature, affable and dignified, he would stand among dignitaries as his equals, and condescend to the lowly with a gentleness which won the attachment of every heart.

In all that constitutes home a source and fountain of hospitable generosities, his amiable companion was quite his equal. With more economy and equal social talent, she managed her household with such skill that the entertained and the entertainers seemed equally happy. In those earlier days, when social habits were not yet costumed into rigid rule, many a traveler urged his journey an hour later and a few miles further to be a guest at his broad hearth-fires. None knew better than the gratefully remembered mistress of that hospitable home, how to "welcome the coming and speed the going guest."

As may well be supposed, on a limited salary, the increasing expenses of his family had not a sufficient foundation. He therefore for a time resorted to merchandise, merely as subsidiary, however, for he never neglected the preaching of the gospel.

In the course of his ministry he traveled extensively. He visited Kentucky, and labored a considerable time among the brethren in that State, and made many friends. The governor of that State received him into his mansion, and showed him marked attentions. He traveled much in Pennsylvania. He crossed the mountains in his saddle many times. At a time when population was sparse, and the mountain passes were infested by robbers, he climbed the craggy cliffs of those mountain barriers to tell to the East the progress of salvation in the West, and to bear

back to the West a share of the harvests the brethren were
reaping in the cities of the East. In these travels he made
the acquaintance of the renowned Dr. William Stoughton.
A lasting friendship grew up between the two ministers,
which Bentley perpetuated by giving to his oldest son the
name of his friend.   Dr. Stoughton was the author of an
abridgment of Dr. Gill's "Complete Body of Divinity,"
a work which, through Mr. Bentley's influence, found many
purchasers in the West.

About the years 1820 to 1825, Mr. Bentley was visiting
the Baptist Church which met near Cleveland's Mills in
the corner of Youngstown. The memory of some yet
living returns with speed swifter than carrier-dove to those
primitive scenes of unsectarianized simplicity. The
groves, "God's first temples," were spacious, and the
umbrageous forests, cleared underneath, lent solemnity
and impressiveness to the scene. I have seen him there
with a wagon for his rostrum, and seats brought from the
adjacent mills for the accommodation of the crowd which
had gathered from miles around. Some leaned at the base,
or sat down on the roots of the trees, whose leafy boughs
interlacing, wove a sheltering protection against the sun's
descending beams. When he stood up to read, all listened ; when he lifted up his eyes to pray, all arose ; when
he announced, in devout accent, the sweet and solemn
hymn, all joined to swell the chorus of praise. Those
days and scenes have been celebrated in poetic lines :

> " I well remember, and I love to stray
>   Down to the grove where BENTLEY used to pray ;
>   Where pious neighbors thronged the place around,
>   And stood, or leaned, or sat upon the ground.
>   I well remember how he used to stand,
>   And hold his Bible in his leftward hand;
>   And use his right to point out what it meant,
>   While lofty oaks in silence waved assent ! "

When the great religious awakening under the Camp-

bells began to make a stir, though cautious, he was one
of the first to accept the principles of a scriptural reform by them so ably propounded. This appeal to primitive ground created much conflict among all the religious
bodies, but especially among the Baptist churches. He
made acquaintance with those eminent men, and so thoroughly had he canvassed the claims of their call for union
on Bible ground, that when the bold and eloquent Walter
Scott came to Warren, Bentley seconded his labors, and
warmly co-operated with him on that occasion. There
followed a great ingathering of souls ; and the whole
church, with scarcely an exception, adopted the platform
of union contained in the New Testament. He continued
to preach with great power and with fresh zeal, now that
the new disclosures of the knowledge of the gospel had
been made known, and many converts came to Christ
under his ministry. In 1829, at the Association in Sharon,
he was chosen along with Scott, Hayden, and Bosworth,
to travel within its bounds.

At the close of the year 1831 he removed to Chagrin
Falls. While laboring to establish himself in his new
home, he "neglected not the gift that was in him." He
preached at every opportunity, not only without regard to
compensation, but rendering such help as his circumstances permitted to lay the foundations of the cause in
that new community.

It will not be possible to follow minutely the active and
useful life of Adamson Bentley. Such a history would
make a volume of considerable dimensions. His interest
in the cause of Christ, and the union of all the Israel of
God on the primitive foundation, never flagged. He had
great assurance of hope in the speedy dawn of the blessed
day for the original union of the people of God to be perfectly restored. His great love of peace, and his ardent,
hopeful temperament led him to indulge bright visions of

the speedy triumph of the pure, primitive gospel of the Lord Jesus Christ.

Age drew on apace, and with it a gradual decrease of his ability to endure field-service under the King. Yet he never desisted. At nearly eighty, decrepitude forced him to retire. The going down of his day was gradual and beautiful, like the decline of the sun, leaving in full play the amiabilities of his fine social nature. Serenity and cheerfulness still held sway, while the eye grew dim, and the natural force abated. While lingering on the shore of the cold stream, he beheld the "shining ones," and longed to be with them. "I rely not on myself; my full and only trust is in the Rock which was cleft for me." Full of hope and full of days, he took his departure for the brighter world, November 2, 1864. He lacked only eight months of eighty full years. For sixty years he blew the trumpet, and led Israel in the glorious combat.

In personal appearance, Mr. Bentley was more than an average man in dignity and comeliness. He was tall, finely proportioned, graceful in manners, and endowed with a remarkably open and engaging countenance. His noble form never stooped, till near the close of life he bowed a little, like a sheaf well ripened for the harvest.

As a preacher, like all men who leave their impression on society, he was like no one else, and no one resembled him. He usually began slowly, with simple and plain statements of his subject, rambling not unfrequently, till warming in his theme, he broke the shackles of logic, and swept on like a swelling tide, bearing his audience along with the vehemence of his pathos and commanding oratory. On such occasions his voice became full, sonorous, and powerful. When the shower was passed, the people not caring to analyze the sermon, or to trace their emotions to logical sources, were delighted and edified, and departed with marked and decided respect for the preacher, and with far higher reverence for the adorable

Son of God, whom he preached and whom he served
He never trifled in the pulpit.   His message was solemn,
and seriously and earnestly did he deliver it.

A life so equable as his, so uniform in its flow, has left
no abruptness or sudden dash; little that is startling to
create a fund of cherished anecdote.   The few that are
handed down bear the impress of his character.   At
one time infidelity, and even atheism, made considerable
headway in Warren.   On a Lord's day he arose in a full
assembly, and after surveying the audience in silence for
a moment, exclaimed: " *There is no God!* "   The people
looked surprised, while wonder and doubt glanced around.
A moment more, and he repeated it with stronger emphasis.   Perceiving the hearers to be thoroughly aroused, he
looked inquiringly into his Bible for a moment.   "But,"
he continued, in a softened tone, " I have omitted a part
of the sentence: 'The fool hath said in his heart there
is no God!' "   The discourse which followed was a clear
and convincing proof of the existence and perfections of
the Creator of all things.

He was one of the original trustees of Bethany College,
and gave his whole influence to the missionary cause.
The following notice of him appeared in the records of
the missionary society for the State of Ohio, for the year
1865.

"Among the memorials of departed worth, a large space
should be allotted to the late, most worthy and patriarchal
brother Adamson Bentley.   Since our last meeting this
eminent man of God has gone to his rest and his reward.
His departure, in happy consonance with the calm and
cheerful dignity of his noble life, was gentle, peaceful, and
blessed.   No man in north-eastern Ohio possessed the weight
of influence with the people that was wielded by this princely
man.   He came to the side of Campbell and Scott in
that early day when such an endorsement of their plea and
work could be appreciated only by those who witnessed

the apostolic labors and struggles which marked the early
epoch of our blessed work.

"Multitudes love to linger around the memory of this
good man. All respected, most loved him. Of him, as
truly as of any other man, it may be said:

> 'Take him all in all,
> We ne'er shall look upon his like again.' "

BIOGRAPHY OF CYRUS BOSWORTH.

CYRUS BOSWORTH, for many years a prominent citizen
of Trumbull County, deserves much more than a passing
notice. Few men in north-eastern Ohio have won more
cordial or more durable respect. None surpassed him in
enlightened views of public enterprise, in energy of character or business capacity. He was twice elected to the
office of Sheriff of the county; served as Colonel of a military regiment, and filled a seat with credit in the Ohio
Legislature; in all which positions he secured the confidence of the people.

He was born in Plymouth County, Massachusetts, April
12, 1791. He early acquired a good English education,
especially in navigation, surveying, and such branches as
would fit him for the seas. Yielding to the entreaty of
friends, he gave up his inclination for a maritime life, and
in 1811, at the age of twenty, he came to "New Connecticut." For a time he engaged in teaching, but the
late war with Great Britain breaking out, he was employed
as express messenger between Warren and Pittsburgh, and
was the first to carry the news of Perry's victory to the
latter place. He returned to New England, married Miss
Sina Strowbridge, and in the latter part of 1813 we find
him, with his parents, again at Warren. He resumed his
former occupation, but soon left it for the battle of life
on more stirring fields. He built the National Hotel,
erected a store, and became a merchant. His election to

the legislature was in 1822. At the expiration of that term, he accepted, at two successive polls, the office of sheriff. He settled on a large farm three miles south of Warren, where, in the more congenial pursuits of agriculture, he passed the maturer years of his active life. He lost his companion after a number of years of happy wedded life, and contracted a second marriage with Miss Sarah C. Case, sister to Leonard Case, Esq., late of Cleveland—a partner who survived him about fourteen years.

He was religiously trained in the Baptist order. In June, 1829, in the general religious interest attending the labors of Scott, he confessed his faith in the Lord Jesus, and was baptized by Bro. Bentley. He never went through the ceremony of a formal reception into the church, insisting that, according to the Scriptures, when we are "baptized into Christ," (Gal. iii : 27,) we are baptized into "one body," which is the church of Christ. (1 Cor. xii : 13.) He was soon called to the eldership of the congregation, and stood in that position many years. Under appointment by the church, he spent much time for several years preaching the gospel. His great weight of character and clear, cogent reasoning, gave a powerful support to the cause in its comparative infancy.

Much as he was respected in public life, to be appreciated, one must see him at home, and mingle in the scenes of the generous hospitality which for many years welcomed the coming guests to his open doors. With equal dignity and grace, he received and provided for the comfort of every one. He, too, was "given to hospitality." The social repast, well seasoned with Attic salt, where intelligence was mingled with agreeable entertainment, made the home of Bosworth known and gratefully remembered in all that region.

In his character there were qualities seldom united. A perfect hater of shams, no one was more lenient to the trivial blunders of humble merit. He could expose hypocrisy with a terrible severity, but he showed to the erring and needy a gentleness and tenderness of heart as beautiful, as they were healing. He had some enemies in a popular sense, for "he could not bear them which were evil;" yet in asserting the cause of the injured, he was prompt and decided. He declared early and openly for emancipation, because "it was right." These elements of character marked his course as a ruler in the church. His-sternness was sometimes the more apparent, but his sympathetic consideration of human weaknesses was never far in the rear. Some feared him, all respected him, the most loved him. For strength of character, force of will, and even consistency with himself, he had few equals.

His health failing, he journeyed to the milder climate of Texas and Mexico. The American Christian Missionary Society employed him to look after the weak churches while on his tour. In this work he was diligent, and proved a blessing. He assisted in the organization of some churches, and the encouragement of many. He returned from that mission in the fall of 1860, improved in health. In January following, he took a severe cold, from which he never fully recovered. Yet he was not confined to his room a day. On the 4th of April he went into his garden, and feeling ill, he turned to come in, and fell in death before any one could come to him. This was in 1861.

East Fairfield.

A quarterly meeting was held in East Fairfield, Columbiana County, beginning February 1st. Bro. Mitchell says:

"Leaving Warren, we went to our appointment in Fairfield, and put up with Bro. John Ferrall. We commenced at candle-lighting, and continued ten days, preaching the same gospel to the people that we did at Warren. The immediate result was thirty-seven additions, all new converts, beside instructing many of the old Christian order in more scriptural views of the gospel, especially in regard to the design of baptism. At this point I parted with Bro. Scott, after enjoying his company twenty-five days, and learning many things more valuable than tens of thousands of silver and gold ; sweeter than honey ; more delicious than the honey-comb. Looking back over forty-four years, and remembering what was the condition of things then, and the present state of affairs, I feel satisfied that the omnipotence of truth has effected it all.''

On the Western Reserve some of the churches originated in reforming Baptist communities. In Columbiana County the "Christian" element predominated. These people were themselves reformers, seeking, in the measure of their light, to return to New Testament usages ; but like most of the efforts to return from spiritual Babylon to Jerusalem, they crystallized around a few items which they capitalized into undue prominence. The great matters of the ancient gospel, and ancient order of the churches, were veiled in obscurity. Earnest and zealous, their public speakers often possessing great exhortatory power, they made many converts. They had a large congregation at Fairfield, and a good meeting-house. The amiable Joseph Gaston was their preacher. Through him, Bro. Scott obtained a favorable introduction among them. These visited the people together, and talked freely on the principles of the gospel. Scott was gifted with conversational powers of great skill and scope, and being full of his subject, he won at every onset. A meeting was called which was attended by the whole church. Scott turned his subject to his master key of Peter, pentecost and pardon. The theme was new, and in his hands the

scriptural scheme of the gospel was so plain and convincing, scarcely a doubt was left in the great audience.
At the close of his sermon, the proposition was made
to take the sense of the church upon the overture
now submitted, to assume the position of a gospel
church, in accordance with the scriptural teaching
they had just heard.   There was almost a unanimous
rising up.   Only five or six refused.   It was a strong
church of strong men.

Not long after this, Elder James Hughes, of Kentucky, came and preached among them.   Learning
the clearer way of the gospel, he adopted it, saying
he always thought the Scriptures connected more
blessing with baptism than they had discovered.   He
continued to thus preach, and to practice as long as
he lived.

According to the order of the "Christian" brethren, the preachers were the elders.   They had deacons to perform the duties common to that class of
officers.   Bringing the church to the New Testament
models, they now appointed William Cunningham
and John Ferrall, who had been deacons, to the office
of bishop, or overseer, and Dr. Amasa Fisher, and
―― ――, deacons.   Joseph Gaston continued to be
their minister.

About this time a colony of Methodists came into
Fairfield, from Virginia.   They had their preacher,
Benjamin Patterson, and were prepared to attend to
the matters of religion in their own way, and keep
guarded against novelties and heresies.   It was not
long before Bro. Benjamin Saunders came, and proclaimed the gospel so clearly and powerfully, he cap-
tured their preacher, and left his flock so shaken, that

10

they became an easy and willing prey. Every one, without an exception, embraced the teachings of the apostolic gospel, and came into the church. Patterson was baptized by Elder John Ferrall.

The subject of "weekly communion," was some time under discussion. It was new; and many thought it too great an innovation on established usages. Some argued that so great frequency would detract from its solemnity. On the other hand, it was steadily and convincingly plead that as the holy apostles, who had been charged by the Lord Jesus with establishing the customs and laws of his kingdom, had ordained that order in the beginning, it was binding still, and that it could not degenerate in solemnity when approached with the true and proper spirit. It was finally arranged, at Bro. Ferrall's suggestion, that the subject should be a matter of forbearance; those who regarded it a duty to show forth the Lord's death every Lord's day, to be permitted to do so; granting the unmolested right to others to come to the table of the Lord at longer intervals, as they had been accustomed to. To this all acceded; and all was harmony. Very soon all the members were a unit in this practice. Would that all differences in religious matters could be settled as amicably and permanently.

The church of East Fairfield has a noble record, and has been a light to the surrounding country. It has been generous in sustaining the "yearly meetings," and all others, for the proclamation of the Word of Life. Our men of name have all preached among them from time time, and assisted the faithful brethren in Fairfield to maintain the "unity of the spirit in the bond of peace."

Bro. J. G. Mitchell spent a long life in the gospel. He began when a youth, and traveled extensively in most of the north-western States. He was equally distinguished for zeal and success. He was small in stature, quick in action and speech, abundant in appropriate anecdotes, and never addressed an inattentive audience. With a kind heart, generous and high minded, few men had more friends. He settled in Danvers, McLean County, Ill., where his most useful life was terminated by a painful disease, which he bore with great patience, July 26th, 1873, in the 68th year of his age.

CHAPTER V.

Churches planted in Salem, Canfield, and Austintown—John
Henry—Origin of the church in Braceville—Sketch of Marcus
Bosworth—Biography of Jacob Osborne.

BRO. SCOTT began his great work in Salem, Columbiana County, in April, 1828, going from his
stirring meetings in Austintown and adjacent regions.
Prejudice preceded him, raised by the misrepresentations of Rev. Vallandigham, a Presbyterian minister, of New Lisbon, the father of Hon. C. L. Vallandigham, of later and wider notoriety. He came and
warned the people against that "apostate" Scott; declaring that he gave out that he would forgive the
sins of the people, with other statements equally
false and ridiculous. A. G. Hayden, residing in the
vicinity of Salem, fell in with Scott at the residence
of his father, Samuel Hayden, in Youngstown. By
him Scott sent an appointment to Salem.

He came, and opened to a full house the watch-cry
of the campaign, the *word of the Lord and pentecost*.
It was heard with mingled delight, wonder and doubt.
People rapidly took sides, some in favor, some against
the new doctrines, as many regarded them. "Why
was this not found out before?" was the cry of many.
"I know not," it was replied, "except that the time
is only just now come for these truths, so long hid
from our eyes, to be found out." "But if it is true,"
said others, "our preachers would have seen it long
ago; it would not have been left for Campbell and

Scott to find it out at this day." "Yes," it was answered, "just so objected all the Catholic clergy to Luther and the old reformers."

The news spread, and converts were multiplied. In ten days he baptized forty souls. The leading Baptists were delighted. Polly Strawn, David Gaskill, and others, came forward with all their influence in favor of the work. Singing and prayer till midnight was heard in many dwellings. The converts were received to baptism on the confession of their faith in the Lord Jesus Christ, without the usual routine of telling an "experience," and a vote of the church.

On a set day, Scott called them all forward to be received as members of the church. After many exhortations, the question was propounded to the church for the reception of the converts into fellowship. It was unanimously responded to in the affirmative; and this great effort, crowned with such blissful results, was about to be sealed up in peace and complete harmony. No creed had been presented for the converts to subscribe. They were baptized as converts to Christ; and in this solemn ordinance they had, as the apostles expressed it, "put on Christ;" to walk in him in all the experiences and duties of a new life. None had demurred, and Scott, feeling that Christianity had now completely triumphed over party, exclaimed, "Who will now say there is a Baptist Church in Salem?"

This gave the alarm. Some of the old leaders thought he was building up the Baptist Church, while in reality he was employed in a much broader and diviner work, that of bringing sinners unto Christ

Jesus, regardless of party names, lines, or limits. The dear name and cherished forms could not be relinquished. Then followed a reaction—a revolution. Then came conclaves, conferences, private and protracted. Mrs. Strawn, a lady of remarkable ability, and a tactician of much shrewdness, was especially active in this crisis. Some Presbyterians sympathized and aided to push the car backward. The old *regime* was restored, and the order was issued that all the new members must appear on church-meeting-day, relate a " Christian experience," and come in by the regular way, as members of the regular Baptist Church.

This was all strange and unexpected. The lambs wanted a sheltering fold. Synods and investigation committees were to them unfamiliar and repulsive. They were disheartened. They scattered ; some went into other churches, some gave up in sorrow, a few submitted to the orders in counsel, and entered by that door into that fold.

Out of this action arose the " Phillips Church," three miles south of Salem. Robert P. Phillips, a man of strong will, and an influential citizen, learned the gospel of Scott, and, with his family, was among the converts. The difference between the gospel and all party unions was clear as a sunbeam to him ; and with an open protest against putting a yoke on the disciples, he and others drew off and stood aloof. But they were far from giving up their faith and hope. He opened his own house where the lambs found shelter. Preachers came: Geo. W. Lucy, J. E. Gaston, J. H. Jones, Whitacre, and many others ; and soon a light sprang up which has continued to this day. Hayden could sing, and soon he was called to be a leader. They organized as a church in the summer of 1829. The unstinted hospitality of Phillips and other brethren, for many years made a home for the itinerant proclaimers of the word of life ; and aided by Hubbard, Allerton, Finch, Hartzel, and Schaeffer, from Deerfield ; by Hayden, Henry, Bosworth, and Applegate, and not a little by George Pow, of Green, this united and affectionate band of Christians became a strong and ruling church. It would take a page to record all who have reaped in this field, and who carry the kindnesses of this church in happy memory. In later years, H. Reeves and S. B. Teagarden have labored there with success. With Bro. White as associate overseer, and such men as Abram Shinn as deacons, this church has won a reputation for "durable riches and righteousness."

" Every wise woman buildeth her house," says Solomon. This church has had a number of " wise women," to whom is due no small share of the credit of building up the Lord's house. To their prudence, piety, sound judgment, and perseverance, much more is owing than will be known till the day of judgment.

After a few years the effort was renewed in Salem, and a church established. Bro. Geo. Pow rendered effective service in planting it, and Alexander Pow also, who is a pillar in the congregation. The brethren, with enlightened liberality, have erected a large, substantial and commodious house. The congregation, under the care of Bro. Spindler, ranks among the most permanent of the churches.

Bro. Geo. Pow, of Green, was long a leader and a stay of the churches in Columbiana County. He was a good scholar, and endowed with a breadth of good sense and candor, which made him superior in counsel. Critically read in literature, and especially in the Holy Scriptures, his speech was remarkable for correctness and richness of instruction. His recent death has left a void which a generation will not repair. The church in Green was much indebted to his wisdom for the strength and prosperity to which it attained.

THE CHURCH IN CANFIELD.

This church was formed January 12th, 1822, in David Hay's dwelling-house. Thomas Miller was the officiating minister. Deacon Samuel Hayden, William Hayden, and John Lane, from the church of Youngstown, and Elijah Canfield, Palmyra, were the counsel. The church was moderatively Calvinistic; progressive in spirit. The principal members were David Hays, William Dean, with their families, H. Edsell, Turner, Wood, and Myron Sackett.

In June, 1829, the following entry is made in the church record:

"The Baptist Church, constituted in 1822, so continued till 1829. During this time, the brethren in attending to the Word of God in search of truth, began to doubt the propriety of having creeds, or articles of faith, as bonds of church fellowship. The result was, throwing them away as useless, believing the Scriptures sufficient to make us wise unto salvation through faith in Christ Jesus. We adopt them as our rule of faith and practice."

In the winter of 1827–8, Bro. Scott opened, at Simmons Sackett's, the plea of the ancient gospel. The second chapter of Acts, the opening of the

kingdom, was his subject. He simplified, and enforced it so pointedly that all saw, and most, on examination, accepted the truth. He showed that all
parties have the elements of the gospel, but differently
arranged; and that as the same letters would spell
different words, according to the arrangement of
them, so these gospel themes, set forth in one order,
formed one theory on which one sect was built; in
another order arose another sect. He contended
ably for the restoration of the true, original, apostolic
order of them, which would restore to the church
the ancient gospel as preached by the apostles.

The interest became an excitement. All tongues
were set loose in investigation, in defense, or in opposition; which foreshadowed good results. Nothing
so disastrous to the sailor as a dead calm. Let the
vessel heave under a tempest, rather. The Bibles
were looked up, the dust brushed off, and the people
began to read. " I do n't believe the preacher read
that Scripture right." " My Bible does not read that
way," says another. The book is opened, and lo !
there stand the very words ! In the first gospel sermon, too—the model sermon—as what " began at
Jerusalem" was to be " preached to the ends of the
earth." The air was thick with rumors of a " new
religion," a "new Bible," and all sorts of injurious, and
even slanderous imputations—so new had become
the things which are as old as the days of the apostles.

Scott's sermons gave a mighty impulse to the work.
Many converts were gained for Christ. Some of the
old members received them with caution, but the
church made them welcome, and, ere long, by the

11

prudent exercise of Christian forbearance, they were, like "kindred drops," all "mingled into one."

Mr. Scott was often eccentric ; but he possessed the talent to sustain himself and turn his eccentricity to good account. On one occasion, when the whole country around was almost tremulous with the excited state of feeling, he managed to slip into the assembly unobserved, and seating himself far back with his cloak well about his face, and his broad-brimmed hat well drawn down, he sat listening to the remarks of the assembling multitude. The reader must remember, as an excuse for the darkness of the room, that the candle was the "light of other days." The illuminating oil still lay concealed in God's great cellar. One man says, in a low tone: "What do you think of Scott ?" without waiting a reply, "I never heard such a preacher ; he is hard on the sects, but he has the Bible on his tongue's end." Another: "I never read such things in the Bible as he is telling us." His quick ear was catching these "droppings" of the people. The room became packed. "Do you think the preacher is coming ?" inquired one. "I wonder if he will not disappoint us to-night ?"

Then rising to full position, still sitting on his seat, laying back his cloak and removing his hat, Scott cried out in his magnificent voice, "And what went ye out into the wilderness to see ? A reed shaken with the wind ? But what went ye out to see ? A man clothed in soft raiment ? But what went ye out to see ? A prophet ? yea, I say unto you, and more than a prophet." Matt. xi. Then with a sweep, and brilliancy, and point that astonished and instructed all, he discoursed on the ministry of John the Bap-

tist ; the preparation of the gospel ; the introduction
of Jesus by him to the Jewish nation; and carried
his audience up to the crucifixion, the resurrection
and coronation of the Lord of glory, and the descent
on pentecost of the Holy Spirit, with the grand events
of that "notable day of the Lord." It is needless to
pause and describe the wonderful effect of this sudden outburst and powerful rehearsal of the gospel
upon his astonished auditors.

There were members here of sound judgment,
conservative, but progressive and thoroughly settled
in the conviction that the Holy Scriptures were a
perfect as well as inspired guide. It is not surprising that with such a people the preaching of Scott
was held under cautious examination. All opposition subsided, however, when they saw the new converts "full of joy and the Holy Spirit," and when
they saw the Scripture language warranted the practice introducèd by the preacher. Such men as the
Deans—father and sons—David Hays, and Myron
Sacket were just the men for a new movement ; slow
to start, but firm as a rock when convinced. These,
with the devoted Ezra Leonard, and a number of
women, such as those of whom Paul makes honorable mention, formed a society as firm and intelligent
as any on the Reserve.

It is to be regretted that history, dealing chiefly
with the outward, sensible phenomena of a movement,
fails too frequently in presenting the subjective part—
the mental and emotional struggles—in which the
visible and tangible facts originate. These heart con
flicts and battles of conscience, are often in the
highest degree instructive. Fortunately we are able

to give something of this inner history of one of these original members of the church in Canfield:

Myron Sacket descended from Presbyterian ancestry, in Warren, Ct. He was early in Ohio. He helped to build the first meeting-house in the center of Canfield, which was erected by the people of his ancestral faith, and in which he piously hoped to be a life worshiper. In 1817, he was married to Miss Orpha Dean, of Baptist principles, and equally conscientious. The discrepancy in their views was a trouble to them; and they sought to reconcile the disagreement, each honestly supposing the other would yield to increased light. He brought pamphlets and sermons, which she read and considered; she resorted to the word of the Lord in its plain teaching on the subject of baptism, and the subjects strictly entitled to it. Sacket was disinclined to discussion, a man of quiet and peaceable, though of very firm habits of mind. He became so aroused to the investigation that he opened his Bible anew. He read the New Testament twice through to find infant baptism, noting carefully every thing bearing on the subject. Many times he turned back and re-read, fearing he might have passed by it. Disappointed and grieved, yet loving the truth rather than the accepted convictions of early training, he resolved now to read it for a far different purpose—which was to learn what are the teachings of the Word of God on the subject. The result was a clear and satisfied conviction that the New Testament contains no trace or evidence of authority for that practice. The struggle was hard. The very firmness of the man, which made him a pillar for long years afterward, made the transition difficult. But the conclusion, finally reached, was never reversed nor regretted. Both himself and wife, now one in faith as well as in matrimonial union, put on Christ in his own holy baptism, on the same day. This was in 1819.

After Bro. Sacket had accepted Baptist principles, an uncle from Connecticut asked him how he could degenerate from the principles of his parental belief to unite with the Baptists, a people of much lower grade of learning and position? His answer was significant: "I read and carefully studied the Word of God for light, and finding no support for those principles, I was compelled to give them up."

Few men ever rendered more efficient and substantial support to the cause of the primitive gospel. His house was long a home for the people of God. The terms, "meekness and fear," applied justly to him. He was slow to accept the light which Scott brought, but step by step he came with the wealth of a ripe Christian experience and sound judgment; and was ever afterward unfaltering in its support.

This church continued to meet in the north-west part of the township, where they built a comfortable meeting-house. At this period, William Hayden was a member of it, though his residence was in Austintown. In the month of May, 1828, the congregation, after full proof of his abilities in public speaking, and recognizing his zeal and knowledge of the Scriptures, gave him their sanction and approval as a minister of the gospel. Thus licensed and commended to other churches, he gave himself more diligently to the work. The eminence which he subsequently attained, justified this action, and vindicated their discernment of his improvable gifts.

In the same vicinity there was forming a community known as "Bible Christians." Wm. Schooley, living in Salem, was their principal preacher. These two churches—the "Christians" and the Disciples—became better acquainted, and Bro. Schooley himself having united with the Disciples in Salem, these communities united as one brotherhood in Christ; thus giving a practical illustration of the union and co-operation of Christians on the original foundation. The Flicks, the Shattoes and all, about twenty, were enrolled with the Disciples, as one people in Christ. This event took place January 23, 1830.

This church was never very numerous, about seventy being the highest number. But they kept up a respectable visibility many years. Their record for the great yearly meetings of the Disciples of the county, is highly honorable. Like many others, she has brought multitudes of converts to the fold of Christ, and has sent out her sons and daughters to carry on the good work in other lands. The church in Center, Rock County, Wisconsin, is a planting from Canfield. The Parmelys, the Deans, Orsemus and his family, while weakening this by their removal, greatly strengthened that church.

In the fall of 1827, some time after his appointment as the evangelist, this church moved Bro. Scott's family into their midst, and contributed liberally to their support. Scott bought, and built a house, intending this as a permanent residence. But his changing field of labor altered his plans. The home talent of the church has always been her chief reliance for edification. But for many years she had the labors occasionally, and sometimes statedly, of the preachers of the county.

As several families resided at and near the center of the township, the church gave consent for them to form a separate congregation. Accordingly, in the spring of 1847, about twenty associated themselves together in that relation. They were organized by Bro. J. W. Lanphear. J. M. Caldwell and Andrew Flick were elders ; Walter Clark and John Flick, deacons. They were aided by the labors of Brethren Pow, Applegate, Belton, Phillips, John Errett, Dr. Hillock, White, F. M. Green, Van Horn, and Edwin Rogers.

The church in the north-west part of the township, reduced by removals—the old members having all gone over the river into the promised land—after struggling in feebleness for awhile resolved to unite with the body at the center. This union was effected October 6, 1867.

THE CHURCH IN AUSTINTOWN

was constituted June 16, 1828. The remains of the Baptist church, once flourishing, lay in a waste and decaying condition over portions of Youngstown and Austintown. In the winter of 1816, a revival occurred under the labors of Elder Joshua Woodworth, a humble and devoted minister. About forty were converted ; among thc converts were William Hayden, then a youth, and others, still younger, of the same family. The counselors of the church thought it necessary to have the young converts instructed in the "doctrines" of the gospel, "election," and kindred themes. So the faithful minister, loved as a father, was dismissed, and Wm. West was called. He was more learned, but straight, cold, Calvinistic. Under his reign the kingdom was dissolved. Zeal languished under doctrinal sermons. Discipline went by rule rather than by love. Covenant meetings became courts. Appeals were taken, and counsels called. The lambs fled from the fold; conversions ceased; the light grew dim, and the church had but a name to live. Elder West was still in the community when Bro. Scott opened the gospel plea there, and opposed his work.

The following sketch of affairs there is from the pen of Walter Scott:

"When called about two years ago, I found the church in a state of entire prostration. For four years they had not eaten the Lord's Supper; all was delinquency—a perfect web of wickedness, the like of which I never had seen. It was an involved labyrinth of personal and family quarrels. For about three weeks I strove to disentangle the sincere-hearted, but in vain. Strife is like the lettings out of water—what is spilt is lost. When the threads and filaments of a quarrel have forced themselves like waves over the whole body ecclesiastic, that body should be dissolved. We accordingly looked upon this institution to be entirely lost, and began to preach the ancient gospel—the word of the Lord as a hammer and a fire. All hearts were immediately broken or burnt; and of that sinful people there have been immersed nearly one hundred and fifty individuals. These have become a church, and are walking in the commandments and ordinances of the Lord, blameless, as I hope. The Scriptures are their sole authority, and they have three bishops, bold in the Lord Jesus, and five deacons."

The religious awakening which restored the church, or rather built it anew on apostolic foundations, began in Austintown, in February, 1828, soon after the great meeting in Warren. A young man by the name of Asa Jones became serious, and, expressing a wish to become a Christian, Bro. Bentley was sent for. He preached in the school-house where William

Hayden was teaching.   When the sermon closed, an opportunity being offered, the young man arose, declared his purposes, expressed much joy in believing, and appealed to his friends to follow him to Jesus. Next day, Bro. Bentley preached and baptized this person and eight others.   John Henry and his wife were of the number.

Bentley returned home, but a work had commenced which was soon to become wide and general.   The converts were clear in their conversion, and active.   William Hayden was greatly delighted by the conversion of his particular associate and neighbor, John Henry, a man of great weight in the community, and possessed of abilities, which Hayden clearly foresaw would be likely to turn to much usefulness.

About three weeks after this, Scott sent an appointment to preach in the "Jones' school-house." He came Wednesday the 19th of March.   A full house was in waiting.   He hurried his audience to the line of decision, classing all the world in two parties—Christ's and the devil's.   He laid the foundations of Christ's kingdom in the grand affair of his death, burial, resurrection, ascension, coronation, and the inauguration of his reign on earth on the day of Pentecost.   Among the startling utterances of that sermon, he said : " We can have a revival of religion whenever we want it !   Strange ! strangely marvelous !   Differing wide as the heavens from all we had ever heard !   Can we obtain this glorious prize—regeneration, pardon, and peace ? "   Thoughts hurried to and fro, as Scott talked on and showed that Christ's work was finished, his sacrifice com-

plete, the "oxen and fatlings were killed," the table
was spread, "all things are now ready," *and had been
ready for eighteen hundred years*—nothing now but
for sinners to hear, and come, and find a welcome to
salvation by the Master of the feast.

This was gospel. "Why have I been waiting so
long? why has no one ever told me that before?"
Thus reasoning and feeling, five came to the decision
and yielded. That night the crowd was increased;
and next day, March 20th, twelve of us were by his
hands lifted into the kingdom.

The whole country was in commotion. Converts
came at almost every meeting. But the excitement
was to become higher, and to penetrate a new class
of society, as I proceed to relate.

Aylett Raines and the Restorationists.

While Mr. Raines was on his tour preaching, and
previous to his baptism by Bro. Williams, he came to
Austintown. It was in April. He already had a
high reputation, especially among the Restorationists,
who were numerous. News circulated that he was
coming to preach his renunciation of Universalism.
A crowd assembled and filled the house. He opened
on the mission of the apostles as the embassadors
of Jesus Christ, the authorized expounders of his
will. Their preaching was the commission carried
out according to Christ's will and intention; as they
were not only commissioned by him, but miraculously
assisted by the Holy Spirit, so that their preaching,
as reported in the book of Acts, is the full, complete,
authoritative guide in preaching the gospel, and receiving sinners to the church; that as they, in the

opening of their mission on pentecost, and always
afterward throughout the world, preached to the believers that they should repent and be baptized, in
the name of Christ, for the remission of sins; this
is our model to the end of time, and, consequently,
no preaching which differs from this model has any
authority in the Word of God.   He concluded his
long and argumentative discourse in these words:

"My friends, I find myself in a strait; I am shut up
in a dilemma; and I can see no way out, with the Word
of God in my hand, but through the obedience of faith
in baptism.   If any of you can see any other, I im-
plore you in the name of my Master to show it to me."

The sensation, which was perceptible in the beginning of the sermon, grew in intensity as he proceeded, till it heightened to a tumult.   As soon as the
meeting closed, persons who had come in big wagons, and had brought their chairs into the house for
seats, jerked up their chairs, started over the benches,
and hurried to their homes.   The medicine was working.   The patients were bilious.   The remedy was
heroic.   Raines was calm.   The Disciples were happy.
The Universalists, who composed the larger part of
the assembly, were disappointed, grieved and chagrined.   Their champion had left them and gone over
to this new and specious heresy.   We can not have
it thus; we will not stop and reason calmly with him
and show him his error, as he earnestly besought us.
"To your tents, O Israel!"   The very horses felt a
touch of the excitement of their drivers!

That discourse worked miracles; that is, if conversion, as we had been taught, was in every case a
miracle.   It had driven nails in sure places, "as nails

fastened by the master of assemblies." Eccl. xii : 11.
William Hayden preached in the afternoon the same
day, and baptized several converts.

The church of Austintown was one of the first in
north-eastern Ohio, built on " the foundation of the
apostles and prophets, Jesus Christ himself being the
chief corner." The day appointed for collecting the
disciples as a church of Christ was fair, and a large
assembly convened. Scott, Bentley, and Raines were
present. After a discourse in the house, we were
called out upon the green in front of it. Here all
the disciples, one hundred and ten in number, were
disposed in a large circle. A space was open on one
side of about twelve feet, in which stood the preachers. Thus, each member, with his right hand clasping the left of the one next him, so stood, that he
could see all the rest, and also the brethren to whom
we owed so much under Christ, and who were, in the
most solemn manner, about to form and declare us
an organized church. Each of the preachers, in turn,
addressed us in the most earnest exhortation, in the
things pertaining to the duties of this new relation,
while all stood uncovered under the open canopy of
heaven. Then followed a prayer by Bro. Scott, implor-
ring blessings unbounded and unending from the
divine Head upon every member of his mystic body.
Then the hymn :

> " Lo ! he comes, with clouds descending,
>   Once for favored sinners slain,"

led by Hayden and Henry, was sung with raptures
of joy. So began the church of Austintown. It was
placed under the care of William Hayden. Bro.
Henry was soon called to his side ; and not long

after, Alexander Spears was chosen also to the eldership.

BIOGRAPHY OF JOHN HENRY.

To few men has it been granted to gain such a celebrity
in so short a time as was won by this gifted man. His
public ministry was only a little over thirteen years, in
which time his personal labors extended from central Ohio
to central Pennsylvania, and into Virginia; and his fame
spanned the continent. In all that constitutes brilliancy,
dash and boldness, he was a very hero. He was born in
Chartiers township, Washington County, Pa., October 1,
1797. It is declared of him that he sung tunes when not
a year old, but he did not talk till he was four. He came
with his father, Francis Henry, to Poland, Ohio, April,
1803. He married Miss Jane Kyle, January 10, 1822, and
settled on new lands in Austintown the next spring.

He was a leader in every thing he undertook. In the
days of military training, he was music-major of regiments.
A few blasts of his bugle would start up every soldier, and
the exact time of his movement infused martial valor into
all around. When he turned to the Lord he quite abandoned this practice, and turned his musical talents, which
were of a high order and well trained, to gather and lead
the bannered hosts of the Lord. As a farmer he did more
work than any other, save one man. He excepted William Hayden. He played on nine kinds of instruments;
his favorites were the violin and the clarionet.

He was trained under the strictest rules of Presbyterianism. As the "Christian Baptist" appeared, William
Hayden passed the numbers over to the hands of his friend
Henry, whose penetrating mind grasped the great principles
it unfolded. He was ripened for the sickle of truth, so that
when Bentley came, he and his faithful wife were among the
converts—the first fruits of a large ingathering. The writer
has the most vivid recollection of the scene, as the excellent

Bentley, tall and venerable, led this man of commanding form, who stood six feet two inches, then in his thirty-first year, and laid him beneath the waters of baptism after the example of the Lord.

He gave himself at once to the diligent study of the Bible. He read little else, he studied nothing else; except, perhaps, church history. His taste was for history, and his sermons were largely historic recitals of the life and work of Christ, and the preaching of the apostles, with historic illustration from the Old Testament, delivered in so fresh, forcible, and fluent a style, that as a speaker, few equaled him in instructive and entertaining discourse. But the power of his sermons was much in the authority with which they were spoken. Without any of the studied arts of oratory, he often moved on great assemblies with a mastery that chained attention for two hours. Without rhetoric, his speech abounded in fine tropes, especially in metaphors; and not unfrequently he arose to a pomp of diction equaled only by the finest orators.

In person he was tall, rather spare, with sandy complexion and sharp features, quick in movement, as in the operations of his mind, and when he walked he planted his feet with a tread which showed the firmness of the man. Cheerful, at times almost to levity, very social, kind hearted, and with wit like a polished rapier, whatever "his hand found to do he did with his might." He was in Smithfield, Jefferson County, when he was informed by a special messenger, March 12th, of the supposed fatal sickness of his wife. He would have started after the night meeting for home, but friends interfering, he rested a time. Before day dawned he was in his saddle, and that night, the 13th, he was at home; a distance of seventy miles. The Yellow Creek was so high it nearly swam his horse. He watched his wife most assiduously, and saw her recovery; then fell a victim to the same disease, typhoid fever, after sixteen days' sickness, May 1, 1844.

His work is interwoven with the groundwork of this cause through the whole Western Reserve. Though un-cultured, he was not rude. He was high-minded and hon-orable, and immensely popular with the people. In the early day he and Mr. Campbell met at the Plains-meeting-house, near Minerva. Many had never seen either of them. Henry preached in the morning, and the people thought it was Campbell. After an interval Mr. Camp-bell preached, and many of the hearers said : "We wish that man would sit down, and let Campbell get up, *for he knows how to preach !* "

There was lamentation in all the churches when he died. The feeling is well remembered and distinctly defined. It was less a murmuring, than a deep, sad, silent grief. Bro. Campbell wrote of him at the time : " Bro. John Henry, as a preacher of a particular order of preachers, had no equal—no superior. He was not only mighty in the Scriptures as a preacher and teacher, but was also emi-nently exemplary in the social virtues of Christianity. His praise is in all the churches in the Western Reserve and circumjacent country."

He was bold, brave, fearless, cheerful and animated ; the life of society, humble, generous, and of unfeigned faith ; of great power, of tremendous force, and mighty and elo-quent in the Scriptures ; he "hewed Agag in pieces, and slew kings in the day of his wrath." All prized and hon-ored him, and the remembrance of him stirs the fainting purpose to unbounded courage. Hundreds yet remember him, as with more prowess than the Knights of St. John, he would return from a successful charge, victor over legions of the king's enemies ; and the blasts of his triumph gave courage to all the faint-hearted. Though not always dis-creet, his bravery was of the first quality. He never lifted his spear but in victory. His enemies gathered near to behold the agile dexterity and massive power with which he felled to the ground the foes of God.

His memory was as capacious as the Mediterranean
Eminently was he, as the orator has it, the "man of one
book." The Bible was his store-house, his treasury, his
exhaustless fountain. He read it morning, at noon and
night, and all he ever read he remembered. He could re-
peat it by chapters and by books. It was his book of history, of archæology, of travels, of biography, of incident,
event and anecdote, of moral power and religious persuasion. Nothing in society for which he found not a coun-
terpoint in that Daguerrean gallery of all truth, all duty,
all motive.

Brief and brilliant his career. The most loved
him—all beheld him with admiration. All love to cherish
and honor his memory, while within a narrower circle, sacred and still as where mourners move, he is the idol of
an affection next akin to the feeling that worships.

Forty-seven years the church in Austintown has
stood against all the forces arrayed against it. It
has never ceased to meet, except by voluntary ad-
journment, to attend the yearly meetings. Under
the wise and careful eldership of Bro. Ira McCollum,
one of its charter members, and Bro. Joshua Kyle,
who for many years have held the helm, she has kept
her course steady and constant toward the harbor.

NEWTON FALLS.

The church in Braceville and Newton Falls was
formed on Baptist principles, early in the year 1820.
The origin of it, and the history of Marcus Bosworth,
can not be dissociated.

Bosworth was born in Plymouth County, Massachusetts,
July 11, 1794. He married Miss Elizabeth Ward, September 9, 1814, and came to Braceville, June, 1816. In
the year 1818, a revival occurred among the Presbyter-

ians, and Bosworth and his wife were among the converts.
Though trained up in the Baptist order, they were willing
to worship with the Presbyterians, and they searched diligently the word of God for sprinkling as baptism; but
they found it not. In the fall of 1819, Thomas Miller,
a Baptist minister, preached at Esq. Johnson's house. By
him, Bosworth and his wife were baptized. "The happiest day of our lives," said the venerable sister Bosworth, who, at the age of seventy-one, recited these scenes.
Next year, under the labors of Mr. Miller, was formed the
Baptist church in Braceville, which called Bro. Bosworth
to act as deacon. Active and warm-hearted, he improved
so rapidly in speaking that the church encouraged his as-
pirations to higher usefulness. He yielded to this decision,
and as much as the care of his farm would permit, he gave
himself to the ministry of the word.

Bosworth attended the ministers' meeting in Warren,
October, 1821, and there made the acquaintance of Mr.
Campbell, and heard much from him on a return to original Christianity, in its form, teaching, and models, as set
forth in the New Testament. His receptive mind heard
attentively and with little prejudice. Yet he prudently
held these views subject to further consideration. The removal to Braceville, in 1825, of Jacob Osborne, gave a
fresh impulse to the scriptural investigations already advancing. Meanwhile Bosworth's improvement of his gifts
in public discourse continuing to be satisfactory, he was
ordained as a preacher of the gospel in October, 1827.
Adamson Bentley and Sidney Rigdon were called by the
church as the council on the occasion.

Bro. Bosworth gave himself ardently to the work of
preaching. His heart was all aglow with the love of souls,
and many were turned to the Lord by him. He traveled
much in other counties and other States; yet he worked
on his farm when at home, to support his family. Preachers received little in those days for their labors. Some-

12

times, in a long trip, he got less than the cost of shoeing his horse. It was the fault of the times that Bosworth, Alton, Applegate, Collins, and quite all the early preachers were suffered to go to the warfare at their own charges. A good wife at home, and a good Father in heaven, kept Bosworth in his saddle. Yet he was much at home, to lead his sons in the needful industries of the farm. For many years coming guests enjoyed the bountiful hospitalities of his home.

He was constant in prayer. He maintained worship daily in his family. His wife frequently heard him in prayer when he thought himself secluded. He often prayed in his house after the family had retired.

He was abundant in labors. He saved not himself, that he might serve the Lord and bless his family. No man need be more tender or amiable in his home. He rode sometimes from New Lisbon home, a distance of about forty miles, after meeting, reaching home past midnight. He was very feeble a year or more before his decease. In the fall of 1846 a cough settled on his lungs, which never left him. June 10, 1847, in the calmest repose in Jesus, he gave his spirit to his God. He was a most agreeable, companionable man, easy and fluent in conversation, mirthful at times, but never trifling. His preaching was more exhortational than argumentative. Frequently his whole audience were in tears, while his own came unbidden, and fell as the rain on roses. He moved amidst new converts. His persuasive appeals to the converted to manifest in their conduct their new life in Christ were most earnest and effective. A godly man with scarce a foil in the bright picture of his life.

At one time he visited a fellow-member of the church, and the conversation turned on the design of baptism as set forth in Acts ii : 38 ; that it is to put the believing, penitent sinner in possession of the joys of pardon through the divine promise. The man could not be persuaded to accept the testimony of the Holy Scripture, and he replied: "You may bring as many Scriptures to prove it as you please, I will not believe it." Bosworth turned away, sad to see men hopelessly wedded to their views and traditions, beyond recovery by the power of the word of God.

Once a Baptist minister paraded himself in front of him, prepared to take notes of his sermon, probably expecting to intimidate the preacher. Bosworth felt a fresh inspiration, and being a clear and rapid speaker, he gave forth his discourse in such copious fullness, the minister failed to keep in sight of him. After the meeting, being asked to show his notes, he turned away, saying, "they are very general, not very plain!"

Though the church in Braceville was originally Baptist in name, its creed was not held rigidly. Love prevailed over law, and the Bible eventually superseded the Confession of Faith. In the discussions which resulted in the displacement of all doctrinal dogmas as grounds of Christian fellowship, this brotherhood bore a leading part. They formally organized as Christians, March 20, 1828, declaring the Holy Scriptures sufficient for all purposes of faith and practice. Their number was then twenty-eight. Marcus Bosworth was appointed the overseer. The church in Braceville was probably the first on the Western Reserve, which formally adopted this divine platform as their only basis. It was increased by twelve conversions at that time.

From this time till the fall of 1839, when they completed the meeting-house at Newton Falls, the church met at different places, mostly in school-houses. Bro. Osborne soon removed to Warren, but other help was not wanting, and all the proclaimers gathered in souls to God in this enterprising church. Yet Bro. M. Bosworth was their constant reliance, who, with all his travels abroad preaching, did far more to sustain the church than any other man.

Amos Clark served as overseer along with Bro. Bosworth ; Joel Bradford also. Henry Harsh and Benoni Johnson were early deacons.

When the congregation established itself in their new house at the falls, they procured more constant preaching, and increased in numbers and in command of the public ear.

Memoir of Jacob Osborne.

His birth dates with the birth of the nineteenth century. His parents lived near Trenton, New Jersey. They were of the Baptist order. His mother was a very pious and active Christian. Early in life their son Jacob was awakened to a sense of his sinful state, and finding hope, he was baptized, and almost immediately entered the ministry. He was licensed to preach when only nineteen years of age. His pure life, reserved, winning manners, devotion to study, and unvarying attentions to the offices of religion, awakened great hopes of his future usefulness. In person, rather tall, very erect, comely of form and countenance, a voice not strong, but clear and very attractive.

In 1821, at the age of twenty-one, he entered Mr. Campbell's seminary on Buffalo Creek, Virginia, along with Joseph Freeman, where he remained two years, making most diligent application in his studies. During this time he employed his talents preaching in localities within reach of the seminary. Becoming acquainted in the family of the McElroys, Washington County, Pennsylvania—a family of marked character for manliness, decision, energy, and promptitude, and for devotion to the principles of religious reform—Mr. Osborne was united in marriage to their sister, Miss Susan McElroy. He was principal of the academy in Wellsburg one year, and preached in that town and vicinity. He came to the Western Reserve, and settled in Hiram, in the fall of 1824. The following year he moved to Braceville. Perhaps Bro. Osborne, more than any other man, prepared the way for the more complete ministration of the gospel which was soon to surprise the churches, and reform their modes of speech and action. He led on biblical investigations quite regardless of the dogmata of creeds and conventional forms of speech. He saw clearly the need of an extensive and thorough revision and correction of the terms and phrases, hackneyed and human, in which people were accustomed to talk of conversion and its kindred themes, and the substitution for them of the more appropriate and divinely authorized language of the Holy Spirit. In all this he was only abreast, scarcely ahead, of many others. At the request of Bro. Bentley, he removed to Warren early in 1827, and taught the academy for a year, still preaching as his health would permit. He was always present at the association and ministers' meetings, and on all occasions took a part more prominent and influential than is usually assigned to one so young and unassuming. For his talent, erudition, and zeal, he stood up as a Barnabas, and all heard him with delight.

His health gave way, and in May, 1829, this young, influential, talented, beloved, Christian gentleman, admirable in all things, in many things a model, fell asleep. His disease was hemorrhage of the lungs. He was only in his twenty-ninth year. He died in Warren.

CHAPTER VI.

THE CHURCH IN WINDHAM.

THE church in Windham was formed Tuesday, May 27, 1828. On the Lord's day preceding, eleven members of the Braceville church requested, and obtained dismissal, to join in the new church. They came together under the wise counsels of Elder Thomas Campbell.

They numbered twenty-eight. Brethren Samuel Robbins, Philander Robbins, and David T. Robbins, with their families, Dr. Thomas Wright, and Bro. Streator, were leading members. David Woolcott, and Samuel Robbins were the deacons. Reuben Ferguson was unanimously chosen overseer.

The beginning and progress of the work which led to the establishment of the churches in Braceville and Windham is well told in the diary of Bro. Samuel Robbins, of Windham. I append some extracts from it.

Lord's day, Sept. 16, 1827. Mr. Walter Scott preached in the school-house, at the center of Braceville, the first time; sent by the Mahoning Baptist Association, by the request of the Garrettsville and Braceville Baptist churches. Text: 1st Epistle of John, chap. iii: 1st verse. A good discourse.

Nov. 25, 1827. Deacon Bosworth preached at the center of Braceville, the first time.

Dec. 2, 1827. Mr. Adamson Bentley and Walter Scott preached in the school-house on Braceville Ridge. Mr. Bentley preached first to a house jammed full—got them

most all asleep—do not recollect his subject. Then Mr.
Walter Scott preached, after reading the second chapter
of Acts. Dwelt particularly on apostle Peter using the
keys of the kingdom of heaven, delivered to him by the
Savior, Matt. xvi: 19. Before he finished his discourse,
a good part of the congregation were standing up gazing
at the speaker. In his remarks respecting Peter opening
the kingdom to the Gentiles, at the house of Cornelius, he
said: "Having no more use for the keys, for aught I know,
he threw them away."

Dec. 23, 1827. Mr. Osborne preached on the Braceville Ridge. He was a good preacher, and a very devoted minister.

Jan. 26, 1828. All the Baptist [church] went from
Braceville Ridge to Warren, to hear Walter Scott preach ;
for they heard he was turning the world upside down.

Feb. 23, 1828. Walter Scott preached on Braceville
Ridge. First-rate attention ; do not remember his subject.
His main object was to convince the people that God meant
what he said in his *Word*, which caused great excitement
among the people in Braceville and Windham ; many sitting up all night reading the Scriptures to see if they meant
what they said ; which resulted in many immersions. It
was a common practice for him to illustrate the *five* items—
viz : Faith, Repentance, Baptism, Remission of Sins, and
the Holy Spirit—by holding up his left hand and using his
thumb for Faith, and so on ; then contrast it with the five
points of Calvinism ; and thus he made the Scripture order of the gospel so plain, that little boys could carry it
home. Great excitement wherever he went.

Feb. 23, 1828. Went from the Ridge to Windham.
In the evening he spoke in the school-room, near Dr.
Thomas Wright's. Father Rudolph and his two sons, John
and Zeb, were present. Spoke first-rate. Remarked he
was like an eight-day clock—he would speak on Faith,
Repentance, Baptism, Remission of Sins, and the gift of

the Holy Spirit, and wind up! Having a desire to hear him through, David T. Robbins and myself went with Mr. Scott to the hospitable families of the Rudolphs; staid all night.

Next day, February 24, Lord's day, we all met at the house of Mr. Chapin, who was a Methodist. Mr. Scott spoke on faith to a room crowded full. Dr. Thomas Wright, myself, D. T. Robbins and others, came forward, which excited Mr. Chapin so he got up and opposed. In the evening met at Mr. Rudolph's : a good meeting.

Feb. 25, 1828. Scott preached in the school-house in Garrettsville—more came forward. Agreed to meet the next Wednesday in the school-house near Dr. Wright's, when Scott would preach and immerse the candidates.

On Wednesday, the 27th, almost the whole town came out. Bro. Scott spoke feelingly. Then Dr. Thomas Wright, myself, David T. Robbins and others, nine in all, were immersed. Ice a foot thick. Great excitement among the people, it being the first immersion in Windham. Very cold; though our hearts were warm and rejoicing.

Tuesday, March 4, 1828. Scott again at the same place ; immersed three more.

March 5, 1828. Preached again; baptized Father Abraham Seymour and three others.

March 10, 1828. Scott went to Braceville. Preached and baptized Philander Robbins and eight others.

Wednesday, March 12, 1828. Bro. Marcus Bosworth preached and baptized three more at the same place. Bro. Scott went home, to Canfield.

Saturday, March 22, 1828. Covenant meeting. It was the custom of the Baptists in those days to tell their experience, to maintain good fellowship with one another, and to be prepared to break the loaf on the Lord's day.

Lord's day, March 23, 1828. We all met in the school-house on Braceville Ridge. Bro. Marcus Bosworth preached and broke bread the first time after the preaching of baptism for the remission of sins.   Joyful meeting.

March 26, 1828.   Bro. M. Bosworth preached—immersed one ; next day, in Braceville, two more, between eleven and twelve o'clock at night.

The diary continues, noting meetings in detail, with additions at nearly every discourse of two or three to ten persons :

"*Lord's day, April* 27, 1828.   Bro. Bosworth preached and immersed seven more, who were added to Braceville church.   Bro. Bosworth administered the Lord's Supper the second time ; glorious meeting."

Old customs are slow to yield.   Monthly communion was still retained.

Elder Thomas Campbell came about this time to the Western Reserve to co-operate in the work.   His visit is thus referred to in Bro. Robbin's journal :

"*May* 1, 1828.   Father Thomas Campbell preached in Braceville, and the next day near Dr. Wright's.   One immersed by Bro. Bosworth."

"*May* 8, 1828.   Father Thomas Campbell preached in Windham.   Baptized Bro. Reuben Ferguson and Bro. Baldwin, of Charleston.   Same day, Bro. Bosworth immersed two."

"*May* 9, 1828.   Father Thomas Campbell preached on Braceville Ridge from Hebrews ; subject : Land of Canaan."

"*May* 17, 1828.   I went to Warren.   Met with them on Lord's day.   Up to this date, one hundred and thirty had been immersed in Warren ; one hundred and five added to the church."

"*Lord's day, May* 25, 1828.   Bro. M. Bosworth preached on the Ridge.   Seven united to Braceville church.   He administered the Lord's Supper the third time."

13

In this manner the work went on through all that region, extending into Nelson, Freedom, Charleston, Hiram, Mantua, and Shalersville.

The church in Windham, like those in Braceville, Garrettsville, and Warren, was in transition. Expiring customs die hard. The " experience " and " covenant " meetings and monthly communion seasons, as occasions of special " fellowship," lingered for almost a year in Windham and Braceville. Robbins writes :

"*March* 22, 1829. Commenced breaking bread every first day of the week. Fourteen added to the church, making in all sixty-five members."

A wise forbearance ruled the church, and they eventually all came to the unity of the faith and practice of the apostolic order.

For many years this church was a shining light. They built a good house at the center of the town, and continued there to worship as late as about the year 1855, when, weakened by removals and other causes, they yielded the ground and ceased to meet as a church. But their works remain. While with sadness they were compelled to abandon the organization, they count with joy on the good they achieved ; and other regions are made strong by the causes which entailed weakness on the church in Windham.

This church raised up and sent forth two able evangelists, Bro. L. P. Streator, long prominent and useful, especially in Pennsylvania ; and Bro. Myron J. Streator, whose abundant labors will never be forgotten. Both arose in Windham, and by this church received their first encouragement and sanction as preachers of the gospel.

Elder Thomas Campbell's Visit.

It is difficult, after the lapse of forty-five years, to realize the commotion consequent on the first work of Scott and his associates. So novel, so bold, and to the candid listeners, so plain and scriptural! The euthusiasm was unbounded. The " zeal," though usually guided by knowledge, sometimes overstepped the limits of prudence; yet it is surprising so few errors became incorporated in the teaching, and that the work was marred by so few cases of indiscretion. The interest in the public mind had swelled to a torrent, whose impetuous rush bore away all before it.

News of all that was going on was constantly transmitted to Bethany, and Mr. Campbell, whose careful and sagacious eye surveyed the movement in all directions with the mind of a general, had some fear lest the impulsive zeal of his ardent and able friend Scott might, in this quarter, wreck the vessel of reformation. At his instance, his father, the venerable Thomas Campbell, saddled his favorite sorrel, and made an extensive tour of these battle-fields. He visited first, New Lisbon, then Fairfield, Warren, Braceville, Windham, Mantua, Mentor, and other places. Nothing could have been more opportune; just such a man was needed; and none who never saw him can well appreciate the great effect of the presence, counsels, and addresses of this noblest of men. Uniting the simplicity of a child with the dignity of a senator, agreeable almost to playfulness, with a piety so pure, sweet, and unostentatious as to command the respect and admiration of all around him, the newly forming churches felt in his presence

the timely aid, encouragement, and counsel which
could be imparted by no other one so well. His
fame and abilities as a scholar and as a speaker, drew
large audiences. Seeing the work before him to be
but an advance step in the great plea of the restoration which he had himself initiated and advocated
twenty years before, after examining the ground with
his usual caution and candor, he gave to it his full
sanction, and entered upon its advocacy with all his
great influence and powers. Soon after his arrival
on the ground, he wrote to his son Alexander from
New Lisbon, under date of April 9th, 1828, as follows :

"I perceive that theory and practice in religion, as well
as in other things, are matters of distinct consideration.
. . . We have spoken and published many things *correctly* concerning the ancient gospel—its simplicity and
perfect adaptation to the present state of mankind, for the
benign and gracious purposes of its immediate relief and
complete salvation—but I must confess, that, in respect
of the direct exhibition and application of it for that
blessed purpose, I am at present, for the first time, upon
the ground where the thing has appeared to be practically
exhibited to the proper purpose. 'Compel them to come,'
saith the Lord, 'that my house may be filled.'

"Mr Scott has made a bold push to accomplish this object, by simply and boldly stating the ancient gospel and
insisting upon it ; and then by putting the question generally and particularly to males and females, old and
young : Will you come to Christ and be baptized for the
remission of your sins and the gift of the Holy Spirit?
Do n't you believe this blessed gospel ? Then come away,
etc., etc. This elicits a personal conversation ; some confess faith in the testimony—beg time to think ; others consent—give their hands to be baptized as soon as conven-

ient; others debate the matter friendly ; some go straight to the water, be it day or night; and, upon the whole, none appear offended.''

He spent the month of May, (1828), in Braceville, Windham, and that region, adding strength and members to the cause, and teaching piety and pure religion from house to house. He preached in Windham, Lord's day, the 8th of May, and baptized Rev. Reuben Ferguson, a Methodist preacher of great moral worth, who began immediately to preach the faith as proclaimed by the apostles at the beginning.

The travels of Elder Campbell were very extensive, and his labors abundant. He visited Chardon, Hamden, and Huntsburg; the latter of which were new and weak churches. He was among the infant churches like Barnabas of the apostolic days. No record can convey a proximate estimate of the blessings of his presence and labors at this juncture. There was probably no man within the reformation who possessed such authority of personal influence ; of noble mien and manly form ; grave and serene of countenance ; courtly in manners, his discourses always religious and instructive, he impressed his hearers always favorably and permanently. The young disciples and inexperienced preachers, who were now springing up, needed such a model ; and it was delightful to see the quiet and profound deference yielded to him wherever he came.

It was during this period of his travels on the Western Reserve that he fell in with Aylett Raines. Bro. Raines may tell his impressions in his own words :

" Not long after this period I made the acquaintance of Bro. Thomas Campbell. He interested himself in my favor, and had me travel and preach with him several months. This I view as a merciful interposition of my Heavenly Father. By day and by night, publicly and from house to house, he was my teacher. I feel that I was greatly benefited, but how much I can never tell. Not only by word, but by example, he deeply impressed my warm and susceptible heart. He was, emphatically, a godly man. He was greatly addicted to private devotions. Often have I seen him, when he had no reason to believe that any eye saw him but that eye before which all things are naked and open, in his closet, prostrate on his face, pouring out his soul in prayer to God. I thank God that I ever made the acquaintance of that great and good man ; and I look forward with bright and cheering anticipations when we may meet to part no more, in the brighter and better world."

Sketch of A. Raines.

This gifted man, destined to rise to a conspicuous place in the advocacy of the gospel, was born near Fredericksburg, Spottsylvania County, Virginia, in the year 1797. At the age of four years, he was led up by his father to the altar, where Parson Boggs "christened" him after the forms of the Episcopal church. It was done amidst many tears from the young "convert," but they were neither tears of joy nor penitence, but of fear and apprehension of something awful about to be done to him, in opposition to which his whole nature was roused. But his pious parents, in fulfillment of obligations which they conceived were resting upon them from the *vows* assumed at his "baptism"—but which, with far more truth, they were under merely as parents—trained him in the principles and paths of strict morality. The pious culture thus obtained, especially from his most excellent Christian mother, was of immeasurable advantage to him. He ever bore toward them the profoundest gratitude for their faithful guardianship. From Virginia his parents emigrated, when he was fourteen, to Jefferson County, Kentucky. Hearing different "orders" of preaching, often contradictory, and presuming, as many do, that the Bible sanctions all, he became skeptical. The reading of Paine's Age of Reason filled him with doubt, and flushed him with conceit. But his mother's pious instructions held him, and finally gained the mastery. He went into Indiana, and engaged in teaching, near Fredonia. His employers being Restorationists, he fell into discussions with them. He felt himself foiled in these contests. Winchester's "Dialogues on Universal Restoration" completed the work, and he came out a thorough and sincere convert to that speculative scheme.

New emotions filled his breast. He obtained the common "evidence" of genuine conversion. He writes:

"I got religion. The sky appeared to be bluer, the leaves looked greener, and the birds sang more sweetly than ever before. I underwent a great moral change. There was much of the love of God in it. Shrouded as I was in error, yet there were apertures through which the love of God passed into my heart, and made me inexpressibly happy."

Persuaded that the numerous friends of Bro. Raines will be delighted with his own statement of his experiences, I continue the recital from his own graphic pen:

"I now commenced the study of the Scriptures in good earnest, and after two years commenced preaching. This, of course, provoked great opposition, and I had a number of debates. In these, one sectarianism was arrayed against another; and those that came plunging and crashing against mine seemed so very frail, and made so feeble a defense, as rather to confirm me in my errors. I preached Restorationism five years. A part of the time I taught school, but the last two years of the five I traveled at large. The expiration of this term brought me to the

Western Reserve, where Bro. Scott and others were preaching the ancient gospel. Hundreds were being baptized. Much interest had been awakened in behalf of the gospel, and bitter was the opposition which had been enlisted against it. Misrepresentations—not to use a harsher term—were as numerous as blackbirds in August, and these too, very often by those who professed to be 'embassadors for Christ,' and who said they were 'the called of God, as was Aaron.' 'Just say you believe, and let a preacher dip you, and there could be no scriptural doubt of reaching—no matter what the life might be subsequently—the heavenly inheritance.' It was strange to me then, and yet passing strange, that good people, when under the dominion of religious prejudice, falsify at a most alarming and extravagant rate. They say that they are 'new creatures;' but if they are, I can. not perceive that the new creature is, in this respect, any better than the old !

"After a few weeks I concluded to hear Bro. Scott for myself. He was to speak at night at Bro. Robbins', in the town of Windham, near where I was at that time sojourning. One object that I had in view was to bring Bro. Scott into a debate; for among other things that I had heard, I had been told that he was a very bold man, and at the close of his discourses he challenged objectors to make known their objections. Here, thought I, will be a good opportunity for me! and hence I let a number of my brethren know that I intended to oppose him. Well, we assembled, a compact congregation. Bro. Scott, after singing and prayer, read first Cor. first chapter. He preached it through, not forgetting to state and defend what he styled the six points of the gospel. I was greatly surprised. But when he called for objections I was confounded. I could see the heads of my brethren moving to the right and left, in the crowd, expecting to see me rise to my feet. But they did n't see me rise ! The reason was, I felt certain that if I *opposed* Bro. Scott I would *expose* myself. His discourse appeared to me, at every point, invulnerable. And so, when we were dismissed, and out in the yard, my old brethren gathered around me and asked, 'Bro. Raines, what do you think of the discourse?' And let me say here that I think my first answer will be my last: 'I can do nothing against the gospel as preached by Bro. Scott; unless I should live to disgrace it; which may our gracious Lord forbid!' Hence I have no sympathy with those who say they can not understand the preachers of the reformation. I understood the first I ever heard a great deal better than I desired.

"The next day I heard Bro. Scott again. His subject was the fifteenth chapter of first Corinthians—the resurrection. Here again I was exceedingly amazed. Germs of truth, and beauties and glories sprang from the bosom of that chapter under the handling of Bro Scott, of which before I had scarcely any conception. 'As in Adam all die, even so in Christ shall all be made alive,' I deemed a passage of cardinal importance, and the whole chapter very good in its place ; but as I did not understand it, of course I saw none of its beauties, and was superlatively ignorant of the meaning of the scrap just referred to, which was one of the proof-texts by which I attempted to prove the ultimate holiness and happiness of all men. At the close of this discourse I felt profoundly interested in the ministrations of Bro. Scott, and resolved to follow him up for some days longer.

"On the next day his subject was the two covenants ; and here again I was amazed, not only in contemplation of the beauty and magnificence of gospel truth, but at my former ignorance, for although I had been a preacher five years, I certainly did not know the difference between the old covenant and the new. I obtained from them a sort of hotch-potch; or rather I made of them a chaos, and preached the darkness that was on the face of the deep !

"In a few days I heard again. His subject was the

eleventh chapter of Hebrews.   He still bore himself aloft in all the grandeur of the gospel, and in the captivating intelligence of the truth as it is in Jesus.   Here I virtually surrendered—not that I was convinced that all men would not be finally saved.   Bro. Scott said nothing on this subject, only that it was a *philosophy*, as was Calvinism, Arminianism, etc., and no part of Christianity.   He convinced me that I ought to lay my philosophy aside, and preach the gospel as the apostles preached, making their discourses a model to be accurately copied by me in all my ministrations.   This was, so far, a capital conquest, for it terminated in due time in the conviction, in my mind, that Restorationism itself, as much as I had formerly idolized it, is founded in error.

"At this juncture it became necessary that I should part from Bro. Scott for a season, for I had a tour of preaching before me, and must fill my own appointments. I resolved that I would preach as Bro. Scott had done, and as I believed the apostles did, and that at the close of each discourse I would call for objections.   And I told my old brethren that I threw myself on their mercy; in other words, that if they believed me to be going astray, in mercy to set me right.   This attempt was often made within this tour, but it only served to convince me more satisfactorily that I was right.   It terminated at the house of brother Ebenezer Williams, in Ravenna, a Restorationist preacher, a good man, and possessing excellent talents. I submitted to him, at his own house, my views of the gospel.   He received them, and we were mutually immersed for the remission of sins.   After this, I immediately retraced my steps, and within five weeks I immersed fifty persons, three of them, counting Bro. Williams, talented Restorationist preachers." *

* Ebenezer Williams, David Sinclair, and Theophilus Cotton.

A. RAINES AND E. WILLIAMS.

Wishing to fortify himself thoroughly on so important a matter as the change in his religious position, and also desiring to keep clear his approaches to his Restorationist brethren, Raines deferred his baptism till he should confer farther with their leading men. He retraced his steps, preaching at points formerly visited, till he came to the residence of E. Williams, of Ravenna, who must now be introduced to the reader.

Ebenezer Williams was born in Warwick, Hampshire County, Mass., March 14, 1793. He came to Ohio, in May, 1815, and settled in Ravenna. Falling in with the views of Winchester on universal restoration, he prepared himself for a life advocacy of that system. He was calm, dispassionate, a candid and sound reasoner, and very conscientious, and was one of the first advocates of that doctrine on the Western Reserve. He was earnest and fluent in speech and persuaded many, and planted communities of converts in Newburg, Bedford, Brimfield, Shalersville, and elsewhere. I will permit his own pen to relate the circumstances which led him to embrace the gospel:

"I will give you a fraction of my history in Shalersville. I preached my first discourse there among the Universalists, at the request of Daniel Burroughs, Esq., who was instrumental in getting the first Universalist preacher on the Western Reserve. In 1828, I was employed in that town one-fourth of the time at one hundred dollars.

"On a pleasant morning in the month of May, I rode from Ravenna to meet my appointment. When I came in sight of the house I saw more people than usual gathered around it. While hitching my horse, two of my friends came up and informed me that Father Campbell and Sidney Rigdon had been holding a meeting there for several days; two young men had been baptized; the meeting had created great excitement; they had dwelt much on the second chapter of Acts; and they requested me to preach from the same, especially the thirty-eighth verse. I informed them I would do so. In my discourse I opened to the tenth chapter, and found that the Gentiles received the Holy Ghost before baptism, reasoning that baptism was but voluntary and quite unessential. I offered the same objections to an immersion in water that I have since so often heard, indulging in some witticisms about going to heaven by water, and succeeded in pleasing the congregation, except the two young men above referred to.

"While going home I reviewed my discourse. Although I had spoken in all sincerity, I became quite dissatisfied with what I had done. My text, and the forty-sixth and forty-seventh verses of the last chapter of Luke, were constantly occupying my mind. I went home quite unhappy. I was familiar enough with the New Testament to recollect the substance of what it contained, and my mind was constantly engaged, day and night, to satisfy myself that immersion could be dispensed with. I had been sprinkled—I had sprinkled others, but in spite of all my efforts my convictions still fastened themselves upon me.

" In the midst of my perplexity one morning, while in the field plowing, a child came and informed me that Bro. Raines was at the house. I went in immediately. We hardly passed the usual compliments, when Bro. Raines said he had been hearing Walter Scott; that he had got into trouble, and wanted me to help him out."

Raines remained with him several days, during which time they gave the subject a thorough examination in the light of the Holy Scriptures. The result is given in the language of Bro. Williams:

"The next Lord's day my appointment was in Brimfield. Bro. Raines went with me. We both preached. After meeting, we walked out, when he inquired of me how I had made up my mind. I informed him I should be immersed. Next morning we notified the friends of our intention, and on our way back to Ravenna, we stopped at Sandy Lake, a beautiful pond in the corners of Brimfield and Rootstown, and taking hold of each other's hands, we walked into the water. I baptized him; he in turn baptized me. I think they were all Universalists who witnessed the scene. Some cried, some scolded. We exhorted them to come and do likewise.

"When the four weeks came round, I went back to Shalersville, and again preached from the second chapter of Acts, but not so much to the satisfaction of the people. Some were angry; many said they would not pay their subscription for such preaching. I told them I did not expect it—the Lord would take care of me. Thus I turned my back on the four hundred a year. I have never since received over half that amount, but having obtained help of God, I continue until this day."

These brethren being now fully emancipated from that useless and pernicious philosophy, went everywhere preaching the word. They were anxious to recover the communities which they had instructed from these errors. There is a worldly and false pride of consistency, which is but the effigy of that true *principle* of "consistency" which is said to be a "jewel," a counterfeit mistaken by many for the genuine. Had Williams and Raines listened to the

voice of that false pride, they would never have encountered the reproaches unsparingly ·heaped upon
them for changing their doctrinal *base*. But this
was their cross, and joyfully for Christ were they
willing to bear it.

The news of their conversion spread every-where,
causing much joy among the Disciples. But the feeling was mingled with a fear that they were not
thoroughly instructed in the foundations of the gospel. It was feared that they were, after all, merely
baptized Universalists. If this was all, it was nothing. Baptized Universalism is Universalism still ; not
the gospel. So baptized sectarianism, in any form,
is but sectarianism at best, and not the gospel of
Jesus Christ. This plea of reformation did not begin nor end in baptism. It saw as its end, and
sought nothing less, than the de-organization of sect,
and the re-organization of the saints on the new covenant, in the express terms and conditions divinely
set forth in the Holy Scriptures. This was clear as
a sunbeam in the preaching and writings of Scott
and the Campbells, and all who were enlisted in the
defense. No marvel then, that even thus early in
our work, no one could be satisfied with the mere
baptism of these men. They wanted proof of their
abandonment of Universalism, and their confession of
Christ and his gospel. They felt as the disciples of
old concerning Saul, of whose conversion and baptism report quickly spread—"they were all afraid of
him, and believed not that he was a disciple." Acts
ix : 26. These noble men, however, had learned and
embraced the gospel as the "power of God unto salvation to every one that believeth." Salvation was

now with them, as with the original preachers,
through faith and obedience ; without which impeni-
tent sinners are still in their sins, and obnoxious to
the judgments of God.

THE CHURCH IN FREEDOM.

The first person baptized in Freedom, after the
primitive order, was Daniel Brown. This was in
1828. Bro. Bosworth sowed the seed and reaped the
fruit. Bro. Rufus Ranney was the next. Then John
Bonney, who heard Scott in Nelson, and was baptized
by him. This post was held by Bro. Ryder and the
itinerant laborers till 1840, when they built and organized. The gospel had made inroads into Charleston also, and brethren Woolcut, Peebles, and Baldwin
associated with the church at Freedom. Daniel
Brown and John Bonney were chosen overseers, and
Lewis Hamilton, Joseph Woolcut, and John James,
deacons.

The church prospered for several years. Two
preachers—O. E. Brown and J. W. James—arose out
of this church, who have been many years in the
work, and proved themselves extensively useful. In
June, 1848, they entertained the county yearly meeting ; their number being about thirty. They afterward rose to fifty. After about twelve years of prosperity, dissensions grew up, and the tie of brotherhood was sundered. For several years the religious
interest was nearly extinct ; but there were a few
names "who had not defiled their garments." The
work has lately been revived, and meetings are again
held regularly.

It is interesting to state that the first disciple in

Freedom still survives, and that the first overseer is elder still.   Bro. Daniel Brown, who in his eighty-sixth year, writes me, "I do not expect to live much longer, but so long as the Lord lets me live, I am willing.   When he calls me I am ready to go."

CHAPTER VII.

Association in Warren, 1828—Principles of Union Settled—Scott
and Hayden appointed Evangelists—Biography of Hayden—
Expectation of the Millennium.

THE association for 1828 was to meet in Warren.
People every-where were looking forward to it
with great expectations. The new converts, now
very numerous, were inspired with the prospect of a
great spiritual convocation. The friends of return
to primitive order were flushed with the victories so
numerous and decisive, and prepared to enjoy that
meeting as a kind of triumphant jubilee; while the
preachers themselves were eager to meet together in
mutual congratulations, to make reports, and to hear
news of the success of the gospel from all quarters.
A few viewed the new movements with fear and
trembling, paused in doubt, and hoped that the
approaching association might interpose some needful checks, and in some way bring the whole work
more within the principles and order which were
still dear to many of the older members.

It is not necessary to conceal the fact that the
writer of these notes was in attendance from first to
last. It will be difficult to convey to the reader the
complex character of that meeting, the important
questions which there called for solution, and the
controlling guidance necessary to maintain unanimity of feeling, that the work so powerfully progress-

14

ing might still go forward. Men for the crisis were demanded. Such men were there.

The association came together purely and simply as an assembly of Christians. Though under the forms and name of a Baptist association, the creed system was abandoned, and neither that denominational name, nor any other, was on its standards. Men of nearly all the religious bodies, many of them leaders therein, leaving the technics of the party, but retaining their faith, hope, and love, mingled together as disciples of the common Lord ; now in the one body, possessing the one spirit, rejoicing in the same hope, submitting themselves to the same Lord, through the one faith and the one baptism, they worshiped together the same God and Father of all Christian people. This great occasion was a grand demonstration of the possibility of the union of Christians on original Bible ground. It was no longer a theory. It was then an actual, accomplished fact. And though by no means the first such example in modern times, this meeting in Warren was, perhaps, the largest assembly, and the most complete, full, and illustrious example of it. The history of it is a triumphant vindication of the principles of the Campbells on this subject, a proof of their practicability, and an illustration of their power. Here were Methodists, no longer Methodists, but still Christians ; Baptists surrendering the title, yet holding the Head, even Christ ; Restorationists, giving up their fruitless and faulty speculations, now obedient to the faith once delivered to the saints ; Bible Christians, recovered from their negative gospel to the apostle's method of preaching, together with very many from other forms of religious belief—all rejoicing together, "perfectly united in the same mind and the same judgment."

Among the seniors were Thomas Campbell and his son Alexander, Adamson Bentley, and Sidney Rigdon, with Walter Scott, to whom multitudes of the young disciples looked with the affection of children to a spiritual father. Of the younger preachers, may be named Jacob Osborne, Marcus Bosworth, William Hayden, John Henry, Symonds Ryder, Zeb Rudolph, John Applegate, John Secrest, A. G. Ewing, as also Aylett Raines, the Cottons, and Reuben Ferguson.

So large a number of Disciples, both of new converts and of persons collected by the appeals for union from various religious beliefs, needed much instruction in the principles of that union, especially in its practical workings. Besides, the doubts and disaffections arising from the introduction of Restorationist ministers began to break forth in out-of-door discussions touching the prudence of such a loose proceeding.

The leading brethren were fully aware of all that was passing. With a correct discernment of the situation, and a profound and far-seeing appreciation of the necessity for a clear and scriptural settlement of the grounds of true *Christian* union, Mr. Campbell, who was to deliver the introductory sermon, prepared to meet the case fairly, fully, and manfully. His sermon was founded on Rom. xiv: 1: "Him that is weak in the faith receive ye, but not to doubtful disputations." He classified under three heads all subjects relating to the Christian religion :—

1st. Matters of knowledge—personal knowledge ;

2d. The things of faith, the facts reported to us, which we accept on testimony ;

3d. Matters of opinion.

The distinctions in these three departments are marked and important. The profound and eloquent preacher, in a lucid and masterly manner, defined them, and showed their application to the present divided state of Christendom, and illustrated the manner in which these principles would solve the difficult problem of the union of Christians, and yet disturb neither the faith nor the piety of any one.

Knowledge, he defined as one's own personal experience. This term is confined to the things which he himself sees, or hears, or discerns, either by his senses, or his own consciousness. A person can testify only to the things which he himself personally knows. It was asserted that the apostles knew the Lord Jesus ; saw him, "handled" him, heard him, and *knew* his miraculous works, and heard his gracious discourses ; so that within their personal knowledge and consciousness they held the absolute certainty of knowledge of him—his character and his claims ; that they were thus qualified to declare the gospel and to be his embassadors, his apostles, and witnesses to the world ; that the apostles knew the gospel to be true, and none but they stood on this high ground of knowledge.

The subject of faith was treated in an equally clear and forcible style. Faith stands on testimony. No testimony, no faith. Testimony is delivered by witnesses. Christ's apostles are his witnesses : "And ye also shall bear witness, because ye have been

with me from the beginning; John xv: 27. "Ye
shall receive power, after that the Holy Spirit has
come upon you: and ye shall be witnesses unto me
both in Jerusalem, and in Judea, and in Samaria, and
unto the uttermost parts of the earth;" Acts i: 8.
Our faith in Christ is founded on the testimony of
his witnesses. The apostles, the men of knowledge,
testified or declared the things which they saw and
heard; we receive their testimony, and thus we believe. "Faith comes by hearing, and hearing by the
word of God;" Rom. x: 17.

It was next shown that as the facts of the gospel
are always one and invariable, and as the apostolic
testimony or declaration of the facts never varies,
the faith of all persons is a unit. The important
conclusion was thus reached, that Christians are not
divided on the faith.

Touching the third division in this classification
of knowledge, faith, and opinion, he showed that
opinion was the fruitful source of all the schism
which checkers, disgraces, and weakens the Christian
profession; that creeds are but statements, with few
exceptions, of doctrinal opinion or speculative views
of philosophical or dogmatic subjects, and tended to
confusion, disunion, and weakness; that as Christ receives us in the faith, without regard to questions of
doubtful disputation, so we should receive one
another, laying the basis of a rational and permanent
union in the faith, in the express matters of apostolic
teaching, on which no differences obtain among the
followers of Christ.

So rational and scriptural a ground of gathering
into the long-desired unity the scattered sheep of

Christ's fold, commended itself to all his hearers as both safe and practicable. But men often approve in theory what they fear to trust in practice. So with Mr. Campbell's views of the grounds on which we were to receive members into fellowship. This, though plausible in theory, was a wide departure from Baptist principles of church-fellowship. So likewise these principles of apostolic teaching would demolish the narrow, restrictive creed policy of all the sects in the land. It was a bold position. It was taken in the face of the embattled array of sect power. It was clear, simple, sensible. But would it bear the strain of the practical tests to which this plan might be subjected? So reasoned many, standing yet in doubt. A trial case was at hand, a case just in point, which served both to illustrate the principles of the sermon, and to test their power. Aylett Raines was present, willing to be counted among the brethren, if he could be received as a Christian without surrendering his liberty in Christ.

The case was called up Saturday afternoon by the careful and judicious Osborne. Raines, it was thought, still entertained Restorationist sentiments. If he should in any wise continue to advocate them, dissension and division would follow. Some were for rejecting him, many were in doubt. But the greater number were decidedly and warmly in his favor. Bro. Osborne was impelled to the measure, less, it is presumed, by his own doubts of the propriety of receiving him, than by the urgency of others who wanted the association to take action in the case.

As we have it in our power, we will gratify the reader by giving Bro. Raines' own recollections of this scene. In a communication of April 6, 1868, he says:

"I went to that association expecting trouble: for, although I did not preach my Restorationist opinions, yet I sometimes told such persons as approached me becomingly, that it was still my opinion that all men would, ultimately, in some distant period of eternity, be saved. Out of this the trouble was to grow. But I resolved to breast the storm. I arrived in Warren, Friday morning. At one o'clock P. M., I had the pleasure to hear, for the first time, A. Campbell. He read the fourteenth chapter of the Epistle to the Romans, and dwelt extensively on a passage in it, which, according to his translation, reads as follows: 'Him that is weak in the faith receive ye, but without regard to differences of opinion.' On this passage Bro. Campbell dilated lucidly, showing the difference between faith and opinion, and between humanisms, or philosophies, and the 'faith once delivered to the saints.' I felt very much strengthened and comforted, knowing, if my case came up in the association, I would have at least Bro. Campbell on my side, and if him, a multitude of our preachers and brethren.

"After hearing the views of Bro. Campbell I thought it probable that my case would be let alone. In this, however, I mistook. Next morning I met Dr. Wright on the street, who said to me: 'I understand that you sometimes tell people that you still believe that all men will finally become holy and happy.' 'I do, sir,' said I. 'What then will you do,' said he, 'with this passage: *These shall go away into everlasting punishment, but the righteous into life eternal?*' 'I will not do any thing with it,' said I. 'If I argue with you in defense of my opinions I shall make myself a factionist. But I have as much right to argue for my opinions as you have for yours; and if you get up an argument with me, be careful, you will make yourself a factionist.' At this the Doctor, seeing that I was not in his trap, became excited, and said : ' Well, sir, I'll see whether this association will fellowship men of your views.' ' See,' said I, ' Doctor, as soon as you please, and I will show you that I will have Thomas Campbell, A. Campbell, Walter Scott, Bentley, and a number of others on my side.' He replied, ' It is impossible.' I responded, ' Well, try it.' Accordingly, not Dr. Wright, but Bro. Osborne, on Saturday afternoon, very lugubriously presented my case. Bro. Thomas Campbell first responded, as nearly as I can recollect, in words following : ' The devil has brought this question into this association to sow discord among brethren. Bro. Raines and I have been much together for the last several months, and we have mutually unbosomed ourselves to each other. I am a Calvinist, and he a Restorationist ; and, although I am a Calvinist, I would put my right arm into the fire and have it burnt off before I would raise my hand against him. And if I were Paul, I would have Bro. Raines in preference to any other young man of my acquaintance to be my Timothy.' Next, Bro. A. Campbell arose, and substantially repeated what he had said in his introductory discourse, on the difference between faith and opinion. Then Bro. Scott arose and said that he concurred with the preceding speakers, and would not have said any thing on the occasion but to give me time for reflection. ' I think,' said he, ' that Bro. Raines has been very badly treated, and I fear that when he speaks he will speak with too much severity.' Then Bro. Campbell requested me to stand upon a bench, * and proclaim to the large concourse present, my own views of my obligations as a Christian and as a preacher of the gospel. This I did briefly, and in effect, as follows : That my Restorationism was a philosophy. That I would neither preach it nor contend for it, but would preach the whole

---

* The better to be heard, the house being very full.

gospel, and teach the whole truth of Christianity according to my best ability, etc., etc.   Bro. A. Campbell then put the question : ' Whether there was any law of Christ by which I could be condemned ?'   The vote was in the negative, and in my favor by an overwhelming majority. This I took to be quite a triumph ; but the end was not yet.

"The next morning I attended sunrise prayer-meeting.   After the usual routine of reading, singing, and prayer, the leader of the meeting, whose name I do not recollect, arose and spoke as follows : ' Brethren, I understand there are certain persons in the fellowship of this association who deny that sinners are saved by grace, and say that those who die in their sins will be purified by hell-fire. I move,' said he, ' that such persons be disfellowshiped.' In a twinkling I was on my feet, and said : ' I second that motion ; for by grace are ye saved through faith, and that not of yourselves : it is the gift of God : not of works, lest any man should boast.   Now,' said I, ' if any member of this association holds any doctrine contradictory to the teaching of this passage, I move that he be immediately disfellowshiped.'   The old Brother who had put the motion, struck a direct line for the door, and the congregation followed him ; and there my association troubles ended. Affairs, however, would probably have taken a very different turn, had somebody else than myself seconded the old man's motion.

"I was dealt with, and my case managed, by Bro. Campbell and all the chief brethren in very great kindness and wisdom.   Had they attempted to brow-beat me I might have been ruined forever.   But treating me kindly, at the same time that they convinced me that my opinion, whether true or false, dwindled into nothingness in comparison with the faith of the gospel, redeemed me.   I became a day and night preacher of the gospel, and my mind becoming absorbed in this vast work, the opinion faded, and in ten months

15

was numbered with all my former errors. The Lord be thanked for his great deliverance. Bro. Campbell, I ought to say, invited me to go to Bethany, and told he thought he could convince me that my Restorationist opinion was false."

"NOTE 1.—I make a distinction between Restoration-ism and Universalism. Opinions are only to be tolerated when they do not subvert obvious facts of the gospel. This Universalism does in its teaching concerning the di-vinity of Christ, atonement, making God the author of sin, denying the remission of sins, and a judgment, and punishment after death. I consider the system no bet-ter than deism.

" NOTE 2.—I remained on the Reserve but a short time after the association. I came to the south part of Ohio and preached in Dayton, Cincinnati, and many other places, with some success ; and finally, in Wilmington, Ohio, in which place and its vicinity I baptized many persons. We used to make our numerous converts at one, two and three days' meetings. Now it often takes two and three weeks' pounding, day and night, with the hammer of the Word to crack the shell of worldliness which surrounds the heart. What shall be the end ?   'When the Son of Man cometh, shall he find faith in the earth ? '   A. R."

The reception of Raines delighted the great body of the young converts and reformers, whose feelings were awakened in his favor. It was also hailed with equal interest by the older and sounder advocates of the plea for Christian union on Christian princi-ples, as it was a clear and conspicuous case in which these principles were strikingly illustrated. They regarded it, therefore, as a marked victory for the truth.

A principal business of this meeting was to hear the report of the evangelist, and to make arrangements for future labors.   We subjoin the

Report of Walter Scott, the Evangelist of the Association.

"Beloved Brethren:—The Christian of the nineteenth century has been permitted to witness the accomplishment of wonderful events. Providence has stationed him on a sublime eminence, from which he can behold the fulfillment of illustrious prophecies, and look backward upon nearly the whole train of events leading to the *Millennium*.

"Afar off, and upon the background of the picture before him, of wonderful extent, and in all the greatness of imperial ruin, appear the three great empires of Babylon, Persia, and Greece. Nearer to hand lies Rome; eternal Rome! terrible in her origin, terrible in her glory, terrible in her *decline* and *fall!* Living and acting through a long series of ages, she approaches the very verge of the present scene of things, till she assumes the distracted form of the ten kingdoms spoken of by Daniel, the remains of which now reel to and fro upon the face of Europe, like a drunken man, ready to be engulphed in the yawning judgments of Almighty God. *Sic transit Gloria Mundi.*

"But from amidst the blaze of her glory, see yet loftier scenes arise. Behold the kingdom of our Lord Jesus, awaking under the eye of the *Cæsars!* Small in its beginning, it rolls forward, it survives all Roman greatness; and that which was yonder a little stone, is here become a vast mountain, and fills the whole earth. The waters which yonder issued from the threshold of the Lord's house, have here arisen; they have become waters to swim in—a river that can not be passed over.

"Here, too, are the impostures of Mahomet and the Pope, with temples having the lowermost part consecrated to God, the upper to the worship of idols. Arrayed in purple and scarlet, decked with gold, and precious stones, and pearls, behold the apostate church, mounted upon her imperial beast, holds forth to the intoxicated nations a golden cup in her hand, full of abomination and of the filthiness of her fornication! On her fair but unblushing forehead is inscribed *Mystery, Babylon the Great, the Mother of Harlots and abominations of the earth.* She shall be thrown down with the violence of a millstone plunged into the midst of the ocean.

"Her portentous offspring also issued to mankind in the mature age of 666, with the head of a lamb and the heart of a dragon: the *Inquisition* raiseth itself on high, with the power, the delusion and cruelty of its parent; it comes roving over the earth, and causeth all, both small and great, rich and poor, free and bond, to receive a mark in their right hand or in their forehead; and that no man might buy or sell, save he that had the mark, or the name of the beast, or the number of his name.

"Here, also, is the French Atheism, filled with all presumption, and magnifying itself above every god; he speaketh marvelous things against the true God; his hands are filled with spears, and his skirts are drenched in blood; but he shall come to his end, says Daniel, and none shall help him.

"All these things, beloved brethren, have passed in review before the Christian of the nineteenth century; but if we have had to witness schemes of policy and superstition so wild and enthusiastic, and apparently so unfavorable to the true religion, we have seen many things introduced also highly conducive to its promulgation and reception among mankind. Above all, we have seen the church in America seated down under a gracious and efficient government, affording her and all men an unprecedented security of life and property; and if her unity be still a desideratum, we ought to remember that the saints, for nearly three hundred years, have been combating tyranny and superstition with astonishing success, until those who despise every name and every phrase, not found in the Scripture, have become, probably, by far the most numerous body of professors in the United States. But who would have thought it remained for any so late as 1827, to restore to the world the manner—the primitive manner— of administering to mankind the gospel of our Lord Jesus Christ! or which of you, brethren, would have thought, two years ago, of men coming from forty to a hundred and twenty miles to the ministers of the Mahoning churches for baptism! Yet these things have actually occurred; and who can not see, that, by the blessings of God, the ancient gospel and ancient order of the church must prevail to the certain abolition of all those contumacious sects which now so woefully afflict mankind?

"Brethren, we have a right to expect great things of our Father, if we are united and stand fast, striving together for the faith of the gospel. And be it known to you, brethren, that individuals eminently skilled in the Word of God, the history of the world, and the progress of human improvement, see reasons to expect great changes, much greater than have yet occurred, and which shall give to political society and to the church a different, a very different, complexion from what many anticipate.

"The Millennium—the Millennium described in Scripture—will doubtless be a wonder, a terrible wonder to ALL.

"The gospel, since last year, has been preached with great success in Palmyra, Deerfield, Randolph, Shalersville, Nelson, Hiram, etc., etc., by Bros. Finch, Hubbard, Ferguson, Bosworth, Hayden, and others. Several new churches have been formed; and so far as I am enabled to judge, the congregations are in a very flourishing condition. Indeed, the preacher of the present day, like the angel of the Revelation, seated on the triumphant cloud, has only to thrust in his sharp sickle in order to reap a rich harvest of souls, and gather it in unto eternal life."

The work in Bro. Scott's hands had prospered so far beyond expectation, that only one feeling prevailed on the question of re-appointing him. When the subject came up, some proposed that he be allowed to travel where Providence opened " a door of faith," not restricting him to associational limits. Others reasoned that there was much work needed in the bounds of the association, and that, as this body is responsible for his support, it had a right to his labors, and it was its duty to direct them. None doubted the power or the propriety of this body taking the work into its hands of sending him out and marking out his field ; but some thought it not advisable so to tie his hands ; that if he saw a door beyond the specified limits, he should not feel forbidden to go over into Macedonia. Rigdon, who had taken no part in this discussion, becoming weary of it, said : " You are consuming too much time on this question. One of the old Jerusalem preachers would start out with his hunting shirt and moccasins, and convert half the world while you are discussing and settling plans ! " Upon this, Bro. Scott arose with a genial smile, and remarked : " Brethren, give me my Bible, my Head, and Bro. William Hayden, and we will go out and convert the world." Then Rigdon, " I move that we give Bro. Scott his Bible, his Head, and Bro. William Hayden." It was settled in a few moments, as Rigdon's resolution was seconded and passed unanimously.

Bro. Scott said afterward, that he chose Bro. William Hayden not because he could preach better than any one else, but for his powers of music ; that there was not a man in the association who could sing like him. Scott showed his discrimination in this choice. People used to come out to their meetings on purpose to hear Hayden sing. He was full of song and full of songs—a ready one always at hand, appropriate to the hearers. Many hearts were first melted with music, and then molded for Christ by the gospel. The preaching was all the better, as both preacher and people were subdued in feeling, and disposed to hear the tidings of salvation with tenderness of heart. The hymns he sang were mostly set pieces, of great beauty and power, and which he " rendered " in a style of surpassing brilliancy and force. On several occasions, when the great name and eloquence of Scott failed to batter down the walls of prejudice, and to get a hearing, he retired from the audience, saying: " I 'll send Willie, and he 'll sing you out! "

It would be difficult to convey to the reader an adequate conception of the power of this great meeting. It was notable for several reasons : The ability and number of the preachers in attendance lifted it into conspicuity above any preceding occasion. The large and enthusiastic assemblage of disciples, newly converted to Christ, or newly from the thrall of sectarian shackles, into the " glorious liberty of the sons of God "—all rejoicing in the fresh views of the original gospel, and the proofs of its power to convert sinners, seen in the hundreds, the fruits of the recent proclamation of it, now here assembled. The Millennium seemed near. The songs, the preaching, and the prayers were well flavored with the ardent hope of it. No song of praise or of hope was so popular as the hymn—

" When the King of kings comes,
  When the Lord of lords comes,
  We shall have a joyful day
      When the King of kings comes :
  To see the nations broken down
  And kingdòms once of great renown,
  And saints now suffering wear the crown
      When the King of kings comes ! "

A new tune for it, composed by William Hayden, was rapidly caught by the people, who swelled the song like a grand jubilee chorus.

BIOGRAPHY OF WILLIAM HAYDEN.

WILLIAM HAYDEN was born in Rosstrevor Township, Westmoreland County, Pa., Lord's day, June 30, 1799. In April, 1804, his father moved to the wilds of the new State of Ohio, and settled in Youngstown, where William, the oldest of the family, experienced the privations of pioneer life. Fond of reading, and having access to few books, he read much in the Bible. He was, when he was young, perplexed with questions about the origin of things, and what shall be hereafter. He was a deist before he was twelve ; then for awhile the gulph of atheism yawned before him. From its frightful chasm he was rescued by the reflection, that " if *nothing had eternally or primarily existed, nothing could have been originated, and that hence a cause uncaused was self-evident.*" He farther reflected that to doubt the existence of a Creator leads necessarily to a doubt of the existence of the creature. For awhile he tried the bold adventure of doubting his own existence. This was impossible. His conclusion, in his own words was, "there is no sense in being a fool!" Cured now of atheism—for deism he found another remedy : "I plainly saw that to turn away from the Bible, we plunge ourselves into darkness, and our only refuge is in our ignorance." " Finally, reading again the narrative of the

inhuman treatment of Christ from the garden to the sep-
ulcher, and seeing how patiently and meekly he endured
it all, his whole life passed in review before my mind. I
was indignant that such a person should be so treated.
What harm had he ever done them? The only perfect
character that ever appeared on earth ; a model of goodness, wisdom, dignity, condescension, and pity—just such
a friend as ignorant, suffering man needed—and to be re-
quited thus ! Till now I had never seen sin in its hateful-
ness, and I felt myself a sinner.''

For four years longer, till he was sixteen, he struggled
in the mysteries of Calvinism ; hoping, if he was one of
the elect, God would impart the evidence of it in a needed
and desired regeneration. A revival occurring, he sought
the coveted relief. At last, he was thoroughly aroused by
the words of Jesus, Matt. xii : 36, 37 : '' I say unto you,
that every idle word that men shall speak, they shall give
account thereof in the day of judgment. For by thy
words thou shalt be justified, and by thy words thou shalt
be condemned.'' He fled for refuge to the hope of the
gospel. He was baptized May 19, 1816, by Elder Joshua
Woodworth, and united with the Baptist church, of which
his parents were members.

December 20, 1818, he married Miss Mary McCollum,
and settled on new lands in Austintown. In the midst
of his work his zeal did not relax. When the church in
Youngstown ran down, he took membership in Canfield.
He studied the Scriptures diligently, and was ready always
to give a '' reason for the hope that was in him.'' I quote
from his own pen : '' I had heard some time before of one
Alexander Campbell. I had read a sermon from his pen,
and now in October, 1821, he was to preach in Warren,
and I resolved to hear him. He was then thirty-three
years of age, the sharpest man I ever saw, both in appearance and in intellect, and I confess I was afraid he might
lead us astray. His first sermon was from the text, 'Thy

kingdom come.' I soon saw what he meant to make out, and I did not mean to believe him; but I could not help believing him. He showed that the kingdom had come. At that meeting, which was for the mutual improvement of the preachers, he made several remarks, which were new and startling, and of infinite use to me. He said 'the true disciple of Christ will follow the truth wherever it leads.' Upon a moment's reflection, I saw there was no safety in doing otherwise. I resolved that whatever the truth would make me, I would endeavor to be. A second was, 'you will notice the apostles in preaching the gospel never said one word about election.' I saw this was true. But then I thought, what is the gospel? I soon saw if the gospel can be preached without election, so can it without any of the 'five points.'"

A person with so tenacious and energetic a mind could not abandon the cherished system of Calvinism without a great struggle. His "Christian experience" had to be analyzed, and every impression and feeling traced to its cause. But the truth *that faith comes by hearing the testimony of God* was revolutionary, and he did not rest till it had gained in his mind the complete ascendency. Every number of the Christian Baptist was thoroughly sifted. No wonder, then, that after seven years of so thorough a schooling he was ready, at the call of the association, to enter unhesitatingly into the work of teaching the true gospel to the world. His own struggles, and his complete mastery of his own difficulties, prepared him to relieve others from similar doubts and scruples.

In May, 1828, the church of Canfield gave him license as a preacher of the gospel. In October following, after his call to ride with Scott, he was ordained, in his own church of Austintown, of which he was then a member and leader, by brethren Scott and Bentley.

From this time his labors were double those of most men. Working with his own hands as much as other men, and yet more in his saddle than most preachers. For twenty-five years he was absent from his own home on an average two hundred and forty days and nights each year. His industry was proverbial. He was incessant in preaching, teaching, and conversation—in public and in private. He created openings—occupied them, and when others could be found to hold the positions, he broke new ground. He was the first man and the chief operator in raising up the churches in Ravenna, Aurora, Shalersville, Akron, Royalton, Warrensville, Solon, and Russell, and several others.

The following from his pen, written near the close of his life, is worthy of careful attention :

"I perceived within six months of the beginning of my labors the necessity of system in our operations, of which we had none—measures to call out and prepare fit men to preach and teach, and to take care of the con-verts—measures to insure a reasonable support for such men—measures to secure harmony of action among the preachers, and for holding the ground already gained. I spoke of all these interests to all the brethren ; but there was only one man who seemed to perceive any sense in what I had to say, and that was Jacob Osborne, one of the most wise, prudent, and godly men we ever had among us ; and he died in May, 1829. For twenty years I urged these things, but they received no encouragement. I was astonished that all could not see the indispensable neces-sity of a matter so in accordance with common sense, and the demands of every-day experience ; for the want of which so many of our churches are languishing almost to dissolution.

"After twenty years hardship, toiling against wind and tide, my brother A. S. Hayden and I resolved that we would lay before the brotherhood the expediency of found-ing an institution of learning—the Eclectic Institute—at

Hiram. It took with the people, and has accomplished much in many ways.

"Isaac Errett responded to the appeal uncompromisingly to aid in getting an association of churches for the purpose of missionary operations on the Western Reserve. Shortly after, in 1852, the Ohio State Missionary Society was organized. It works well, and is likely to live and prosper; for the brethren are forced to see, after so long a time, the need of united action. But, oh how much the cause of Christ has lost! and how many have died ignorant of the gospel! and how many more will, for not having had a good system of management from the commencement!

"But now my labors are about ended, and I am beginning to see the brethren act like men of common sense. One whole generation has passed away, and we are not quite ready to begin to act with efficiency in this great work of showing our contemporaries the true gospel in contradistinction from the speculations of men about the gospel. Until the true gospel is honored by its friends, it will not be heard so as to be understood; and, until it is understood, faith that justifies will be supposed to come by prayer and the mysterious work of the Spirit; and while that is so, the evidence of prophecy and miracle will not be taught the people. Consequently, ignorance, unbelief, division, and iniquity will abound, as it is at this day.

"No man has labored so wisely and so successfully as Alexander Campbell, to show the true gospel and its evidences, and how men become Christians, since the great apostasy commenced; and almost no man appreciates his labors! He has left nothing to be done by any other reformer who may come after him; and I fear it will be another generation before those who acknowledge him a reformer will organize, so as to be as efficient as all other people are in conducting their affairs."

His teaching on the whole question of conversion, was so clear and thorough, few who heard him candidly failed to see the difference between the teaching of the Scriptures on this important subject, and the mystic theories of regeneration which bewilder the mind and perplex the conscience. His converts were, therefore, thorough and decided, like himself. One of these, Jewett Frost, of Richfield, could not rest till his brother and other friends in Riga, New York, should hear the same truth. At his instance, Wm. Hayden went into that State in 1832, and afterward, alone or in company with others, he made many and extensive trips in most of the Western counties of the Empire State, and in Canada, where he powerfully proclaimed the gospel, and rendered the most efficient service in establishing the cause of reformation. In western Pennsylvania, Virginia, and in all the region of North-east Ohio his pioneer labors laid the foundations for others to build upon. Some of his most stirring and profitable tours were into Michigan and Wisconsin; so that from Syracuse to the Mississippi River, and from Canada to Virginia, he "fully preached the gospel of Christ."

The following account of him is from the Millennial Harbinger, to which it was sent by the writer, 1863, just after his death:

During his ministry of thirty-five years he traveled ninety thousand miles, full sixty thousand of which he made on horseback—that is, by this mode of travel— a distance of more than twice around the world! The baptisms by his own hands were twelve hundred and seven. He preached over nine thousand sermons, that is, over two hundred and sixty one discourses per annum for every year of the thirty-five years of his public life. He once preached over fifty sermons in the month of November alone. Besides all these pulpit services, his private labors were abundant and incessant. He had a peculiar turn for winning attention, and imparting instruction in

the social circle, mingling the humor that charms with
the experience which teaches. Few could relish or relate
an anecdote better, or apply one more appropriately for
purposes of illustration. Yet he never indulged in recitals of any in which the adorable Name, or any of the
titles of the Most High, were even playfully, much less
irreverently, introduced; a practice against which he bore
frequent and forcible testimony.

His mental powers were most rapid and energetic in
action. His method of reasoning tended to generalization, embracing a great variety of subject and method.
Though not educated, in a scholastic sense, his taste, discernment, and industry very fully supplied this deficiency,
and stored his mind with much general information and
critical historical learning. The master quality of his
mind was his almost matchless memory—memory, both
of history and chronology. He made no memoranda of
his sermons, yet he could report at any time, promptly and
accurately, the number of his discourses, baptisms, and
multitudes of incidents, and all without pen or pencil to
aid him. It were vanity, perhaps, to assign him a place
in this respect with Macaulay or Johnson; but all who
knew him wondered at his power—a power which was at
his command, with undiminished force, up to the hour of
his death. In his character were chiefly discernible firmness, decision, boldness in enterprise, and sturdy honesty.
He was eminently social and hospitable, compassionate
and kind-hearted. His religion was conscience and reverence; his humanity, a tender and systematic benevolence. He gave freely for humane, religious, and educational objects.

More than a year previous to his death, he was afflicted
with a gradual weakening of the muscles, which pervaded
the whole system, affecting his speech in common with
every other muscular action. Without pain, and with the
full exercise of his mental powers, he died at his home,

at Chagrin Falls, easily and tranquilly, in full hope of immortality, April 7, 1863, in the sixty-fourth year of his age.

EXPECTATION OF THE MILLENNIUM.

The ardor of religious awakening resulting from the new discoveries in the gospel was very much increased about the year 1830, by the hope that the millennium had now dawned, and that the long expected day of gospel glory would very soon be ushered in.   The restoration of the ancient gospel was looked upon as the initiatory movement, which, it was thought, would spread so rapidly that existing denominations would almost immediately be deorganized; that the *true people*, of whom it was believed Christ had a remnant among the sects, would at once, on the presentation of these evidently scriptural views, embrace them, and thus form the union of Christians so long prayed for; and so would be established the Kingdom of Jesus in form, as well as in fact, on its New Testament basis.   All the powers in array against this newly established kingdom, whether in the churches of Protestantism or Romanism, would soon surrender at the demand of the King of kings.

The prospect was a glorious one, springing very naturally from the discovery of the complete adaptation of the gospel to the ends for which it was given. This hope of the millennial glory was based on many passages of the Holy Scriptures.   All such scriptures as spoke of the " ransomed of the Lord returning to Zion, with songs and everlasting joy upon their heads : that they should obtain joy and gladness, and that sorrow and sighing should flee away," (Isa. xxxv : 10,) were confidently expected to be liter-

ally and almost immediately fulfilled.   These glowing
expectations formed the staple of many sermons.
They were the continued and exhaustless topic of
conversations.   They animated the hope, and inspired
the zeal, to a high degree, of the converts, and many
of the advocates of the gospel.   Millennial hymns were
learned and sung with a joyful fervor and hope surpassing the conception of worldly and carnal professors.   One of these hymns, better in its hope than
poetic merit, opened as follows :

> " The time is soon coming by the prophets foretold,
> When Zion in purity the world will behold,
> For Jesus' pure testimony will gain the day,
> Denominations, selfishness will vanish away."

The Scriptures, especially the prophetic writings,
were studied with unremitting diligence and profound
attention.   It is surprising even now, as memory returns to gather up these interesting remains of that
mighty work, to recall the thorough and extensive
Bible knowledge which the converts quickly obtained.
Nebuchadnezzar's vision of the four great monarchies,
with the accompanying vision of the kingdom of the
stone (Dan'l ii) and the visions of that prophet
himself (chapters 7 and 8), became generally familiar,
and were, in the main, it is presumed, correctly understood.   Many portions of the Revelation were so
thoroughly studied that they became the staple of the
common thought.   The " two witnesses," their slaugh-
ter, their resurrection after three and a half days ;
their ascent in clouds to heaven in the sight of their
enemies ; the woman that fled into the desert from
the flood of persecution poured out to engulf her ;
her abode and nourishment there for a "time, times

and the dividing of time;" her blissful return from
her wildnerness retreat, and the prophetic acclaim :
"Who is this that comes from the wilderness leaning on the arm of her beloved, fair as the sun, clear
as the moon, and terrible as an army with banners?"
all these and many others constituted a novel and
voluminous addition to the stinted Bible knowledge
and the stereotyped style of sermonizing which then
prevailed.

Some of the leaders in these new discoveries, advancing less cautiously as the ardor of discovery increased, began to form theories of the millennium.
The fourteenth chapter of Zechariah was brought forward in proof—all considered as literal—that the most
marvelous and stupendous physical and climatic
changes were to be wrought in Palestine ; and that
Jesus Christ the Messiah was to reign literally "in
Jerusalem and in Mt. Zion, and before his ancients,
gloriously." The glory and splendors of that august
millennial kingdom were to surpass all vision, as the
light of the moon was to be made equal to the light
of the sun, and the light of the sun would be aug-
mented "sevenfold." William Hayden went to New
Lisbon to fill an appointment. Calling at Bro.
Jacob Campbell's, we found Bro. Scott. Mrs. Campbell was a Christian lady of much brilliancy of talent,
and intelligent in the Holy Scriptures. Salutations
over, she broke forth in an animated strain : "Bro.
Scott and I have just been contemplating how joyful it will be in the millennium—mortals and immor-
tals dwelling together!" Bro. Scott then, with great
fluency, discanted upon the prophecies of Jeremiah
and Ezekiel, relating to the return of the Jews and

16

their re-establishment in the Holy Land, the coming of the Lord, the resurrection of the saints, and the gathering together unto him on the Mount of Olives. Scott had a vein of enthusiasm, to which these millennial prospects were very congenial.   He was led on in the brilliant expectations by the writings of Elias Smith, of New England, whose works had fallen into his hands.   In a letter to Dr. Richardson, written in New Lisbon, April, 1830, he says the book of Elias Smith, on the prophecies, is the only sensible work on that subject he had seen.   He thinks this and Croly on the Apocalypse all the student of the Bible wants. He strongly commends Smith's book to the Doctor. This seems to be the origin of millennial views among us.   Rigdon, who always caught and proclaimed the last word that fell from the lips of Scott or Campbell, seized these views, and with the wildness of his extravagant nature, heralded them every-where.

These hopes were much confirmed and increased by the publication, about this time, of " Begg on the Prophecies," a small, but vigorous and confident work, excessively literal, by James Begg, of Paisley, Scotland. A cheap edition of it was brought out by the author's brother, William Begg, a recent convert from the Presbyterians.   The announcement and favorable notice of this work in the " Millennial Harbinger," together with the taste for such reading now prevalent, introduced this book widely, and it became a powerful auxiliary of the doctrines and aided to crystallize them into definite theory.   About the same time appeared the essays on the millennium, by S. M. McCorkle, a " sturdy layman."   His trumpet blew no uncertain sound.   Its blast was fierce and fiery as the noise of the ram's horns around the walls of Jericho. His essays, which were published in the "Millennial Harbinger," produced a wonderful effect. Many thought the day of the Lord just at hand. They prayed for it, looked for it, sung of it. The set time to favor Zion had come. The day of redemption was near. It only awaited the complete purification of his church—which meant the removal of sects and the union of Christians on the "Bible alone." Preaching against "sectarianism" was now more frequent and vehement. The legitimate and needed work of preaching the gospel of Christ, and of correcting the errors which lie directly in its way and impede its progress, was not abandoned, but more attention was now bestowed on the task, assumed as necessary, of clearing off the whole body of sectarianism. "Cast ye up, cast ye up, prepare the way, take up the stumbling-block out of the way of my people." Isa. lvii: 14. This was the text of many a sermon. The sects, it was assumed, are the stumbling-blocks in the way of the chariot of the coming king. This assault on the denominationalism of the times, by which Christians are separated from one another, is so nearly in line with the true work of the restoration of primitive Christianity, that this mistake of its purpose was very easy. Yet the difference is neither small nor unimportant. It is one thing to introduce light into an apartment, and thus remove the darkness, and quite another to attack the darkness hoping to remove it and thus make way for the light. This reformation, so called, is not a negation—a mere protest against sectarianism. This is not its prime, or originating impulse. It is a plea for the

Christian religion as a whole. Its defenses are defenses of Christ, of his apostles, of their authority, their claims and their teachings, as set forth in the volume of inspiration. If obstacles are in its way, it seeks their removal, whether they be Protestant, Romanish, Jewish, or Mohammedan. But these are resultant and consequential to its primary and direct aim, and not for a moment to be confounded with it.

Many sagacious brethren perceived with regret the new turn things were taking, and rightly judging that these Millennial theories would not tend to develop the work so auspiciously begun, but rather divert the minds of the people from it, they began prudently and cautiously to correct the aberration, and draw attention away from untaught questions and visionary anticipations of the future to the real purposes of the work of Christ now on hand, the preaching of the gospel for the salvation of sinners, and building up of the saints on the most holy faith. Some supposed Mr. Campbell to be in sympathy with these views ; and, indeed, some plausibility was lent to this opinion by the title of his new periodical, " The Millennial Harbinger."

Mr. Campbell, whose eye was fully open to all, was not slow to perceive all this, and he felt called to undertake the needed correction. He commenced, in the " Millennial Harbinger," for Sept., 1834, a series of articles under the title of " The Reformed Clergyman," which, while they held McCorkle's essays on the literal interpretation of prophecy directly in review, had for their aim the wider purpose of correcting the errors entertained and propagated to the detriment of the practical work of the gospel. These essays were written with marked ability. They immediately arrested universal attention, and were read every-where. For prudential reasons the writer sought to veil his style, evidently desiring that no bias might be given to his reasonings from personal considerations. Their drift and aim were soon discovered; and the positions assumed, and rules of prophetic interpretation set forth, were so consistent and evenly balanced, that the "second sober thought" coming to the rescue, the effect was salutary and the remedy complete.

Mr. Campbell's *non de plume* of "Reformed Clergyman," was not to all a concealment of the real author of the essays. His style betrayed him; and it was amusing to hear the discussions—the hints and guesses on the subject of their authorship, and the merits of the essays themselves—which were carried on with Mr. Campbell and by others in his presence, before he was suspected as the writer of them. A sagacious Scotch lady, in the city of Pittsburgh, of great positiveness, berated him soundly for his indiscretion in permitting that "Reformed Clergyman" to publish such erroneous doctrines in his paper. My eyes stole over Mr. Campbell's face the while, and from the tokens there I saw, first and plainly, a confession of their authorship. The hits and jibes were sharp as from a polished quiver, and somewhat rude, withal. It was matter of much joy to many when this result was reached, and the brethren began to turn their thoughts and talents more directly to the preaching of the gospel. Among them, William Hayden should be named, as he saw and sorely felt the evil, but had not power to stay the tide; and, in like manner, others who saw not the evil tendency so plainly, now that

the remedy had wrought its cure, could see more
clearly than ever the importance of adhering closely
to the plain New Testament teachings, taking Christ
as the only interpreter of type, shadows, and prophecy
in the Old Testament; and the inspired apostles as
the divinely authorized and commissioned interpre-
ters of Christ.

CHAPTER VIII.

The Church in Mentor; and Biography of M. S. Clapp and other
Advocates of the Gospel.

FOR several years previous to the establishment
of the reformatory doctrines in Mentor, there
had been a Baptist church in town, considerable
both. for numbers and influence. It had Elders
Woodworth, West, Abbott, and Freeman as its ministers. Near the time of the appeal for the union of
Bible men on Bible ground, it was served by the
good Warner Goodall. His death, in June, 1826,
was the occasion of calling Sidney Rigdon, then residing in Bainbridge, to preach his funeral sermon.
The church called Rigdon as its pastor in the fall of
that year.

During the winter of 1825–6, Corbly Martin, who
became extensively useful in the reformation in Ohio
and Indiana, resided in the hospitable family of
Judge Clapp, a prominent member of the church.
Bro. Martin preached there during that season. A
conversation between him and a Mrs. Rexford is reported, in which she urged the practice of "close
communion" in the church as an objection to her
becoming a member. He failed to remove her objection, and she remained to be a first convert when
the gospel offering a free salvation to all who would
receive it was first proclaimed in Mentor.

Sidney Rigdon was an orator of no inconsiderable

abilities.   In person, he was full medium height,
rotund in form; of countenance, while speaking, open
and winning, with a little cast of melancholy.   His
action was graceful, his language copious, fluent in
utterance, with articulation clear and musical.   Yet
he was an enthusiast, and unstable.   His personal
influence with an audience was very great; but
many, with talents far inferior, surpassed him in
judgment and permanent power with the people.
He was just the man for an awakening.   He was an
early reader of the " Christian Baptist," and admiring
its strong and progressive teaching, he circulated the
paper, and brought out its views in his sermons.
Whatever may be justly said of him after he had
surrendered himself a victim and a leader of the
Mormon delusion, it would scarcely be just to deny
sincerity and candor to him, previous to the time
when his bright star became permanently eclipsed
under that dark cloud.

In March, 1828, he visited Scott in Warren.   He
had been with him on former occasions, and had
adopted fully his method of preaching Christ, and
of calling the awakened and penitent believer to an
immediate obedience of his faith for the remission
of sins.   The missing link between Christ and convicted sinners seemed now happily supplied by the
restoration of the way of bringing converts into the
knowledge of pardon, which was established by
Christ himself in the commission.

Rigdon was transported with this discovery.   On
leaving Warren to return to Mentor, he persuaded
his brother-in-law, Adamson Bentley, to accompany
him.   This was a visit to that town of no ordi-

nary importance. Bentley was a gentleman of cultivated manners, tall, of benign aspect, and of commanding presence; and, as a preacher, dignified, solemn, and often very impressive. But more, they were both ablaze with the new developments of gospel light which was shedding its effulgence rapidly over the country.

The trumpet which they blew gave no uncertain sound. It was the old jubilee trumpet, first sounded by the fishermen of Galilee on the day of Pentecost, announcing glad tidings to the nations that the year of release from bondage in sin had now come, and calling ransomed sinners to return, freely pardoned, to their homes. They spoke with authority, for the word which they delivered was not theirs, but that of Jesus Christ. The whole community was quickly and thoroughly aroused. Many turned to the Lord. The first person to accept the offered boon and lead the people to Christ, was an intelligent young man, M. S. Clapp, then in his twenty-first year, son of Judge Clapp. His older brother, Thomas J. Clapp, had been baptized in June previous. Twenty persons were baptized the first time they repaired to the Jordan. The immediate result of the meeting was the conversion of over fifty souls to the Lord Jesus.

It is impossible to describe the agitation of the public mind. The things which they heard were so new, yet so clearly scriptural, that, while some hesitated and many wondered, they could not gainsay it; and nearly the whole church accepted cordially the doctrine of the Lord, exchanged their "articles" for the new covenant as the only divine basis for

17

Christ's church, and abandoned unscriptural titles and church names, choosing to be known simply as the disciples of Christ.

From Mentor they went to Kirtland, where almost an equal ingathering awaited them. The fields were white for the harvest. At the first baptizing here, twenty souls were lifted into the kingdom. Others followed, and soon the numbers so increased that a separate organization became a necessity—so mightily prevailed the word of the Lord.

The news of this great overturn spread quickly through the country, up and down the lake shore. Bentley went to Painesville. The rumor of the revival in Mentor preceded him, with some exaggerated and perverted accounts of the preaching. He delivered a few discourses on the first principles of the gospel, and left them to leaven the minds of his hearers.

The church now contained over a hundred members. The following were prominent ; many of whom became leaders of the host, and pillars in churches. The head of the family is named. Their wives, and generally their families, were also in the church: Deacon Benj. Blish, Deacon Ebenezer Nye, Orris Clapp, Jonathan Root, Joel Rexford, Thomas Carroll, Asa Webster, Sidney Rigdon, Deacon Champney, Amos Wilmot, Osee Matthews, Eggleston Matthews, Joseph Curtis, Anson Matthews, Sylvester Durand, ———— Tuttle, Warren Corning, Amos Daniels, Samuel Miller, Ezra B. Violl, Noah Wirt, David Wilson, Danl. Wilson, Alex. P. Jones. To these are to be added, Mrs. Moore, Mrs. Randall, Mrs. Waterman, Mrs. Rexford, Calista M. Lewis, Morgan Lewis.

Few communities have been so stable ; the families here named have composed the staple of membership, and the support of the church from that time to the present. This congregation has long stood as a light-house. It was shaken as by a tempest under the outbreak of Mormonism ; but it is to be noted that few of its members were led astray. While the church in Kirtland, with less experience, and more immediately in Rigdon's power, became engulphed, and has never since been recovered, the church in Mentor, with stronger material, withstood the shock. They were much aided in their resistance by the presence of Elder Thomas Campbell, who spent several months there and in the vicinity during the agitation which it produced.

Bro. M. S. Clapp came rapidly before the public, and soon attained prominence by his zeal and ability. In the year 1834, Bro. E. Williams was settled as pastor and elder, with Benj. Blish. He served the congregation, yet preaching much abroad, till his removal to Chardon, in 1856. Bro. Blish not only won, but retained the fullest confidence, not of the church only, but of the whole community, for his prudence in management, his judicious counsels, and godly life. After having won the crown, he died universally beloved, February, 1864.

Her long-time laborers were brethren Clapp and Williams. But a page would scarcely hold the names of all who have gleaned in this harvest-field. Few churches have possessed a membership of more ability. In a community noted for its social culture, it has maintained its position with credit. For integrity, benevolence, and as a leader in the cause of temperance, antislavery, and measures that look to the lifting up of the world from wrong and oppression, no brotherhood has a brighter record.

Three preachers arose in Mentor, whose names are known afar—M. S. Clapp, A. P. Jones. and J. J. Moss. Bro. Moss was in the employ of Bro. B. Blish, in the summer of 1829. Raised in Presbyterianism, he had a spasm of horror when he learned that he had engaged himself to work for a very leader of the new and hated heresy of "Campbellism." The first evening, greatly to his surprise, as he had been told "Campbellites" never prayed, Bro. Blish gathered his household, with the word of God in every hand. But Moss, still doubting, stood bolt upright, while all around him knelt. The service, so simple, sincere and earnest, melted his heart. Ashamed of his prejudice, the next time he joined, and knelt, and prayed. His Bible was now read while others loitered. He soon heard Bro. Collins. His acute, quick mind saw, understood, and grasped the immense difference between all forms of sect-organization, and the simple, entire system of Christianity as a whole. The sun was now risen upon his understanding, and the twinkling lights of Babel-sectarianism faded. September, 1829, he came to Christ, and was baptized into his name, which, with him, meant the entire consecration of all his powers to his honor. The thousands by him turned to God in Ohio, New York, Canada, Kentucky, and other States, attest the fidelity of his heart to that plighted vow. A history of his life would fill a volume. He was the first man to raise a testimony against Mormonism. With the elements of character for pioneer work, he has, to an extent which can be affirmed of few men, extended the limits of the kingdom into new regions, and defended it in the arena of controversy against every form of assault, with a mastery and success above the reach of most men. He has not always had the gratitude of those whom he has served, nor the support of the churches he has planted. He was born July 13, 1806, in Onondaga, N. Y., and after forty-five years of toil and privations, he is still in the field.

Bro. A. P. Jones, equally bold and with more learning, was his true yoke-fellow. They were both teaching in the vicinity of Kirtland, when Mormonism invaded the place, and hand in hand, though young, they often put its champions to flight. Bro. Jones married Miss Irene Gilbert, of Newburg, and soon afterwards he gave himself to the service of the new churches in western New York, where his name is still cherished with great respect. He finally settled in Platteville, Grant County, Wisconsin, where he preached for several years. He has recently fallen asleep in the Lord.

BIOGRAPHY OF MATTHEW S. CLAPP.

If "a good man's steps are ordered of the Lord," as says the prophet, "his death also is precious in His sight."

Bro. Clapp was born in Mentor, February 1, 1808. His father, the late Hon. Orris Clapp, was called by his fellow-citizens to serve as Judge of the Court; which trust he discharged, with honor. Matthew's early life was passed amidst the scenes and privation of that early day. His boyhood passed during the war of 1812–14 and the years subsequent, when the chivalrous anecdotes and the military deeds of that stirring history formed the staple of conversation of the times. With eager ear and acute mind, he caught up the recitals of those exploits and deeds of valor—a discipline for achievements on a far different field.

In March, 1828, in the great religious awakening in Mentor, under Bentley and Rigdon, the amiable M. S. Clapp was the first to yield. He was baptized by Bro. Bentley. Many predicted for him a bright course as a herald of the gospel. The late venerable Thomas Campbell fully confirmed his purpose to devote his talents to the ministry of the Word. Under this devout and superior man, Clapp began his study of the classics. He availed himself of whatever aids were within his reach, yet in this instance the student was himself the chief teacher. His application was so complete, that he became not only a respectable Greek scholar, but also a good Latinist. During all these studies he was preaching, visiting the newly-founded churches, and increasing the number of the converts.

In the fall of 1830, he married Miss Alicia Campbell, sister of Alexander Campbell. This proved a happy union. He spent some time in Bethany, West Virginia, where he diligently improved the favorable opportunities which he found in Mr. Campbell's family, for enriching his stores of knowledge, and for forming acquaintance with gentlemen of education, who were almost constantly guests in Bro. Campbell's family. He also resided a year or more in West Middletown, Pennsylvania, with Matthew McKeever, Esq., another brother-in-law, while "Father and Mother Campbell," models of gentleness, dignity and Christian excellence, were in their full ripeness and strength, sitting as king and queen amidst the family.

After this short episode, he returned to Mentor, which became his permanent abode. He continued his public labors, visiting weak communities of brethren, receiving little compensation, often none, for his labors. From necessity, quite as much as from choice, he resorted at times to farming, interlacing its labors with his public duties. Experience proved to him as it has to thousands, that the world will not pay for its own reformation ; that the pioneer advocate of new and revolutionary principles must go forth, like the martyr-apostles, suffering and to suffer.

Bro. Clapp saw—rightly saw—in the Christian religion the germs of all good to man in this world, as well as the sure and only basis for hope hereafter. Every attack upon its claims he was consequently prompt to repel. Jesus of Nazareth was the Son of Man, as well as the Son of God, and he lived for the good of the world in every possible condition. As a friend to his race he must defend the Lord Jesus, the helper of the poor, the Savior of the world. So when a shrewd, young, accomplished, eloquent, lawyer in Elyria, Joel Tiffany, Esq., walked into the arena, and threw down the glove, M. S. Clapp took his "sling and five smooth stones gathered from the brook," and stood before the boaster. He so fully exposed the dark counsels of atheistic sophistry, that Mr. Tiffany declared at the close of the discussion, " It is the last time I will ever stand in opposition to the Christian religion." And it was. Soon after he was baptized in Elyria, and became a *quasi* member of the Episcopal church.

His happiness in his family was not suffered to continue without interruption. A sad day came. He looked for the last time on the living form of his excellent companion. One by one all the children of his first marriage went before him down to rest. The last of them, Campbell Clapp, was killed in the State of New York, by the falling of a cattle train through a defective bridge. He was a young man of much promise. A large concourse attended his funeral services in Mentor.

April 26, 1840, he married Miss Lucy A. Randall, of Mentor, a union whose felicity was not marred or broken till the last sad stroke which left her a widow, and her four living children without a paternal head. The winter after their marriage they spent in Pompey, Onondaga County, New York, laboring in the gospel. The friendship they established there with many of the citizens continued through life. The next season he spent, by invitation, preaching for the church in the city of New York. Here his skill as a peacemaker found scope for useful exercise. His ministrations for good were signally blessed, less in gathering many into the fold than in purifying and regulating the fold itself. His friends, Drs. Eleazer and Samuel Parmly, received him with marked and merited hospitality. His residence in the great commercial metropolis was a bright and useful epoch in his history. While in the city, he received instructions in Hebrew under Sexias, a Hebraist of note, the very same son of Abraham who came to Kirtland, Ohio, in 1830, and instructed the Mormons in the "unknown tongues," the boasted proof of inspiration of the disciples of Smith, and the marvel of many well-duped outsiders.

It should be noted that Bro. Clapp was not a clergyman in any restricted or exclusive sense. His eye was open to the widest views. He was ready to second all legitimate measures for the elevation and amelioration of men in all departments of society. With him the pulpit was not a theological chest, or box, containing a few well assorted and labeled wares to be cried on sale. It was rather a veritable throne of power, and the incumbent was bound to deal with all the active, moral questions that affect society. Hence his early, and open, and unconquerable opposition to intemperance. Hence, also, he stood out, when he had to stand quite alone, on the antislavery question. Of these and kindred subjects he took the broadest views. The poorly-paid laborer, the unpaid seamstress, were objects of lively and sympathizing interest to him. He had faith in appeals to heaven for their redress; but with equal faith, he appealed to the benevolence and conscientiousness of men for their relief. So ardent were his feelings, so fixed his principles, that he took radical ground, and plead so uncompromisingly that at times he provoked the charge of ultraism. Yet no such charge moved him. His principles in regard to war were equally radical and decided. He opposed all war, at all times for any purpose. It is due him to say that all these great moral subjects he viewed from the Bible ground, and not as a partisan, or in coalition with any special organization, social or civil. Yet his known opposition to war, slavery, and intemperance, brought him at times alongside persons whose advocacy of these reforms was prompted by no higher than merely temporal, and sometimes selfish, considerations.

It was his conviction that he could serve these great ends in a wider and different field, which gained his consent to a nomination as candidate to the Legislature. The polls confirmed the nomination. His acceptance was upon a platform which, in his judgment, invited the play of his principles on a grander stage. He returned from Columbus conscious of having performed his duties faithfully, and satisfied with the general approval of his constituency.

The last few years of his life he spent in Detroit, preaching, and in various ways shedding the light and warmth of his genial and religious nature on society around him. During the last year before his death, it became apparent that his "natural force was abated." As the progress of his frailty rendered his departure an event more and more certainly near, the anchor of his hope maintained the steadiest hold on its deep fastenings in the Rock. The

calmness of his mind was wonderful. "I do not ask
you to pray for my recovery," he said to his brethren,
"but that with unfaltering trust and bright hope I may
pass into the world of light."

He had often expressed a feeling of the happiness it
would afford him to be summoned away to the Lord just
in the midst of the memorial scenes of the Lord's Supper.
His thought was an accepted prayer. His departure to
Jesus was on the Lord's day. One week before he died
the brethren assembled in his room and partook with him
the loaf of blessing. The next week, December 17th, at
his request, they came again, and again the blessed Supper
was administered. All bore witness of the deep earnestness of his devotions. His voice was almost too feeble
for utterance. He spoke but little. All seemed aware
that the messenger was at the door. The service ended;
scarcely had the communicant members reached their
homes when the word came that he was at peace in Abraham's bosom.

His remains, accompanied by his family and his friend,
Colin Campbell, of Detroit, were brought to Mentor, the
home of his childhood. Many of his early friends came
and stood silently and sadly around him. Six preachers
participated in the funeral services, when we consigned to
the dust the remains of this patriotic citizen, this generous friend and devoted preacher.

He had nearly completed his sixty-fourth year. His
memory was capacious, retentive, and peculiar. It was
remarkable for its verbal power. It was richly stored with
the exact language of the Holy Scriptures. From his copious stores he could draw with great readiness and correctness. His scholarship in general history, and especially in English literature, was very complete. He had
read with care the standard poets, and was familiar with
the opinions of the leading critics on most subjects of interest. His own taste, critical and chaste, furnished him

a style in writing and public address, correct, pure, and expressive. He was often ornate, sometimes eloquent, but never pompous nor declamatory.

His manners were simple, dignified, urbane, courteous to inferiors, respectful to all. His conversation and his speeches were marked by delicacy, flavored with wit and anecdote, always pure, and manifested great liberality of views. His piety and honesty held sway supreme among his qualities of character. Sometimes his ardor led him to undue bounds—but none could feel more keenly the excess, or make amends more heartily when convinced of overstepping the limits of prudence.

Few men among us were more widely known or more sincerely respected. For him no monument is needed, especially in his own dear family, where he is embalmed in the tenderest and most durable affection.

When the call was sounded for a return to Jerusalem and Pentecost, it called out many noble advocates. Some of them had "professed religion," as the phrase ran, but they lay in spiritual torpor under the confused and bewildering exhibitions of Christianity which they were accustomed to hear. When they saw the gospel scheme, the Bible became intelligible; and under the impulse of their joy at the discovery, they "did run to bring the disciples word" of the clearer views of the gospel which gave them such joy. These men are worthy of a good record.

In the fall of 1821, William Waite, emigrated from Saratoga County, New York, on the head waters of the Susquehanna, and settled on the plateau since known as Waite Hill, in Willoughby. He and his wife were Baptists. His sons, Erastus and Alvan—the latter in his eighteenth year—had come in advance, in February before. The next autumn, his son-in-law, Dexter Otis, in his twenty-eighth year, arrived and settled in Kirtland. Otis united with the Baptists under the preaching of Elder Stevenson, better satisfied with the scriptural mode of baptism, than with the creed and close communion, matters on which his mind was never at rest. Elder Goodall came to Waite Hill, baptized Erastus Waite and others, and so arose a church in the Baptist order. When Elder T. Campbell came to Mentor, soon after, these brethren, E. Waite and D. Otis, were so delighted with the new light which beamed on the gospel from his preaching, that they pressed him to come to Waite Hill. His sermons made a marked impression, powerfully advancing the more liberal and correct views of the New Testament order of things. Rigdon coming in about that time, and following up the well begun work by his earnest and animating appeals, several were baptized, among whom was Alvan Waite, then in his twenty-sixth year. This was in 1829. In the same movement, and by the same hands, E. B. Violl, Samuel Miller, and Noah Wirt were brought into the kingdom. This was the beginning of the Church of Christ on Waite Hill.

These men all made their mark. Dexter Otis was appointed overseer, and he soon began to preach. In 1835 he moved to the township of Chardon, and there gathered a church. It flourished while he lived—it declined at his death. He worked hard with his own hands, yet he was so diligent in study that he became a good Bible scholar, and was well informed in history as it relates to prophetic subjects.

His candor was proverbial. He was conscientiously opposed to display in dress, and to all forms of pride, and was himself in these respects a consistent example. He was so humble, zealous, earnest, and instructive in his lectures on Bible themes, that all heard him with delight. His speech, like his garb, was plain, but it went to the hearts of the people. He turned many from infidelity to the faith, and from sin to righteousness. His very useful life terminated March 15, 1845. His works follow him, and the memory of him is a fragrant odor in all that region.

Equally useful, but a different type of manhood was Alvan Waite. He was a man of full size and manly form, a man of superior judgment and great weight of character. His timidity kept him in the shade, till strongly urged, especially by Bro. Otis, he took a bolder and more public stand for the gospel. All the rising churches around him felt the weight of his presence and edifying sermons. Candor, kindness, sincerity, and good sense prevailed in his instructive discourses. He was cheerful, hopeful, and confiding. In 1844 he went with William Hayden, in a tour through western New York, in which he gained much respect for his affectionate manners, and his clear exhibitions of the truth. Soon after, consumption began to appear. In the summer of 1846, he journeyed to the new West in hope of recuperation, visiting the churches in northern Indiana and Lake County, Illinois, and helping them by his wise counsels. He steadily declined till May 20, 1847, when he passed in among the shining ones. He died at his home on Waite Hill, with his affectionate family, surrounded by many friends who mourned the loss of so useful a man.

Ezra B. Violl who came to Christ with these noble men, and who was their close companion all the way, was still left in the field. He had consecrated the powers of intelligible speech and sound reasoning, which God gave him, to the proclamation of his truth. He traveled into other counties, and was abundant in labors in his own regions. He was born in the year 1806. He turned to God in 1829, and began almost immediately to hold forth the word of life. He preached with great fervor, not only in Willoughby and Mentor—in Perry also, and Euclid, and is gratefully remembered in Camden and other towns in Lorain County. He served in the campaigns for about twenty years. He fell a victim to the fatal malady consumption, which terminated his days on the 9th of April, 1851. He was visited near the time of his departure by Bro. M. S. Clapp, whose conversation cheered the feeble saint. Bro. Clapp said to him: "Bro. Violl, it must seem hard to you to leave the world in the midst of your life and usefulness, and to part with your kind and affectionate companion!" "Yes, Bro. Clapp, it is hard in that view, but not so hard as you think. I used to think so when I was out there where you are; but when you come in here where I am, you will not find it so hard!" Strikingly coincident were the closing scenes of these dear friends. In about twenty years, Bro. Clapp came by the same path in slow approaches to the dark stream. Perhaps he then thought of his friend Violl's words, and had an experience of their truth!

Samuel Miller, of the same church, was the peer of these noble men, in all that constitutes broad and generous manhood. His parents—John and Catharine Miller, came into Ohio when it was yet a territory, from Gettysburg, Pa., a place now memorable in American history. They settled in Willoughby, where Samuel was born, August 30, 1802; the first white male child born in that town. The country was a wilderness, and the red man, with the game he chased, ranged the interminable forests. February 26, 1828, he was married to Miss Maria Storm. He had been trained in the Lutheran church. When in 1829, the great wave of religious reformation broke along the shore of the lake, he heard, examined, and with his usual independence, candor, and decision, he confessed the Lord; his wife joining him in this consecration to Jesus Christ; also Bro. Violl, Wirt, and others, who were his companions in the support of the gospel. When the overflowing scourge of Mormonism burst forth, these three men, with Otis and Waite, withstood the shock, though Rigdon himself, their leader to Christ, had reeled and fallen under its blow.

Bro. Miller was distinguished for superior business capacity, great probity, and for his consistent and liberal benefactions. Hiram College and the Ohio Christian Missionary Society received liberal donations from his hand.

He lived to bow at the grave of nearly all who started with him in the gospel. As he saw the painful disease leading him slowly and certainly to death, with wise forecast he made ample provision for the comfort of his faithful wife, and left the balance of his property in the hands of a faithful and competent Christian friend, A. Teachout, to be used for the gospel. Business done, his attentions were devoted to his friends as they came about him, and to contemplations on the things that are eternal, in the heavens. In the calmness of an unfaltering trust he fell asleep, September 6, 1867, aged sixty-five years.

The church on Waite Hill was organized in 1830. Dexter Otis and Steven Tinkham were the overseers, and John Violl and Noah Wirt, deacons. Bro. Wirt was afterwards called to the eldership. His active life in the ministry was a great support to the church till his removal to Wisconsin.

With these, Bro. Ransom R. Storm was long associated. He was a man of superior gifts, an easy speaker, and a pointed reasoner. He was born in 1818, in Shenango County, New York, but was brought up in Ohio. He confessed his faith in Christ in Mentor, under the preaching of Bro. Williams, and soon began to proclaim the gospel. He became much devoted to his work. At the call of some churches in Lake County, Illinois, he settled among them, where he spent the last years of his ministry. Disease seized him, and as he became weaker, he was brought, by his desire, to pass the last of his days among his numerous friends in Willoughby, where he died June 1, 1871, in the full hope of immortality in Christ.

CHAPTER IX.

THE ADVENT OF MORMONISM.

THIS was in the fall of 1830. This coarse imposture was not born of chance. Characterized by much that is gross, and accompanied by practices repulsive for their lowness and vulgarity, it yet had a plan and an aim, and it was led on by a master spirit of delusion. It marked out its own course, and premeditated its points of attack. Its advent in Mentor was not accidental. Its four emissaries to the "Lamanites" in the West, like the four evil messengers from the Euphrates (Rev. ix: 15), had Rigdon in their eye before leaving Palmyra, N. Y. On his part, Rigdon, with pompous pretense, was travailing with expectancy of some great event soon to be revealed to the surprise and astonishment of mankind. Gifted with very fine powers of mind, an imagination at once fertile, glowing and wild to extravagance, with temperament tinged with sadness and bordering on credulity, he was prepared and preparing others for the voice of some mysterious event soon to come.

The discomfiture he experienced at the hands of Mr. Campbell at Austintown, when seeking to introduce his common property scheme, turned him away mortified, chagrined and alienated. This was only two and a half months before he received, in peace, the messengers of delusion. Another fact: A little

18

after this, the same fall, and before the first emissaries of the Mormon prophet came to Mentor, Parley P. Pratt, a young preacher of some promise from Lorain County, a disciple under Rigdon's influence, passing through Palmyra, the prophet's home, turned aside to see this great sight. He became an easy convert. Immediately an embassy is prepared, composed of this same P. P. Pratt, Oliver Cowdery and two others, for the " Lamanites."

The next scene opens in Mentor. About the middle of November, came two footmen with carpet bags filled with copies of the book of Mormon, and stopped at Rigdon's. What passed that night between him and these young prophets no pen will reveal ; but interpreting events came rapidly on. Next morning, while Judge Clapp's family were at breakfast, in came Rigdon, and in an excited manner said : " Two men came to my house last night on a c-u-r-i-o--u-s mission ; " prolonging the word in a strange manner. When thus awakened, all around the table looking up, he proceeded to narrate how some men in Palmyra, N. Y., had found, by direction of an angel, certain plates inscribed with mysterious characters ; that by the same heavenly visitant, a young man, ignorant of letters, had been led into the secret of deciphering the writing on the plates ; that it made known the origin of the Indian tribes ; with other matters of great interest to the world, and that the discovery would be of such importance as to open the way for the introduction of the Millennium. Amazement ! They had been accustomed to his stories about the Indians, much more marvelous than credible, but this strange statement, made with an air both of wonder and credulity, overcame their patience. "Its all a lie," cried out Matthew, quite disconcerting the half apostate Rigdon ; and this future Aaron of the new prophet retired.

These two men who came to Rigdon's residence, were the young preacher before named, P. P. Pratt, intimately acquainted with Rigdon, and therefore, doubtless, chosen to lead the mission, and Oliver Cowdery. This Mr. Cowdery was one of the three original witnesses to Mormonism ; Martin Harris and David Whitmar were the other two. Harris was the first scribe to record the new Bible at the dictation of Smith ; but through carelessness he suffered the devil to steal 116 pages of the manuscript, and then Cowdery was chosen in his stead.

These men staid with Rigdon all the week. In the neighborhood, lived a Mr. Morley, a member of the church in Kirtland, who, acting on the community principles, had established a " family." The new doctrines of having " all things in common," and of restoring miracles to the world as a fruit and proof of true faith, found a ready welcome by this incipient " community." They were all, seventeen in number, re-immersed in one night into this new dispensation.

At this, Rigdon *seemed* much displeased. He told them what they had done was without precedent or authority from the Scriptures, as they had baptized for the power of miracles, while the apostles, as he showed, baptized penitential believers for the remission of sins. When pressed, they said what they had done was merely at the solicitation of those persons. Rigdon called on them for proofs of the truth of their book and mission. They related the manner in which they obtained faith, which was by praying for a sign, and an angel appeared to them. Rigdon here showed them from Scripture the possibility of their being deceived: "For Satan himself is transformed into an angel of light." "But," said Cowdery, "do you think if I should go to my Heavenly Father, with all sincerity, and pray to him, in the name of Jesus Christ, that he would not show me an angel—that he would suffer Satan to deceive me?" Rigdon replied: "If the Heavenly Father has ever promised to show you an angel to confirm any thing, he would not suffer you to be deceived; for John says: 'If we ask any thing according to his will, he heareth us.' But," he continued, "if you should ask the Heavenly Father to show you an angel, when he has never promised such a thing—if the devil never had an opportunity before of deceiving you, you give him one now."

This was a word in season, fitly spoken; yet, strange enough! "two days afterward he was persuaded to tempt God by asking this sign. The sign appeared, and he was convinced that Mormonism was of God! According to his own reasoning, therefore, Satan appeared to him as an angel of light. But he now imputed his former reasoning to pride, incredulity, and the influence of the Evil One."

The next Sunday Rigdon, accompanied by Pratt and Cowdery, went to Kirtland to his appointment. He attempted to preach; but with the awful blasphemy in his heart, and the guilt of so shameless an apostasy on his conscience, how could he open his mouth in the name of the insulted Jesus? The eloquent lips which never stammered before, soon became speechless, and his tongue was dumb. The faithless watchman, covered with the shame of his fall, surrendered his pulpit and congregation to the prey of wolves. Cowdery and Pratt did most of the preaching; and that day, both Mr. and Mrs. Rigdon, with many of the members of the church in Kirtland, were baptized into the new faith.

"Scenes of the most wild, frantic and horrible fanaticism ensued. They pretended that the power of miracles was about to be given to all who embraced the new faith; and commenced communicating the Holy Spirit, by laying their hands on the heads of the converts, which operation, at first, produced an instantaneous prostration of body and mind. Many would fall upon the floor, where they would lie for a long time, apparently lifeless. The fits usually came on during, or after, their prayer-meetings, which were held nearly every evening. The young men and women were more particularly subject to this delirium. They would exhibit all the apish actions imaginable, making the most ridiculous grimaces, creeping upon their hands and feet, rolling upon the frozen ground, going through all the Indian modes of warfare, such as knocking down, scalping, etc. At other times they would run through the fields, get upon stumps, preach to imaginary congregations, enter the water and perform the ceremony of baptizing. Many would have fits of speaking in all the Indian dialects, which none could understand. Again, at the dead hour of night, young men might be seen running over the fields and hills, in pursuit, as they said, of the balls of fire, lights, etc., which they saw moving through the atmosphere."— *Mormonism Unveiled*, pp. 104, 105.

These ridiculous practices were performed in Mr. Rigdon's absence. About three weeks after his adoption of the delusion, he went to Palmyra to see

Smith. The prophet was rejoiced at his coming, and had a revelation all ready for him, just suited to his own purpose and Rigdon's vanity. The beginning of it is here transcribed:

"A commandment to Joseph and Sidney, December 7, 1830, saying: Listen to the voice of the Lord your God: I am Alpha and Omega. Behold! verily, verily, I say unto my servant Sidney, I have looked upon thee and thy works; I have heard thy prayers, and prepared thee for a greater work: thou art blessed, for thou shalt do great things. Behold! thou wast sent forth even as John, to prepare the way before me and Elijah, which should come, and thou knewest it not. Thou didst baptize with water unto repentance, but they secured not the Holy Ghost. But now I give unto you a commandment that thou shalt baptize with water and give the Holy Ghost by laying on of hands, even as the apostles of old. And it shall come to pass that there shall be a great work in the land, even among the Gentiles."

Mr. Rigdon tarried with Smith about two months, receiving revelations, preaching in the vicinity, and urging proofs of the new religion. His knowledge of the Bible enabled him to pervert many scriptures to this end. Soon after his return to Ohio, Smith and several of his relatives arrived. "This being the 'promised land,' in it their long cherished hopes and anticipations of living without work were to be realized. Thus, from almost a state of beggary, the family of Smiths were immediately well furnished with the 'fat of the land' by their fanatical followers, many of whom were wealthy."

The new delusion immediately assumed an aggressive attitude. A hierarchy was formed consisting of several orders of priesthood and grades of eldership. New converts began to come up to the " New Jerusalem," to behold the miraculous wonders that busy rumor reported to be of daily occurrence, and to worship under the eye of the prophet of the "Latter Day Saints." Rigdon's reputation lifted it at once into notice. New members, with incredible haste, were solemnly ordained to the eldership by the high priests, and sent out every-where to propagate the faith. Their gravity and apparent candor, coupled with a degree of ignorance which was ostentatiously paraded as evidence that they were not deceivers, gave them great credit with a superstitious class of people who are ever ready to be duped by supernatural pretension.

Though coming into Ohio first among the disciples, and introduced to their attention in a well-planned and artful manner, very few of the leading members were for a moment deceived. After its first approach, it boasted of few converts from any of our churches. Rigdon, Pratt and Orson Hyde, the last two young and but little known, were the only preachers who gave it countenance.

The opposition to it was quick on its feet, in rank, and doing effective work to check the imposture. J. J. Moss, at the time a young school-teacher in the place, pelted them, but not with grass. Isaac Moore stood up, and became a shield to many. The vigilance of the Clapps prevented any serious inroads into the church of Mentor. Collins forbade its approach to Chardon, and it merely skulked around its hills. Alexander P. Jones was there also, young, shrewd, and skilled. In many an encounter he was left with-

out a foe. But the misfortune governing the case
was that many people, victims of excitement and
credulity, and taught in nearly all pulpits *to pray
for faith*, now found themselves met on their own
grounds, and so finding an emotion or impulse an-
swerable to an expected response from heaven, dared
not dispute the answer to their own prayers, and
were hurried into the vortex. The reason the delusion made little progress among the Disciples, save
only at Kirtland, where the way for it was paved by
the common-stock principle, is to be found in the
cardinal principle every-where taught and accepted
among them, that *faith is founded on testimony*. This
is the law of faith, both in things divine and human.
This fundamental principle of the " current reformation," so rational, as well as so scriptural, was every-
where proclaimed and accepted among the disciples.
It constitutes the *divergent* truth lying at the basis
of their views of conversion, and by which they are,
on that subject, distinguished from other bodies of
religious people. They never " pray for faith," since
" faith comes by hearing, and hearing by the word of
God." Having obtained faith by the appropriate testimony, they pray, in the exercise of that faith, for
all the rightful objects of petition.

No marvel, then, that when the Mormon preacher
approached a disciple, with the proposition to pray
for a sign, or evidence of the truth of his system, he
was met with an intelligent refusal so to " tempt the
Lord his God."

The venerable Thomas Campbell, hearing of the
defection of Rigdon and the progress this silly delusion was making, came quickly to the front. He

spent much of the winter in Mentor and vicinity.
His wise counsels and great weight of influence in-
terposed an effectual barrier against its encroachments.
He addressed a communication to Rigdon so firm,
so fatherly and characteristic, that the reader shall
have the pleasure of perusing it. Its great length
will apologize for the omission of a portion of it.
Soon after his return to Kirtland, Rigdon fulminated
a pompous challenge to the world to disprove the new
Bible. On this Mr. Campbell wrote him, as follows:

"MENTOR, *February* 4, 1831.

"MR. SIDNEY RIGDON,

"DEAR SIR:—It may seem strange, that instead of a con-
fidential and friendly visit, after so long an absence, I
should thus address, by letter, one whom for many years
I have considered not only as a courteous and benevolent
friend, but as a beloved brother and fellow-laborer in the
gospel; but, alas! how changed, how fallen! Nevertheless, I should now have visited you, as formerly, could I
conceive that my so doing would answer the important
purpose, both to ourselves and to the public, to which we
both stand pledged, from the conspicuous and important
stations we occupy—you as the professed disciple and public teacher of the infernal book of Mormon, and I as a
professed disciple and public teacher of the supernal book
of the Old and New Testaments of our Lord and Savior
Jesus Christ, which you now say is superceded by the book
of Mormon—is become a dead letter; *so dead* that the belief and obedience of it, without the reception of the latter, is no longer available for salvation. To the disproof
of this assertion, I understand you to defy the world. I
here use the epithets infernal and supernal in their primary
and literal meaning, the former signifying from beneath,
the latter from above, both of which are truly applied, if

19

the respective authors may be accredited; of the later of which, however, I have no doubt.   But, my dear sir, supposing you as sincere in your present, as in your former profession, neither yourself, your friends, nor the world are bound to consider you as more infallible in your latter than in your former confidence, any further than you can render good and intelligible reasons for your present certainty.   This, I understand from your declaration on last Lord's day, you are abundantly prepared and ready to do. I, therefore, as in duty bound, accept the challenge, and shall hold myself in readiness, if the Lord permit, to meet you publicly, in any place, either in Mentor or Kirtland, or in any of the adjoining towns that may appear most eligible for the accommodation of the public.   The sooner the investigation takes place the better for all concerned.

"The proposition that I have assumed, and which I mean to assume and defend against Mormonism and every other *ism* that has been assumed since the Christian era, is the all-sufficiency and the alone-sufficiency of the Holy Scriptures of the Old and New Testaments, vulgarly called the Bible, to make every intelligent believer wise to salvation, thoroughly furnished for any good work.   This proposition, clearly and fully established, as I believe it most certainly can be, we have no more need for Quakerism, Shakerism, Wilkinsonianism, Buchanism, Mormonism, or any other ism, than we have for three eyes, three ears, three hands, or three feet, in order to see, hear, work, or walk.   This proposition I shall illustrate and confirm, by showing—

"1. That the declarations, invitations and promises of the gospel, go to confer upon the obedient believer the greatest possible privileges, both here and hereafter, that our nature is capable of enjoying.

"2. That there is not a virtue that can happify, or adorn the human character, nor a vice that can abase and dishappify, which human heart can conceive, or human lan-

guage can express, that is not most clearly commanded or
forbidden in the Holy Scriptures.

" 3. That there are no greater motives that can possibly
be expressed or conceived, to enforce obedience, or dis-
courage and prevent disobedience, than the Scriptures most
clearly and unequivocably exhibit.

" These propositions being proved, every thing is proved
that can effect our happiness here or hereafter."

He next tells Mr. Rigdon the course he proposes
to pursue in exposing the claims of Mormonism:

1. By examining the character of its author and his ac-
complices ;

2. Expose their pretensions to miraculous gifts, and the
gift of tongues ; and will test them in three or four foreign languages ;

3. Expose their assertion, that the authority for administering baptism was lost for fourteen hundred years till restored by the new prophet, by showing it to be a contra-
diction to Matt. xvi : 18 ;

4. That the pretended duty of " common property " is
anti-scriptural, and a fraud upon society ;

5. That re-baptizing believers is making void the law
of Christ ; and the pretension of imparting the Holy
Spirit by imposition of hands, is an unscriptural intrusion
on the exclusive prerogative of the primary apostles ;

6. That its pretentious visions, humility and spiritual
perfection, are nowise superior to those of the first Shakers,
Jemima Wilkinson, the French prophets, etc.

" In the last place we shall examine the internal evidence of the book of Mormon itself, pointing out its evident contradictions, foolish absurdities, shameless pretensions to antiquity, restore it to its rightful claimant as a
production beneath contempt, and utterly unworthy the
reception of a school-boy."

He concludes:

" I remain, with grateful remembrances of the past, and best wishes for the future, your sincere friend and humble servant, THOMAS CAMPBELL."

Mr. Rigdon read a few lines of this communication, and then hastily committed it to the flames!

Perhaps in no place, except Kirtland, did the doctrines of the " Latter Day Saints" gain a more permanent footing than in Hiram. It entrenched itself there so strongly that its leaders felt assured of the capture of the town. Rigdon's former popularity in that region gave wings to their appeal, and many people, not avowed converts, were under a spell of wonder at the strange things sounded in their ears. The following communication from Bro. Symonds Ryder, living in the midst of the scenes he describes, will be read with interest, especially by those who knew the high and indubitable integrity of the writer:

" HIRAM, *February* 1, 1868.

" DEAR BRO. HAYDEN :

". . . To give particulars of the Mormon excitement of 1831 would require a volume—a few words must suffice. It has been stated that from the year 1815 to 1835, a period of twenty years, ' all sorts of doctrine by all sorts of preachers had been plead ; ' and most of the people of Hiram had been disposed to turn out and hear. This went by the specious name of 'liberal.' The Mormons in Kirtland, being informed of this peculiar state of things, were soon prepared for the onset.

" In the winter of 1831 Joseph Smith, with others, had an appointment in the south school-house, in Hiram. Such was the apparent piety, sincerity and humility of the speakers, that many of the hearers were greatly affected, and thought it impossible that such preachers should lie in wait to deceive.

"During the next spring and summer several converts were made, and their success seemed to indicate an immediate triumph in Hiram. But when they went to Missouri to lay the foundation of the splendid city of Zion, and also of the temple, they left their papers behind. This gave their new converts an opportunity to become acquainted with the internal arrangement of their church, which revealed to them the horrid fact that a plot was laid to take their property from them and place it under the control of Joseph Smith the prophet. This was too much for the Hiramites, and they left the Mormonites faster than they had ever joined them, and by fall the Mormon church in Hiram was a very lean concern.

"But some who had been the dupes of this deception, determined not to let it pass with impunity; and, accordingly, a company was formed of citizens from Shalersville, Garrettsville, and Hiram, in March, 1832, and proceeded to headquarters in the darkness of night, and took Smith and Rigdon from their beds, and tarred and feathered them both, and let them go. This had the desired effect, which was to get rid of them. They soon left for Kirtland.

"All who continued with the Mormons, and had any property, lost all; among whom was John Johnson, one of our most worthy men; also, Esq. Snow, of Mantua, who lost two or three thousand dollars.

"SYMONDS RYDER."

The subsequent history of this modern imposture of most blasphemous pretension, is before the world. It is not a little curious that it has become the groundwork of many publications and much romance. A very full and complete history of it, full of incident and personal allusion, came out a few years ago in France, in two elegant volumes. Its research is minute and extensive, giving with remarkable accuracy and fullness sketches of many leading actors, with accounts of the religious societies from which they deflected. A copy of the work is in the library of Congress, at Washington, as I learn by a note from Gen. Garfield, who writes: "It was published in French, at Paris, in 1860, and about the same time in English, in London. The London edition is entitled 'A Journey to Great Salt Lake City, by Jules Remy and Julius Brenchley.' It is published at London by W. Jeffs, 15 Burlington Arcade—imprint, 1861."

CHAPTER X.

The Church in Chardon—Wm. Collins—Pastors—The Church in Munson—Leading Men—The Cause established in Burton.

THE Baptist church at Chardon was formed October 1, 1817.   On the eleventh of that month the church met in the court-house, and appointed Elders Hank and Rider to represent them in the Grand River Conference, and act for them in forming the Grand River Association.

Mr. Campbell's visit to Chardon at the ministers' meeting, June, 1824, produced a marked and permanent effect.   The ground principles of all this grand movement—that the Bible is a self-interpreting book ; that it is not to be interpreted in the interests of any party, or any received system of theology ; that a correct and faithful use of it would lead back the divided saints into the original apostolic " unity of the spirit in the bond of peace," a glorious consummation, and so bring about the long prayed for union of God's people—these views, so clear, so desirable, and so in harmony with the Holy Scriptures, were warmly cherished and much discussed.   Mr. Campbell's " Christian Baptist," several copies of which were taken and critically read, kept alive the discussions, and added very much to the power and boldness with which they were asserted and defended.   Lucius Smith was in the habit of taking his copy of it to the neighbors and reading it to

them. He came frequently to John C. Collins', father
of Elder Wm. Collins, who was brother-in-law to the
brothers King, where many an evening was profitably spent in searching the Scriptures. It must not
for a moment be supposed that the truth gained an
easy victory. So far from it, many of its early and
life-long supporters arrayed themselves at first
against the alleged innovations, and yielded their
opposition only when they could withstand no
longer. Zadok and George King were among the
earliest and firmest opponents.

The hymns reflected the doctrine of the day.
There were few more popular than the following : —

> " Awaked by Sinai's awful sound,
> My soul in bonds of guilt I found,
> And knew not where to go ;
> Alas ! I read and saw it plain
> The sinner must be born again,
> Or sink to endless woe ! "

All the points in the process of conversion passed
through the most thorough ordeal of analysis and
examination. That the Law of Moses was ever delivered to any nation but the Jews, or that it was
ever intended to bring repentance, was questioned,
doubted, denied. But " the law is our school-master
to bring us to Christ," was quoted triumphantly by
preacher, deacon, and disputant. " It does not read
so," says one in the audience. " Take that man out,
he disturbs the meeting."

Mrs. Lucius Smith was no less interested than
her husband in the clearer views of gospel light advocated in the " Christian Baptist." She was a Presbyterian, a person of clear apprehension, and of

much independence of character. She saw the truth in regard to the law, and usually replied to the argument by quoting correctly: "The law *was* our school-master," and asking, "What have we, under the gospel, to do with the law?" Quoting further: "The law was given by Moses, but grace and truth came by Jesus Christ." The people were walking on the sharp edge of the controversy about legal and evangelical repentance; about saving faith, evangelical faith, historic faith, and many such needless distinctions unknown to the gospel, and which served only to confuse the mind, and render the way of salvation a mystery.

Nathan Porter, who not long before had come from the East, young, ardent, ready in speech, and ready to learn, took hold with fresh avidity of the new principles. He was commended for ordination, and was formally set apart to the work of the ministry, June, 1824. He was prompt to publish and defend the teaching of the Holy Scriptures touching the points under discussion, little caring what the doctrinal standards taught.

WILLIAM COLLINS, familiarly known as "Elder Collins," was born in Enfield, Connecticut, September 24, 1799, but brought up in Suffield. His parents were Presbyterians. When he was about fourteen years of age an extensive religious awakening arose among the Baptists in Suffield. Many turned to the Lord, and young Collins, in the language of that day, become "hopefully converted." Like Timothy of Derbe (Acts xvi: 1) he began at once to exercise his gift of exhortation. His zeal impelled him forward. It is related of him that when the tide of feeling was high in the community, he arose in a

crowded evening assembly, and stretching both arms side-
ways to full length, he cried out : " Jesus of Nazareth is
passing by ! " His voice was full and clear, and the
speech produced a profound sensation. He followed with
an exhortation twenty minutes, so pertinent, earnest, and
persuasive, that many made note of it as preluding eminence in the Christian ministry. In the year 1816, when
he was some seventeen years old, his father, John C. Collins, emigrated to Ohio, and settled in Chardon. John
King, father of Zadok, George, and Harvey King, and
father-in-law of John C. Collins, had removed to Chardon
from Connecticut the year before, and settled on "King
Street." The land was all a wilderness. Teams of oxen
and horses brought their families and their few necessary
" goods " all the way, and their own axes underbrushed
the way many miles for their wagons. These firm, persevering men brought excellent muscle for the clearing off
of the forest, and laying the basis of the agricultural
wealth of the country. Their moral and religious principles, in which they were equally heroic, was the groundwork of a future eminently noble society, in which were
secured the right culture and development of their children's children. The writer of these memoirs was not
born out of due time to see and converse with grandfather
and grandmother King. George King, long an elder and
active member, died June 8, 1862, at nearly sixty-nine
years of age. Harvey King, unexceptionable in upright-
ness and piety, died joyfully, December 15, 1872, at seventy-five years ; while " uncle " Zadok still survives, a
veteran of three generations, like a tree with its root in
one, its trunk and bloom in another, and its ripe fruit in
the third.

Wm. Collins was employed in industrial pursuits for
several years. In the winter of 1821-2, Chardon was visited by a deep religious revival. Elder Warner Goodall,
of Mentor, was the mover in it, a man of plain, broad

common sense, of no mean abilities, widely esteemed for
his godly behavior. He so preached that a large part of
the Presbyterian membership came like Jesus the blessed,
and exchanging the bowl for the Jordan, followed their
leader into it. Collins had never lost the impressions
produced in old Suffield. He came also, and on the 17th
of March, 1822, he was baptized by Elder Goodall.
Again his tongue was loosed. He was young, ardent, devotedly pious, of brilliant imagination, commanding a
copious flow of language, and of manners that awakened
great hopes of his future usefulness. He was licensed by
the Baptist church, November 3, 1822, when about
twenty-three years of age. He was warmly commended
to prepare for the ministry in their theological school at
Hamilton, New York. Elder Rufus Rider, the Baptist
minister, was active in securing these advantages for
him. This outlay of means yielded a rich harvest ; though
probably not precisely in the channel of the counsels
which urged him to Hamilton—the only difference, yet
important, consisting in the fact that he returned to
preach the gospel as he read it in the New Testament, not
as it is interpreted in the confession of faith.

When he returned from college he found the community all alive, and agitated with these doctrinal discussions. With a readiness of insight possessed by few
men, and with the promptitude and frankness for which
he was ever distinguished, he examined, accepted, and
began openly to defend the Scripture models as the true
standard of conversion, rather than the experiences of
men formed as they are by the standards of their respective systems. In this progress of religious intelligence the
main portion of the church were with him. He was duly
set apart by ordination to the life work of the ministry
of the Word, October 26, 1826.

Just the month previous to his ordination, he was married to Miss Ann Eliza Haynes. In her he found a

Christian companion, whose life flowed evenly with his. They were one in life; in death they were not long separated. Their demise was only three weeks apart. He fell asleep in Chardon, June 26, 1860, aged sixty years; and on the twentieth day of July, twenty-four days after, she followed him to their final reward. The funeral services of both of them were performed by Bro. J. H. Jones, in presence of a great concourse of weeping and admiring friends. Few persons ever passed to their graves more universally respected and lamented.

Collins won all to him by his kind, genial, social nature. He was very quick in discernment, abounded in humor, and was highly entertaining, either as guest or host, by his wit, anecdote, and unfailing supply of sensible and instructive conversation. One less hopeful would have sank down under the hardships and lack of compensation, an experience in which he had his full share in common with the generation of preachers who founded and built up the churches. He did not exceed a medium height, was finely formed, his countenance comely and benevolent. Few men ever preached so many funerals. His abundant, practical common sense, his excellent vocal powers and fluent speech, his firmness of principle, activity in the gospel, his love of men, and devotion to Christ as his servant, made him universally acceptable, and with very many a favorite.

-For thirty-four years he proclaimed the gospel. Most of this time he served as pastor of the church. In 1853, J. W. Errett was settled in the church, and served three years. James Encell followed him; then R. Chapman, who died there. Orange Higgins succeeded him for two years. J. W. Ingram next. After him W. S. Hayden, two years; then R. S. Groves.

For many years the church has had the benefit of the invaluable life and labors of Bro. Dan. R. King, who, as a preacher, the peer of any of them, has borne burdens when others laid them down. At intervals, when no preacher was employed, he has himself blown the silver trumpet, and, "without murmuring and complaining," has stood always ready to serve for Christ. Present Elders, D. R. King and C. D. Spencer; deacons, Henry Bartlett, L. G. King, O. C. Smith. Seth Sawyer, clerk. Membership, about two hundred.

THE CHURCH OF CHRIST IN MUNSON.

Both in its origin and subsequent support this church is much indebted to the faithful William Collins. Living near by, and being extensively acquainted, and respected by all, he was a pillar of strength to the cause. The first visible awakening was in January, 1839, by Bro. J. P. Robison, who preached one Lord's day, and baptized Miss Jenett Hamilton. He visited them again in the spring, added several, and left a church of twenty-two members; with Alonzo Randall and Orrin Gates as elders; and Milo Fowler and Halsey Abrams, deacons. The visits of E. Williams, W. Collins, and Dexter Otis kept the fire alive. In June, 1840, brethren Bentley, Collins, and Robison, conducted a meeting with seventeen additions. In March, 1841, J. Hartzel came among them. The Presbyterian church was obtained, and a large hearing secured. His lucid statements and able defense of the truth won confidence and converts. In five days, twenty-one souls yielded to Christ. Being compelled to leave, the church sent Adolphus Morse, who was then preaching there, to Mantua for A. S. Hayden, to carry the work forward. The first evening the house was filled with people, who had waded through blinding storms and deep snow—such was the inter-

est in the public mind. Rev. Mr. Pepoon, the Presbyterian minister in the place, a man clearly honest
in his convictions, but blinded by prejudice, came to
hear and to oppose. Honor to the man, who, while
opposing what he conceives to be dangerous error
hath yet an honest heart to listen and to learn.
Here was an example: This gentleman was hostile;
but years afterwards he became calm, and worshiped,
and helped on the work. At this visit of three
days, nine more were baptized into Christ.

On the 20th of May following came Henry.
His royal blade of tried temper was never drawn but
in victory. He staid from Friday till Monday, the
time of a long meeting then ; produced an immense
interest, added a number, and left the church all
alive. There occurred a passage at arms between
him and Rev. Pepoon, which was rather hot than
healing ; but the times then permitted some things
over which these days would throw the veil of charitable oblivion.

In September following Hartzel returned, bringing
Bro. C. E. Vanvoorhis with him. But the meeting-
house was now closed. A store-room just erected
was fitted up, and filled with hearers ; of whom some
were obedient to the faith. W. A. Lillie, a school-
teacher and student at law, whose inquiring mind had
been tossed on the ocean every-where agitated by opposing winds of doctrine, heard Hartzel with delighted
relief of mind, as he saw in his exhibition of the gospel a rational system which he could embrace under
the laws of evidence without violence to common
sense. He immediately confessed his Savior. As
in the case of Paul, so in his, the law was aban-

doned for a higher and nobler pleading. He became
a minister of Jesus Christ, and his labors have long
been fruitful, both in converts and counsels. The
churches of Munson, Chester, Russell, and Mogadore,
especially, as well as many others, have received
much aid by his judicious instructions.

Not only he, but Bro. Orrin Gates came up to
usefulness in this church of Munson. Gates was
born in Windham County, Connecticut, May 17,
1815. He was brought up among the Methodists.
He sought earnestly among that people the joys of
salvation ; but he failed to obtain under their teachings the anxiously-sought blessing—the evidence of
pardon. He heard on King Street, Chardon, the
rapid Henry ; and his interest grew to astonishment
as he listened to the unadorned proclaimer of the
gospel. The King brothers there, and Collins, were
faithful with him, and he was compelled to investigate. The very plainness of the gospel stumbled
him. He fell sick ; and his conscience so re-
proached him with neglected duty, that he resolved
to obey the gospel the first opportunity. This was
afforded him in the great yearly meeting in Euclid,
September, 1837.

His position as elder of the church, to which he
was called soon after its organization, compelled him
to take a public stand, and called him to exercise his
good, natural gifts of exhortation.

The outburst of "Come-outer-ism" during the
presidential campaign of 1848, was a sore trial to the
church in Munson—good men staggered, and many
were swept away by it. His associate elder bowed
under it. He girded up his soul, and aided much to

steady the ship over the rocking billows. It was long before the dissidents resumed their seats in the congregation.

His preaching was now no longer confined to a local congregation. In the winter of 1854, he was formally ordained in the church of Chardon, of which he had become a member, by brethren Isaac Errett, John W. Errett, William Collins, and Zadok King, the time-honored elder of that church. His field enlarged. He was the chief agent in founding the churches in Trumbull, Denmark, and Harpersfield, Ashtabula County, and Montville, Geauga County. His work in Munson, Hartsgrove, Bloomfield, and Bazetta will be long remembered. In Bazetta he had an ingathering of fifty souls at one meeting, and afterwards lived among them eight years.

In 1842, the church in Munson had acquired sufficient strength to erect a good house. Bro. Hartzel came to the dedication of it in November. He preached with such power that fifteen turned to God, among whom were Jas. G. Coleman, and Henry, Thomas, and James Carroll. William Hayden, returning from a tour of preaching in the State of New York, arrived in the midst of the meeting, and preached from the words of the prophet, ". . . . . *to this man will I look, even to him that is poor, and of a contrite spirit, and trembleth at my word."* Isa. lxvi: 2. In his sermon he urged strongly the needs and uses of the Sunday-school.

A great move was made among the people in March, 1843, by Dr. Robison. He began meeting the twenty-fourth of that month, and in ten days he had brought seventy-six souls into the kingdom. Elder Collins stood closely by his side, and the presence and prayers of Otis the meek, a part of the time, helped forward the work.

No marvel that in June following this flood tide, when the yearly meeting for Geauga County was to be held in this church, Bro. Robison was the picked standard-bearer for that occasion—the church selecting A. S. Hayden as his associate; these brethren, with those residing near by, discoursed during the four days to the great congregation. There were twelve conversions at that time.

During this year, Dexter Otis was employed by the church to preach one-fourth of the time for fifty dollars.

The brotherhood here have had the labors of most of the preachers. Besides the names already given, men who have been much among them, we mention Bro. M. S. Clapp, E. B. Violl, and Ransom Storm; nor should William Hayden have been omitted as among the earlier and most efficient factors in these results. A. B. Green also, and Washington O'Connor have gathered stars there for Immanuel's crown. Alvin Waite preached stately for some time, alternating with Bro. Otis.

Among the home forces, much credit is due to Thomas Carroll, who has long been at the helm. His patience, faithfulness, and good judgment are not easily overrated. Milo Fowler left his post as deacon and finance agent many days ago; but he held it faithfully till his hand was enclasped by the touch of that of the angel who bore him to paradise. James G. Coleman also, for many years an

20

elder and counselor, and who, by preaching and teaching kept the membership together, will never be forgotten.

No man has been more faithful, or more useful than Allen Harper, one of the first members ; he has borne the burden· at all times so faithfully and uncomplainingly that he stands among the first in the gratitude of the church. And many others, who, with equal fidelity and perseverance have stood firmly by the cause for many years, doubtless have their names graven on the palms of Immanuel's hands.

BURTON.

From Chardon, as from the church of the Thessalonians, the "word of the Lord sounded" out into surrounding townships. In the year 1835, John A. Ford, of Burton, and his wife, Mrs. Eliza Ann Ford, attended a meeting on King Street, in Chardon ; and hearing, they "believed and were baptized" by Bro. Collins. Her sister, Adaline Barnes, afterward Mrs. Hoadley, made her confession of Christ the same time. Mr. Ford was a prosperous farmer, of Presbyterian connections, and a member of the most influential family, and pioneers in the settlement of Burton. His brother, Seabury Ford, Esq., was subsequently chosen by the suffrages of the people to be Governor of the State of Ohio.

Mrs. Ford was a woman of warm friendships, of quick and correct perceptions, and by her decision and energy, she was a great help to her husband in the effort to bring to their neighbors the knowledge of the gospel as preached by the apostles. Almost the whole town was under the influence of the Presbyterian church, and the numerous and wealthy family of the Fords were its chief support. This deflection from ancestral faith by John and his wife, was looked upon as close akin to a family reproach, and many times they were made to feel the slights and taunts of offended sect pride, as a penalty for their independence and the legitimate exercise of their rights of conscience.

Wishing the gospel, as they now plainly saw it, to be heard by their neighbors, they invited Collins to come and preach, who promptly responded to the call. In 1838, Ford moved from his farm to the center of the town, where, in his new house, with better accommodations, the people came to hear, and there in the autumn of that year Elder Collins constituted the church, consisting of twenty members.

Bro. John A. Ford and Bro. Joseph Woodward, a man of much religious worth, formerly a Baptist, were very appropriately intrusted with the oversight of the young community. These men would be entitled to respect for their sound judgment and weight of character in any community. Their families heartily co-operated with them in maintaining the ground under great disadvantages for many years. Bro. Henry Pifer was the deacon. After a time, Bro. Hoadley, brother-in-law to Bro. Ford, located in Burton, whose firmness and ability in counsel and address, with the musical talent of his amiable companion, were no small assistance.

The church was sustained by the occasional and sometimes stated help of the preachers—Collins, Williams, Hartzel, Belding, the Haydens, and others— so that they became well established in their own

neat and comfortable meeting-house.   Soon after the
establishment of the Eclectic Institute at Hiram,
this church obtained help from that source.   It never
grew to be large, but for twenty years conversions
and other accessions repaired the loss by disinte-
gration ot various kinds.   At length, when these two
leading families began to separate, the congregation
declined, and their dismemberment eventuated in
that of the church.   In 1858 they ceased to meet.

CHAPTER XI.

The church in Mantua—D. Atwater—Churches in Hiram and Garrettsville—Biography of Ryder—Origin of the Eclectic Institute.

A BAPTIST church was formed in Nelson, July 30, 1808, called "Bethesda." It was the first church of any "order" in the county of Portage. Its members resided in Nelson, Hiram and Mantua. It was gathered chiefly through the influence of Deacon John Rudolph, who, in 1806, moved from Maryland to Hiram township, and settled near the site of Garrettsville. Of this church, William West was pastor for a few years. He was followed by Thomas Miller, a warm-hearted man, who brought in converts. Darwin Atwater, of Mantua, was baptized by him in February, 1822. The principles of reform breaking out about this time, the dismemberment of the Bethesda church followed.

That portion of the members who maintained the sufficiency of the revealed will of God for all purposes of "faith and practice," formed a church in Mantua, January 27, 1827, "on the principle of faith in Jesus Christ as the Son of God, and obedience to him as taught in his word." It consisted at first of nine members, viz: John Rudolph, John Rudolph, Jr., Zeb Rudolph, James Rudolph, Darwin Atwater, Laura Atwater, Cleona Rudolph, Elizabeth Rudolph and Patta Blair.

The first year eighteen members were added, including Seth Sanford, Seth Harmon, Lyman Hunt and Mrs. Judge Atwater. Sidney Rigdon was their stated, though not constant, minister. In February, 1828, soon after his great meeting in Warren, Scott visited Nelson, Hiram and Mantua, and many turned to the Lord.

In May, of this year, the church was favored with a visit from "father" Thomas Campbell. The infant cause derived great advantages from this visit. He "set in order the things that were wanting," confirmed the faith of the members, and new converts were added to the congregation. Under his counsels, brethren Zeb Rudolph and Darwin Atwater, young men of commendable gifts, studious and of blameless reputation, were chosen by the church, and set apart as "teachers;" and John Rudolph Jr., and Lyman Hunt were appointed deacons. This was done Saturday, May 24, 1828. The next day, Elder Campbell preached in a barn belonging to Jotham Atwater, to a large concourse of people. Symonds Ryder, of Hiram, whose mind had been tossed with conflicting doubts, seeking to find the "right way of the Lord," heard him with fixed attention, and his difficulties being all removed, he confessed the Lord that day, and was baptized by Bro. Reuben Ferguson.

The converts increasing in Hiram and Nelson, a petition for the formation of a new church in Hiram was laid before the congregation; which, being granted, thirty-seven were dismissed for that purpose, and organized April 18, 1829. Another portion were dismissed to unite in Shalersville. Gamaliel H. Kent, and his wife Anna E. Kent, took letters to Aurora.

The church in Mantua was thus much reduced, but her light has never gone out.

The following statement from the hand of that pillar of truth and justice, Bro. D. Atwater, just lately (May 28, 1873) laid down to rest, will be read with special interest:

MANTUA STATION, *April* 26, 1873.

DEAR BRO. A. S. HAYDEN:

. . . . The infant church at Mantua was left small and inexperienced. I was the only one who had been accustomed to take an active public part. There were Bro. Seth Sanford, and Bro. Seth Harmon, both very young in the Christian profession, with a number of excellent sisters. In our weak state, in the midst of so much opposition, we were poorly prepared to take care of the church. March 21, 1830, I was ordained elder, (in my youth), and Bro. Seth Harmon was ordained deacon—Adamson Bentley officiating.

At this time, Oliver Snow, an old member of the Baptist church, united with us. His talents, age and experience, ought to have been very useful to us, but they were more frequently exercised in finding fault with what we attempted to do, than in assisting us. This only increased our embarrassment. Soon after this, the great Mormon defection came on us. Sidney Rigdon preached for us, and notwithstanding his extravagantly wild freaks, he was held in high repute by many. For a few months before his professed conversion to Mormonism, it was noticed that his wild, extravagant propensities had been more marked. That he knew before of the coming of the book of Mormon is to me certain, from what he said the first of his visits at my father's, some years before. He gave a *wonderful description* of the *mounds* and other antiqui ties found in some parts of America, and said that they must have been made by the Aborigines. He said *there was a book to be published containing* an account of those things. He spoke of these in his *eloquent, enthusiastic* style, as being a thing *most extraordinary*. Though a youth then, I took him to task for expending so much enthusiasm on such a subject, instead of things of the gospel. In all my intercourse with him afterward he never spoke of antiquities, or of the wonderful book that should give account of them, till the book of Mormon really was published. He must have thought I was not the man to reveal that to.

In the admiration of Sidney Rigdon, Oliver Snow and his family shared very largely ; so, when he came with his pretended humility, to lay all at the feet of Mormonism, it caused a great shock to the little church at Mantua. The force of this shock was like an *earthquake*, when Symonds Ryder, Ezra Booth and many others, submitted to the "New Dispensation."

Eliza Snow, afterward so noted as the *"Poetess"* among the Mormons, led the way. Her parents and sister, and three or four other members of the church, were finally carried away. Two of these were afterward restored.

From this shock the church slowly recovered. Bro. Ryder returned and exposed Mormonism in its true light. The Mormon character soon exposed itself.

Marcus Bosworth continued to preach for us. Symonds Ryder soon resumed his public labors with us, and regained the confidence of the community.

In the year 1834, there were several additions to the church. Its growth has never been rapid. We never had very large accessions, or very low depressions.

In 1839, we built a meeting-house at the center of Mantua, and commenced to occupy it late in the Fall. It was soon after this that you labored for us. About this time, (January 19, 1840), John Allerton and wife, from the church at Euclid, and Selah Shirtliff and wife united, from the church in Shalersville—all the same day. Of the events during your labors for the church at Mantua, in 1840 and 1841, I need not write.

After much prayerful consideration, the church ordained Selah Shirtliff and John Allerton as elders, and Seth Sanford, deacon. This was done August 21, 1841.

In the above, I should have mentioned that Walter Scott preached for us several times. Father Thomas Campbell a number of times. Alexander Campbell once, and Bro. Alton once. Jacob Osborne several times before our organization, and once afterward. Adamson Bentley once or more. John Henry one meeting of days. William Hayden many times. D. ATWATER.

This congregation affords an instructive example to show that the leaders of a church usually impress the strong features of their character on the membership. No community presents greater uniformity in its history. Firm, unwavering, moderately aggressive, she has maintained her ground and gradually extended her borders. Her house of worship was too small. and after some years it was enlarged. Chiefly from Mantua, came the agencies which established the church in Auburn. She has not been behind in works of benevolence, and her contributions for missionary enterprises, for the translation and circulation of the Bible, and for the support of the ministry, are a memorial to her honor. Among the earliest and strongest advocates of temperance, antislavery and kindred moralities, this brotherhood will be remembered when some communities of more pretension, but far less merit, shall pass away and fade from memory. Bro. Darwin Atwater, for more than forty-three years, was the honored teacher, elder, and counselor of the congregation.

21

This church of Mantua has given to the public three educated men of much promise for ability and for a thorough training in the principles of the Christian religion. These are the three sons of the elder Atwater: O. C. Atwater, John M. Atwater, and Amzi Atwater—the last a professor in the University of Bloomington, Ind., and a preacher; the others are proclaimers of the gospel in New England.

Sketch of Darwin Atwater.

Bro. Atwater's life was in many ways remarkable. Very seldom has a man appeared, and disappeared from the scenes of life's activity with so little of cloud or fleck upon him. Finely formed, of full size, an open, frank, yet grave countenance, his presence was noble, commanding always the respect of the people.

He was the only son of Hon. Amzi Atwater, who for a time filled the position of Associate Judge, and of Sister Huldah Atwater, whose time-honored home was in Mantua. His father, the late Judge, being one of the original party of surveyors to survey into townships the country called New Connecticut, or "Western Reserve," the party landed at Conneaut, the 4th of July, 1799, and proceeded to their work. This done, Amzi Atwater married Miss Huldah Sheldon, and settled on the banks of the Cuyahoga, where his son Darwin was born, September 11, 1805.

He availed himself of such facilities for learning as the country afforded. 1822–23 he spent some time in the academy in Warren. Afterward, in company with his friend, Bro. Zeb Rudolph, yet surviving, he took a course of study in language and the Bible, to fit himself for preaching.

He found a congenial companion in every good sense, and for every good purpose, in Miss Harriet Clapp, daughter of Judge Orris Clapp, of Mentor, whose family are known as widely as the cause of the reformation.

When the church of Mantua was formed, Bro. Atwater was appointed its elder. The history of the church from that day was the history of Bro. Atwater. Other elders there have been—and good ones—yet the uniformity of his life, his undeviating devotion, his high and consistent manliness and superiority of judgment, gave him an undisputed pre-eminence in the church, and wherever his noble qualities had legitimate exercise.

Few men ever lived among us who understood better the gospel of Christ. Though conducting successfully a large farm, his study of the Scripture was constant, thorough, and unremitting. In the earlier part of his life he gave considerable time to preaching, and all his life the church received much of his attention. As a speaker he was slow, but his speech was so candid and so seasoned with good sense and godly counsel that it was always profitable.

He died on Wednesday, the 28th of May; was buried Friday, the 30th. Bro. A. B. Green preached on the occasion to the largest assembly ever convened on such an occasion in the town. The preacher was much weighed down, saying to me afterward, "I felt as though I was preaching the funeral of my own father."

His first family consisted of three sons and one daughter. The sons are all preachers and holding important positions. His daughter Mary is Mrs. Neely, lately among the freedmen in Alabama, now of North Carolina. She was, through distance, denied the sad privilege of mingling her tears with the family at the burial. The others came, but some of them too late to have the coffin-lid lifted to behold his face in death.

Bro. Atwater died within twenty rods of the spot where he was born. The home virtues were pre-eminent. Such a home! And such generous hospitality! For much more than forty years the welcome guest has bathed at his fountain and been refreshed, equally at his table and by his Christian, hospitable welcome.

Many years ago he lost the faithful wife of his youth. Another was given to him, who let not down the standard of home virtues and comforts He married the second daughter of the beloved Marcus Bosworth, Mrs. Betsy W. Treudley, whose children found a home and counsel invaluable to them.   About eighteen years the new went on so steadily and uniformly, it seemed but the first continued—not two families; one continued, unbroken chain of affection through all.

HIRAM.

The history of the church of disciples in Hiram is so intimately interwoven with that of its first and long its only elder, Bro. Symonds Ryder, that we shall follow the thread of his life in giving this history to our readers.   In doing this, we shall draw freely from the biographical sermon delivered by Pres't B. A. Hinsdale, of Hiram College, on the occasion of the funeral of Mr. Ryder, August 3, 1870, slightly abridging some paragraphs.   We do this with the more pleasure, as in the discourse Pres't Hinsdale gives in its true light, the "momentary tripping" of Bro. Ryder, with the correct explanation of his deviation ; a circumstance, which, at the time it occurred, as I distinctly remember, created a marvel of astonishment in the minds of the disciples and of all who knew the manly consistency of his character.   This discourse repeats a few facts already recorded, but in such connection that the repetition will be fresh. The length of the sermon will not be considered objectionable, in view of the valuable lessons which it impresses from the life of the man of whom it speaks.

LIFE AND CHARACTER OF SYMONDS RYDER.

A FUNERAL SERMON PREACHED IN HIRAM, O., AUG. 3, 1870.

BY B. A. HINSDALE.

And thou shalt go to thy fathers in peace ; thou shalt be buried in a good old age. Gen. xv : 15.

Thou shalt come to thy grave in a full age, like as a shock of corn cometh in, in his season. Job v.: 20.

Nothing has occurred in the history of this community for many years so fertile in suggestion, as the event which has called us together.

Here lies one who has attained to the age of nearly eighty years—who was but three years younger than the American Government. Not many men are left to us whose recollections go back to the closing years of the great life of Washington—to the time when Adams, Jefferson, and Hamilton, were in the fullness of their strength ; not many who read in the newspapers the history of the wars of the French Revolution ; not many are the lives that have spanned the eventful period reaching from the time when the first Napoleon was an unknown subaltern in the French army, to the time when the third Napoleon is marshaling his troops for the great struggle with Germany.

The man whom we bury to-day was an object of interest in himself. He was no ordinary man ; his was no tame or common life. What he was in himself, the relation in which he so long stood to this community, and especially to this church, make the present an occasion of unusual interest and solemnity.

His Early History.

SYMONDS RYDER was born in Hartford, Windsor County, Vermont, on the 20th of November, 1792. He was of

Puritan stock, being a lineal descendant of a Ryder who came over in the Mayflower. His father, who had moved from Cape Cod to Vermont, was a man of considerable influence and property. The decay of his father's fortune threw young Symonds wholly upon his own resources. At the age of fifteen he entered the service of Elijah Mason, the father of Carnot and John Mason, long citizens of this town; the father, also, of Mrs. Charles Raymond and Mrs. Zeb Rudolph, who are present with us to-day. So soon as he had attained his majority, having served Mason six years, Ryder started for the West. His entire property consisted of the clothes he wore, the horse he rode, and a little money in pocket—all together amounting to one hundred and thirty-three dollars. It is worth remarking that he passed through the village of Buffalo on the 28th of December, 1813, the evening before it was burned by the British. The next day the fleeing population overtook him, while yet in sight of their burning homes. He arrived in Hiram, January 6, 1814. He purchased some land, and set to work to create a home in the forest. In the winter of 1814–15, he returned to Vermont.

Gathering the family about him, he started a second time for the West; now to plant his father and mother, brothers and sisters, in the new home which he had partially prepared for them. Here, in due time, the Ryder family found themselves in Hiram, surrounded by the wilderness, surrounded too, by old acquaintances; for Hiram was a Vermont colony.

In his efforts to restore the fortunes of his family, he was supported by his younger brother, Jason, long a deacon of the church.

In 1818, he married Mehetabel Loomis, who struggled up the rugged steeps of life side by side with him for more than fifty years; who survives her husband, and is here to-day to weep over his bier.

In the early history of Hiram, he was, perhaps, the

best educated man in the township, and was, of course, well fitted for the public duties which his townsmen called him to discharge.

His Religious Life.

His early teachings and impressions of religion were of the severe puritanical sort which prevailed in New England during the last century. His nature was susceptible to religious ideas, and he recognized the necessity of religion as a conservative influence on society.

One of the oldest churches of the Mahoning Association was the Church of Bethesda, in Nelson, Portage County, founded in 1808. The reformed views effected a lodgment among the members of this church early in 1824, and after a series of struggles to reconcile differences of opinion on the question of creeds, and on some points of doctrine, seventeen members were excommunicated for heresy. The heretics represented the largest share of the intelligence and piety of the Bethesda Church ; moreover, but eight votes were cast for the exscinding resolution. They were citizens of Nelson, Hiram, and Mantua ; and being devoted to the Bible and the religion of the New Testament, they met successively for worship on Lord's days in these townships. In those meetings they studied the Word, and strengthened each other by prayer and exhortation. There was at first no man among them of sufficient age and experience in public speaking to warrant his election to the office of Elder or Overseer. But Darwin Atwater, John Rudolph and his two sons, John and Zeb, (and we have reason for gratulation that the first one and last two are with us to-day), were leading members. The little band continued to meet and increase in numbers, though without any regular and formal organization. They were occasionally visited by evangelists and preachers, who had adopted the advanced views of Campbell and Scott, whose preaching, together with the reading of the "Christian Baptist," kept them informed of the progress of the new movement.

In June, 1828, Bosworth preached in Hiram. Symonds
Ryder heard the sermon, and at its conclusion, called Zeb
Rudolph aside, and asked his opinion of the views submitted. The subject was briefly talked over, and they
agreed to meet on the following Saturday to consider the
matter further. It is worth remarking, however, that at
this interview he expressed himself as being better satisfied with this presentation of the gospel than with any
other that he had heard. Suffice it to say, it presented
something tangible to the hearer, and appealed powerfully
to the objective mind.

On the Saturday appointed, it so happened that Thomas
Campbell was to preach in Mantua, and on his way to the
meeting Rudolph called on his friend Ryder early in the
morning. He found him with the New Testament in his
hand, studying the theme of Bosworth's discourse. On
the following day Ryder went to hear Mr. Campbell, who
preached in the barn of Jotham Atwater. The venerable preacher read the two first chapters of Genesis and
the last chapter of Revelations—chapters which give the
history of the creation of man, and an account of the
New Jerusalem. He then remarked—holding the intervening portion of the Bible between his thin hands—that
had it not been for sin there would have been no need
for any other revelation than the three chapters he had
read ; all the rest was to unfold the scheme of redemption.
He said that in his earlier years he had often wished he
had lived in the days of the Jews, that he might offer his
sacrifice at the altar, and know by the direct assurance of
God that his offering was accepted. Then, quoting from
the sixth of Jeremiah the words: "Stand ye in the ways,
and see, and ask for the old paths, where is the good way,
and walk therein, and ye shall find rest for your souls," he
proceeded to unfold the law of Pardon as taught in the

gospel, and concluded with an invitation to sinners to obey. Before the first line of the hymn was sung through, Symonds Ryder went forward to confess his Master, and the same day was baptized in the Cuyahoga River by Reuben Ferguson, of Windham.

The accession to the cause of a man of Symonds Ryder's age, influence, and force of character was the signal for a more systematic organization ; and before one year had elapsed, the hitherto floating band of worshipers was divided into two churches. One of these was the Mantua church, at Mantua; the other the Hiram-Nelson, at Hiram. Of the Hiram church, Bro. Ryder was chosen and ordained the first overseer. This church continued to maintain its joint character till 1835, when the Nelson element withdrew and formed a separate organization at Garrettsville. So far as I have been able to ascertain, the Mantua and Hiram-Nelson churches were the first which were established in this part of the Western Reserve distinctly and avowedly on the basis of the Bible alone.

From the moment Bro. Ryder obeyed the gospel, he expressed himself satisfied with the views taught by the Disciples on all points save one. He read in the New Testament of the gift of the Holy Spirit; and, in his mind, it was in some way associated with the laying on of hands, and with some special spiritual illumination. The words, "These signs shall follow them that believe," seemed to him not yet to have been comprehended or realized. For years, this mystery of the Word was the subject of frequent thought and conversation. I have been careful to state this fact, because it furnishes the key to a remarkable episode in his life.

In the latter part of 1830, the founders of Mormonism began to effect a lodgment in northern Ohio. Sidney Rigdon, a preacher among the Disciples, of great eloquence and power, had joined them, and commenced preaching their doctrine. Whatever we may say of the moral character of the author of Mormonism, it can not be denied that Joseph Smith was a man of remarkable power—over others. Added to the stupendous claim of supernatural power, conferred by the direct gift of God, he exercised an almost magnetic power—an irresistible fascination—over those with whom he came in contact. Ezra Booth, of Mantua, a Methodist preacher of much more than ordinary culture, and with strong natural abilities, in company with his wife, Mr. and Mrs. Johnson, and some other citizens of this place, visited Smith at his home in Kirtland, in 1831. Mrs. Johnson had been afflicted for some time with a lame arm, and was not at the time of the visit able to lift her hand to her head. The party visited Smith partly out of curiosity, and partly to see for themselves what there might be in the new doctrine. During the interview, the conversation turned on the subject of supernatural gifts, such as were conferred in the days of the apostles. Some one said, "Here is Mrs. Johnson with a lame arm; has God given any power to men now on the earth to cure her?" A few moments later, when the conversation had turned in another direction, Smith rose, and walking across the room, taking Mrs. Johnson by the hand, said in the most solemn and impressive manner: "*Woman, in the name of the Lord Jesus Christ, I command thee to be whole,*" and immediately left the room.

The company were awe-stricken at the infinite presumption of the man, and the calm assurance with which he spoke. The sudden mental and moral shock—I know not how better to explain the well attested fact—electrified the rheumatic arm—Mrs. Johnson at once lifted it up with ease, and on her return home the next day she was able to do her washing without difficulty or pain.

In addition to this striking occurrence the Mormon Bible professed to be a continuation of the revelations which God had made to the Jews and their descendants. Two

questions of great historic interest, which appealed strongly
to the imagination of all students of sacred and profane
history, it professedly solved. It gave a history of the
lost tribes of Israel; and it accounted for the red men of
the new world, the mound-builders of Mexico, and of the
great valley of the Mississippi. The revelations made to
these wandering Israelites, it was claimed, had been preserved for the saints of the latter day, who should inhabit
the new wilderness of the West, and upon whom God
would pour out his Spirit in fullness and power. Ezra
Booth became a convert and an elder, May, 1831. Coming to Hiram in the same month, he attended church, and
at the conclusion of Elder Ryder's sermon, sought and
obtained permission to make an address, in which he
stated in the strong, clear language of impassioned enthusiasm, the ground of his new faith, and the inspiring
hopes which it gave him. A deep impression was made
upon the minds of many who heard him. Elder Ryder
was himself staggered; and "lest haply he should be found
even to fight against God," he sat in silence, neither ap-
proving nor disapproving. Determined, however, to
know the truth and follow it wherever it might lead, he
made a journey to Kirtland, and heard for himself. On
his return, he seemed for a short time to have rejected
the claims of Mormonism; but in the month of June, he
read in a newspaper an account of the destruction of Pe-
kin, in China, and he remembered that six weeks before,
a young Mormon girl had predicted the destruction of
that city. Shortly after this, he openly professed his adhesion to the Mormon faith; but he and Ezra Booth, who
were most intimate friends, promised that they would faithfully aid each other in discerning the truth or the falsity
of the new doctrine.

Booth was soon commissioned to go to Missouri to ex-
plore the new land of promise, and lay the foundations
of the new Zion. Ryder was informed, that by special

revelation he had been appointed and commissioned an elder of the Mormon church. His commission came, and he found his name misspelled. Was the Holy Spirit so fallible as to fail even in orthography? Beginning with this challenge, his strong, incisive mind and honest heart were brought to the task of re-examining the ground on which he stood. His friend Booth had been passing through a similar experience, on his pilgrimage to Missouri, and, when they met about the 1st of September, 1831, the first question which sprang from the lips of each was—"*How is your faith?*" and the first look into each other's faces, gave answer that the spell of enchantment was broken, and the delusion was ended. They turned from the dreams they had followed for a few months, and found more than ever before, that the religion of the New Testament was "the shadow of a great rock in a weary land." A large number of the citizens of Hiram had given in their adhesion to the doctrines of Smith and Rigdon, but the efforts of Ryder and Booth went far to stay the tide, and lead back those who had been swept away on its current.

It may seem strange that a man of Father Ryder's strong mind and honest heart, could even temporarily have fallen into the Mormon delusion. Let us not fail to remember, however, that Mormonism in northern Ohio, in 1831, was a very different thing from Mormonism in Utah, in 1870. It then gave no sign of the moral abomination which is now its most prominent characteristic. Besides, it was a formative period in religious history: new ideas were fermenting in the minds of men; and, considering the facts before stated, it is not inexplicable that so strong a nature should have given way to the fanaticism. It is greatly to his credit that he so soon discovered its true character, and had the honesty to say to the community that he had been deluded. He did not, like so many others who found that their faith had been

trifled with, renounce religion.   He immediately returned
to the church, but in contrition and meekness.   His conduct showed plainly that he felt he had in some degree
forfeited the confidence of the brethren.   Had he been
repelled as an apostate, his heart might have broken, or
he might have drifted off into godlessness.   But the
brethren treated him kindly—he regained confidence,
took his old place in the church, and labored for its welfare with increased energy.   Counting from the date of
his election as overseer, for a full third of a century he
was the strong tower of the church—its defender, teacher,
preacher, and, till 1852, its only elder.   In addition to
his work in Hiram, he labored extensively in other fields.
He was well known to most of the churches in north-eastern Ohio.

His Later Life and Relations to the Hiram Church.

Here the facts are less striking, and they must be
passed over in silence.   They are familiar to many of you.
You remember the giving way of his constitution—his
retirement from public duty—his confinement at home—
his terrible suffering from disease—his happy faith—his
triumphant and blessed death.

Here I should speak more particularly of Father Ryder's
relations to the church, especially with reference to one
point.   As he was an influential citizen at the time of his
conversion, he was justly regarded as an important acqui-
sition to the cause.   He took from the beginning, the
leading position.   The brethren were few in number, and
poor in goods.   He served the church, as was his duty,
with little or no reward.   The more the church grew,
the more it seemed to need him.   He was first the eldest
brother, then the father, finally the patriarch.   What followed was natural : he did too much for the church ; the
church did too little for themselves.   Their sense of satisfied dependence, together with his thrifty maxims, led

to illiberal contributions for the support of the gospel, and to inefficient business management. A mistake was made, into which almost all the old churches fell: no suitable provision was made for a new and different age. The church failed to discern the signs of the times. He, too, failed to discern them; or discerning them, gave no warning; or, the warning being given, it was not heeded. At all events, the church was not educated up to the wants of the coming time, and its force is weakened, and its usefulness impaired to this hour.

His Character.

I pass on to present a hastily prepared analysis of his character. I shall seek to speak of him as he was. This is the only course he would approve if he could be consulted; for he was of the Cromwellian class, whose motto is, " *Paint me as I am.*"

First of all, *his physical constitution.*

His large frame, powerful muscular organization, and great power of endurance, furnished the physical basis of his long and laborious life. If this were, as is sometimes falsely charged, an age of physical degeneracy, it were the more worth remarking that Father Ryder never could have done his work as a citizen and a Christian without his great vital power. The picture of him that I shall carry through life is the one which he stamped upon my mind when he was about sixty years of age. I was then a young student, and he alternated with the principal of the school in the preaching. I remember him as he stood in this pulpit—rather in the pulpit in the midst of whose ashes this pulpit was reared—hale of body and vigorous of mind, scourging popular errors and follies, and exhorting to righteousness, temperance, and preparation for the judgment to come. It seemed that nature had stored up in his strong body force enough to supply the vital mechanism for a century. He lived, indeed, to a good old age. Nevertheless, I find myself asking, why did he not attain to the age of one hundred years? Two facts are a sufficient answer to the question. He was one of the most laborious men of that generation which bore off upon its broad shoulders, as Sampson did the gates of Gaza, the heavy forest which covered this land—the generation that made possible that home in which we live to-day—the generation which performed the most wonderful work of the kind that history has witnessed; for in no age, and in no country, has the face of nature been so suddenly transformed as in the Northern States of the American Union. He was also identified with a religious work, somewhat akin to the other, and no whit less laborious. To this he gave his time, his energy, and, no doubt several years of natural expectancy of life. If the pioneers gave us the homes in which we dwell, no less did these pioneers of religious reform give us the churches in which we worship.

In the second place, *his mental characteristics*.

Father Ryder's mind, also, was organized on a large plan. He lacked only the discipline of study and the culture of the schools, to fit him for prominence in any community where the fortunes of life might have called him. I say he lacked only these; for his logical cast of mind, great common sense, and simplicity of character would have fortified him against the warpings and effeminacy which the schools sometimes engender. I have mentioned his logical cast of mind. Every thing was brought to the test of reason and common sense. His own life was ruled by his judgment, not by his sentiments or emotions. Besides, his mind was eminently honest and practical. He followed the convictions of his reason ; he brought things to the test of utility.

He had no confidence in sensational religion, or in sensational preaching. He feared the influence on the church of high religious excitement. " Let us have no excitement here!'' he cried, almost in the tone of command, when in a great congregation that throbbed with religious feeling, one of his sons came to confess Christ. "Let us have no excitement here,'' and the tension of his own frame, and the tears that coursed down his cheeks, showed how deeply he was himself moved. If he allowed the logical faculty to reign too absolutely in the realm of religion—as was no doubt true—it must be remembered that this was a natural result of his own mental constitution, and of his early religious training. The practical character of his mind was also seen in his preaching. In his preaching he was in the habit of dealing with a class of themes that receive too little attention in the pulpit. He brought religion into the store, the shop, the field, the granary, and the kitchen. He thought it had something to do with the manufacture of wagons, the weighing of sugar, the measuring of grain, the cording of wood. Industry, economy, honest dealing, the obligation to pay debts when due—those old-fashioned virtues formed the theme of constant discourse. A very competent judge has expressed the opinion that the marked honesty and thrift of the citizens of Hiram are largely due to his teachings and example. Here again, in his later years, he no doubt committed some excesses. His mind revolted at the exhibition of what he thought the extravagance, wastefulness, indolence, and recklessness of the new generation, and his honest nature poured itself out in warning and rebuke. No doubt he exaggerated the vices of the new time ; but much of his admonition was called for, and the remainder can be pardoned when we remember that it is a rare occurrence for one to see and understand two generations.

In the third place, *his moral and religious character.*

The basis of his moral character was integrity. So far as known to me, no man has ever charged him with a deflection from the strict line of right. He never had a lawsuit in his life; dying, he leaves no enemy. This was largely owing to the fact that he always so regulated his life that he *could* be straightforward and honest. He never allowed the situation to become his master. He was so careful in making contracts; so wary of promising when it was questionable whether he could perform; so prompt in meeting his engagements, that it was always easy for him to be upright and honest. He understood thoroughly that it is possible for a man to commit himself to a logic of events that is sure to embarrass and perhaps destroy him. A fact will illustrate this characteristic: For several years he was the Treasurer of the College. For a man in his circumstances at that time, this was a very considerable responsibility. He carried the institution money in one end of a wallet, his own in the other. He never used the College-funds in his own business; never changed a large bill in one end for smaller ones of equal value in the other. Most men will smile at this refinement of scrupulousness; but let me say to all— especially to the young men present—this sort of men never become unknown debtors to the money-drawers of their employers, or defaulters to the public treasury.

To sum up in a few words, Symonds Ryder had *character*. He did not drift on the current; he set currents in motion. He did not rest on the sentiment of the community; he formed sentiment for the community. He was not the creature of circumstances; he made them bow to him. As a citizen and a Christian, *he had root in himself*. Of course he had a will; a man of his stamp always has; without it, character is impossible. His will may have run into excess; no doubt it did; but it was the inevitable play of a powerful and indispensable faculty. A man who was never firm even to obstinacy, never plain even to severity, never truthful even to unkindness, could not have done his work.

22

THE LESSON OF HIS LIFE.

There is one lesson still to be gleaned. So long a life has a sermon in itself: *The duty of living for old age.*

History teaches us that the average of human life is lengthening. Nor are we left in doubt as to the reason : fevers are becoming less frequent and less murderous ; plagues do not desolate cities as in the middle ages ; men wear better clothing, live in better houses, eat better food ; in a word, they live more as God intended they should live. In the Bible an abundance of old men is made an evidence of peace and prosperity—a sign of God's presence with his people. "There shall yet old men dwell in the streets of Jerusalem, and every man with his staff in his hand for very age." This language points to contentment, peace, and godliness. "Behold the days . . . . . come that there shalt not be an old man in thine house forever." This points to scenes of violence, bloodshed, and sin. Intemperance, lust, ungoverned passion, consume the oil that should fill the lamp of life ; industry, temperance, godliness, feed the flame. " The fear of the Lord prolongeth days ; but the years of the wicked are shortened." "For as the days of a tree are the days of my people, and mine elect shall long enjoy the work of their hands." Accordingly, " Godliness is profitable unto all things, having promise of the life that now is, and that which is to come." Hence the relative number of old men in any community is a good measure of that community's physical, mental, and moral health.

"The hoary head is a crown of glory, if it be found in the way of righteousness." This is a description of the old age of the father whom to-day we commit to his rest. We do not weep or shed unnecessary tears ; we rejoice that he lived so long, and lived so well. His usefulness was past. The age was calling for a different type of men, when increasing infirmities compelled him to retire from the field. We judge him by his generation—not by ours. He has gone to his father's in peace ; he is buried in a good old age. He has come to his grave in full age, like as a shock of corn cometh in his season. God grant that we may do our work as well as he did his ; then we may go to our graves in equal peace.

This church has never been subject to much acceleration or retardation in its movements, another example of the leading authority in a community governing and moderating the tendencies of the people. Constantly and faithfully supplied with home talent, it has suffered few fluctuations. The brethren here have received accessions to their numbers at various times, from the labors of most or all the preachers who for a period of thirty years were the stay of the churches. In the founding of the Eclectic Institute, the church and community in Hiram proffered a larger donation for establishing it than was offered by any other of the seven contestants for the location ; nearly every dollar of which was paid. And during the twenty-four years of its life, this community has responded liberally from time to time to its necessities.

Soon after the Institute was established, A. S. Hayden was elected co-elder with Bro. Ryder, and preached in alternation with him during the seven years of his connection with the Institute. Since that time brethren Perry Reno and Hartwell Ryder have presided as elders. Bro. E. H. Hawley served the church one year as elder and pastor. At present, Bro. B. A. Hinsdale, is employed as elder and preacher. Brethren Jason Ryder and Erastus Young have long served as the faithful deacons of the church.

THE CHURCH IN GARRETTSVILLE.

In 1835, the members increasing, a new church arose in Garrettsville. The veteran "Father Rudolph" and his family, Bro. Hunt, Isaac Mead, and the brethren Noah were principal members. John Henry and William Hayden were early helpers. In July, 1838, a meeting was conducted by J. Hartzel and M. Bosworth, which imparted great strength to the cause, and added eleven souls. The church flourished for several years under the charge of Bro. Zeb Rudolph, with John Rudolph, Jr. and Michael Pifer as deacons. Bro. H. Brockett held some meetings with marked success; also Allerton, Hubbard, Moss, Green, and most of the proclaimers of the Word.

The brethren built a good house for meetings, which was formally dedicated by Bro. J. Hartzel and A. S. Hayden.

The congregation prospered for about twenty years; till by removals and death it was so reduced that the meetings were closed, and the meeting-house eventually was sold.

ORIGIN AND ESTABLISHMENT OF THE ECLECTIC INSTITUTE.

Hiram College flourished seventeen years under the title of the Western Reserve Eclectic Institute.

In tracing the earliest impulses in which the school arose, it may be sufficient to state that several men seemed to be impressed nearly simultaneously with

the necessity for it. A. S. Hayden had been for
years corresponding with leading members of the
church in North-eastern Ohio, on the advantages to
the cause of Christ of such a work; fixing his
thought, however, on a school for qualifying preachers of the gospel for their duties. His brother, Wm.
Hayden, entered fully into his views, and promised
liberal pecuniary assistance.

The first direct practical suggestion for realizing
these views, is due to the late A. L. Soule, Esq.,
then of Russell. At the yearly meeting in Russell,
June, 1849, he proposed that the matter be stated publicly, and a call be made for all who were interested
to meet at his residence on Monday morning of the
meeting, to take the subject under consideration. It
was agreed that A. S. Hayden should make the statement and present the call for this meeting.

On Monday morning, June 12th, at eight o'clock,
there was a full meeting of the councillors of the
church. There were present: A. Bentley, Wm.
Hayden, A. L. Soule, Myron Soule, Benj. Soule,
Anson Matthews, Zeb Rudolph, A. S. Hayden, W.
A. Lillie, Alanson Baldwin, E. Williams, F. Williams, E. B. Violl, M. J. Streator, W. A. Belding, A.
B. Green, and many others. A. L. Soule was appointed chairman, and A. S. Hayden, secretary.
The movement was unanimously approved, and a
resolution was passed to take steps immediately for
founding such a school as was in contemplation. The
secretary was instructed to prepare and send to the
churches an address stating the object in view, and
inviting delegates to a future meeting in which the
views of the people might be fully ascertained.

At this meeting, which was held in Bloomfield at the yearly meeting, the last of August, the same year, the response of the people was unanimous and decided in favor of the project ; and a call was issued for delegates to meet at Ravenna the next October, for maturing plans to accomplish it.

This adjourned meeting assembled in Ravenna, Wednesday, October 3, 1849. Dr. J. P. Robison was chosen chairman, and A. S. Hayden, secretary. It was found that there was a general interest in the enterprise. The delegates discussed various questions relating to it, one of which was the grade or rank of the contemplated institution. Two classes of views were represented there. Some proposed the founding of a college, asserting our ability to create an institution of that grade; others were in favor of establishing a school of high grade, but not to clothe it at first with collegiate powers. Those latter views prevailed, and the sense of the convention was expressed nearly unanimously in a resolution to that effect.

This meeting appointed five of its members a delegation to visit all places which solicited the location of the school, to investigate and compare the grounds of their respective claims, and to report at the next delegate meeting, when the question of location was to be decided. This delegation consisted of Aaron Davis, Zeb Rudolph, B. F. Perky, Wm. Richards, and ―― ――.

No fewer than seven towns came in as petitioners for it, viz.: North Bloomfield, Newton Falls, Hiram, Shalersville, Aurora, Russell, and Bedford. The members of the delegation were sound and discern-

ing men. They performed their duty faithfully, and
prepared an able report. Much interest was awakened on the question of location, and many awaited
with anxious expectation the decision of that question. The next convention met in Aurora, Tuesday,
November 7th. Thirty-one delegates from as many
churches were in attendance; also many other
friends of the enterprise, whose presence testified
their great interest in the subject. The meeting organized by appointing Dr. J. P. Robison, chairman,
(J. G. Coleman presiding part of the time,) and A. S.
Hayden, secretary.

The whole day was spent in hearing and discussing the report of the visiting delegation, and in settling the plan of procedure. The balloting occupied
much of the night. After thirteen ballotings, the
choice resulted in favor of Hiram. The last vote
stood ten for Russell and seventeen for Hiram, four
delegates having returned home before the final vote
was taken.

The convention adjourned to meet in Hiram, December 20th.

This meeting at Hiram was the last delegate assembly. It elected a board of twelve trustees, viz.:
George Pow, Samuel Church, Aaron Davis, Isaac
Errett, Carnot Mason, Zeb Rudolph, Symonds Ryder, J. A. Ford, Kimball Porter, William Hayden,
Frederick Williams, and A. S. Hayden; and appointed Charles Brown, Isaac Errett, and A. S. Hayden, a committee to draft a charter for the school.
This committee, with the assistance of Judge King,
of Warren, prepared the charter, which, with a few
slight changes, received the approval of the Board.

The name of the institution, WESTERN RESERVE EC-
LECTIC INSTITUTE, was suggested by Isaac Errett.
The provision in the charter that the Holy Scriptures shall forever be taught in the institution as
the foundation of all true liberty, and of all moral
obligation, was inserted on motion of Wm. Hayden.
He strongly urged that this must ever be the characteristic dignity of this institution, the perpetual
safeguard of social happiness, benign government,
and religious freedom.   The charter was forwarded
by A. Udall, Esq., to the hands of Hon. George
Sheldon, of Mantua, who then represented Portage
County in the legislature, through whom it received the sanction of legislative enactment, March
1, 1851.

The corporators met in Hiram the same month,
and, in anticipation of the confirmation of the charter, they appointed the following gentlemen a building committee, viz.: Jason Ryder, Carnot Mason,
Alvah Udall, Zeb Rudolph, and Pelatiah Allyn, Jr.
At the same time Wm. Hayden was appointed a so-
liciting agent to procure funds for the building.
They also purchased of Thos. F. Young, Esq.,
grounds for the school, at the center of Hiram.   In
the midst of that beautiful plateau of about eight acres
the edifice of the Eclectic Institute was erected.

On the 27th of November, which had been announced as the day for opening—a full suite of
rooms was ready for the reception students.

At the first meeting of the Board of Trustees the
position of Principal was unanimously tendered to
A. S. Hayden, of East Cleveland.   He accepted the
position for five years, not doubting that in that time

the institution would be firmly established, and permit
him to return to his chosen life work of preaching
the gospel.   This period of five years was extended
to seven, when his original purpose to retire was
fulfilled in his resignation, June, 1857.   At the same
meeting the Board unanimously elected Thos. Munnell, an honorable graduate of Bethany College, to
the chair of ancient languages.   Mrs. Phebe Drake
was called to be Principal of the primary department.
With these teachers, on the 27th of November,
1850, the Western Reserve Eclectic Institute commenced its career.   Eighty-four students were enrolled the first day.

The natal day of the Eclectic was celebrated by
a meeting of the trustees, friends of the institution
from abroad, and of the citizens of Hiram, held in
the meeting-house.   Able addresses were delivered
by Wm. Hayden, A. B. Green, J. H. Jones, and
others, upon the principles and objects of the school.
The speakers proclaimed it the completion of long
cherished purposes, the realization of many anxieties
and hopes.   It was the accomplishment of a fact
which would centralize our labors, quicken our hopes,
and animate our pleadings for the gospel.   This hill,
it was predicted, would yet become a Minerva, a
center and source of light, of literature, and of refinement.   From this place would go forth men of
ample moral and mental growth, to fill stations of
honor and usefulness in all departments of social
life.   The churches would send young men to gain
here the skill and power to plead the gospel, and to
lift up the cause of human redemption.

The students increased so rapidly that the cura-

23

tors were obliged to call, during the first term, the assistance of C. D. Wilber who had just gone to complete his course of study in Bethany College. A few weeks after, Miss Almeda A. Booth was added to the corps of instructors. The next term the influx oi patronage justified the Board in electing Norman Dunshee to the chair of mathematics and modern languages.

From this period the Institute has been before the eyes of the public, and its history is in the hearts of thousands of admiring students, who have from time to time enjoyed the benefits of its moral instruction and intellectual culture.

CHAPTER XII.

The cause planted in Sharon—Four evangelists in the field—The
church in Hubbard—John Applegate—Bazetta receives the
word—Biography of Calvin Smith.

IN Sharon, on the Shenango, over the border in
Pennsylvania, was a church under Baptist col-
ors. It was constituted in 1804, with twenty-eight
members. In 1806, it sent Thomas G. Jones, A.
Bentley, then young, Jesse Hall, John Morford and
Ed. Wright, as messengers to the Red Stone Association, in Brooke County, Va. In 1814, Isaiah Jones,
the father of our J. H. Jones, appears as its messenger. For a few years before the principles of reformation made a stir, this church had associated with
those on the Western Reserve. The elements in it
were not harmoniously blended. The family of Mc-
Cleery had emigrated from Tubbermore, Ireland,
where they had profited by the instructions of that
profound teacher, Alexander Carson. Holding clear
views of the Bible, they responded promptly to the
call for setting the churches in order, according to
New Testament usages. The father, John McCleery,
to venerable years added intelligence and decision.
His sons, George, a preacher, and Hugh, a genial,
and also an influential member, and others of the
same enterprising family, were awake to the reformatory movement which was making conquests in all
quarters. The opposition was aroused to prevent

the spread of these new doctrines ; but these brethren plead for the justice of a fair hearing of them,
before they should be condemned.   Hugh McCleery
went to Warren for Bentley and Scott, who were
soon on the ground, and who preached in Sharon the
same gospel which began in Jerusalem eighteen hundred years ago.   The same results followed ; for
" those who gladly received the word were baptized ; "
and had the church been the same as that at Jerusalem, it might have been said, " and the same day they
were added " to the church.   But the church utterly
refused them admittance, because they had not come
before the members, told a " Christian experience,"
and been accepted by a vote of the church.   Bentley
had already gone, and Scott left them immediately
after these conversions.   Elder Thomas Campbell
then came, but all his influence for reconciliation was
unavailing.   He wrote to the church a very concilia-
tory letter, deprecating division, and beseeching them
to shelter the lambs.   The reply was a stern refusal.
Meanwhile, the time arrived for the " June meeting "
of the Baptists, to assemble in Sharon.   Scott and
Bentley had returned, but the hostility was now so
bitter that these three excellent and venerable ministers, as also all who sympathized with them, were
expressly refused admittance into their meeting-house.
The excitement in the community was running high,
and Daniel Budd, Esq., a reputable gentleman, fitted
up his barn and opened it to the reformers, where,
on Saturday, Sunday and Monday, they proclaimed,
to a multitude of people, the ancient gospel, which
had filled the Roman Empire with its conquests before any of the modern sects arose.   On Monday, the

fourth one in June, 1829, on the bank of the river, after the baptism of some converts, was formed the church of Christ in Sharon.   They were forced to this step, after much persevering effort to prevent a separation.   Seventeen of the Baptist members united then, and more soon afterward.   About thirty were that day enrolled with devout invocations by these three brethren, for blessings upon them from the Head of the church.   George Bentley, Bashara Hull, with their families, and the McCleery family, were in the newly organized church.

The declared policy of the old church was non-intercourse.   A resolution was passed excluding the wives of Benjamin Reno and James Morford, for breaking the loaf with the disciples.   The former, who was a deacon, arose and protested against such an unchristian act, and announced his withdrawal from their fellowship.   Morford, a deacon and clerk, laid down his pen, his office and his membership, refusing to be a party to such a proceeding.   Both became pillars in the new organization.   The church, by resolution, excluded all who united with the disciples.

The new church had considerable talent in its members ; and they were firm, zealous and united.   Converts were multiplied.   Hayden came often among them, as did Henry also, and the persuasive Bosworth.   Applegate was near, and was quick to help.   Allerton visited them and brought in a large number.   And "having obtained help from God" through the hands of many of his servants, they continue a prosperous brotherhood in Christ.

These brethren have done much for Christ.   Two

ministers have arisen among them, Prof. Amaziah
Hull, of Oscaloosa, Iowa, and J. B. McCleery, of
Kansas. Many of great usefulness in the West were
trained for their work in Sharon.

The association was appointed to meet in this
(Baptist) church in Sharon, August, 1829, little an-
ticipating the revolution which was to take place in it
before that time. When that body convened, it found
a new church, just organized on purely gospel grounds,
all alive and strong in faith, ready to give it welcome.
A very large and joyful meeting was the result. It
was attended by T. Campbell, Scott, Bentley, Hayden, Henry, Bosworth, Applegate, McCleery, and
many others. It kept no records; nor did the great
one at Warren transmit any account of its transac-
tions. This was doubtless an error and a misfortune.

The reports from all parts of the field were highly
encouraging, and the association felt called upon to
send out more reapers into the ripening fields. It
selected four brethren, Scott, of Canfield; Hayden, of
Austintown; Bentley of Warren; and Bosworth of
Braceville; all of Trumbull County; and sent them
out under the seal of her sanction and authority to go
forth "to preach and teach Jesus Christ."

A System of Itinerary.

These four proclaimers formed for themselves, and
followed during the greater part of the years 1829–30,
a very complete and simple plan. It was understood
to be chiefly the work of William Hayden. The writer
of these notes, from an original sketch put into his
hands by him, prepared a copy of it for each of the
evangelists.

A circuit was established, including sixteen stations at convenient distances apart. It was arranged that four of the places should have preaching every Lord's day ; and also, that in the course of a month each of the sixteen places would be favored with a Lord's day service. The other days of the week being also employed, all of these posts had frequent preaching.

Several advantages resulted from this arrangement :

1. As the preachers followed one another in a regular and fixed order, the churches always knew who was coming ;

2. They had regular times for the preaching and knew when to expect it ;

3. Each preacher knew, at any time, where each one of the others was ;

4. It afforded a profitable variety of talent and instruction, giving to each community the benefit of all the talents ;

5. It removed any grounds of dissatisfaction arising from the practice of limiting the more brilliant speakers to the stronger communities, leaving to the weaker places the less eligible gifts ; a practice which has caused many a well begun opening to wither, and forced many an honest and earnest worker out of the field.

This scheme of " circuit preaching" pleased as long as it lasted. But there was no general manager who, as openings were made beyond these limits, could " send forth more laborers into the vineyard." Moreover, the "laborers were few ; " consequently, as the Macedonian cry came up from all quarters, by letters and by messengers, it became impossible to confine these evangelists. They could not resist these ap-

peals.   Scott, somewhat erratic, distanced all bounds.
He was moved at beholding the whole country a prey
to sectarianism, and having the jewel of the "ancient
gospel" in his possession, he was confident it would
soon turn the whole mutilated and dismembered profession of Christianity back to the original apostolic
unity.   So, like a hero dismantled of arrangements
which he felt to be an encumbrance, he flew where
the finger of God directed, and stirred the land with
the tidings of the gospel.

The others maintained their course for awhile.
But one after another they yielded to calls for help,
and so fell this first attempt at systematic order in
preaching the gospel.

The Church in Hubbard.

Jesse Hall, for more than fifteen years, had been a
member of the Baptist church in Sharon, Pa., and
though living about six miles distant he was a regular attendant.   He was a man of unblemished character, of broad sense, zealous, and given to hospitality.
Such a man could scarcely fail to gather Christian
people around him.   In the year 1820 a church, of
the same name and order, was formed at his residence
in Hubbard, in which himself, A. K. Cramer, Archibald Price, James Price, Walter Clark and Silas Burnett, with their families, were prominent members.
Jesse Hall was, by far, the most influential man in
this organization, and as deacon, he was the leader,
councillor and chief manager.   For a considerable
time it was the "church in his house."   He was just
the man to welcome the "Christian Baptist;" and
though he was very firm in purpose, the floods of

light poured upon the world by that work revealed to his penetrating mind, a Bible basis for the Church of God not yet fully discovered by the rival sects of Christendom. In 1828, when Walter Scott came among them, as the evangelist of the association, most of the members were prepared to receive him warmly. His forcible preaching compelled a crisis, and the whole church, eight or ten only excepted, discarded the creed and the name of the party, and adopted the New Covenant as the divinely appointed basis of the church, with only such names as the New Testament writers employ to describe the people of God.

The church thus newly formed had about forty members. Jesse Hall and John Applegate were appointed the overseers. They served with great fidelity for about twenty-five years. Their successors were Oliver Hart and Warren Burton. Orenous Hart and David Waldruff have served the church in the same capacity. And now, James Struble, H. Green and A. K. Cramer, Jr., are the acting elders.

Under the efficient management of her officers the church grew in grace and in numbers. The zeal of the brotherhood knew no bounds. Applegate, under the judicious counsels of his able co-elder, soon became a preacher who, while he traveled much abroad, served his own church in public instruction for at least twenty years. But they were not stinted in their views, and in the earlier days Hubbard gained great renown for the victories in behalf of the truth through their own prayers and activities, and the cooperative labors of Scott, Bentley, Hayden, Henry, Hartzel, Alton, Saunders, and both the Bosworths ;

and a little later, of John T. Smith, Brockett and
Perky. Bro. J. W. Lanphear is cherished for his
able defenses of the truth in that place. In after
times, W. T. Horner, William S. Winfield, Willard
Goodrich, Matthias Christy, Harmon Reeves, C. C.
Smith and J. A. Thayer have co-operated in extending and building up the church.

In August, 1837, the yearly meeting for Trumbull
County met in Hubbard. It was one of the largest
assemblies ever gathered on the Reserve. Preachers
and people came from far in those days, creating great
enthusiasm. To this one came Campbell, Bentley, the
Bosworths, Henry, Hartzel, G. W. Lucy, Applegate,
Clapp, Rudolph, J. J. Moss, and A. S. Hayden ; nearly
all of whom preached, exhorted, and held evening
meetings during the great occasion. There were thirteen converts.

Two years later, this church had an accession of
several members during a meeting in Youngstown,
conducted by A. Campbell. Among them were Jesse
Hall, Jr., Aaron Smith, James Struble, Moses Cole
and Jesse Hougland.

The growth of the church has been gradual. No
root of bitterness has ever sprung up to cause a division. They began without any church property.
For a few years, they held meetings in a building
rather useful than costly, owned by the elder Jesse
Hall, and which he finally deeded to the trustees,
with the grounds belonging to it. Subsequently,
they erected on eligible grounds a permanent and
valuable edifice ; and with a present living membership of one hundred and seventy five, the church in
Hubbard seems likely to pass from the present into

the hands of the next generation, a light and a blessing to that whole country.

SKETCH OF JOHN APPLEGATE.

"Tell us the story of the earlier times. Describe the men who lived in them, and relate to us their deeds." So cry out thousands, to whom the stirring events and the struggles which made and marked our early history have come down in mere fragments of information. It is not mere curiosity which prompts the call for this knowledge. It is a just and laudable desire for a knowledge of the causes and conditions which originated this great work, the effort to recover the Christian institution, in all its parts, from the mixture and corruptions of the long, dark day of papal superstition. Gratitude, doubtless, also mingles in the demand, that due honor may be rendered to the moral heroes to whom this generation is greatly indebted for their prompt espousal of the truth, then freshly brought out from the sacred Scriptures, and for their able, untiring, and self-sacrificing advocacy of it amid fearful struggles and against formidable foes.

Beloved among these memorable men, and distinguished in the circle of his labors, was Bro. John Applegate. He was born May 13, 1797, in Bordentown, N. J. Cradled in the lap of frugal industry, he early saw the practical side of life, from the necessity imposed on him to contribute to the wants of the family. Ohio, at the time of his removal into it, had been only five years a member of the Federal Union. Its fertile soil was the El Dorado of hope to the working people in the States of the sea-board. The Western Reserve, in particular, was receiving large accessions to its young population by immigration from New England and other portions of the East. To this inviting land came the Applegate family, when John, the subject of this

sketch, was only ten years of age. They settled in Hubbard, Trumbull County.

Through his father he inherited the Baptist faith. His
mother was a pure-minded, conscientious adherent of the
Quaker doctrine. John, very early in life, was the subject
of deep and pungent religious convictions. From about
the fifteenth year of his age up to his twenty-first year,
the tempests of religious conviction, with all their harass-
ing doubts, despondencies, and dimly gleaming hopes,
swept across his breast. The gospel of his day was moul-
ded in the most rigid school of Calvinism. Its doctrines
resounded in thundering tones in groves, under forest trees,
and in school-houses, by the Knox-like preachers of that
early time.

No sweet voice from Calvary came to his terrified conscience. He languished for relief. Sometimes he quite
resolved to abandon hope, and yield; to sink down among
the eternally lost. Then from this vortex he fled, shud-
dering at the horrible despair. He saw Calvary, and the
meek sufferer there, "but, oh! for the elect alone he
suffers there and bleeds. Oh! that I could but know it
was for me! 'Come,' he says, 'come unto me—you shall
find rest.' But, then," his soul in anguish cried, "that
blessed voice is for the elect alone; I may not be one; I
dare not stir to go." If some earnest comforter spoke of
the loving Jesus, and of his invitation to sinners—"Yes,
but I know not the way—I can do nothing but wait; if I
am to be lost, I can but fulfill my destined doom." A
genuine "experience" it was, according to the standards
of that day. Much of it ever remained a blessed memorial
in his humble and truly Christian heart. Yet how much
of needless torture might have been saved him; how much
earlier he might have found "peace in believing," had the
plain gospel plan of salvation been pointed out to him in
the hour when he was seeking to "flee from the wrath
to come!"

At length the "darkened cloud" withdrew, and peace shone in on his soul. He gave in his experience, was received by the vote of the church, and was baptized in a stream in the vicinity of his residence, in the month of March, 1818, by Elder West. He was then in his twenty-first year.

About the same time he was married to Miss Fanny Cramer, a woman worthy of his affections, and who, with even step and equal hand, bore her full share of the hardships incident to her position. Abounding in the domestic virtues, she managed her household with great prudence and discretion, and lived his faithful companion in all his life-work till very near his own departure.

Immediately after his conversion, he began to "exercise" in meetings. He was a rapid and ready talker. His articulation was very distinct and complete. He commanded a good voice, penetrating, and very agreeable to the ear. He was a singer of more than common excellence. He soon filled his soul, and the meetings, too, with the songs of joy in which he expressed the peace and hope, and love of a new-born soul.

He continued to work among the Baptists for six or seven years, distinguished for great activity and a burning zeal. Wherever a word could be spoken for the Master, his diffidence yielded to the pressing sense of duty and the earnest impulses of his warm Christian heart.

The churches and ministers in all North-eastern Ohio were beginning to be agitated by certain views—by some, looked upon as dangerous, by all regarded as novel and bold—of the Campbell's, father and son. In the year 1826, Applegate heard these gifted men in Warren. His free mind was, by his own reading of the word of God, partially prepared to receive some modifications of those rigid views which had caused so much trouble in his own experience, and he went with the determination to hear fearlessly, and give due weight to all he heard. But he was cautious; and on returning, he received the faithful chidings and reprimands of the older brethren for giving heed to new things.

Soon after this, Walter Scott came to Austintown. He was producing there a great *stir* among the people. This was the spring of 1828. All the way from Hubbard to Austintown came Applegate to hear Scott. He was afraid of him. Bentley, from Warren, and Schooley, from Salem, were also there. After the hearing, Applegate drew the sword and joined in battle. The method of enlisting converts was too quick. Genuine conversion could not be so short a work. Faith, "with all the heart," in Jesus was not enough to prepare for baptism, without relating an experience, such as the fathers and mothers in Israel could approve. So went the investigation. He thought he "whipped them all out;" and, reiterating the ancient cry, "To your tents, O Israel," he took leave of them and departed. Riding on a few miles, his horse went slower, as he thought over what he had heard. At length he halted, and resolved to return and give these brethren a farther hearing. This he did, and on leaving them a second time, Scott and Bentley sent by him an appointment for Hubbard.

He addressed himself with new zeal, with deep and prayerful interest, to the study of the word of God, resolved to be fully prepared to meet and discomfit them. But this reading partially disarmed him. He decided to "let them alone," lest he might be fighting against the truth.

The winter of 1829–30 saw the full consummation of these changes in his views. Bolder now became his testimony. He read the Word of Life to the people, and testified publicly every-where. Authorized by the church, he went to other places to teach the way of life; and without any direct intention on his part, and before he was aware of it, Applegate "was among the preachers." He visited

Brookfield, Hartford, Fowler, Bazetta, and many other places, exhorting the brethren ; and wherever he went he revived the spirits of the fainting, and poured the oil of joy into the souls of the Lord's people.

Few men were ever more patient, persevering, or enduring of privation and toil, in fulfilling the duties of the Christian ministry. Unpaid, yet uncomplaining, he traveled on horseback, often afoot, over the rough roads of a country yet new, never failing to meeet his appointments. Impelled by a lofty and sacred sense of duty, he denied himself the happiness of a home, whose limited store of earthly wealth was sweetened by the endearments of pure, genial and religious affection, that he might teach sinners in the great congregation the plain way of the Gospel of God's salvation. In those days preaching " paid " poorly in the pocket. Nor was fame reaped from it. Surely the long-continued toils and hardships of the preachers of that early day of the Reformation vindicate them from all imputations of selfishness, and stamp them with a lofty zeal and heroic chivalry worthy of all admiration.

Among all our early preachers no one had less of vain ambition. Without guile and without envy, he was happy when others preached. If any surpassed him in apparent public usefulness, or won more rapidly the favor of the people, his joy at the success of the Master's work suffered no abatement through envy. He esteemed other preachers better than himself, and voluntarily chose the lower seat at the great spiritual feasts when many proclaimers of the gospel and multitudes of souls assembled at the great yearly meetings of North-eastern Ohio. Yet was he not the less esteemed, and the greetings of the people testified the depth and sincerity of their affection for him.

In the spring of the year 1866, he removed from Hubbard, so long his home, to Iowa, to reside with his youngest son Charles, near Monticello, Jones County. Two years after his removal came the time of his mourning for the death of his wife. During their long pilgrimage, so complete had been their union in life, so like a stream without a ripple or an eddy had flowed their mutual affection, that her death was a shock almost insupportable. Five or six months after this event, in the fall of 1868, he returned to Ohio, visited well-remembered friends, and extended his journey to his original home in the State of New Jersey. In the spring of 1870 he returned again to Iowa, and made his home with his sons, James and Charles. Though age was now on him, and the " outer man" beginning to show signs of decay, he still preached almost every Lord's day. A peace-maker still, as in all his life, he labored to reconcile differences among brethren, some instances of which, among the very last acts of his life, are cherished with gratitude by the brethren where these ministrations of mercy were performed. He preached his last sermon at Nugent's Grove, Linn County. Overexertion and a sudden change of weather caused a severe cold. Typhoid fever followed, from which he never recovered. Nearly eight weeks he languished under this terrible scourge. His love of singing continued to the last. Frequently during his sickness he raised his feeble voice in melodious praise.

Near the closing scene he was visited by Rev. —— Wilson, a Presbyterian minister, who asked him if he knew him. By a nod of the head he gave the affirmative reply. Mr. Wilson then repeated a part of the twenty-third Psalm: " The Lord is my shepherd ; I shall not want." The dying hero waved another response, and soon the vessel of clay alone remained.

Thus died, on the 17th day of February, 1871, in Scotch Grove, Jones County, Iowa, at the residence of his son James, Elder John Applegate, in the seventy-fourth year of his age, having been a preacher of the gospel over forty years.

BAZETTA—BACONSBURG.

The Baptist church here was formed January 22, 1820—eight members. James and Dorcas Bowen, William and Anna Davis, Samuel and Rachel Hoadley, and Samuel and Elizabeth Bacon, were dismissed from the church in Warren for that purpose. These, with Asher and Esther Coburn, Samuel B. Tanner and Anna Tanner, Martin Daniels and a few others, composed the church. Four persons, baptized the day previous, of whom Eben R. Coburn and John F. Coburn were two, were received that day. Bro. Bentley officiated. Asher Coburn and Samuel Hoadley were the first deacons. No bishops were appointed, the Baptist order recognizing no such officers apart from the preachers.

This church continued till the "times of reformation." Her highest reported number, at any time, was forty-four. Bro. Edward Scofield, one of their number, was an earnest Christian, a man of liberal views. Being a good exhorter, he was very useful. He got hold of the "Christian Baptist." Its editor, in his triumphant vindication of the scriptural baptism in his debates with Walker and McCalla, had made a highly favorable impression on the Baptists every-where. He had thus gained their confidence, which gave a wide circulation to this his first periodical. The reformation for which he plead was not a negation. It consisted in a well matured effort to introduce Bible views, and to establish New Testament Christianity. Such views, so clearly propounded, and so well sustained by argument and Scripture, created a commotion every-where—some advo-

24

cating, some opposing them.   The brethren in Bazetta were not behind in these investigations.   The
traditions of less favored times were losing their hold
on the people.   The great stir in Warren, in January,
1828, shook the church in Bazetta like the heavings
of an earthquake.   Indeed, its impulse spread like a
tidal wave over the country.   It was a time of Bible
research, such as had not been known.   The emancipation from the traditions of the church was complete—deference to the teachings of God's word was
equally complete.   The "lively oracles" were accepted
as meaning what they said.   This grand principle
brought all parties face to face on the Bible.   People
studied it as they never had before.   It was customary to keep a copy at hand, on the desk, or the coun-
ter, that every-where, and on all occasions, the appeal
to it could be instant, and its decision was final.   The
disciples were becoming strong in the faith ; many
of them able to teach others.   The church divided
on these principles—the greater part moving on under
the leadership of the apostles, a small minority adhering to the received standards.

Among the converts in Scott's meeting, in Warren, were Enos Bacon and Daniel Faunce.   At their
invitation, Scott and Bentley came to Bazetta in May,
and added a number more ;   who, taking membership in the existing church, were counted as Baptists.
In the fall Thomas Campbell came and organized the
present Church of Christ in Bazetta.   Bro. Aaron
Davis writes : " He had to fight every inch of ground.
There was division in the ranks of the Baptist church,
but most of the members fell in with the ' new doctrines,' as they were called.   This stirred the ire of

Elder Woodworth, the pastor. The contest was sharp for awhile, as he said he would have a fair fight in an open field. And surely it was sharp for a time, but he was soon vanquished ; and most of the church fell in with the 'new doctrine.'"

The church numbered twenty-eight at the beginning. They found in the Scriptures that, under the apostles' teaching, there were elders in every church. Proceeding to organize on the divine model, they elected Samuel Bacon, Samuel Hoadley and Asher Coburn, bishops or elders ; and James Bowen and Asher W. Coburn, deacons. This was done in Father Bacon's barn, the only place they could get for their meetings. In the fall, when cool weather came, they repaired to his house. Finally a school-house was obtained, which served, for a few years, till a meeting-house was erected. During this period, and for many years, they had no regular preaching. They were served in occasional appointments, and two days' meetings, by the preachers then in the field ; and, later, by Green, Jones, Brockett, Phillips, James Calvin, Gates, Henselman, Dr. T. Hillock and I. A. Thayer.

Several churches arose from this one. West Bazetta, Fowler, Mecca and Greene, started with members from this hive. In respect to its officers, fewer changes have been made than in many churches. After Samuel Hoadley, one of the first overseers, John Sanders was appointed. He served a few years. After him Aaron Davis, who has stood as an elder about thirty-eight years. In the place of Samuel Bacon, Calvin Smith was chosen. In the place of Asher Coburn, the lamented Daniel Faunce was

elected overseer. At his demise, Otis Coburn.
Then, after him, Seth Hulse, who serves now with
Davis. The present number is about one hundred
and eighty. A good house, and Bro. R. T. Davis for
settled preacher.

Several preachers have arisen from this church.
The wise and excellent James Hadsel, of Indiana,
arose in this church. John T. Phillips began here,
though he was not sent out by this congregation.
Here Harvey Brockett—the sainted Brockett—was
helped on his feet. They found him in Farmington,
showing zeal and ability in exhortation, which gave
promise of a bright future. They moved his family
to Bazetta, and with some help from abroad, they
purchased and gave him thirty-five acres of land for
a home. And Calvin Smith, famous above his associates.

The church in Bazetta has long been generous in
sustaining the yearly meetings of the county; one
held in August, 1841, is spoken of with much interest. It was attended by Henry, Lanphear, S. Church,
Green, Jones, Dr. Robison, Winfield, Brockett and
others. There were thirty-nine conversions; Bro.
John T. Phillips was one of that number.

Biography of Calvin Smith.

Among the unchronicled dead, whose labors will be held
in perpetual remembrance, is the name of Calvin Smith.
He lives in the affectionate remembrance of the many
whom he turned to righteousness. Very many churches
throughout North-eastern Ohio, with some in the East, to
New York and New England, and in the West to Wisconsin and Iowa, will never cease to cherish the memory of
this remarkable man.

Calvin Smith was born October 30th, 1813, in the township of Vernon, Trumbull County, Ohio.   His father died when he was between five and six years old.   He continued to live in poverty, with his mother, until he was eleven years of age, when he went to live with Ezekiel Beach, of the same town.   When he was nearly fourteen, his mother was married again to Isaac Meecham, of Kinsman.   He chose his step-father for his guardian, who bound him out to learn the blacksmith trade.   During the six years he remained at this business, he was employed less at the anvil than at the desk, as an accountant.   But other impulses fired his soul.   His quick discernment and penetrating mind surveyed the wide domains of our intellectual nature, and he longed to enter, possess, and cultivate that prolific soil.   During the time of his apprenticeship, he omitted no opportunity to read and study.   With a temperament immensely active, with a keen and quick discernment and a most retentive memory, he gathered knowledge as the miser gathers gold.   At twenty he bought his time and commenced teaching school, still employing every available opportunity to advance in education.

March 19th, 1835, in his twenty-second year, he was married to Miss Maria Meecham, whose tastes and intellectual endowments were in perfect coincidence with his own.   This proved to be one of the happiest of unions.   With views, aims and purposes the same, and both possessed of great energy, and abounding in hope, they accumulated a competence, founded a house, and established a name which will long survive their own generation.   For two or three years he taught winters, and summers gave his energies to the clearing of his forest farm.

But, though ambitious, his purposes of life had not been lifted above the attainment of a comfortable home and an honorable position in society.   His heart was yet unblessed with the light and truth of the gospel.   I quote here his journal : " I was wild and unconcerned about Christianity

most of the time.   When I was about nineteen, I attended
a meeting or two held by Foot, a revivalist of the Presbyterian order, and did all they told me to do, but did not
get an evidence of pardon, and was afterwards rather
skeptical.   I occasionally heard the Disciples preach, and
on the 28th of May, 1837, I was immersed by John Henry,
and united with the church.''

It is of special interest to pause and note the workings
of his mind, and the disposing causes which acted in this
happy and eventful change in his heart and life.   In him
existed that rare and admirable adjustment of the moral
and the rational natures by which faith is sought, but
which refuses to believe without rational evidence.   He
longed for ''religion.''   He sought for ''grace.''   But though
he eagerly and earnestly sought, human promises and ex-
pedients failed to satisfy his strong mind, which desired a
firm foundation on which his soul could lean so important
a trust.   Hence his disappointment; and hence his relapse
into skepticism—a dark and dismal despondency from
which a rare man and mighty power alone could lift him.
In the guidings of a good Providence, such a man came.
In this state of his heart, John Henry, whose name is a
synonym for peerless power, came to ''the Burgh,'' in Bazetta, to preach the gospel.   When Henry preached all
men heard.   Smith came, heard, learned, and believed.
Such preaching he could understand.   It was the word of
the Lord, instead of the word of man.   The men were
much alike in mental activities and social life.   It was
David and Jonathan.   Each kindled life in the other, and
both were greater men.

From this time forward, Calvin Smith was a new man ;
but his great work of life had not yet commenced.   June
26, 1839, he was chosen Justice of the Peace by the suffrages of his townsmen.   This office he filled for nearly
eight years, and discharged its duties with fidelity and popularity.   ''During this period,'' he says, ''I paid ,more

attention to the law than the gospel." In truth, he was rising into acquaintance and esteem with the business men and leading citizens of the county. The difficult and trying duties of his office he managed with skill in some important legal cases which came before him; and, young as he was, he manifested no ordinary talent in that position. He won the confidence of the members of the legal profession, and he began to be talked of as a candidate for the legislature.

But other honors awaited him, and another destiny was before him. "Before honor goes humility." The applause of the world is not the praise of God. In the midst of all his duties now rapidly accumulating, he never wavered in his faith in the Lord Jesus, nor in his walk with the church. The church was much enlivened and edified by his zeal. He preached occasionally for them till, December 19, 1844, the church gave him letters as an evangelist. This widened his sphere of usefulness. He visited other churches, preaching on the Lord's day, and contributed very much to their growth in grace and knowledge. About four years he spent in this manner, dividing his time between preaching and the labors of his farm. At length the time came for him to cut the cable and launch upon the sea.

November 30, 1848, commenced his first protracted meeting. He was now thirty-five years old. It was not far from his own home, a place on the line between the townships of Champion and Bazetta. No church was there, and every thing seemed discouraging. Storms swept along the sky and over the earth, so that the meeting, which was opened with a fair attendance, dwindled down to eight persons. A noble opportunity to prove the sterling qualities of character, which won the victory for him on many a hard contested field! On the sixth night, only eighteen auditors, and four of them yielded to the gospel appeal and confessed the Lord. This meeting resulted in twenty-seven conversions, and the establishment of a new church of thirty-five members, which has continued in existence ever since. Before this time, however, he had seen souls awakened and converted through his ministry. In the summer of 1848, in company with Bro. James Hadsell, he held a meeting in Johnson, in his own township, with sixteen conversions.

From this time may be dated the commencement of that brilliant career in the gospel which has made the name of Calvin Smith so widely known, and so dear to thousands. His active and energetic labors spread over a period of about ten years; but as his health was very poor during the last two years, only about eight years can be assigned for the achievements of Herculean labors which are a source of amazement. Wherever he went crowds gathered, and seldom did he quit the field without many captives for Christ. Often a single discourse in a place would bring several souls to repentance. His travels included most of the counties in North-eastern Ohio, and extended to the mountains in Pennsylvania, to New England, New York, and beyond the Mississippi in the West. The labors of a long life were condensed into these eight or nine years.

In his trip to New England he was accompanied by Bro. J. T. Phillips, of New Castle, Pa. They started in November, 1853, and spent about two months. The chief object of this visit was not so much immediate conversions, as the sowing of seed to ripen into a harvest for others to reap; still there were a number brought to Christ during the trip. He made a trip to Eastern New York, and conducted a meeting in Poestenkill, December, 1855.

His longest trip abroad was one of five months, the utmost terminus of which was Dubuque, Iowa. He started on this tour August 14, 1855, and arrived at home January 30, 1856. He intended to visit his particular friends, the Soules, and the Robinsons, late of Russell, Ohio, and hold a meeting at their present residence in Iona County,

Michigan; but finding sickness among them, he tarried a few days, and proceeded westward to Wisconsin, and made a stand at Hazle Green.   Here he preached twelve days and visited fifty-three families to converse with them on the gospel.

He went to Lancaster and to Platteville.   At the latter place, sect prejudice raged so violently that the Methodist and Presbyterian meeting-houses were both shut against him.   He began in a school-house, but after a few days this also was closed.   The citizens then rallied, obtained a hall, fitted it up commodiously, and the meeting went on without the interruption of a day.   The meeting was a great success in teaching the people and in gathering souls into the kingdom.   January 4th, 1856, he commenced a meeting in Dubuque, Iowa, and continued it twenty-three days, closing on the 27th of the month.   The interest arose to a great height.   There were seventeen additions.   The cold was intense, the thermometer some days 30 below zero.

This was his last meeting for a year; and, indeed he never recuperated from the overpowering drafts on his physical energies.   He preached during that meeting every day—yet he spit blood daily, and was constantly taking medicine.   From this time to the close of his life he was able to preach but little.   The last of his preaching was in his own church in Bazetta, February, 1867, of one week preparatory to a meeting held there by the writer of these sketches; and one in Lordstown of a few days, to which he went while I was yet in Bazetta.   I well remember him as he was then, emaciate and frail, but abiding in faith, and abounding in zeal, as when health was his in fullest measure.   It is a touching remembrance to call to mind how we endeavored to dissuade him from going to Lordstown, and his replies from a voice once so ringing and clear, now so consumptive and plaintive: "I shall live only a little time," he said, "and I may do some good by going."

25

He went. Let his own hand tell the rest, in a note written by him two months afterward:

"Came home, had an attack of lung fever; sick a long time, and from this sickness I shall never recover. It is now December 15, 1858, and I have not been able to speak a discourse or do any labor; and now I am confined to the house, and will ere long die with consumption. When I die, I hope some one will record my death, and I will leave the record for those interested in it."

This is his last written note of his life. The next lines are by another hand:

"Died on the 13th of January, 1859, Calvin Smith, in the 45th year of his age, of consumption. His work is done, and he is entered into rest. He lived and died a Christian—labored for the good of man—stood up for Jesus, and went home to heaven.

"Keep us, O Lord, that we may meet him at thy right hand."

A few weeks before his death he gave his Bible to Bro. Edwin Wakefield, with a request that he preach his funeral from the following words: "Blessed are the dead which die in the Lord, from henceforth; yea, saith the Spirit, that they may rest from their labors and their works do follow them." Rev. xiv: 13. This solemn duty was ably performed in the presence of a large and weeping assembly. His widowed companion, six daughters and an only living son, followed him, and "beheld where they laid him."

"Alas! alas! my brother," wrote Bro. *William Hayden*, who visited him a short time before his death, "how was my spirit crushed in parting with thee! How sweet was thy spirit! How true was thy devotion to that gospel which pours floods of light and immortality on death's dark hour! Thou hast obtained the true ambition. On thy tombstone it should be written: 'He died at his post;' and in heaven it will be said, 'He turned many to righteousness.' How blest the righteous when he dies! How good to be embalmed in the affections of the pure in heart! May my memory be blest as thine, and my last hours be like thine, my brother.''

It would be impossible to convey in words an adequate conception of his state of mind at departing. So calm, so serene, so strong in faith, so cheerful in hope! Most tenderly devoted to his family, he heard no murmur or sigh. His religion was not a mere sentiment nor a passion. It was a faith which actualizes the "things hoped for''—a faith which saw the things invisible. What a heaven was that home for weeks before his departure! Few visitors could be admitted, but it was all the better; he was all the more sacred to his dear companion, who would have died with him, and to his children, to whom, in the serene blessedness of these most hallowed scenes, he was illustrating the faith in Jesus which he had so extensively preached to the world.

The hour came, and he slept; slept sweetly and in peace. Aged 45 years, 2 months, 14 days.

Though short the time of his ministry, *fifteen hundred and thirty-six souls* were by him turned to God, and baptized into the Lord Jesus, besides over *three hundred* who united with the churches during and under his labors. He was an early and decided friend of the Missionary cause. He saw in this effort to associate the brethren in a great evangelical enterprise, a coming hope for the churches, to lead them into a closer unity and a better order. A large proportion of his great and successful labors was under the auspices of the Missionary Society.

Bro. Smith was, in person, of full medium height, in weight about one hundred and fifty. His eye was the picture of quickness and ready discernment; his countenance was highly engaging and agreeable. He was a ready talker, blunt and rapid in speech, exhaustless in illustration and anecdote. There was a fine flowing vein of humor in his heart, which, with his hopeful and cheerful temperament, made him a most animated, social, and instructive companion. His intuitive perception of character was a marked trait of his mental capacities. He was seldom mistaken in his man.

It is needless to say that a nature so decided and marked in peculiar features, carried itself into his audiences, and under the animation of the force and enthusiasm with which he commonly moved on in his sermons, he bore the delighted hearers along with him to the conclusions which he sought to impress.

In this place it would be wrong to omit mention of some of the causes of his marvelous *effectiveness* in his work. Among these, his habit of visiting the people wherever he went, should be prominently mentioned. He was an untiring and most industrious visitor. He always visited; went every-where; made religious calls among the people, in their houses, at their workshops, on their farms. Wherever they were, he found them, talked with them, and often prayed where prayers were never before heard. These were not dull, dry, demure visitations. He was a man of the people, with the people. They saw this. He could tell them about common things, and showed himself a man with them in the experiences and knowledges of common life. His abounding sympathies went to the house and home of poverty, and cheered into life and hope hearts that never felt their blessed warmth before. It was nothing uncommon for him to visit thirty, forty and sixty and seventy families during a single meeting. The highest number I see recorded in his journal is one hundred and six during a single meeting. In these labors from house to house he omitted none, of whatever rank, or condition, or creed. He broke through all barriers, nor allowed either prejudice or religious belief to prevent his getting to the people. Christ died for them,

and his it was to reach all, teach all, convert all it was
possible to gain.

Be sure—ye indolent, ease-loving sermon makers, that
the people are God's great militia ; they are his army.
And the man who interests himself in the people, will
find the people interested in him and his message to them.

His style of speech was plain, clear, pointed and forcible.   Though rapid in utterance, his enunciation was perfectly intelligible.   The words came full and rounded from
his tongue.   He had no pedantry nor artistic airs.   His
illustrations, always pertinent and pointed, were from common things.   They were so clear and appropriate, the
people felt in them the force of demonstration.

He believed what he preached.   The intense earnestness
of his faith carried its convictions to every mind.   None
doubted his sincerity.   All saw his earnestness.   The subordinate arts of embellishment were nothing to him.   "I
believed, therefore have I spoken."   The word of God
was true ; he knew, he felt it true, and he made the people
feel it too.   The grand realities of heaven, of hell, life,
death, eternity and a judgment to come, were no toys in
his hand.

"When the son of man cometh, shall he find faith in
the earth?"   Much of the preaching of this age can
scarcely be called even a solemn farce !   So vapid and
volatile, trope, phrase, and dignity in *relief;* Christ, sin
and salvation shaded in the background !

I am conscious this sketch will, by some, be regarded
as long drawn out.   But to thousands, it will be felt to be
far too meager, while to one precious circle, where he was
vastly more than king, it will seem all imperfection.   I
dare not say how much I loved him.   Let this and a thousand other precious memories be as seed sown, to spring
up into a full harvest of joy and holy fellowships when the
saints arise in the likeness of Jesus, who is our life and
our everlasting hope.

CHURCHES FOUNDED BY HIM.

1. Between Champion and Bazetta, 35 members, December, 1848.

2. Fowler, 33 members, March, 1851.

3. Mecca, 23 members, March, 1851.

4. Auburn, De Kalb County, Iowa, June, 1852.

5. Jackson, 50 members, September, 1852.

6. Russell, 23 members, October, 1852.

7. Elmore, March, 1853.

8. Bristol, 32 members, May, 1853.

9. LaGrange, September, 1853.

10. Chester, October, 1852.

11. West Arlington, Vt., January, 1854.

12. Kenton, Hardin County, 26 members, Feb., 1854.

13. Hartsgrove, 33 members, November, 1854.

14. Rome, 60 members, February, 1855.

15. New Lyme, 18 members, March, 1855.

16. Jefferson, 28 members, August, 1855.

"Gone to thy heavenly rest!
    The flowers of Eden round thee blooming,
And on thine ear the murmurs blest
    Of Siloa's waters softly flowing
Beneath the tree of life, which gives
To all the earth its healing leaves,
In the white robe of angels clad
    And wandering by that sacred river
Whose streams of holiness make glad
    The city of our God forever!

"Oh! for the death the righteous die!
    An end, like autumn's day declining,
On human hearts, as on the sky,
    With holier, tenderer beauty shining;
As to the parting soul were given
The radiance of an opening heaven!
As if that pure and blessed light
    From off the eternal altar flowing,
Were bathing, in its upward flight,
    The spirit to its worship going."

CHAPTER XIII.

Great Meeting in Austintown, 1830—Dissolution of the Association—Defeat of Rigdon's Community Scheme—The Church in
North Bloomfield—Benjamin Alton—The Cause in Farmington—Harvey Brockett—The Church in Green—W. Bartlett—
E. Wakefield.

FOR numbers, ardor of enthusiasm, and important results, no meeting on the Reserve surpassed the great assembly in Austintown, in 1830.
It was still called the association. The church at
that place had built a meeting-house, the first one
erected by the Disciples on the Western Reserve.
It was completely filled Friday afternoon. Not fewer
than twenty preachers attended it, and crowds of
people from long distances. Yet the hospitality of
the people provided for all. Father Hayden furnished provisions for uncounted numbers, and lodged
a hundred and fifty ; bringing into requisition for that
purpose not only every floor and room in his house ;
but the barn also—empty, swept, and furnished. All
vied with each other in the profuse generosity which
bid all a hearty welcome.

The meeting opened with salutations, songs, exhortations, and reports. The next day Henry stepped
up quickly into the pulpit where were sitting the
older preachers, and said in a low but energetic tone,
" I charge you to look out what you are about to do
here ; we want nothing here which the word of the
Lord will not sanction." They smiled at his bold

independence as he returned to his seat. His meaning was apparent when he arose, soon after, and
moved that the association, as an advisory council,
be now dissolved. The resolution was offered, put
and passed so quickly, that few paused to consider
the propriety or effect of it. The most seemed
pleased ; but not all. The more thoughtful regretted
it as a hasty proceeding. Mr. Campbell arose and
said : " Brethren, what now are you going to do ? are
you never going to meet again ? " This fell upon us
like a clap of thunder, and caused a speedy change
of feelings. Many had come forty or fifty miles, in
big wagons even, so eager to enjoy this feast of love.
Never meet again ! For a little time joy gave place
to gloom. Campbell saw there was no use in stem-
ming the tide and pleading for the continuance of the
association, even in a modified form. The voice of
the reformation, at this juncture, was for demolition,
and Scott was thought to favor the motion. Mr.
Campbell then proposed that the brethren meet annually hereafter for preaching the gospel, for mutual
edification, and for hearing reports of the progress
of the cause of Christ. This was unanimously approved. Thus ended the association, and this was
the origin of the yearly-meeting system among us.

As this action and this occasion became a turning
point in our history, a few remarks upon it are demanded :

1. For three years of unparalleled success we had
organic unity of the churches, and harmony of action
among the preachers. At New Lisbon one evangelist was sent out ; at Warren, two ; at Sharon, four :

the association in this acting as a delegate body only for evangelical purposes.

2. At the dissolution of the association the system of evangelization under the auspices and direction of the brotherhood ceased and perished. No one was sent out by that body, as it ceased to be ; nor by the yearly meeting, for no such power was then assumed by the "yearly meeting," nor has been since.

3. Then perished the principle of concert of action among us for evangelical purposes; and it lay dormant for years.

4. Therefore we have been, in this respect, in a state of apostasy from our first principles.

5. Due discrimination was not made between the evangelical, which was right, useful, and not liable to dangerous results; and the ecclesiastical, against which the opposition was directed; and that in the overturn of the one, which was, perhaps, liable to objections, the other was destroyed, which was the true principle, and ought to have been carefully preserved, guarded, and, perhaps, improved.

6. Efforts, unavailing, were often made in our yearly meetings afterwards, to revive the evangelic feature of the lost association ; pleaded for by our own example and history, and by the increasing testimony of our experience.

7. Wise men saw the evil, and deplored the result at the time and afterwards ; as Benajah Austin, William Hayden, whose persistent appeals for its resuscitation provoked many, and by Mr. Campbell, who writes thus in the *Millennial Harbinger* for 1849, p. 272 :

"I have before intimated my approval of the Baptist associational formulas, pruned of certain redundencies and encroachments upon faith, piety, and humanity. I was present on the occasion of the dissolution of the 'Mahoning Baptist Association' in 1828,* on the Western Reserve, State of Ohio. With the exception of one obsolete preacher, the whole association, preachers and people, embraced the current reformation. I confess I was alarmed at the hasty and impassioned manner in which the association was, in a few minutes, dissolved. I then, and since, contemplated that scene as a striking proof of the power of enthusiasm and of excitement, and as dangerous, too, even in ecclesiastical as well as in political affairs. Counsel and caution, argument and remonstrance, were wholly in vain in such a crisis of affairs. It would have been an imprudent sacrifice of influence to have done more than make a single remonstrance. But that remonstrance was quashed by the previous question, and the regular Baptist Mahoning Association died of a moral apoplexy in a quarter of an hour.

" Reformation and annihilation are not with me now, as formerly, convertible or identical terms. We want occasional, if not stated, deliberative meetings on questions of expediency in adaptation to the ever-changing fortune and character of society."

There occurred at this meeting a passage at arms between Mr. Campbell and Mr. Rigdon. It was only about two months previous to the fall of that star from heaven. On Saturday, Rigdon introduced an argument to show that our pretension to follow the apostles in all their New Testament teachings, re-

---

* As it relates to forms and reports of its doings, it ceased at Warren, 1828. But the resolution for its dissolution was passed at Austintown, 1830. Bro. Campbell was present on both occasions

quired a community of goods ; that as they established this order in the model church at Jerusalem,
we were bound to imitate their example.   The sagacious mind of Mr. Campbell saw at once the confusion and ruin that would result from such doctrines
plausibly presented before a large, eager multitude,
many of whom were new converts.   He arose and
offered a correction of the mistake.   This did not
satisfy the zealous Rigdon.   He rejoined.   Mr. Campbell felt the necessity of settling the matter, and in
a half hour's speech he set forth the following
points :

1. The "community system," in the second of
Acts, was formed not to make property, but to consume it, under the special circumstances attending
that case.

2. The matter about Ananias and Sapphira put an
end to it.

3. Sundry passages in Corinthians and elsewhere,
calling for contributions for benevolent objects, show
that no such system prevailed in the primitive
churches.

This put an end to it.   Rigdon finding himself
foiled in his cherished purpose of ingrafting on the
reformation his new community scheme, went away
from the meeting at its close, chafed and chagrined,
and never met with the Disciples in a general meeting afterward.   On his way he stopped at Bro. Austin's, in Warren, to whom he vented his spleen,
saying; "I have done as much in this reformation
as Campbell or Scott, and yet they get all the honor
of it!"

On Lord's day, from a stage prepared in a grove,

the addresses were delivered to an immense concourse. Mr. Campbell's discourse was based on the language, "*This is a faithful saying, and worthy of all acceptation, that Christ Jesus came into the world to save sinners.*" 1 Tim. i: 15. Two propositions, he affirmed, are in the passage : 1. That the gospel is *true ;* 2. That it is *good.* Taking the first proposition, he delivered a sermon of great power on the evidences of Christianity.

About a thousand conversions in the previous year were reported ; over forty united on that occasion. For many years this meeting was referred to as conspicuous among the joyous religious festivities so numerous on the Western Reserve.

North Bloomfield.

Benjamin Alton was born February 22, 1799. His early life was spent in Genesee County, New York. At the age of eighteen, he was a zealous exhorter among the Methodists. Falling in with Elder Wm. True, of the " Christian Connection," he was baptized by him, and continued to preach the gospel as he understood it.

About the year 1827, he moved to North Bloomfield, Trumbull County. He was a man of marked abilities, full size, finely formed, and possessed most winning manner and tender speech. He had been very successful as a revivalist among the " New Lights " or " Christians." In the process of his ministry he became convinced that something was radically wrong in the exhibition of the gospel in these times, as no case is to be found in all the history of the apostles' preaching of penitent sinners mourning for days and nights, and sighing for undiscovered pardon. The sensitive heart of the sympathetic Alton was overwhelmed, as he saw many souls weeping under conviction for sin, crying out to know what they

should do, while the only answer ever given was to continue in that very condition of agony, and that relief some
time and in some way might be expected. Disgusted and
discouraged, he resolved to hide himself away in a
"lodge" in the wilderness, and there in quietness and
seclusion, to live for his family and heaven. He settled
on lands in the dense forests of Bloomfield. He had
traveled much, and witnessed with grief and shame the
sectarianisms of the day; and, moreover, he thought it a
great mistake that the gospel contained no express provision by which a repenting sinner might be assured at
once of the forgiveness of his sins. He was fast tending
to skepticism, and might have been swept into the vortex
of infidelity, but for an incident which called him forth to
the light and to great usefulness.

About the year 1829, the good people of Bloomfield
called a public meeting, and resolved to-unite in raising
a fund to support preaching, and all go to meeting together. It was an effort, after its kind, to form a union
for religious purposes; a union out of diversity. But the
union not arising out of previously existing unity—the only
condition of a permanent union—it proved of short duration. Yet they entered into the enterprise in good
heart, with good intentions, and good omens. As the
Presbyterians were the most numerous, they were to have
the house half the time; the Baptists and the Methodists
one quarter, and the Unitarians the other quarter. Squire
Brown, a prominent citizen, was to secure the Unitarian
minister. By some of the more rigid in sentiment he
was thought to be skeptical; but he entered heartily into
the arrangement as a means of the moral improvement of
the town. By him Benjamin Alton was engaged. Alton,
thus called from his coveted retreat, consented to gird
himself again in the panoply of the gospel. He came
regularly to his appointments. He would sit quite a
while in the pulpit, and then, rising, proceed to preach

without singing or prayer. He usually preached on the prophecies, and many became interested in his sermons.

About this time William Hayden preached at the center of Bloomfield, and staying over night with Alton, these two Bible men spent much of the night searching the Scriptures in relation to the ancient gospel, particularly as it relates to the manner in which the apostles preached it, and brought convicted sinners into the light and peace of pardon. In the course of the same year, Alton heard Thomas Campbell. In that discourse he saw the scriptural plan of salvation. The darkness, which like a cloud had rested on the Bible, cleared away, and he discovered, to his great joy, that God had not left us ignorant of what to do to be saved. Like Saul, when the scales fell from his eyes, he forthwith preached the gospel after the models found in the sermons of the apostles.

The alarm was sounded at once. The people had never agreed to hear a "Campbellite." The union exploded and went to the four winds. The people called another meeting, dissolved the covenant, and each party agreed to support its own meeting.

Alton kept up his appointments. Four or five were baptized this season. In 1830–1, some others were converted. In 1832, Bro. Alton preached half the time, and began to attend regularly to the Lord's Supper. They were now meeting in a school-house, where they continued several years, during which time they were growing strong and more numerous, under the visits of Hayden, Henry, the Bosworths, Applegate, and others.

In 1836, Bro. Alton moved to De Kalb County, Indiana. There he displayed the same zeal which had always warmed his own heart, and melted the hearts of hundreds. Suffering all the hardships of pioneer life in a densely wooded country, contending with marsh and miasm, he still found time to preach the gospel and plant churches. With a numerous family, little money in the country, and nothing to sell to procure any, his fare was the plainest, and his costume any thing but clerical. Sometimes without a coat—but a wrapper instead—a shoe on one foot, the other honored with a boot, he traveled afoot to his appointments. His genial disposition, manly form, sweetness of countenance, and earnest, convincing pathos, full of Scripture withal, brought many from far to hear his sermons, and many turned to righteousness. Some of the churches planted by him in that wilderness, are yet standing and flourishing.

As illustrative of the straightened condition of those days, a young man wished Elder Alton to perform for him the marriage ceremony. Unable to pay money for the service, he stipulated to compensate him with pumpkins ! The service was rendered cheerfully, to the satisfaction of the happy bridegroom, and the next day he brought a large load of selected "fruit of vine," and delivered them to the very needy and equally gratified parson.

Exhaustive toil, and the malaria of the rich opening soil, undermined his naturally hardy constitution. He sank gradually to a feeble state from which he could not rally. His wife, the faithful sharer of his life and fortunes, sank with him and before him. She died March 24, 1847. He survived thirteen days longer, and fell asleep, April 7th, aged only a little over forty-eight years. He was universally lamented. His talents commanded the respect of the people, who sought to put him on the ticket for political fame. But he chose to suffer reproach with the people of God. Like all men who move men for God, he was a most devoted Bible student. It is said he had the whole New Testament by heart. His family are religions, and his youngest son, Cyrus Alton, is devotedly engaged in the ministry of the gospel.

The little band in Bloomfield had organized as a worshiping assembly with eleven members. Among them were Nelson Works, Bro. Netterfield and his wife, Mary Sager, Polly Green, and Mehitabel Thayer. Bro. Works was appointed to take the lead of the meetings. Bro. Alton's removal left them much discouraged; but they were not cast down nor forsaken. In October, 1836, Marcus Bosworth visited them, and learning the condition of the church, thought it necessary to take steps to complete their organization, their number being now considerably increased. This was done the nineteenth of that month. The following new names were taken at this time, viz.: Zephaniah Luse, Ruhama Luse, Wm. M. Bellows, Benjamin Bellows, Josiah Bellows, Rachel Bellows, Mary Ann Bellows, Henry G. Neal, Clarissa Neal, Wm. Parker, Charles Thayer, Clarissa Wilder, Candace Green, Nancy Green, Anna Sager, Rebecca Sager, Miriam Smith.

The church has never lost its identity. It was assisted by the preaching brethren of the time; the brethren Hayden, Henry, Hartzel, Applegate, Cyrus and Marcus Bosworth, Clapp, Collins; and a little later by Lucy, Brockett, Perky, Calvin Smith; and later still by Edwin Wakefield, W. A. Belding, C. C. Foote, and H. Reeves.

In the winter of 1848, Bro. Isaac Errett held a meeting in the Congregational church at the center of the town. Bro. Charles Brown made every arrangement to secure for him a favorable hearing. The church was doubled in numbers, and the cause of religious reformation lifted up to the notice of a large number of the people in the township. Their place of meeting in the school-houses was too small for the assemblies, and in 1849, the meeting-house at the center was built, and Bro. Errett moving there in October, that year, he became the first pastor of the church. He remained two years, adding numbers and strength to the congregation, preaching also in other communities, so that the principles of this religious reformation were established in various places. The church in Green was formed chiefly under his ministry.

April 19, 1840, Nelson Works and H. G. Neal were appointed Elders. William Parker served also awhile in that capacity. In 1842, John Sager was elected deacon. These, and others after them, performed the duties of their respective offices without ordination. Some new officers having been selected, the church set apart April 19, 1854, for the purpose of ordaining them after the scriptural example. On that day Bro. Edwin Wakefield was, by imposition of hands, with prayer and fasting, set apart to the "work of an evangelist;" brethren Nelson Works and Charles Brown were, in like manner, ordained as elders; and John Sager, David Snyder, Chester Howard, and N. B. Ferry were ordained deacons. Brethren Cyrus Bosworth, M. S. Clapp, Isaac Errett and B. F. Perky were the officiating ministers.

This church owes much to the unwavering faithfulness of her time-honored elder, Nelson Works. Through all her trials he has held firmly the standard, its honored flag unfurled and aloft. Around it, with supporting encouragement, a number of the sisters, whose names are in the book of life, have as faithfully rallied, displaying a zeal, constancy, and devotion worthy of special commendation. In this connection also, the godly zeal and cheering voice of

26

Brockett comes to remembrance. In the darkest
days he would cheer the little company of believers
with assurances that the gospel would yet triumph
in Bloomfield. And when at length the day dawned,
and such an ingathering attended the labors of Bro.
Errett, " he is but reaping," said the sincere Brockett,
"the fruits of the sowing of others."

THE CAUSE IN FARMINGTON.

Like most of the churches the congregation in
Farmington is an example of Christians coming together in gospel order from different "orders," so
called. In 1818, Abijah Lee came into that town
with his family. He was a Baptist. His son, Isaac
Lee, who had embraced religion among the Methodists, went after a few years to Kirtland. There in
the great reformatory movement under Bentley and
Rigdon, in 1828, he saw the great difference between Christianity as a unity, as contained in the
Holy Scriptures, and an organized "branch" of the
church. He dropped the terms and title of schis
matic party, and stood for uniting Christians in
Christ Jesus. He returned to Farmington in the
spring of 1829, and found a young man, Harvey
Brockett, much awakened on the subject of religion.
Lee found little trouble in teaching him the "obedience of faith" as now re-proclaimed by the disciples. He received the truth "with all readiness of
mind" and was baptized by his friend Isaac Lee.
Meantime Father Abijah Lee, his family and others
there, were reading the "Christian Baptist." The
powerful stimulus of that revolutionary periodical
awakened inquiry in the minds of many. Soon Ben-

jamin Alton was on the ground, and to full houses
announced the call to the Bible—to Pentecost—to
Christ. A local Methodist preacher confronted him,
but God in his truth was mightier than man in his
ignorance of it; and the people "heard him gladly."
In 1830, a church was formed, with Abijah Lee as
leader, which met every Lord's day according to the
commandment, to keep the ordinances as they were
delivered to the church by the apostles. With no
chart but the unerring Word, they launched on the
ocean under the pilotage of the Captain of salvation.

They numbered at the beginning about twenty.
The Baptists gave them Abijah Lee and wife, and
Daniel Davidson and his wife. Isaac Lee, for a little
with the Methodists, and Harvey Brockett also now
rallied with them and the new converts around the
"ensign" lifted up for all nations on the day of Pentecost, A. D. 33.

Alton did not forsake them, nor were they wanting
in zeal nor gifts among themselves. They lost no
opportunity to teach the people; and they were constant in mutual edification. The sincere Applegate,
the tender Bosworth, the rapid Henry, and the energetic Hayden, labored among them early and with
much success; as did also Collins, Clapp, and Hartzel.

SKETCH OF HARVEY BROCKETT.

All honor to the church that could produce a Brockett!
He was a man of attractions. Few men in so short a career have left so lasting results to witness for their devotion to Christ. He was born April 13, 1806, in Onon
daga County, New York. In 1821, he came with his
parents to Farmington. When he was ten years old, his
mother, a devoted Christian, gave her son to God, and

bidding him follow her, she left him, and was borne to her grave amid plentiful tears. From that day, heaven was to him a dear place. The Savior was precious; the Bible was sacred; but confused by the teaching of the day he found no peace, till in his twenty-third year he obeyed the Lord Jesus Christ. His way was now clear, and the young disciple and future preacher of righteousness studied diligently the Holy Scriptures, and began to exhort sinners to turn to God. He rose rapidly. His whole nature was aglow. Gifted with great copiousness of language, and fluency of speech, his natural timidity yielded to his mastering zeal, and he was heard gladly wherever he went. The church of Bazetta caught hold of the hand of this young Timothy, gave him a home among them, and helped him on his way.

For about twelve years he was among the churches. And who shall describe the swell of holy enthusiasm which every-where attended his labors? Converts came like the dew-drops of the morning. In his hands the gospel was luminous and tender, melting the heart, and convincing the judgment with such a power, and an array of evidences so abundant and pungent, that all who heard admired, and many yielded to his trumpet call to repentance. He preached twice a day, sometimes thrice, sung much, was a great talker, and not having, like Paul, a Silas or Timotheus to baptize his converts, his personal administrations of that sacred ordinance were almost daily.

He was cheerful, but never trifling, serious, and most earnest, with a voice of good compass and charming tone. His pathos excelled his logic, in which, however, he was not deficient. His sermons were long, closing up with exhortations of warmth and power. He overworked; his constitution lost its iron, and he became a prey to frailty and fever. On the 12th of September, 1848, his most active and useful life closed at his home in Sharon, Pennsylvania. He was twice married; the last time to Mrs.

Margaret McCleery, relict of Hugh McCleery, of Sharon. She was much respected for her benevolence and steadfastness in the faith, and has recently joined him in the promised rest.

THE CHURCH IN GREEN FOUNDED.

The church in Green, Trumbull County, was organized the first Sunday in January, 1851, by Isaac Errett and C. Bosworth. The following eleven persons were the members : Walter Bartlett and Prudence Bartlett, Wm. D. Morris and Mary A. Morris, Edwin Wakefield and Mary Wakefield, Eldad Barton and California Barton, Austin Dean, Deborah Curtis, and Polly Smith. Walter Bartlett was chosen overseer, and Wm. D. Morris, deacon. There were twenty additions during the year ; ten in a meeting held by Calvin Smith in November after this organization.

Bro. Edwin Wakefield, widely and favorably known for his success in the gospel, was baptized here in the spring of 1845, by the able Perky, in a meeting held there by him. Bro. Bartlett has from the beginning held a leading position. He was born 1801, and came to Mecca with his parents in 1818. In 1821, he heard Mr. Campbell deliver two discourses in Warren, which were " nails driven in sure places " with him. He united with the F. W. Baptists, and preached among that people a few years. His associations and reading opened his mind to the plea and principles of the disciples ; and as he earnestly sought only to know and teach the truth, he sometimes proclaimed sentiments not in the theological system of that sect. He was arraigned in the quarterly meeting for heresy, and after various hearings, they refused to renew his license. They granted him a letter, and as the brethren in Bazetta had been kind to him, he presented to them his letter, was received, and after due time was ordained an elder in the congregation. This was in 1836. Though no church was established in Green till the year 1851, as above related, Bro. Bartlett's tongue was not silent, nor his light under a cover. There was occasional preaching there by Alton, Brockett, Perky, Hartzel, and Bosworth. Wm. Hayden and Elder T. Campbell explored the land as early as 1828.

The church numbers about eighty members. Bro. E. Wakefield has long been a "captain of hundreds" among them, and his son, E. B. Wakefield, is rising to usefulness as a proclaimer of the gospel. Bro. A. C. Bartlett, son of Bro. W. Bartlett, for many years before the public, is a gift to the cause from this church.

Bro. W. Bartlett writes: "It is wonderful to see what great results sometimes spring from small causes. I can not doubt that my hearing A. Campbell in 1821, was the cause of my withdrawing from the F. W. Baptists and uniting with the Disciples ; and this led me to labor for an organization in Green, which, through the blessing of God, I have seen accomplished. The seed, after passing through more than one crucible, and occasionally watered, not only brought forth the blade in 1836, but the full ear in 1851, and has produced fruit ever since. How little did I think when I was listening to those sermons that they were to have an influence on me through all my life! But I now know that this has been the case. It has taught me to sow the seed of the kingdom wherever I could, for I knew not how much might fall on good ground, and bring forth fruit in the salvation of souls."

CHAPTER XIV.

Primitive Christianity in Deerfield—E. B. Hubbard—Experiences of J. Hartzel—Church formed—Scott's Sermon—Captain Allerton surrenders—John Schaeffer relieved of Lutheranism.

EPHRAIM B. HUBBARD was born in Duchess County, New York, February 28, 1792. His father, of Connecticut ancestry, moved to Deerfield, Portage County, Ohio, in 1802, Ephraim being then ten years old. His early life was the usual toil and privations in a new country. His education was gained in the primitive log school-house. But the thirsty soul can drink water from goblet or gourd. Hubbard learned rapidly, and acquired information which placed him high among his fellow-citizens, and eventually raised him to a seat in the Ohio Legislature.

July 1, 1817, he married Miss Mary McGowan, whose father was an early emigrant from Maryland. After raising eight children, and filling faithfully the duties of domestic and social life, she fell peacefully asleep, October 13, 1839. Hubbard was re-married to Miss Jerusha Reed, and is enjoying life at eighty-three.

The Methodists pre-empted Deerfield. The Hubbards gave assent to their assumed claim, all except Ephraim. He held membership with them about four years, but he openly protested against the creed and discipline as a direct challenge of the rights of the King. He felt relieved, however, of responsibility on the subject, as he had been cordially received with expressed opposition to it as an unauthorized usurpation of the place of the Word of God in the government of his church.

About this time a Methodist class was formed in Smith Township, under the leadership of Gideon Hoadley. This class solicited Hubbard to unite and assist them. To this he consented on condition that he should not be required to assent to the "discipline." This band of Christians, acting on their inherent rights, and, in this act, setting aside the rules of the Methodist church, unanimously agreed to his terms. Accordingly, himself and his wife, who was a Baptist, became members the same day. With the same noble sentiments, his brother-in-law, Samuel McGowan, a Baptist, and his wife, a Presbyterian, offered themselves for membership. Some demurred, alleging that the rules of the church should be enforced. Bro. Hubbard asked them to delay a decision for two weeks, and to search the Word of God for authority to guide their action. To this they assented ; and at the end of that time, no precedent or other authority for a period of probation being found, McGowan and his wife were cordially received.

As soon as this was known by the authorities of that church, Presiding Elder Swaize came with the circuit rider, Rev. Mr. Taylor, denounced these whole proceedings as a violation of the rules of the discipline, and declared the class dissolved.

But this was not the last of it. The most of the class were so dissatisfied with this invasion of their rights as men and Christians, that they held them-

selves aloof from any farther union with the M. E.
Church, and stood ready for the coming light, which
was soon to result in a practical and permanent union
of these and many others on New Testament
grounds. The leader of the class, Bro. Hoadley, being one of this number.

As the history of a religious movement is identical
with that of its chief actors, I insert some notice and
experiences of Bro. Jonas Hartzel, associated with
the origin of this church, and long identified with it.

He was born October 19, 1803, in North Hampton County, Pa., In 1805, his parents settled, with
several other families of the same name and kindred,
in Deerfield, then quite an unbroken wilderness.
Now let his own pen continue the recital:

"On the second day of June, 1825, the marriage con-
tract between myself and Miss Alice Wallahan was con-
summated. In religious profession we were divided; but
in religious tendencies, industrial habits, domestic economy, and love of home, we were happily united.

"Soon after this my mind became more seriously affected with my religious condition. My wife being a
Methodist, we occasionally attended Methodist preaching.
This brought before me the complications of Calvinism
and Arminianism. *Sovereign grace* put on the more orthodox face, but *free grace* wore the more pleasant smile.
But the effect was uncertainty and doubt, and this was
followed by skepticism in the current religion of the
times. Meanwhile I said nothing in relation to my
troubles, until in an evil hour I communicated the state
of my mind to my father. It was, as we then called it,
a sacramental occasion. I attended all the sessions until
Monday morning.

"My father saw from my movements that I did not

27

intend to go to meeting. He came to where I was at work, and asked: 'Jonas, an't you going to meeting to-day?' To which I said: 'Father, you know my business is urgent, and going to meeting is doing me no good; I go to our meeting, and our preacher preaches unconditional election and reprobation; I go to Methodist meeting, and the preacher will preach an opposite doctrine from the same text. Father, there is something wrong. We all say we are influenced by the same spirit; we are all reading the same Bible; we are all traveling the same road to the same heaven. The different parties acknowledge each other to be Christians, but each party says my way is the right way, and I can not tell which way is the right one.' To this my father made no reply, but as he turned away, I saw the falling tear. My regret for this freedom was bitter. I threw down my tools, and I was in the meeting-house as soon as himself.

"Not long after this a new trouble sprang up. Having returned from meeting, and dinner over, my wife asked: 'What evidence is there for infant baptism?' This question, coming from this source, produced strange emotions. Knowing that the subject of baptism was not under discussion in our respective families or neighborhood, added no little to my surprise. 'Alice,' I said; 'why do you ask me this question?' 'If there is any evidence in the Bible for infant baptism, I want it, for I never had any confidence in my baptism,' was her reply. 'Well,' I replied, 'I can satisfy your mind.'

"I took down the Scriptures, and read those passages upon which I had always relied for defense. I read them, but the reading was of no avail. I must draw inferences. The Lord only knew the deep mortification I suffered. My witnesses were against me. I saved appearances as best I could, laid up the book, and said we would talk upon this subject at another time. I now saw the differ-ence between the controversialist and the impartial instructor. I could no more mislead my dear wife, than my own soul. Before this, I saw infant baptism in 'Suffer little children to come unto me,' in the baptism of Cornelius, Lydia, the jailer, Stephanas, and their households ; and when hard pressed by an opponent I could find it in circumcision, but under these new circumstances it had departed, given up the ghost without a struggle or a groan, and left me in mourning.

"Between denominational pride and conviction there was a fierce contest for a short time. But I finally resolved to be true to my convictions, and I made an honest surrender. I said, 'My dear wife, I can give you no Bible evidence for infant baptism, for there is none. I am now convinced that it is a human device; and neither we, nor so much as one of our extensive family connections are in the church of Christ, according to the law of the Lord.'

"I now became more confirmed in the conviction, that there was something wrong in the denominational exhibitions of Christianity. I had been misled by wise and good men. I also discovered that I had never read the Scriptures, to form sentiments for myself. My religion consisted in opinions, rather than faith. I had been acting upon the credit system, and I was determined to abandon it at once. This led us to the only reliable source of knowledge. We now began to read the Bible as we had never read it before. The question of infant baptism was now disposed of, and we regarded ourselves as unbaptized. Then we examined the specific passages in the New Testament on faith. This was the subject of my greatest trouble. Sometimes I thought I had a hope, and again I doubted. I knew I had never felt and experienced what others said they had, and I attributed my darkness to unbelief. Yet I knew I did believe. But, in our classification at that time, there were four kinds of faith—speculative, historical, dead, and saving faith—the latter only was of saving value. This faith I supposed I had not, and had no means of obtaining. The first three might be the result of the Scriptures, and were of no avail; while saving faith was the direct gift of God. This gift was the burden of my daily prayer. In our course of reading we came to this Scripture: 'And many other signs truly did Jesus in the presence of his disciples, which are not written in this book: but these are written, that ye might believe that Jesus is the Christ, the Son of God; and that believing ye might have life through his name.' John xx: 30, 31.

" I exclaimed! 'This faith I have had from my childhood!'

" I said, adopting the language of David, ' The Lord has brought me into a large place.' This discovery came like a flood of light. The gospel in all its facts and phases assumed new and lovely aspects. The gospel appeared intelligible, and its promised blessings accessible. This was to us the beginning of a new life and new joys. We had new incentives to read the Bible."

Samuel McGowan was a devout man, possessed of solid mind, with great power of analysis. One day he met Jonas Hartzel, his brother-in-law, and said: "I fear Alexander Campbell has fallen into a grievous error." "What is it?" "In the last number of the 'Christian Baptist' he maintains that baptism, preceded by faith and repentance, is for the remission of sins." Hartzel replied: "I have advocated that for some months past myself. In defending anti-pedobaptist views with other folds, I referred to Acts ii: 38; where it says, ' Repent, and be baptized in the name of Jesus Christ for the remission of sins.' I found this to be a new and unanswerable argument against infant baptism."

"Well," said McGowan, "I guess you'll read the 'Christian Baptist' now!"

Thus the investigations ran, till the Hartzels, Hubbards, McGowans, Finch, and others agreed to form a society for the investigation of Scripture subjects. They were fully awake to the sad condition of the Christian churches, so called, divided, alienated, contradictory in doctrine and work, and that this state of things was not only unauthorized by the word of God, but contrary to it. And they were equally convinced both of the truth of the Holy Scriptures, and the unity of their teaching on all practical subjects. This noble band of men and women bound themselves together to find out that truth, and to walk together in it. They resolved to meet weekly, and semi-weekly when convenient. This was in March, 1827. Bro. Hartzel's pen may proceed with the story:

" There were in this little band the following persons: Cornelius P. Finch, a Methodist preacher, and his wife; Ephraim B. Hubbard and his wife, he an active Methodist and his wife a Baptist; Samuel McGowan and wife, he a Baptist and his wife a Presbyterian; Peter Hartzel and wife, he a Presbyterian and his wife a Baptist; myself and wife, myself a Presbyterian, but not a communicant, and my wife a Methodist. There were a few others. The first three named were our chief speakers. We assumed that the Christian religion, in its fullness and perfectness, was recorded in the New Testament, and what could not be there found, or what could not be read from this book was no part of Christianity. We also assumed that this was an intelligible document, for, if not adapted to the common intelligence of mankind, it could not be received as a revelation from God to man.   In these predicates we agreed.

"Our work was now before us, and we had a will to do it.   But little did we know of the magnitude or the difficulties of the work to which we had committed ourselves. Our meetings increased.   Some came in from feelings of opposition, others from motives of curiosity.   Stephen M. Hubbard, a Methodist preacher and a worthy man, attended occasionally, and participated freely and affectionately in our discussions.   Our number at one time, I think, was twenty-two.   The three most popular church parties were all represented among us, both in number and intelligence ; therefore our discussions took a wide range. Sometimes we discussed the intelligibility of the Scriptures, their all-sufficiency for the purposes of enlightenment, conversion, Christian perfection, church government.   Then the 'special call' to the ministry ; how does faith come ; how many kinds of faith ; which is first in order—faith or repentance ; can a sinner believe and obey the gospel, acceptably and savingly, without some super-added spiritual influence from above; should an unbeliever pray for faith ; is the gospel a dead letter, or does it possess inherent, quickening power; when, where, and by whom was the gospel first preached.   The difference between the first and second commission which Christ gave to his apostles; apostolic succession ; the abrogation of the Mosaic dispensation ; the subjects, mode, and design of baptism ; should a sinner be baptized on the confession of his faith in Christ, or on an approved experience. All these subjects were under earnest discussion for about one year.

"These were great questions, and on account of our old theologies, they were exceedingly perplexing.

"No doctrinal standard was appealed to.   All human authorities were ignored.   The Bible was our book ; Jesus Christ and his apostles were our umpire; and our work

was personal in its object. We were sick of denominationalism. All save Bro. Finch and his wife, had a religious opponent in his or her own bosom. Primarily our
objects were to save our souls from sin, and to sweeten our
domestic enjoyments by a return to that gospel which was
from the beginning. We had but two alternatives between which to choose; either to transmit religious party-
ism, with all its bitter fruits, to our rising families, and
live and die in that state of doubt and uncertainty, vascil-
lating between hope and fear, the inevitable result of a
mixed profession, or to find relief by going back to the
old record, to 'look up the old paths and walk therein.'

"Now for the practical results. In the month of May,
1828, we determined to enter into church relations. The
question of baptism came up. It was suggested by one of
the senior brethren who had been immersed, that those of
our number who did not yet see their way clear, might
come into membership on their former baptism, until such
time as they might see their duty more clearly. To which
I replied, that myself and wife had been desirous to be
baptized for some months past, but were waiting an opportunity; and we would not stand out-door and do in-
door work. This at once settled the question in favor of
immersion as a condition of membership.

"Immediately brethren Hubbard and Finch were requested by the meeting to visit Adamson Bentley and
Marcus Bosworth, to obtain their attendance to preach for
us, and administer baptism, and assist in a formal church
organization on the New Testament basis. On Saturday,
preceding the second Lord's day in June, 1828, these
brethren came. Before preaching, a few were baptized,
and more on the day following. Then thirteen 'gave
themselves to the Lord and to one another.'

"The test to which our investigations conducted us
was a rigid one. To abandon long cherished opinions,
and to dissolve endeared church relations, requires strong

faith and great conscientiousness. Especially is this true
in the case now before us. One profession may be exchanged for another, one creed for another, and one party
name for another without much sacrifice or loss of reputation. But to abjure party, creed, and name, and espouse
the simple gospel, involves reputation, and, in the case of
ministers, standing, character, and support.

". . . . . This congregation grew in favor with
all who gave us a candid hearing. In less than six months
our number was about sixty. Seven of these were strong
men, and did more or less evangelical work in the region
round about, and the Deerfield church became a radiating
point, a center of Christian influence."

November 7, 1828, Walter Scott first preached in
Deerfield. His reputation had preceded him, and
expectation was high. The house was filled densely
at an early hour. His victories in other fields plumed
his hopes, and prepared him for the occasion. It is
to be spoken of that remarkable man that he seldom
came into an assembly unprepared. Though attentive to all that was about him, his theme absorbed
him, and it was matured. I have often seen him
with his face bowed almost to his knees as he sat
waiting the moment for opening, with his hands
covering it, evidently lifting his soul like Jacob for
a blessing. On this occasion the people were on his
heart, and each soul was a kingdom to be won for
Christ. His first sentence commanded every ear.
" The world has been wrong three times, it has been
well nigh ruined a fourth." Proceeding through the
Patriarchal, the Jewish and Christian dispensations,
he shed on each such a flood of light, that the whole
Bible seemed luminous. The sermon lasted three

hours. At the end of his discourse on the Patriarchal dispensation he paused, and turning to Sister
Jane Davis, a sister from Wales, of fine musical powers, he said: "Sister Jane, sing us one of your
songs." Then resuming, he opened the Jewish age
to their understanding. "Sister Davis, another of
your beautiful songs." Then gathering up his
strength he presented the Christian institution, the
full and complete development of God's mercy to lost
man.

The effect was perceptible every-where. Eleven
souls accepted the offered mercy. Capt. Amos Allerton and Capt. Horace Rogers were of the number.

Capt. Allerton was an influential citizen, of fine
social qualities, good intellectual abilities, high toned,
generous, sensitive, quick of discernment, and frank,
almost to a fault. Tall, heavy frame, not muscular,
but of immense physical power. Yet this fine ship
carried no faith. Having heard of Scott and his doings, that he baptized people and promised them
heaven, sometimes taking them by force into baptismal floods, he went to the meeting fully intent on
seeing fair play, and not permitting such perform-
ances in Deerfield. And he was just the man for
such a venture, had there been a call for it. How
was he taken aback when he beheld a small man, of
gentlemanly manners equaled by few, delicate in
build, with every evidence in lineament, and form,
and speech of the gentlest and the noblest of natures! He was disarmed of all his useless purposes,
and he resolved to hear him carefully and candidly.
He caught his first word and his last. As the great
dispensations moved on before him in that grand

discourse, like panoramic illuminations, he saw what he never saw before—order, system, plan, arrangement, and development in the Bible history of human redemption. As the eloquent preacher approached the conclusion, Allerton's skepticism had vanished, and he felt his heart moved, as never before, by the view of the Savior, suffering on the cross for the sins of the whole world, opening there the fountain where all must come, and wash and be clean.

As the preacher said, "Clear the way and let the people come and confess their faith in Jesus Christ and be pardoned," Allerton started with a decision so quick, and a step so prompt, that Scott felt alarmed at seeing him crowding so resolutely along. No sooner was he seated than Scott's fears subsided, and he felt as Ananias after the Lord had said to him " Behold, he prayeth !"

This community presents a favorable example of steady and continued growth. Her elders, C. P. Finch and E. B. Hubbard were men of distinction as speakers. Bro. Finch had been a circuit rider among the Methodists. With the frankness of character for which he was distinguished, he quickly saw, and promptly embraced the principles of this appeal for a restoration of primitive Christianity. "Ye may all prophesy, one by one, that all may learn, and all be comforted," (1 Cor. xii: 31.) No church better exemplified this Scripture. Thus the church was able to " edify itself in love ; " and moreover from them "sounded out the word into every place." All the churches within a radius of thirty miles felt the power of this congregation. Many became highly competent teachers, as Peter Hartzel, Samuel

McGowan, Alex. Hubbard; and several rose to eminence, such as E. B. Hubbard, J. Hartzel, A. Allerton, C. P. Finch, and John Schaeffer. From her came the Laughlins—Milo Laughlin, of Missouri, and A. J. Laughlin, of Indiana. While depending on their regular steady meetings, they have enjoyed the labors of most of the preachers—Henry, Hayden, Bosworth, Brockett, Lanphear, Perky, the Erretts, Belding, M. L. Wilcox, Streator. And time would fail to tell of their glorious work in Christ. From her have gone, besides those named, W. W. Hayden, W. L. Hayden, and M. P. Hayden, the three sons of Daniel Hayden, all fully educated, and all giving themselves to the ministry.

It should be recorded in honor of the power of woman, too frequently left in the shade, that to the influence of one female in their number is largely and justly due this early Christian enterprise. The firmness of character needed to support faltering resolution was found in the inflexible purpose of heart of Mrs. Polly Hubbard, the wife of Bro. E. B. Hubbard. To her devotion to truth, to her clearness of perception of it as taught in the gospel, to her marked and consistent evenness of character and firmness of mind, her husband was greatly indebted for encouraging support in many an hour of fierce trial, to which their position and principles were subjected in those times of conflict and debate.

The same honorable mention should be made of several others, the wives of men whose names have won renown. To their prudence, firmness, and cheerful devotion to the cause, and endurance of toil and reproach, equal to their husbands, is to be cred-

ited a full measure of the success of the gospel in
Deerfield.

In the year 1834, there was an accession to the
reformation from the ranks of Lutheranism of one
of their ministers. The recital of his change of
views presents so much information, that it can not
rightfully be withheld from the reader. We refer to
the case of Rev. John Schaeffer, of Columbiana
County. We are thankful that we can give it from
Bro. Schaeffer's own candid and careful pen:

" DEAR BRO. HAYDEN:

"By your request I will give you a brief history of my
life, exclusively on those points you suggest.

" 1. The place of my nativity is Westmoreland County,
Pennsylvania. My religious training was that of the most
ultra order of the Lutherans. Being of poor parentage, I
did not enjoy the advantage of a collegiate education. At
the age of twenty, I was placed under the theological instruction of Rev. John Wagenhals, a fine scholar from
Germany, and a gentleman in the true sense of that word.
I studied the theology of the Lutheran church one year,
after which, by his influence I obtained, when examined,
a license to preach, sprinkle infants, catechize, and sol-
emnize marriage contracts; but denied the right of administering the Lord's Supper, and a voice in the synodi-
cal and ministerial sessions. This was to assist me in the
prosecution of my studies for another year. After which
I obtained license after being examined in theology, by
which I was clothed with all the ministerial functions, save
a voice in the ministerial session, which privilege was consequent upon ordination; and by this license I was constituted a candidate for ordination, and put on probation
in the ministry for three years; after which term, upon
examination of my orthodoxy in the Lutheran faith, I

was ordained, by the imposition of the hands of the ministerium, to the office of pastor. I remained with the society but one year in the capacity of a pastor. My entire stay with that religious order was five years, save two months; viz. : one year as catechist, three years as candidate on probation, and one year as ordained minister or pastor.

"2. The agencies that led me to reform in many of my religious views were, briefly, these : While yet on probation, on a visit to my father-in-law's house, I had an introduction to Bro. Jonas Hartzel by his sister, who, after a few months, became my companion for life. Our conversation soon turned on the subject of religion, which was the common topic of those days, and in the course of our interview he propounded this question : 'Which in the order of salvation stands first, faith or repentance ? ' I answered in all the honesty of my soul as I was taught, and as I was teaching, not suspecting, in the least, the possibility of a negative to my answer, 'Repentance precedes true and evangelical, or saving faith.' Bro. Hartzel replied : 'Do you hold that repentance is pleasing to God ? ' 'Most certainly, else he never would have commanded it.' Bro. Hartzel replied : ' The apostle Paul says, Hebrews eleventh chapter : *Without faith it is impossible to please God.*' This was enough for me on that subject. I confessed my error, and from henceforth I no more preached repentance before faith, nor justification by faith alone.

"This was the first time my confidence in Lutheranism was ever in the least shaken. I felt the very platform on which I stood tremble beneath me. My mind became much agitated. The idea of being wrong on this cardinal point, prompted the inquiry, may we not be in error in others also ? Moreover, the whole religious world was arrayed before me, in all their diversified views and opinions on. religion. They all lay equal claims to divine truth and right.   I was forced to lay aside all my former prejudices, and come to the charitable conclusion that we are all alike but *sects* and *parties*, and all wrong, being in opposition to each other.   With me it was a settled logical fact, that two opposites can not both be right; it is possible that both may be wrong, but impossible for both to be right.

"From these reflections I came to the conclusion, that Lutheranism may be as rich in error as any other *ism*. Hence the word of God was my only refuge; for all regard the word of God infallibly true.

"After I became connected with the Hartzel family I was brought into frequent contact with Bro. J. Hartzel. The main difficulties in my way were the questions relating to infant church membership, predicated on the perpetuity of the church state, which received its visible form when Abraham was ninety years old, and received the covenant of circumcision.   These were the topics discussed when we met.   Our debates were warm and animated, and I thought that neither of us had much to boast when we laid our armor off.   His sister, my wife, who was a Disciple sentimentally, long before we were married, also greatly aided in revolutionizing my views on these subjects, by propounding questions, and leaving me to struggle under their weight to work out a solution, without ever attempting a vindication of her questions.   This prudential course had its desired effect.   I never had any difficulty respecting the action of baptism.   I well understood before I completed my theological studies, that pouring and sprinkling were substituted for baptism by the authority with which the ministers professed to be clothed; believing themselves to be the successors of the apostles in office, embassadors of Christ, having the keys of the kingdom of heaven committed to them.   Believing all this, I was fully satisfied that I was doing God service in sprinkling a little water on the face of an innocent babe in the name of the Father, Son, and Holy Ghost. Bro. Hartzel and I engaged in a written debate on these subjects, during which time I availed myself of all the aids in my power, both from books and from my preaching brethren. I did this in disguise, not wishing that the secret workings of my mind should be made manifest. It was customary with the ministers when they met on a visit, in order to pass the time more pleasantly and profitably to themselves, to take up a debatable question and discuss it. On one occasion I took the negative of infant baptism with the pastor of the German Reformed Church of New Lisbon. He being a scholar, and a man of experience, I discussed it with a good degree of energy, paying due deference to his age and superiority. He frankly confessed that infant baptism could not be positively sustained from the New Testament, and closed the debate with this remark: 'It is a good old practice, and I would have my children baptized if the whole world should repudiate the practice. On another occasion, with the pastor of the Lutheran church in Carrollton, I took the negative of the same proposition. He made the same concession as the former, but his concluding remark differed, viz.: 'So we believe and so we preach.' I will refer to one more case: Conversing with the pastor of the Lutheran church in Canton, he discovered in me what I did not so fully realize myself, and thought my sentiments ran in the direction of my arguments. When we gave each other the parting hand he said: 'I fear the next time I shall hear from you, it will be *John the Baptist*'—my name being John. So the aid I sought against my opponent, made me weaker.

"In the meantime I had in charge about thirty catechumens, instructing them in the religion of our fathers, qualifying them for the act of confirmation, in which act they voluntarily assume their baptismal vows made in their infancy by their sponsors or god-parents. The time

had arrived when it became my duty to ascertain whether
they were all baptized. After asking several in the class
and receiving an affirmative answer, the following col-
loquy ensued : A young lady whom I asked, Are you baptized? answered, 'I do not know !'

" *Ques*. 'Do you not know that you were baptized?'

" *Ans*. 'No.'

" *Ques*. 'Did your parents never tell you that you were
baptized ?'

" *Ans*. 'My parents told me that I was sprinkled when
I was a baby, but I know nothing at all about it.'

" The argument was overwhelming. A personal duty
changed into an item of faith, robbing the believing penitent of one of the greatest privileges, to know that he
has put on Christ in baptism through faith in him. It
clinched the nail Bro. Hartzel had so skillfully driven.
I immediately dismissed my class, returned home, and
said to my wife, 'I shall never sprinkle another infant
while I live.' She congratulated me on my resolution,
expressed her gratitude and joy, and remarked ; ' I never
believed you would remain a pedobaptist many years.'
This resolution of mine soon became public. On the
night of the same day, Mr. Stewart, one of the deacons,
called on me to come and baptize an infant of his brother's, which lay at the point of death. I informed him I
could not comply without a divine warrant; I am fully
convinced that heretofore when I sprinkled infants I did
it in ignorance, on human authority. I gave him my reasons. The effect this announcement had on his feelings
could not easily be described. He left. The child died
that night. It was buried the next day, and I was not
called upon to conduct the funeral services. In a very
few days it was published throughout all my congregations that I had refused to discharge the ministerial obligations I was under to the Lutheran church.

" I wrote a letter to Bro. Hartzel, informing him of

my full conviction of the truth, and desired him to send an appointment and baptize me. This brought our debate to a close. He cheerfully responded to my call, sent an appointment to the Phillips congregation, filled it in company with Bro. E. B. Hubbard; preached on a subject adapted to the occasion, after which my happy wife and myself were immersed by Bro. Hubbard, in the presence of a goodly number of my Lutheran brethren and sisters, March, 1834.

"In the month of June following the Synod convened in New Lisbon. I addressed a letter to their honorable body, presenting it by the hands of Bro. Benj. Pritchard. The proposition for a hearing was discussed, and when a vote was called, the *nays* had it by a good majority of the preachers. Thus I was excluded from their fellowship as a heretic, greatly to the dissatisfaction of many of the laity, who judged that I ought to have had a hearing, and the right of self-defense. Thus ended forever my religious connection with the Lutheran church.

"You ask me to relate some of my struggles and privations connected with this part of my history. I will answer you briefly: When this religious tie was sundered I was left in a very destitute condition. My salary at the time was four hundred dollars, which, added to marriage fees and other perquisites came to near five hundred dollars. My year was expired within two months when I came out from among them. My convictions of truth did not allow me to dissemble, and preach, and practice error two months longer for the salary. Neither did I ever receive a farthing of it, though it was collected in several of my congregations, and ready for delivery.

"I had thirty acres of land, less than half paid for, without team or means to cultivate it. I was without money; forsaken of fathers and mothers. But my friends did not all forsake me. The Lord reserved to me two very wealthy men, members of the church from which I

28

seceded—Mr. Brinker and Mr. Switzer. They ever were and they remained, my warmest friends. My departure from their doctrine only heightened their respect for me. They claimed it was the strongest evidence of my candor and honesty to leave a society that supported its ministers, and become identified with a people that repudiated salaried preachers. They both lent me generous, substantial aid, and remained my most ardent friends till their death. Some of the brethren were also benefactors to me, especially George Pow and A. Campbell. The church of Bethany presented me one hundred dollars, besides some valuable gifts.

"I preached every Lord's day, and sometimes during the week. The brethren received me kindly, heard me gladly, thanked me heartily, invited me cordially to preach for them, but never seemed to consider that I lived just like themselves, by eating and drinking, and that my time was my only means of support. Consequently I had to 'dig.' I was not ashamed to *dig;* but one thing I plainly discovered and felt most seriously, that my sun had forever set so far as time for suitable preparation to hold forth the word of life was concerned. One of the congregations agreed to pay me one dollar a visit every four weeks, or one-fourth of my time. This was ominous of better times. Another congregation promised me fifty dollars for one-fourth of my time. A certain brother and sister, who always appeared to have a very high regard for me, were exceedingly hurt because Bro. Schaeffer was receiving a salary for preaching. I received only thirty-seven dollars of the amount, and unwilling to give further offense, I never asked for the balance.

"I am glad that a change has been effected in this particular. Ministers are now cared for as justice and equity demand.

"In reflecting on the past and the present, my losses

and privations, I always come to the conclusion that I
was the gainer. The exchange of error for truth, I esteem a great gain. When my spirit has been almost
crushed, and my physical nature almost exhausted by
hard work, the consideration that I have found the light
of the gospel has always revived and strengthened me.

"Yours fraternally,

"DEERFIELD, O., *August*, 1872. JOHN SCHAEFFER."

The writer of these chronicles regards it important to present a correct, if not an exhaustive, history of the struggles and self-denials of the early
preachers of the "reformation." Bro. Schaeffer's
modesty would not have permitted him, unsolicited,
to speak of his own case as he has in the above communication. From one, learn all. His story is not
an exception. To a great extent they all went to
the warfare at their own charges. The growth of
justice in this particular was slow, and not a few
were compelled to abandon the ripened fields of evangelical enterprise by the stern law of necessity. It
is certainly ground of much regret that a brother of
Bro. Schaeffer's excellent endowments of mind, manners, and education, a gift to the cause while he was
young, a fluent speaker in his native German, could
not have been amply supported, and employed to
open the gospel to his own people, a work for which
his experience was so good a preparation.

CHAPTER XV.

Churches established in Palmyra, Shalersville, and Randolph.

THE first year of Bro. Scott's travels, he and
William Hayden went together to Palmyra.
There was no small stir concerning "this way."
They came with the King's message, and they proclaimed it with authority. In few places could so
little be done with the old professors. The Baptist
church, which existed as far back as 1818, under the
charge of the benevolent Thomas Miller, and which,
in 1825 entertained the association, had lost its savor.
The religion of peace was poorly represented. Shame-
ful quarrels were perpetuated in the separation of
the church into two fragments, in which personal
ambition and family strife prevailed. The patience
of many was exhausted with evils which they could
not cure, and they stood aloof from the churches,
waiting a better hope and a truer gospel. These
messengers of Christ's gospel, not wishing to identify
their mission with such a state of things, soon abandoned all hope of reconciling these old professors,
and opened on new grounds the claims of the gospel.
Their boldness and zeal, supported by the charms of
music and the attractions of eloquence and, still
more, by the plain, pungent truth they proclaimed,
brought multitudes to hear, and many to yield to
Christ. The conquest was complete, but it was
achieved in much sharp opposition. The piercing,

piquant speeches of Scott provoked some of the people. One man, who had been on bad terms with his neighbors, objected to Scott's preaching, saying: "I want to see more heart religion in it." "Aye," said Scott, "and I want to see a man not keep all his religion in his heart, but let some of it come out so his neighbors can see it!" A Methodist lady retorted upon him: "You have to sing our songs!" "We ought to, madam," he replied; "we get your converts!"

A church soon arose, formed of the new converts and a large proportion of the old members. Britton Fisher and Iliff Garrison were appointed the overseers of it. Robert Calvin, Marvin Gilbert, George and Nicholas Simons, William Shakspear and E. Fisher, with their wives, were among the early members. It was established in 1828.

They received help from the brethren who founded the congregation, especially from William Hayden. John Henry helped them much also, as did the brethren in Deerfield—Allerton, Hubbard, Finch, Hartzel and McGowan; A. B. Green also, with Brockett, Reeves, and M. J. Streator. Dr. Robison is remembered for valuable help. In September, 1840, A. B. Green and A. S. Hayden conducted a meeting in Palmyra. A wide hearing was gained, and seventeen converts came in. The church then counted a membership of seventy-four persons.

Like all churches unsupported by pastoral labor, their course has been fluctuating. The lamp has nearly ceased to burn at different times; but much of the true salt is yet to be found in the church, which to this present day meets every Lord's day to keep the ordinances as they were delivered.

A church was started in the south part of Palmyra almost as early as that in the north. Elijah Canfield, Horace Western, and Andrew Sturdevant were the leaders. It sustained itself a number of years, but succumbed at last to the common enemies of embodied societies—emigration, death, and neglect.

The Church in Shalersville.

Some time in the fall of 1828, as William Hayden was riding through Windham he met Isaac Mead. The surprise at meeting was mutual. Mead, accosting Hayden, said: "Bro. Hayden, is that you?" "Yes, it is I." "What's the matter? I see your garments are wet!" "I preached back here last night, and a person coming to Christ, I have just been baptizing the convert; and having no opportunity of changing my garments, I am going on to find a place to preach. Do you know of any opening?" "Yes, in Shalersville; I am just from there, and there is a good opening. Go on, and call on Davis Haven, and tell him I sent you." "Good bye," said the vigorous preacher, and applying his spurred heels to his horse he was soon out of sight.

Late in the spring of 1828, Thomas Campbell and Sidney Rigdon had preached a few discourses in Shalersville, taught the people the way of life, and baptized two young men. In the summer, E. Williams delivered a number of sermons, but his former Universalian friends, incensed by his renunciation of their fruitless speculations, were not favorable to his message. But the labors of these men, and Scott's success in adjacent towns, had opened the public ear. So when Hayden came to plant the standard of the cross he had an audience. The ardor of his nature was equal to his powers. He double shotted every piece, and directed his artillery against skepticism and sectarianism ; and in contrast with the darkness of the one and the demoralizations of the other, he vindicated the credibility of the apostles and prophets, and asserted and defended the rightful claims of Jesus Christ to the throne of the universe.

In one of his trips Scott came with him. Here it was Dr. R. Richardson, then of Pittsburgh, seeking Scott in New Lisbon, "to be baptized of him," and not finding him there, came and found his preceptor and friend in the midst of an animated meeting. Scott mêt him with great joy, for his soul was toward him like that of David to Jonathan. When the congratulations were over, said Scott, aside, to Hayden, " O, that the Lord would give us that young man !" not yet aware of the purpose of his visit. He had been brought up strictly in the Episcopalian order ; but having his attention called by Bro. Scott, sometime previous, in a conversation with him at Pittsburgh, to the original term for baptism, his fine scholarship enabled him to investigate its meaning ; and finding its current use in the Scriptures and every-where else to be immersion, he conscientiously followed the light, and sought Bro. Scott for baptism at his hands. On going to the Cuyahoga to baptize some converts, Richardson made known his wishes ; when, with the others, he was buried by baptism into the death of the Lord Jesus.

Bro. A. B. Green was early in Shalersville. The

brethren in Deerfield, also C. P. Finch, E. B. Hubbard, and A. Allerton, helped much both to sow, to water the seed, and to gather the harvest. For several years William Hayden, having planted the church, looked after it as a nursing father.

The citizens of the township having erected a good Town House, it was proposed that it should be dedicated. At the instance of prominent citizens, Hubbard and Allerton were invited to hold a meeting in it. They solicited me to accompany them. Closing up my winter school Friday night, we mounted our horses early Saturday morning, and at noon we were on the ground. The meeting was held three days ; and many heard out of regard to the nature of the occasion. This was the last of February, 1834.

All this time, and for years afterward, the church had no settled minister. The preachers came among them frequently ; but the church, like most of the congregations, had learned to "edify one another in love." This reliance on the talent of the church quickens the zeal and develops the abilities of the members ; and if it is not depended on to the exclusion of preaching, it is a direct and powerful means of imparting strength and permanency to the churches.

At one of Bro. Green's meetings there was a Miss Langworthy among the converts. The Congregational minister, all praise for his zeal, became much excited at seeing the people so deluded and led away into error. Green had taught the converts simply to believe on the Lord Jesus Christ as their Savior, and to trust honestly to his gospel word of promise, " he that believeth and is baptized shall be saved." This minister came in the crowd to the meeting, and knowing Miss Langworthy, he called her attention to the danger of the error she was embracing. " Why," she innocently responded, " has not the Lord told us to come and be baptized?" " O, I tell you," said the minister, "it is a most pernicious doctrine, and you are exposing yourself to the danger of being damned if you believe it." " But, the Savior said 'he that believeth and is baptized shall be saved;' and now, if I believe on him with all my heart, and am baptized, will he damn me?" This was enough. The strength of "orthodoxy," so called, was weakness before the word of the Lord. Bro. Green and all around heard the conversation, but he said not a word, perceiving this child of mourning and of joy, in her tears and simplicity, was effectually defending the faith. The converts were then baptized; they were full of joy, and new songs were heard in many homes.

In 1835, the yearly meeting for Portage County was held in Shalersville, which increased the number of converts, and imparted strength to the church. Again, in 1837, the churches of the county came up here to hold their annual convocation. It was a large and impressive meeting. Many public advocates of the gospel attended it. Both the Town Hall and the Congregational church were filled to overflowing on the Lord's day.

In February, 1843, Harvey Brockett, by invitation of the elders, Milo Hoskins and Davis Haven, came to Shalersville. There was a great shaking among the people. Brockett's earnest and persuasive eloquence, with his instructive exhibitions of the gospel,

29

enlightened many and brought them to Christ. An event occurred in the midst of this meeting, which brought out the whole town to hear. It was the death of William Coolman, Esq. This gentleman, unpretentious, well educated, and kind-hearted, was deservedly held in high esteem. His residence was also the home of his widowed daughter, the excellent mother of Bro. C. C. Foot. Brockett's sermon at the funeral of Bro. Coolman was all aflame with light on the resurrection and eternal judgment. Many towering imaginations were brought low, and many hearts were humbled. The seeds of this sowing came up for reaping in many subsequent harvests.

From this place Bro. Brockett went to Ravenna two weeks. Additions followed his labors there. He returned to Shalersville for one week. Exhausted and obliged to leave, Bro. M. L. Wilcox came in and finished up this extraordinary series of successes.

Eighteen months afterward, February, 1845, Brockett responded to the urgent calls of the people, and conducted another meeting. Among the souls brought into the kingdom at this time, was the youthful Charles Coolman Foot. He soon manifested inclinations for the ministry. Availing himself of all the means of education and spiritual improvement within his reach, his "profiting" began to be apparent to the church. He persevered in his preparations, and has become extensively useful in the gospel.

Bro. T. J. Newcomb grew up into religious activity in this church. He confessed the Lord Jesus, and turned his talents to build up his cause in the hearts of the people.

In the year 1849, Bro. W. A. Belding began his labors in this church. It was much reduced, and the fine gold had become dim. He immediately began to " revive the spirit of the contrite ones." His practical addresses, enforced by an assuring confidence of the value of Christianity, by a cheerful manner, and many a sweet, enrapturing song, soon brought about a reformation. The house was filled once more. Many wanderers were brought back to the fold, and conversions were again frequent. During the seven years of his residence in Shalersville, there were one hundred and fifty additions.

Bro. Belding's labors have been very abundant and successful. He was sometime in Mentor, where the church was greatly enlarged; one hundred and seventy-seven souls being added in eighteen months. In many other places he has a grateful remembrance among the people. He is the youngest son of the late Dr. Rufus Belding, of Randolph; a gentleman of rare excellence, serenity, and dignity of character.

The church in Shalersville was long under the counsels and management of Milo Hoskins, Davis Haven, and Isaac Mead, as overseers; of E. B. Chapin, James Coit, Decalvus Root, John Haven, Chester Cooley and others, as servants of the congregation. From this community emigration has carried the message of life, and built up in other counties and other States the cause of the Lord Jesus Christ. The Cooleys, the Havens, the Nicholls and Streators, in North Eaton, early lifted the standard, and they have, with the blessings of God upon them, established a church which is now one of the strongest on the Western Reserve. Some of the same families are in Bloomingdale, Mich., with a good house of worship, and a faithful and united brotherhood in Christ.

RANDOLPH.

Deacon William Churchill moved into Randolph from the State of Connecticut in 1812. He died in that town August 30, 1846, at the advanced age of 81 years.

In 1819, he, with others, constituted a small Baptist church in Randolph, of which he was both deacon and clerk. When the "*Christian Baptist*" made its appearance Churchill obtained it, and the new light it shed on gospel themes was welcomed by this inquiring community of believers. They had come together under the name of Baptist, but their single aim was to be only Christians, and to be led only by the revealed will of God. This membership was the basis and the beginning of the large and flourishing church from which, for forty-five years, has radiated the light of the gospel. The church was formed on New Testament principles, July 20, 1828. The record reads as follows : " On this day came forward the baptized disciples of Jesus Christ our Lord, and acknowledged him to be their only Teacher and Lawgiver, and the Holy Scriptures to be their only guide, and agreed to maintain Christian worship according to the aforesaid declaration."

The following names composed the new congregation. All were previously members of the Baptist church, viz. :

William and Polly Churchill, Philo and Rosanna Beach, Calvin and Polly Rawson, Elisha and Sophia Ward, Bela Hubbard and Levi Huggins. William

Churchill and Calvin Rawson were appointed deacons.   C. P. Finch, E. B. Hubbard and Samuel McGowan were present and "gave the right hand of fellowship."

Bro. Amos Allerton, also of Deerfield, was an early and able advocate of the gospel in Randolph, contributing much to the growth of the body.   Indeed, the church of Randolph was fostered by that in Deerfield, as in turn the one in Randolph became the mother of those in Mogadore, New Baltimore, Suffield and Rootstown.   The latter two have dissolved.   The others have never failed to meet, and have generally flourished.

Early in their history, William Churchill was elected to fill the office of overseer, and Elisha Ward was appointed deacon.   The first meeting-house was erected in 1830, and finished in 1832.

Although the trumpet call to religious reformation and return to the Jerusalem model of the church, had been sounding only four or five years, it had spread far abroad, and was echoed by hundreds of willing tongues.   New churches were starting up in many quarters, and old ones were throwing aside their creeds and adopting the New Testament as their only guide.   The Disciples all looked to the *yearly meeting* as the means of social and religious union, like as the great festivals of the Jews, even more than the uniformity of their rites and ritual, cemented their nationality.   Those great anniversaries, by the acquaintances formed and the consequent interest they awakened in one another, became a real and lasting bond of union among the advocates of the "ancient order of things."

To Randolph all eyes were directed this year (1832), for here, the last of August, was to be the annual gathering. For the first time in seven years, Mr. Campbell was not present. But the strength and hope of this cause was in its divinity and truthfulness, not in man. There was no diminution in numbers, nor enthusiasm. The freshness, ardor, and simplicity of the meetings in those days was beautiful to behold. Here assembled "the disciples," all on an equality, many of them the recruits of the past year, for edification, for fellowship in Christ, and for increase of their animating hopes.

The following public speakers were present: Symonds Ryder, William Hayden, Marcus Bosworth, Amos Allerton, E. Williams, E. B. Hubbard, C. P. Finch, Jonas Hartzel, John Henry, J. J. Moss, A. P. Jones, A. B. Green, John Applegate, A. S. Hayden and Eli Regal ; some of whom were only beginning the work of preaching.

The following report of this meeting will be read with interest :

STREETSBOROUGH, PORTAGE CO., O., *Aug.* 28, 1832.

DEAR BRO. CAMPBELL:

Our general meeting closed yesterday. Such love, such union, not of opinion, but of faith and Christian feeling, zeal and intelligence, I never saw but among the disciples of the ancient mold.

We met on Friday, at 1 o'clock P. M. ; and though disappointed by not seeing you, we proceeded to do as well as we could. Bro. Bosworth gave the first discourse, and seven or eight other brethren spoke during the meeting in daylight. Preaching in four or five places each evening.

On Lord's day, Bro. Ryder gave us a masterly discourse from the second chapter of 1st Timothy. His first effort was to show the fallacy of Universalism ; 2nd, of Calvinism. In the third place, an exhortation to prayer; and, finally, female character and influence as Christians—and why? That as the woman was the first in sin, and has ever since been oppressed by the man ; that as the female was by Christianity raised and honored with the place, privileges and influence which naturally and originally belong to her, it, by all reasons, behooves the sex to honor Christianity in turn by showing all contempt for the trifles which charm the eyes of the vain and the irreligious ; that they should delight to honor the gospel with a display of benevolence, rather than of dress.

He succeeded in every point to the great satisfaction of all the disciples, especially the sisters. The discourse was followed by appropriate exhortations; and, in short, the whole day was filled up with much valuable instruction. Nineteen were immersed during the three days. On Monday our time was devoted to hearing the reports of the itinerants, and making arrangements for future operations. This was the most interesting day of any, and probably more profitable for the interest of truth than all the rest together.

It appeared from the reports, which, from personal knowledge I know to be correct, that the apostolic gospel and order of things are gradually and regularly gaining influence among us ; and, although in many things we are quite in the rear of Christian perfection, yet one good sign is that all see it, and all unitedly urge an advance. The present reformation is in this different from all the Protestant reformations, whose leaders, when they had taken a few steps from their former ground, halted, and determined the people of God should learn and do no more of the Lord's will than they had already attained to. The teaching brethren understood Christianity better.

Public opinion is turning rapidly in favor of the ancient gospel and order; and I think there is a growing liberality among the brethren.

The subject of itinerancy was spoken of with warmth and an unanimity of judgment and feeling never before equaled among us. The whole community, teachers and taught, were much affected with the great responsibility we are under to present to the world the ancient religion of Christ. It was proposed the itinerants should go two and two; but when we beat for volunteers, it was found there were but two whose circumstances would permit them at present to make it their sole employ to proclaim the word. These two, Bro. Moss and myself, are to go together wherever a door opens and labor is most needed, and not to neglect the churches. The brethren and sisters most honorably signified their approbation of these laborers, and gave good evidence of their readiness to assist them in all things necessary. Besides these two, brethren Allerton, Williams, Henry, Hartzel, Bosworth and Applegate, expressed themselves willing and able to devote a share of their time—some of them the greater part; and from their known gifts, were assured by the disciples present of their willingness to sustain them. After these matters were dispensed with, an invitation was tendered to any who wished to obey the Lord, when six or seven came forward. We went to the water, and continued instructing and exhorting until eighteen were immersed, making in all thirty-seven.

Yours, as ever,
WILLIAM HAYDEN.

Among the converts at this meeting was Bro. W. A. Belding, who has since become widely known as an able minister of the gospel.

For many years this church moved on in great harmony, receiving increase of members almost constantly. In 1845, the withering blight of "Come-outerism" fell upon it, causing alienations, dissension, and division. Its advocates were infidels. While pleading for the abolition of slavery and for temperance, they hurled their deadliest daggers at the churches and gloried in the demolition of the organized Christianity of the land. Many excellent men were caught in their snare. Many here and elsewhere went out with them. This wild impulse became a sore trial to the faith and patience of the churches. Brethren Moss, Perky, and others came to the defense of the congregations. They met the fiercest advocates boldly in debate, and mended the breaches these assailants had made in the walls. Most of the disciples who were shaken for a time, returned into peace and order.

Since that period the church, like a well-manned ship, has held steadily to its course. It outgrew its discouragements in a few years, and established itself more firmly than ever. In 1860, the brethren built, at the center of the town, a new and much better house of worship. In 1871, the record showed sixty-two members. In the winter of that year, there was a great ingathering, under the labors of Bro. F. M. Green; within a few weeks sixty-seven were converted, forty-one of whom were heads of families. Bro. W. H. Bettes is now the overseer.

This church owes much to the prompt, manly zeal of Bro. Bela Hubbard, who, with his family, gave no uncertain support to the cause at the start. Also, the families of the Churchills, the Rawsons, the Wards, the Beldings and many others, hold a high place in the grateful memory of the people.

CHAPTER XVI.

The Churches in North Perry, Painesville, and Eagleville.

THE church of Christ in Perry was organized by S. Rigdon, August 7, 1829. It had twenty-seven members; among whom were Ebenezer Joy and his wife, David and Eliza Parmly, Sam'l W. and Lovinia S. Parmly, Ansel and Desire Ryder, John Brooks, Ezra Isham, Orvis and Rufus Call, Clinton and Sottle Butler, Leonard, Bradbury and Sallie Sinclair, Lydia Wood, and Deborah Bacon.

There was soon a large increase of members, embracing the following and other names: David Dodge, Rufus Neff, —— Rose, Shubal Lincoln, Elisha Colton, Levi S. and Eliza Parmly, Eleazor and Ann M. Parmly, Lewis, Lewis B. Levi, S. and Otis M. Wood, with the families of Sinclair and Call.

Among the causes which brought the reformation into the Baptist church in Perry, was the liberty taken by one of its members to "commune" with Christians who were not of their "faith and order;" though they were "baptized believers," in the Baptist sense of that term. David Parmly, a correct and zealous Baptist, having heard of the great revival in Mentor, went over from Perry to hear the advocates of the "new" doctrine, as it was called. Pleased with the preaching, and finding the spirit of the Lord among them, he ventured to "commune" with the Disciples.

News of this act came quickly to Perry. It was too much ; David Parmly was an offender, and a "labor" was taken up with him. Bro. Parmly plead his right as a free man in the Lord, to hold Christian fellowship with brethren who are believers in Christ, and who, as well as themselves had been "buried by baptism into his death." His plea was of no avail. A church meeting was called to try him on the following charge of heresy : "Bro. Parmly is charged with communing with the Campbellites, and believing in the doctrines of Alexander Campbell.' He admitted the act of communing with Christ's people, and that he believed in the Lord Jesus, in all he teaches in his word, and declared his willingness to be subject to his brethren in all things, only " in the Lord." No defense was admitted. This warmhearted Christian of unblemished reputation, was declared guilty of the charge of " heresy." While the trial was proceeding Parmly asked to read, without remark, a few portions of the word of God. This was refused. When the act of exclusion was accomplished, he walked out of the house, Bible in hand, and taking his position under the shade of a goodly tree, he read the word of life to many people, who followed him with eager interest.

The exclusion of Parmly hastened matters to a crisis. Rigdon soon was there, and a church was formed, bringing into it a large number of the Baptist members, who saw too clearly the spirit of the inquisition, in the exclusion of an upright Christian man for no other crime than holding fellowship with the people of God.

Before the organization of the church, the five

Parmlys—David, Levi, Eleazor, Jehiel, and Samuel W.—erected a comfortable meeting-house on the lake shore, which was afterward moved to the place where it now stands, and formally opened for worship, August 22, 1841, at which time the church was re-organized with David Parmly, Asa S. Turney, and Lewis Wood, overseers; and Jehiel Parmly and Otis M. Wood, deacons. It counted about fifty members.

In December 8, 1850, the brethren who had been meeting on the " Dock Road," in Madison, united with the church in Perry, which swelled the number to about one hundred.

During many years of its earlier history this church had the labors of all the earlier preachers. A little later came Jones and Green. But Bro. Clapp stood by them as a chief dependence, and Bro. Violl also. Rodney Veits and Abram Saunders, espec-ially the former, preached much there. For two years they located among them Edward H. Webb, from Huron County. This noble young brother, possessed of many promising gifts, went to his re-ward early in life, just as he was ripening into ex-tensive usefulness. Bro. Turney stood by them many years as a leader and counselor.

This church has maintained an unbroken testi-mony for a period of over forty-five years. Her later history, like her beginning, has been marked by joyful ingatherings of souls into Christ's king-dom. A meeting, conducted by Bro. W. A. Belding, in 1855, resulted in many conversions. Afterward Bro. John Encell and M. S. Clapp brought a large number into the faith. Bro. R. G. White, five years their efficient pastor, will long be held in grateful remembrance.   Bro. W. O. Moore succeeded him as minister in the church.

PAINESVILLE.

This town felt the impulse of the great movement which began in Mentor early in 1828. A. P. Jones, a young man then in the printing office, heard to profit, turned to Christ, and became extensively useful. This beginning was followed up by brethren Clapp, Collins, Hayden, and Moss, who occasionally preached in this town. A "meeting of days" was conducted in the village by Wm. Hayden and his brother, in November, 1842. A few converts were gained at that time, as there had been by others before. Bro. Joseph Curtis, moving with his upright family into the environs of that thriving town, a more formal occupancy of the ground was decided upon. A meeting was held in the month of January, 1843, by E. Williams and Abram Saunders, of Saybrook ; and on the twenty-ninth of that month, under the counsels of these brethren, the church was established. As overseers, brethren Joseph Curtis and William Harrison were unanimously selected ; as deacons, Thomas Smith and Lyman Durand. There were thirty-six members.

From the beginning the church has maintained a uniform and consistent policy. Brethren Williams, Clapp, Collins, and Violl aided to keep the fires burning on the altar. Protracted meetings have enlarged their borders from time to time, conducted by W. Hayden, Isaac Errett, J. Encell, H. W. Everest, K. Shaw, and others. As pastors, Bro. E. H. Hawley served them from 1855 to 1859. Bro. John Encell settled with them about two years, followed by his brother, James G. Encell. After these, Bro. L. Cooley about three years, closing in 1866. Then came Bro. J. B. Knowles. Bro. L. F. Bittle labored there from 1868 till 1870, when they secured Bro. J. W. Ingram for three years. Bro. F. H. Moore, the present pastor, began in 1873.

With all encroachments on their numbers they still have about one hundred and eighty. The church was incorporated in 1851, and their present comfortable meeting-house, in a very good site, was completed and dedicated in the summer of 1853, Bro. Collins officiating on the occasion.

This church has mourned the loss of some of her noblest men : Her first elder, whose enterprise contributed much to found the church, Bro. Curtis ; and more recently the first deacon, the lamented and upright Lyman Durand; Bro. Tuttle likewise, one of the oldest members, sleeps in the hope. And the venerable brother, Jehiel Parmly, full of days and hope.

With the Parmlys, A. Teachout, Dr. Stebbins, Dr. Pancoast, and the others who stand with them, the church has a fast hold on society.

EAGLEVILLE.

This church came into existence amidst a " great fight of afflictions." Here, as in many other places, the cardinal principle of Protestantism, the right of private judgment, was the ground of the agitation which resulted in the dismemberment of the Baptist church, and the formation of a religious community on New Testament principles.

As early as 1825–6, the "Christian Baptist" had many readers and many admirers in that Baptist community. But toleration toward it was of short duration. The pastor, Silas Barnes, a man of narrow views, supported by others equally opposed to progress in religious light, determined to purge the church of this leaven.

On the 21st of January, 1833, members of the Baptist church met to consult on the dangers to be feared from the new doctrines, and to devise methods to remove the evil. For six months or more the church had innumerable "covenant" meetings, church meetings, and councils. Sometimes they met three times a week. Early in the course of the proceedings the following resolution was passed : " *Resolved*, That we do not fellowship the doctrines and sentiments published and advocated by Alexander Campbell and his associates. Neither will we fellowship as members in our church those who patronize or make a practice of reading his periodical publications, or those who are in any way trammeled with his doctrines or his sentiments."

The church, having passed a law to fit the assumed case, a law conveniently vague, was now prepared for victims. John D. Foot was cut asunder with the long knife of excommunication. Martin Mills was next cited ; but he returned such answers to the committee, that the church forgave his temerity, and removed from him her censures.

Not so the chief offender. This was Bro. Eben A. Mills. He was a man of good abilities, firm, earnest in his purposes, of quick and correct discernment. and a devoted Bible student. He was the *quartz*, with pure gold in every vein. With a Christian wife, morally and intellectually his equal, both blessed with admirable good nature, he carried public sympathy with him in the trying difficulties through which he was about to pass. He sought no rupture in the church. A sincere adherent of the "faith and order" of the Baptists, he contributed more by his zeal and tireless activity to build up that "Zion" than any other private member. As clerk of the church, he had charge of her records. Devoted to music and an adept in that charming accomplishment, he and Mrs. Mills seemed inseparable from the life of the church. But "orthodoxy" had no mercy, and quite as little wisdom ; and it came to Mr. Mills requiring him to desist reading Mr. Campbell's "Millennial Harbinger," to put away the new translation, and abjure the alleged heresies.

He plead: 1. His liberties as a Christian to "prove all things" by the infallible standard of the Word of God, and to "hold fast that which was good ;" and 2. His rights and liberties as an American citizen to the unmolested use of all things which tended to the injury of no one, or the restraint of no other person's privileges.

It is needless to detail all the proceedings which make this a marked case. It was prolonged till the church almost to a man had become enlisted. No charge was hinted against the character of Mr. Mills. It was a case, pure and simple, of creed—orthodoxy in array against liberty of conscience. The following note of his exclusion is copied from the church record : "March 2, 1833. It was then motioned and seconded that, as Bro. E. A. Mills will not con-

sent to abandon the reading of Mr. Campbell's
' Millennial Harbinger,' which we think is leading
him from the gospel and the faith of the regular Baptists, we withdraw from him the hand of fellowship.
The vote was then tried and carried by a considerable majority. The office of clerk being now vacant, Cornelius Udall was unanimously chosen clerk."

The new clerk, some time afterward, embraced the
sentiments for which Mills was excluded. But he
suffered less persecution—a new class of men having
come into power.

Pending the motion for the exclusion of Mills, he
made a most manly appeal, and an able defense of
Mr. Campbell and his work. It was printed and circulated, but it could not avert the premeditated blow.

This act of exclusion was a heavy stroke to many
of the members. A remonstrance was prepared and
sent in to the church, signed by eighteen names. It
was mild and respectful ; yet, strange to say, it was
the death-knell of every one of them. They were
all, without exception, and without any other offense,
excluded from the church.

This declaration of exclusion was signed by nine
names, and was silently acquiesced in as the action
of the church without approval or demur. Thus nine
members excluded eighteen, the number who had
signed the remonstrance; the rest of the church,
eighty members, taking no active or recorded part
in the proceedings.

These rejected members, cast down, but not forsaken, could not let the light within them become
darkness. Hearing of a church in Mentor, meeting
just as the disciples of the Lord Jesus Christ,

30

they sent an invitation for a man to visit them. Bro.
M. S. Clapp came, preached, and organized a church
of seven members, with Bro. E. A. Mills, elder, or
bishop, and Michael Webster, deacon. This took
place October 5, 1833. Bro. Webster was soon associated as overseer. A. J. Hall and Alfred Mills
were chosen deacons.

Thus originated the church of Christ in Eagleville,
which for forty years has continued to hold the
ground under great discouragements, and to send
forth the light of the gospel into other towns in Ashtabula County.

The preachers for the first few years were Alton,
Saunders, Collins, Hayden, Henry, Hartzell, Clapp,
Brockett, Smith, and others. But Bro. Mills was
their reliance for years, in the absence of other aid.
He preached, sung, visited, and entertained the
preachers who visited them. His hospitality was
unstinted. He paid freely to sustain the cause in all
things; was an example to the flock, till broken in
health, and partly in fortune, he went West, and
ended his days in the unfading hope of immortality.

Bro. Jacob Bartholomew was called to preach for
them in 1846. For many years he has been the minister of the word among them.

CHAPTER XVII.

The Church in Middlebury and Akron—A Church arises in Mogadore—In Wadsworth also, with Sketches of Elder O. Newcomb
and A. B. Green.

IN August, 1829, E. B. Hubbard and Wm. Hayden delivered a few discourses in Middlebury.
Some of the people were so much interested they
desired to hear them more fully, and when they departed, Levi Allen and William Pangburn went with
them to Mogadore. The good seed had fallen into
good ground. The next month Bro. Hayden returned, when Levi Allen and Mrs. Pangburn became
obedient to the faith. Some time previous to this,
Mr. Wm. Pangburn and Mrs. Judge Sumner had
been baptized by Elder Newcomb. February, 1830,
Bro. Marcus Bosworth came : others now yielded in
obedience. Williams visited these old battle-fields,
where, in former days, in the defense of Restorationism he had driven Calvinism to the wall. In the
advocacy now of something better than human theories, he desired to lead the people to the Lord Jesus.

About this time Tillinghast Vaughan, a young
Methodist preacher of considerable ability, falling in
with Mr. Campbell in Virginia, was baptized by him,
and returned to the Western Reserve. He preached
in Middlebury about a year. But he forsook the
faith, and embraced some scheme of Universalian
skepticism, and drew away a number from the gos-

pel. Vaughan's defection disheartened many; yet though cast down the cause was not destroyed. The well instructed disciples never wavered, nor for an hour doubted the triumphs of the scriptural principles they had embraced. Bro. A. B. Green was often with them, whose clear presentations of the gospel aided in building up confidence. Bro. M. L. Wilcox moved into Middlebury, and while "working with his own hands," he also gave a strong impulse to the struggling cause by his able and eloquent defense of it. A litigious preacher of the M. E. church, by the name of Thomas Graham, sought a discussion with Wilcox. The young mechanic shrunk not from this public appeal to defend the faith. The preacher plumed himself in high feather, expecting certain victory, and to gain the coveted mead of public applause for crushing the noxious heresy, as he assumed to call the ancient gospel. But "the race was not to the swift, nor the battle to the strong." Wilcox was panoplied in the armor of light. He brought such a compact array of Bible truth, enforced with an argumentative eloquence and brilliant original wit, against his clerical assailant as to compel him to forsake the line of serious investigation, and resort to ridicule. Rising in full figure, in his dignity he assured his audience that it was beyond all reason to expect that a common laboring man should understand theological subjects, as did one whose whole life had been devoted to such studies. "It is absurd to suppose that a mechanic, who makes barrels for a living, however respectab'e his talents, or sincere his intentions, should be skilled in the profound themes of theology." Wilcox bore the jibe with undisturbed equanimity. In reply, he awarded his opponent even more than his arrogance claimed, of learned preparation for the occasion, and skill gained by many encounters. " I am a mechanic. I claim to be nothing above a common laboring man—an honest cooper. And yet my trade may be of use in this discussion ; for if my opponent swells much more I may have to hoop him ! " This sally of wit " brought down the house." " Hoop him ! " cried one. " Hoop him, Wilcox, hoop him ! " shouted others. The crowd became almost hilarious. Graham tried to rally. But it was useless. He was whipped by the half-suppressed " hoop him ! " from all sides. His feathers drooped, and he retired from the contest.

As may be well supposed the result of the few evenings spent in this investigation turned decidedly in favor of the original gospel.

In the year 1834, Mr. T. H. Botsford came to Middlebury. Mrs. Botsford was a firm disciple. With a clear perception of the principles of the reformation, and with unbounded confidence in their truthfulness and power, she could not remain quiet and see the disciples scattered, and the cause prostrate. She found another whose heart was as her own, in the burden that lay upon them to arouse the members to the work of the Lord. This person was Mrs. Eliza Parker, consort of Dr. Parker. She was a lady of intelligence, accomplished in her manners, good conversational ability, and, like Mrs. Botsford, had consecrated herself wholly to the Lord. These Christian women visited personally all the disciples in Middlebury, Akron, and the township of Coventry, inviting them to Mr. Botsford's own house to revive the meetings. At the first there was no brother to read, sing, or pray. With trembling heart, but unfaltering purpose, the worship was conducted by the sisters. No breaking of bread yet. That altar was not yet rebuilt. These appointments continued. Brethren Samuel and Elisha Bangs and Dan Moulton came over from Akron and gave them aid. A. B. Green, Wm. Hayden, A. Allerton, and others, threw in appointments. Bro. Green was employed for a considerable time. William Hayden came frequently during the year 1836. The audiences increased, and the ordinances of the house of the Lord were again regularly observed.

These were the days of heart-songs and heaven-reaching prayers. And the preaching! It was hail mingled with rain! The prolonged hour flitted away unconsciously. The group of disciples tarried, exhorted each other, sung warmly and feelingly a parting hymn, and with a final, earnest supplication they commended one another to the Good Shepherd, and separated. But they were unspeakably happy! Poor pay the servant of the Lord received for his pocket, but he saw such eagerness to hear ; such evidences that his ministrations were thankfully appreciated ; such proof that he had resolved a doubt, confirmed a soul, lifted a heart into new light and comfort, that he went on his way rejoicing in a labor which was reducing him every week into straitness and want. Such was the experience in all parts, but in no region more than in the district of country of which Akron was the center.

This effort by the sisters to revive the church,

which constituted the second stage of its history, was made early in the year 1836. In the course of three years considerable accessions had been made to their numbers, and a new organization was demanded. Bro. Bentley and Bro. Bosworth were called, who confirmed them in the faith, and appointed Levi Allen and Samuel Bangs, overseers, and W. B. Storer and Jonah Allen, deacons. Their number was then thirty-two. This was in 1839. The year 1843 is memorable in the annals of that congregation. It was the year of expectation. The attention of the people of the whole country, from New England to the western prairies, was arrested by the bold position of the sincere, ardent, but mistaken William Miller, of Low Hampton, New York, that the coming of the Lord and end of the world would occur in that year. Great religious awakenings pervaded the country. Multitudes, who had no sympathy with Mr. Miller on the time of the Lord's advent, drank into the spirit of revivalism which stirred all churches. Preachers were stimulated to extraordinary activity, by the calls for meetings, and the many doors opening to them, and their labors gathered in converts every-where.

The church in Middlebury sent for Bros. J. H. Jones and Dr. J. P. Robison, who were wholly devoted to preaching, and whose meetings were crowned with many conversions. These brethren were engaged in Pittsburg. Conferring with Bro. Samuel Church, they sent John Cochrane to answer the call. Bro. John Taffe being there at the time, he accompanied Cochrane to Middlebury. The meeting arose to high interest, conversions were taking place daily, and the brethren finding more help needed, sent an express call for Bro. John Henry. That mighty man, "quick to hear," but not " slow to speak," received the word Saturday night. He preached three times Sunday at home, and at 1 o'clock Monday, he was at Middlebury, a distance of over forty miles. He dismounted only once on the way. His movements were like an electric flash. Before the hour for evening meeting the community were all apprised of his presence, and he began his sermons with no diminution of the crowd. There were forty-nine conversions, and one other addition.

Henry's horse was like his rider, gay with life, eager for the track. The morning of starting home, the moment his bit was released from the hand that held him, he was galloping away, while Henry's long surtuit streamed back on the wind, presenting an amusing spectacle to the people along the street.

Early in 1845, Dr. Wm. F. Pool moved into Akron. With the healing art, which was his profession, he united the diviner art of healing the souls of the people, and during his residence he was a great support to the church. In the winter of 1849–50, Bro. M. J. Streator became the pastor of the flock, and remained about ten months. The last of January, 1854, W. S. Gray commenced his labor in the church, which continued about three years. Subsequently they have had Bro. J. C. Stark, J. G. Encell, J. O. Beardslee, L. Cooley, J. F. Rowe, and R. G. White, under whose able administration the congregation has tripled its membership.

THE CHURCH IN MOGADORE, SUMMIT COUNTY.

As the leaven, so works the gospel in the hearts of men. Near Mogadore there lived a disciple from Canfield, by the name of Conrad Turner. At his invitation, E. B. Hubbard and C. P. Finch preached there one Lord's day, in the summer of 1828. Just before this, Benj. Green had put the "Christian Baptist" into the hands of William Richards, a candid man, not a professor, stumbled by the schismatic state of Christendom. To him, the preaching of Finch and Hubbard seemed rational. Hayden soon came, and made monthly visits. Seeing the interest, he returned in the spring, bringing Scott with him. They held a two days' meeting in the midst of the week, in J. Anson Bradley's new barn. The audience was large: they were on the King's business, and they "hurried the people away to the valley of decision." There was some opposition, but it turned to the advance of the truth; as the preachers, instead of giving their opinion on the points of inquiry, read the word of the Lord, which effectually silenced controversy.

The vine was planted and watered, and soon it began to bear fruit. Hubbard returned and baptized Mrs. Wm. Richards. Then, on subsequent occasions, came Mrs. J. A. Bradley, Joseph Baird, Isaac Miller and his wife. In September, Wm. Richards obeyed. Then J. D. Green and his wife, Allen and his wife, and J. Anson Bradley. There were now thirteen of them. They naturally, in much opposition, came together for encouragement and sympathy. The aged Bro. Churchill, of Randolph, came

31

among them, and under his counsels these new converts stood up before all the people, and entered
solemnly into the holy obligations of a church of the
Lord Jesus Christ. The organization took place in
the year 1832, in the school-house near Mr. Asa
Young's residence.

They chose Wm. Richards with one voice as their
leader, and Benjamin Green as deacon. It was a
day of great responsibility ; and so felt each one of
that little fraternity. The opposition was violent, if
not formidable, and this was to all of them an untried
step. Many pronounced in anticipation a failure of
the attempt to gather disciples, and regulate the affairs of a church without rules written out and
adopted by which to be governed. But this was one
breastwork of the battle of that day. Relying on
the wisdom of the Founder of the church for the
sufficiency of the rules he has left in his Word, they
clasped hands and held the grip till their hearts beat
in unison in the same sublime trust in God and his
Word. Their opposers were false prophets. The
continued success of this church in all the following
years has vindicated this action of these disciples.

The church in Mogadore has borne her testimony
unbroken from the beginning. In meetings and
works of enterprise she has not been behind. All
the preachers have gleaned sheaves in this field. In
1835, Elder T. Campbell, on a tour among the
churches, came among them. His gravity, gentleness, and authority enforced his instructions on the
whole community. In 1836, they erected their house
of worship. For several years the brethren who
planted the church kept watch of their welfare. In

1839, Dr. M. Jewett settled there, a brother, who by the skill of W. Hayden, chiefly, had been rescued from the wilderness of doubt, engendered by the confusion in the religious world. Uniting his influence with that of elders Richards, Baldwin, and J. D. Green, the church increased. A. B. Green was then visiting them a fourth of the time. Bro. Ryder followed for two years, half the time. Robison and M. L. Wilcox gave them much help. Brockett and Philander Green are cherished in grateful memory. J. Henry held a great meeting in 1843, with forty conversions. All the brethren from Deerfield were instant in their support. Bro. Moss for a time lived among them, as did Bro. Lillie also, both adding converts. Bro. J. H. Jones has here gathered many souls for Christ.

To the faith and perseverance of the resident brethren already named, and the female members, whose names seldom appear in earthly chronicles, is mainly due the permanence and prosperity of this church. In later times the mantle has fallen on Bro. Simon Laudenslager, and the brethren Isaac and James Monroe, who, as officers and leaders, are holding well the ground. Bro. J. M. Monroe, of California, is a gift to the world from this church, and from the family of Bro. Isaac Monroe.

THE CHURCH IN WADSWORTH, WITH SKETCHES OF A. B. GREEN AND ELDER O. NEWCOMB.

A. B. GREEN was born in Litchfield County, January 12, 1808. His parents moved into Ohio in 1811, and settled soon after in Norton, Medina County. Amidst the hardships of life in a new country, he was brought up;

and in the midst also of the conflicts of Calvinism and
Arminianism, and the resultant compound, Universalism.
No wonder that, like many others, he became skeptical.

On Sunday, his father, a steady church-goer, said,
"Almon, are you not going to meeting?" "No, father,
I think I will stay at home and read." The "Family
Testament," a new translation of the New Testament by
Drs. Campbell, of Aberdeen, Macknight and Doddridge,
compiled and published by Alex. Campbell, had recently
made its appearance, and was attracting much attention.
During the quietness of that blessed day, whose associations all are favorable to calm and candid contemplation,
Green read this new and attractive book. New light came
into his mind, and a new interest was awakened in his
heart. He arose after hours of serious perusal of it, exclaiming aloud to himself, "No uninspired man ever
wrote that book." The stormy and dangerous cape of
infidelity being "doubled," he sailed rapidly past the
shoals and sharp rocks of "total depravity," "final perseverance," etc., the drift and debris of theological periods, into safer channels. Reading regularly on, with interest deepening at every step, he came to Acts ii: 38;
"Repent, and be baptized every one of you in the name
of Jesus Christ for the remission of sins, and you shall receive the gift of the Holy Spirit." He asked Elder Newcomb what this Scripture means. "It means what it
says," replied the Elder, with his characteristic promptness. This reply sent the meaning deep into his heart.
In a few days he sent a letter to Elder Newcomb asking
for baptism at his hands, which event took place December 28, 1828.

His mouth opened in praise, and in pleading the claims
of the Savior of sinners. He soon went by invitation to
Chippewa, Granger, and other places. Elder Newcomb
was his counselor and steady help. Moved by him, the
church granted a letter of commendation to the young

Timothy, to go forth proclaiming the glad tidings. His first mission-trip opened at Stowe, September 10, 1833. One came for baptism. This was his first baptism. His tour was about three weeks; from it he returned, his natural timidity having yielded very much to an assured confidence that God was opening the way for him into fields of extensive usefulness.

From this period he has belonged to the public. In all the counties of North-east Ohio, much in other parts of it, in other States also, and in Canada, he has "fully preached the gospel of Christ." For more than forty years he has been zealously engaged and personally identified with all the movements—missionary, educational, and social—tending to build up the churches, and extend the knowledge of the Redeemer's kingdom.

The church in Wadsworth arose as follows: There had been a Baptist church in the community, principally in the care of Elder Obadiah Newcomb, a very worthy man, of good gifts and excellent sense. In the fall of 1818, he came from Nova Scotia to Pittsburg, where he preached for a time, and associated with the ministers of the city. He came to Wadsworth in the spring of 1822, where he planted a Baptist church. The "Christian Baptist" appeared soon after, and Mr. Newcomb obtained and read it. Its views of New Testament truth arrested his eager attention. Too conscientious to preach the doctrines of the "creed," now that he found them not among the apostolic "traditions," he slackened in his ministry till these new and scriptural views became well formed in his mind. The church ran low. The "Elder" was nearly silent, save at funerals and special occasions. But the "Christian Baptist" was faithful in its visits. It was read by him, by his family, and by others. William Hayden came among the people about this time, and the smoldering fires burst forth in flames. There was agitation every-where. Mr. Newcomb exchanging the mien of a clergyman for the panoply of the gospel, lifted the sword of the Spirit and went into the battle. Green was baptized; others followed. Williams came, and in Wadsworth, where the people formally heard Universalism from his eloquent lips, they now heard the original gospel in its simplicity, as it was first told by the holy apostles.

The church of Wadsworth was formed in February, 1829. The first day there were eight members: Obadiah Newcomb; his two daughters, Statira and Matilda, recently baptized; P. Butler, Samuel Green, A. B. Green, and John and Sarah Bunnell. Bro. Newcomb was appointed elder, and John Bunnell, deacon of the new organization.

This church soon became a strong pillar. William Eyles, late judge of court, soon united with his family. Conversions were almost constant. The opposition was active, vigilant, and often virulent, but over all the gospel made steady and triumphant progress.

The first yearly meeting held in Wadsworth was in September, 1833, in a new barn belonging to Bro. William Eyles. The meeting was noted for the numbers who attended it, and for the stimulus it gave to the cause of reformation. Being quite removed from the sources and center of the work, the proclamation was new to large numbers who came a long distance to attend it. A. Campbell was present; also William Hayden, John Henry, Marcus Bosworth, E. B. Hubbard, J. J. Moss, and many others. There were many converts.

An incident occurred at this time which displays Mr. Campbell's character for discernment and candor. Aaron Pardee, a gentleman residing in the vicinity, an unbeliever in the gospel, attracted by Campbell's abilities as a reasoner, and won by his fairness in argument, resolved to obtain a private interview, and propose freely his difficulties. Mr. Campbell received him with such frankness that he opened his case at once, saying: "I discover, Mr.

Campbell, you are well prepared in the argument and defenses of the Christian religion. I confess to you frankly there are some difficulties in my mind which prevent my believing the Bible, particularly the Old Testament." Mr. Campbell replied: "I acknowledge freely, Mr. Pardee, there are difficulties in the Bible—difficulties not easy to explain, and some, perhaps, which in our present state of information can not be cleared up. But, my dear sir, when I consider the overwhelming testimony in their favor, so ample, complete, and satisfactory, I can not resist the conviction of their divine origin. The field of prophetic inspiration is so varied and full, and the internal evidences so conclusive, that with all the difficulties, the preponderance of evidence is overwhelmingly in their favor." This reply, so fair and so manly, and so different from the pulpit denunciation of "skeptics," "infidels," etc., to which he had been accustomed, quite disarmed him, and led him to hear the truth and its evidence in a much more rational state of mind. Within a year he became fully satisfied of the truthfulness of the Holy Scriptures, and apprehending clearly their testimony to the claims of Jesus of Nazareth as the anointed Son of God, he was prepared to yield to him the obedience of his life. At a two days' meeting held there by Bro. A. B. Green and A. S. Hayden, Mr. Pardee and four others were baptized.

Elder Newcomb being fully relieved of the irreconcilable perplexities of the Calvinistic system, was now like an eagle fresh from the moulting. His joy was unbounded, and his zeal was equal to that of a new convert. He rode horse-back sixty miles, to the great meeting in Austintown, in 1830, accompanying a full two-horse wagon, loaded with members of his own family and others, to the same meeting. .He preached, visited, and talked continually. He had an element of sternness in his character. Going to the school-house early Sunday to meeting, he took his usual seat.   He descried a young man across the room with a flashy guard-chain displayed in a conspicuous manner over his vest.   He looked at his Testament, then cast a glance to the gay toy.   After a few moments he closed his book, walked across the house, and without uttering a word, gathered the glittering ornament off the young man's neck, put it all down into the owner's pocket out of sight, then walked back to his seat, and quietly resumed his preparation for the meeting.

He once accompanied Bro. Green in a preaching tour to Bethany and the region round about.   At a night meeting on Salt Run, Ohio, he arose before a full house, announced the hymn in usual manner, and requested some brother to " set the tune."   No one starting, he repeated the first two lines, saying: "I hope some brother will raise the tune."   All were silent.   Closing the book he said: "The apostle James says; ' Is any merry, let him sing psalms; is any afflicted, let him pray.'   I think the people here must be afflicted—let us pray!"

This excellent man passed away universally respected. He died October 4, 1847, aged seventy-four years.

The congregation in Wadsworth has been a light to all the region round about.   It is mother of churches, and mother of preachers.   The following proclaimers of the gospel received their earliest aid and encouragement there, and some of them were brought forth almost exclusively by this church: A. B. Green, Wm. Moody, Holland Brown, Philander Green, B. F. Perky, and Pardee Butler.   Bro. L. L. Carpenter, also, from the church in Norton, a daughter and dependency of Wadsworth, gained his guiding impulse there to his distinguished usefulness.

CHAPTER XVIII.

The gospel in Ravenna, in Aurora and Stowe, Franklin and Hudson.

THE CHURCH OF CHRIST IN RAVENNA.

THIS is one of the most stable of the churches. From its establishment, early in May, 1830, to the present time, a period of over forty-five years, it has never once ceased to meet on the blessed Lord's day, except as they agreed to omit in favor of the regular yearly meeting.

The conversion and baptism of Ebenezer Williams, the Restorationist minister, living in Ravenna, by Aylett Raines, has already been mentioned. From this event the work opened, as Bro. Williams immediately began to preach the gospel which he now understood, and most ardently loved. His preaching being mostly abroad, no stand was taken for the apostolic gospel in Ravenna. In the winter of 1830, Marcus Bosworth sent an appointment to the Clement district, three miles north-west of the town of Ravenna. His audience was small, but it yielded the fruit of one conversion, a brother Jonathan Stewart. The 12th of March, William Hayden came. Seven souls turned to the Lord. From this time the tide of interest swelled. The subject of the new preaching was in every one's mouth. No lack of hearers now, and there were converts at every ap-

pointment.   The seeds of a pernicious infidelity had
been early sown in Ravenna.   They were bearing
their bitter and baleful fruits in a reckless indifference
to all sacred things, and the revolt of the soul from
all religious obligations.   Hayden was the man for
such a people.   Well prepared on the evidences of
the Bible, and very expert in exposing the subtle and
sophistical refuges of the unbelieving heart, his sermons were heard with great satisfaction and profit.
Early in May, he collected the disciples together, numbering twenty-six, and formally set them apart as a
church of Jesus Christ.   Bro. Sturdevant, a licensed
preacher of the Baptist order, uniting, the new
church was placed under his charge.   It continued
to prosper, gathering additions almost every time a
preacher came in among them.   Bros. Ryder, Atwater,
Green, and the Deerfield brethren came, like Apollos
and Timothy, to comfort their hearts and confirm
their faith ; but Hayden and Bosworth were their
chief reliance.   In the absence of a preacher, the
members assumed the duties of edification, and broke
the loaf of blessing among themselves ; a practice in
which the disciples on the Western Reserve were
correctly taught in the beginning.   In the summer
of 1830, Scott delivered a discourse in the Methodist
church, in the village, to a full and delighted audience.
Fisher, of Kentucky, was with him.   It was here he
compared the creed to a silver quarter-dollar, which,
though small, may be held so close to the eye that
the sun can not be seen.   Thus the creed, though a
little thing, may hide the Bible from sight.

In June, 1831, Mr. Campbell came to the Western
Reserve.   Mormonism had recently burst forth, and

the emissaries of that crude and strange delusion were every-where active in calling victims into the snare. On his way he made Ravenna a point for a few addresses. William Hayden, with whom he had communicated in regard to his trip, obtained, with the assistance of the brethren, and fitted up with seats a grove in the environs of the town. A vast crowd of people came to hear the gifted advocate and defender of the Bible. The bold and prattling infidelity, rampant in Ravenna, found no quarter at his hands. Like a pestiferous atmosphere, it was poisoning and demoralizing all piety, all truth, all moral health, and was destructive to all social order and happiness. Mr. Campbell was at home in this department of Christian labor. He surveyed his audience, and directing well the range of his artillery, within two hours and a half the flotilla of their skeptical crafts was shattered and sunken. "Heavens! what an eye he has!" said one of the master men to F. Williams; "he scorches wherever he looks!"

Court was in session. The presiding judge sent a note of invitation to Mr. Campbell to deliver a discourse in the court room—the court, under resolution, adjourning for that purpose. He accepted the invitation, and on opening the service, with full and ringing emphasis, he read the hymn:

> "I'm not ashamed to own my Lord,
> Nor to defend his cause!
> Maintain the honor of his word,
> The glory of his cross!"

His masterly and convincing argument for the truth of the Bible, founded on prophecy, was then delivered in his own best style. Mr. John Harmon was then publishing, in Ravenna, a little paper, the "Ohio Watchman," an infidel sheet of some pretensions. The editor was in the assembly. In the sermon, Mr. Campbell, having made a climax in his argument, paused on it, remarking : " He who can not see this, has closed his ears and shut his eyes, and is blind—as blind"—gathering force by delay, "as blind as the 'Ohio Watchman!'" At the dinner table, at the hotel, where the judge and several of the lawyers were dining, the argument of Mr. Campbell was the topic of conversation. One of the young lawyers remarked : "I could not see the point of Mr. Campbell's argument to-day!" "Very likely," replied the judge ; "arguments are always obscure to persons who can not understand them!"

Frederick Williams, long a prominent citizen of the county, an elder and useful preacher, was born in Hampshire County, Mass., March 2, 1799. He came to Ravenna, July 2, 1815. On the 17th of September, 1828, he married Miss Marcia Underwood, an alliance of uninterrupted happiness to the present time. His mind had been imbued with Winchesterian Universalism, but on hearing the gospel as proclaimed by the apostles, his candid heart laid hold of it. In the year 1833, he and his wife were baptized in Sandy Lake by Amos Allerton.

Bro. Charles Judd, a man of good sense, an excellent heart and devout mind, entered the kingdom about the same time. The accession of these two men added much weight to the cause. Father Sturdevant had been the chief presiding officer. These brethren were soon called to the bishop's chair, in which position, they co-operated by counsel and by public discourse to maintain the church for a whole generation. Few churches have been blessed with so judicious and efficient elders. Bro. Judd, full of honor and of hope, went to await his crown, November 17, 1864, and was laid beside his foster son, the beloved and lamented Sterling McBride. Bro. Williams tarries yet a little longer.

The Congregation continued to meet in the Clemment district about ten years, when they moved into the village. They built their house in 1844. Bro. A. B. Green conducted the dedicatory exercises in December, from which time they have not only held the ground but gained in numbers, wisdom, and social power.

Bro. John T. Smith was employed, Bro. Charles McDougal also. Bro. C. C. Foot served four years. He was followed by Bro. A. B. Green—five years. Bro. Lowe and Bro. Amzi Atwater came afterward. The congregation now flourishes under the administration of Bro. George Darsie.

The first yearly meeting held in Ravenna was in June, 1838. It was held in a large barn fitted up for the purpose. The preachers in attendance were Hubbard, Marcus Bosworth, William Hayden, Moss, Allerton, J. W. Lanphear, A. B. Green, Robison, Moody, A. P. Jones and A. S. Hayden.

Ravenna church has always hospitably entertained the brethren, and numerous conventions have, from time to time, found there a welcome.

Present overseers: George Darsie, Albert Underwood, Samuel J. Gross. Deacons: John Mahard, R. B. Johnson, Whiting Carter, P. P. Dawley, E. C. Belding, Alex. Clements. Members: 319.

Among the early fallen is Bro. S. McBride, reared in this church, the foster son of Bro. and Sister Judd. His serious and contemplative character in youth gave promise of a devout and earnest manhood. After progressing far in his studies in Hiram, he was graduated in Bethany, and immediately devoted himself to preaching.   In many places, especially in Salem and New Philadelphia, he gained for himself the permanent esteem of the people for his amiable manners and efficient services in the gospel.   He died of a fever while young.   Intelligence of his death was received while the preachers' meeting was in session in Newburg, October 4, 1864.   "A committee was appointed to report resolutions expressive of the merited respect we owe to the memory of our dear Bro. Sterling McBride, just this day laid in the grave :

"*Whereas*, We have learned with great sorrow of the unexpected death, only day before yesterday, of our beloved fellow-laborer in the gospel, Bro. Sterling McBride ; therefore,

"*Resolved*, That we fully appreciate the great loss we have sustained in the sudden demise of that brother, of gentle and amiable spirit, a highly appreciated preacher of the gospel.   With great assiduity he struggled under pecuniary embarrassments till he gained a college diploma, and with it a clear and sound education.   Of modest manners, an earnest and confiding heart, firm and decided in character, he possessed a high and honorable friendship, and a well regulated Christian character.   As a preacher he already controlled a wide influence.   We feel that the churches in Ohio have suffered a great loss in the fading from our sky of a bright star ; and we in this meeting also, as he was one of the most diligent members of this association.

"*Resolved*, That we have a deep sense of the loss sustained by his afflicted wife and children, in the early demise of her devoted husband and their affectionate father.

	A. S. HAYDEN,	⎫
F. M. GREEN, *Sec.*	E. H. HAWLEY,	⎬ *Com.*
	L. COOLEY,	⎭

THE CHURCH IN AURORA.

This church was established October 17, 1830, by the indefatigable William Hayden. He laid his plan and pursued it. He visited the community at regular intervals, and by much private conversation, as well as by his cogent and instructive discourses, he laid the foundation of a permanent work in the solid instruction of the people. No man has less confidence in mere revival processes. No one ever had more in the illumination of the understanding as the method of reaching the heart and persuading the will. Discarding the arts of revivalism, he was strong in reasons for his statements, and often attained a high degree of argumentative eloquence in his appeals. To such a nature, a measure of opposition was necessary to awaken his reserve forces and to marshal them in the best position and order. This stimulus was not wanting in Aurora. No wonder, then, that the city of the great King was built up there on granite, and that it has remained to this day. The earlier converts included some of the most sensible, shrewd, and intelligent citizens of the community. Upon the organization of this congregation, they had such men as Gamaliel Kent, Russell G. McCarty and Samuel Russell, to whom, as elders, they committed the management of their affairs. For four years the church met in the south school-house, by Eli Cannon's; after this they moved the meetings to the center of the township.

Bro. Marcus Bosworth was early on the ground. Happy the people who heard the weeping Bosworth. He was brimful of tenderness. "Little children, let us love one another, for love is of God;" came as naturally from him as from the lips of the beloved disciple. He and Hayden were greatly attached, and they were counterpointed in a most admirable manner to be co-workers in the gospel. Soon after the church got under way the serene and stately Bentley came among them, adding the weight of piety, experience, and great personal dignity, elements both needful and rare, to enforce and carry on the work of reform.

The following were the original members: Isaac H. Streator and his wife Clarina Streator; their children Charity, Cyrus and Marius Streator; Alonzo Root and his wife; Whitney Smith and his wife; Simon and Sally Norton; Polly Ruggles, Mary Lake, Gamaliel H. Kent and his wife; Russell G. McCarty and his wife; Samuel Russell, Joel Giles, and Sophronia Stanton. In a short time, both Henry and Alanson Baldwin, with their wives, came in. For many years they were leading men, and their bountiful hospitality was an efficient means of sustaining the cause. Bro. Henry Baldwin, for many years one of the overseers, moved twenty years ago to Niles, where he fell peacefully asleep June, 1875, aged 82 years.

The next year, June, 1831, following the outburst

of Mormonism, there was held a grove meeting in
Aurora, east of the center.   Mr. Campbell was present, as were likewise many of the preachers.   Hon.
A. G. Riddle, in his recent work, entitled :· "The
Portrait : a Romance of the Cuyahoga Valley," has
written so truthfully concerning it that I transfer his
description to my page :

"The woods were full of horses and carriages, and the
hundreds already there were rapidly swelled to many thousands ; all of one race—the Yankee ; all of one calling, or
nearly—the farmer ; hardy, shrewd, sunburned, cool,
thoughtful and intelligent.   The disciples were, from the
first, emancipated from the Puritan slavery of the Sabbath ;
and, although grave, thoughtful and serious, as they were
on this Sunday morning, it was from the gravity and se-
riousness of the occasion, and little from the day itself—
an assemblage that Paul would have been glad to preach
to.

"At the hour of eleven, Mr. Campbell and his party
took their places on the stand, and after a short, simple,
preliminary service, conducted by another, he came forward to the front.   He was then about forty years old,
above the average height, of singular dignity of form, and
simple grace of manner.   His was a splendid head, borne
well back, with a bold, strong forehead, from which his
fine hair was turned back ; a strong, full; expressive eye,
aquiline nose, fine mouth, and prominent chin.   He was
a perfect master of himself, a perfect master of his theme,
and, from the moment he stood in its presence, a perfect
master of his immense audience.

"At a glance he took the measure and level of the
average mind before him—a Scotchman's estimate of the
Yankee—and began at that level ; and as he rose from it,
he took the assembled host with him.   In nothing was he
like Rigdon ; calm, clear, strong, logical, yet perfectly sim-

32

ple.   Men felt themselves lifted and carried, and wondered at the ease and apparent want of effort with which it was done.

"Nothing could be more transparent than his statement of his subject; nothing franker than his admission of its difficulties; nothing more direct than his enumeration of the means he must employ, and the conclusions he must reach.   With great intellectual resources, and great acquisitions, athlete and gladiator as he was, he was a logician by instinct and habit of mind, and took a pleasure in magnifying, to their utmost, the difficulties of his positions, so that when the latter were finally maintained, the mind was satisfied with the result.   His language was copious, his style nervous, and the characteristic of his mind was direct, manly, sustained vigor; and under its play he evolved a warmth which kindled to the fervor of sustained eloquence, and which, in the judgment of many, is the only true eloquence.   After nearly two hours, his natural and logical conclusion was the old pentecostal mandate of Simon Peter, and a strong, manly and tender call of men to obedience.   There was no appeal to passion, no effort at pathos, no figures or rhetoric, but a warm, kindling, heated, glowing, manly argument, silencing the will, captivating the judgment, and satisfying the reason; and the cold, shrewd, thinking, calculating Yankee liked it.

"As the preacher closed and stood for a response, no answering movement came from any part of the crowd. Men were running it over, and thinking.   Unhesitatingly the orator stepped down from the platform upon the ground, and moving forward in the little open space, began in a more fervid and impassioned strain.   He caught the mind at the highest point of its attainment, and grasping it, shook it with a half indignation at its calculating hesitation, and carrying it with a mighty sweep to a still higher level, seemed to pour around it a diviner and more radiant light; then, with a little tremor in his voice, he implored it to hesitate no longer. When he closed, low murmurs broke and ran through the awed crowd; men and women from all parts of the vast assemblage, with streaming eyes, came forward; young men who had climbed into the small trees from curiosity, came down from conviction, and went forward to baptism; and the brothers and sisters set up a glad hymn, sang with tremulous voices, clasping hands amid happy tears.

"Thus, in that far off time, in the maple woods, under the June sun, the gospel was preached and received."

For the next three years there was a steady increase. In June, 1834, the yearly meeting was in Aurora. It was one of much historic importance; a large number of preachers attended it, many of whom, before this, were nearly strangers. Hymns and tunes, known by leaders, were caught and transfused throughout the mass of eager disciples, and carried home to animate the rising churches everywhere. Chauncey Forward, from Somerset, Pa., was present as the chief speaker. Aurora was his home in his youth. He had attained a distinguished position at the bar and in Congress; but having confessed the Lord Jesus, he renounced the professions of law and the rulership of men, and he appeared on this occasion among the scenes of early years, to plead the cause of primitive Christianity. His abilities as a reasoner and eloquence in appeal, commanded the profound attention of large audiences daily. There were thirty-one converts, some of whom afterward became public advocates of the gospel.

In the year 1837, under the charge of Henry and Alanson Baldwin and A. V. Jewett, as building committee, the meeting-house was erected, and dedicated by John Henry. The next year, brethren Clapp and

Green held a meeting in it, with thirty conversions. In 1855 it was burned. A better one was immediately erected at a cost of $1500, and dedicated by A. S. Hayden. In 1843, a great meeting was conducted by Bros. J. H. Jones and John Henry, which brought in thirty additions. The same year, M. L. Wilcox came and preached for two years with great acceptance.

There were churches formed in Streetsborough and in Bainbridge in the year 1845, which drew members from this church and reduced its strength. These societies, after flourishing a number of years, have both become extinct; but the parent church, though weakened, has never failed to keep the light burning. "From first to last the church has had as teachers, William Hayden, M. Bosworth, A. S. Hayden, A. Bentley, J. J. Moss, John Henry, Charles McDougall, J. T. Smith, T. Munnell, J. Hartzel, A. Allerton, A. B. Green, W. Collins, B. F. Perky, M. L. Wilcox, N. Dunshee, T. J. Newcomb, H. W. Everest, J. A. Garfield, C. P. Bowler, E. Doolittle, S. A. Griffin, B. A. Hinsdale, O. C. Hill, and some others." But to the home membership all credit is due for faithfulness and devotion to the cause in all times and amidst many trying discouragements.

A good story went the rounds, in early day, of one David Shepherd, a blacksmith, who came into Aurora about the beginning of this Bible reform. His wife and a female relative of hers, professors of religion, were, before coming into town, warned by their friends against the "Campbellites," and straitly charged, and were put under formal pledge, not to hear them. Having received so strict a charge, they retired into the inner prison, secured by high and strong walls of prejudice. Isaac Streator, Esq., already a convert to the faith, coming to Shepherd's shop on business, talked freely about the preachers, the preaching, and the interest aroused on all sides. He concluded by inviting Shepherd to come to the south school-house and hear John Henry, a man of native wit, of good sense, and great power. Shepherd went, timidly. Unexpectedly he was greatly pleased, hearing for the first time a gospel he could understand and read in his Bible. Buying a cheap testament, convenient for the pocket, he examined the passages referred to in the sermon, and found, truly enough, the doctrine of baptism of the repenting person for the remission of sins clearly and fairly taught by the apostles. He ventured to read the portions of Scripture containing this truth in the presence of his family. They "pitched into" him. "There, you have gone and got one of those Campbellite testaments, which they have made just to suit their doctrine! I wonder you are not afraid to have it about you. That reads so, of course, and teaches the doctrine, for they made it so." Shepherd smiled, but only inwardly, willing to bear the reproach, for he wished to enjoy the joke a little longer. At length, he asked them to take the old family Bible, which they were sure contained no such awful heresy, and carefully compare the two. They consented, and the comparison began. Passage after passage was slowly read over, word by word. To their utter amazement and confusion the good old trusty Bible actually contained the very words and language, and of course the doctrine, denounced as "Campbellism!" What was to be done? They could scarcely believe their own eyes. His testament was then examined. It was found to contain the imprint of the " American Bible Society!" They saw the "situation"—their ignorance of their own Bible and its plain teaching. He relished their confusion, but was generous enough to listen to their earnest and repeated charges to "tell nobody!" But it told itself. They came out to hear, and all of them obeyed the gospel, despite protests, vows, and cautions, choosing nobly and rightly to obey God rather than man.

Another incident is related of a woman of good sense and intelligence, who came to Aurora from the State of New York to visit her relatives. She was at once told of the new heresy—that they took the people, and if they just said they believed, they baptized them without any change of heart, and then they were sure of heaven.

This woman, in deep astonishment, said: "Surely they get no persons of intelligence or respectability to follow them?" "O, yes, some of the best and most substantial people in town are among their converts." She replied, "There is certainly something wrong about this; for no person of common sense can believe such things as you tell me they preach: I must hear them myself." She went, heard, saw the truth, obeyed it, and returned home rejoicing in the new light of gospel truth which shone upon her heart.

RISE OF THE CONGREGATION IN STOWE.

In 1831, the gospel was introduced into Stowe by William Hayden. David Darrow was the first fruit. All who knew him counted him just the man to break ground. Honest, frank and decided, he grasped the gospel with wonderful energy. The cause owed much to his zeal and decision. John Henry was also early on the ground. At one time Henry, Hayden, and E. Williams met here by agreement, when many heard the truth and several converts were gained. Rev. A. Bronson, presiding elder of the M. E. Church, had an appointment in the house at the same time. No little stir was created, as the militant elder had already gained a reputation for zeal against the disciples. He used every opportunity to attack the new doctrine, as he represented it. In this case the appointment of these brethren was prior to his, but they yielded to his contentious determination, and sat down to hear him. In opening, he announced with full voice the hymn :

"Jesus, great Shepherd of thy sheep,
    To thee for help we fly,
Thy little flock in safety keep,
    For O, the wolf is nigh!"

No one doubted to whom he meant to apply the term wolf. But like the terms orthodoxy and heterodoxy, its meaning depends much on who uses it. The shrill-voiced singers in the audience, looking up to the large, dark form of the preacher, sang " wolf " as well as he. Henry, in reporting it, said they all sung "wolf," "wolf," but himself; and he neither sung *wolf* nor howled! The sermon which followed was a perversion of the views of the disciples. But ample correction followed, and the cause of reform gained by the opportunity.

In September, 1833, Green preached here and baptized his first convert. The cause gained constantly,

forcing its advancement through intense opposition
Students, and occasionally a professor, from Hudson
college, only a few miles distant, practiced their skill
in attempted refutation of an imaginary novelty which
they styled "Campbellism." The converts, however
were too well grounded in the Scriptures to be
alarmed by these misdirected assaults. If the school-
houses were closed, private houses were opened
The Darrows, the Sawyers, the Starks, the Stowes
the Thomases, the Lindsays, and the Gaylords received
the truth in the love of it, and soon united to sustain
meetings on the Lord's day. In June, 1834, Timothy
Wallace obeyed the gospel in Aurora, at the yearly
meeting. These principles were making progress at
the same time, and by the same agencies, in Franklin, and in Hudson township. In the north-west part
of Hudson, Williams and Hayden were successful in
teaching the people the difference between the church
of Christ founded on the New Covenant, and all ecclesiastical organizations established on human foundations. Zina Post and his family, with his son-in-
law, Bro. A. E. Foote, "hearing, believed and were
baptized;" Sherman Oviatt also, and others, in such
numbers that they founded a church there which continued many years. In Franklin the Converses, the
Wadsworths, the Clapps, and the Burts were the beginning of the congregation known afterward as the
church in Kent.

Among the proclaimers who aided in planting the
churches of Stowe, Hudson, and Kent, were Allerton,
Hubbard and F. Williams also, of Ravenna. Wm.
Hayden and A. B. Green were the most frequently
with them. Several times in the great yearly meet-

ings Bro. D. S. Burnett, of Cincinnati, has plead here, with his great abilities, the claims of the Lord Jesus.

Over the most of this region the sentiments of Universalism prevailed. With these the principles of the gospel came in sharp collision ; constantly in private, and several times in public, there were discussions on the subject. A debate of several days was held in Franklin between A. B. Green and Rev. Davis, which opened the eyes of many to the dangers of the slippery rock on which they were standing, and led them to Christ.

After several years, the church in Stowe suspended meetings as the result of removal and other causes. But the remaining members kept the fire burning, and a reorganization of the church was made January 9th, 1844. It was effected during a meeting held by Charles F. Bartlett, J. P. Robison and A. S. Hayden. The members then, were David Darrow, Zebulun Stowe, Eli Gaylord, B. Stark, C. Thomas, J. C. Willis, Datus E. Lendsay and Constant Rogers, with their wives, and Miss C. Stark—sixteen members. In April, 1873, twenty-nine years after, it had one hundred and twenty members.

This church has long been a light to the county. With lavish hospitality the members have repeatedly welcomed the great Tent meetings, and have been richly repaid in the fruits of edification and conversion. Among its honorable and most useful names now gone to rest, should be mentioned David Darrow, Zebulun Stowe and Edwin Wetmore, faithful leaders, who long, zealously, and cheerfully gave a powerful support to the cause. These, with the names of many others, are cherished in grateful hearts.

33

As resident preachers, they have had W. T. Horner, S. R. Willard, A. C. Bartlett, H. J. White; while scarcely any of the preachers known in north-eastern Ohio can be named who have not aided them in meetings. This church is the religious birth-home of L. Southmayd and J. C. Stark, brethren who have done, and are still doing, effective service as preachers of the gospel.

Her present elders are U. Marvin, A. S. Wheeler, and William Southmayd. Deacons, A. C. Stowe, J. R. Ream, and L. Hartle. They have sustained a lively Sunday-school for twenty years, and have a valuable church property with a parsonage.

CHAPTER XIX.

Origin of the Church in Bedford—Yearly Meetings—Sermon by A. Campbell—Bartlett—Robison—Jones—Prominent Preachers— The Gospel in Newburg—Great Yearly Meeting—Quarterly Meeting—Incidents.

THE congregation in Bedford arose in the following manner: E. Williams came in May, 1830, and preached the way of salvation, where formerly he had taught Restorationism. Newell C. Barnum was the first convert. He came monthly during the summer; and in June, Enoch Allen and some others were baptized. In July, Mrs. William Williams, of Newburg, Livonia Payne, "Grandmother Barnum," Julia Barnum, and Laura Gould came in. In the fall, Wm. Hayden held a meeting and baptized eight, and from this time he held the ground. In November, 1832, he held a meeting with Bro. Moss, and in the following month he formed the church with twenty members. Thomas Marble was chosen the overseer, and Enoch Allen and Geo. M. Payne, deacons. Bro. Green, on his first tour of preaching, came in September, 1833. The next year Moss became a resident of Bedford, and for five years he assembled with them and taught many.

In August, 1835, a new appointment of officers took place. Allen Robinett and Enoch Allen were elected overseers; Samuel Barnes, N. C. Barnum, and W. W. Walker, deacons. These served till December, 1837, when Sidney Smith and James Young were chosen to serve as the bishops, and Enoch Allen, Alanson Gray, George Comstock, and Charles F. Bartlett, who was baptized the month before, came in as deacons.

In July, 1840, James Young and Sidney Smith were re-appointed elders, together with C. F. Bartlett and R. S. Benedict, while the ever-faithful Enoch Allen continued to serve the church as a deacon, his co-deacons being now S. F. Lockwood, Augustine Collins, and S. A. Hathaway. The congregation had now become numerous, and in her board of rulers were men of much solidity and judgment.

The year 1837 was one of marked prosperity for the church. In August, James Young and his wife united, also Dr. J. P. Robison, Sidney Smith, and others, whose position gave weight to their influence. In November, Chas. F. Bartlett and John S. Young came to Christ. Two of these, Robison and Bartlett, arose to extensive usefulness as proclaimers of the gospel. About thirty souls united between August and December. The church, thus lifted up to great strength, and filled with a zeal "according to knowledge," added constantly to her numbers, seldom a week passing without accessions.

The year 1838 was no less prosperous. In March, of this year, James Egbert, moving in from Salem, and finding the liberty of the gospel as a ground of union and fellowship among Christians more congenial to his views than the creed basis of his former profession, he gave up the sect for the church of Christ. Mrs. Fanny Willis, a person of intelligence, and a worthy member of the Baptist church, laid aside the name and terms of party in favor of the union of Christians in the new covenant.

This enterprising church opened a " door of faith" in school-houses and private dwellings, in all available places, and by unremitting appeals the community became thoroughly leavened.

The yearly meeting for Cuyahoga County was held with the church in Bedford, in the year 1839, its first assembling in that town. It was held on the Lord's day beside the meeting-house which was erected by the generosity of Sister Willis, a house intended for the use of the Baptists, but which, with her change of views, became the property of the Disciples. This house was filled on Friday the first day of the meeting. After a discourse by Bro. J. Hartzel, and an exhortation by Bro. M. Bosworth, Bro. Campbell followed with a eulogium of much power, beauty, and eloquence on the Holy Scriptures.

This meeting was noteworthy for several reasons : The principal men of the Western Reserve who had risen up for the advocacy of the gospel were present. Some came from Canada and the State of New York. Bro. Joseph S. Havener, now of Barnwell District, S. C., then young, recently arrived from Ireland, added interest by his gentle and genial speech. But the overmastering attraction of the occasion was due to the presence and discourses of Mr. Campbell. With all the great powers of his manhood in full energy, he came before the vast auditory as comes a man only once in an age. His attendance at the first yearly meeting in the county, in Newburg, in 1835, at the still greater occasion at Euclid, in 1837, and more especially his defeat of the allied forces of infidelity in the city of Cleveland, in June, 1836, gave him a reputation all along this region of the lakes, as the first and ablest of living orators.

His discourse on Saturday was from Jer. vi : 16 : "Thus saith the Lord, Stand ye in the ways, and see, and ask for the old paths, where is the good way, and walk therein, and ye shall find rest for your souls. But they said, We will not walk therein." This subject was taken at the instance of Cyrus Bosworth, and grandly did he plead that day for a return to "the good old way" of the Savior and his apostles. On Lord's day he held the great audience of five thousand in fixed attention for two and a half hours by the watch, in a discussion of the atonement, a theme offering little attraction to a popular assembly. Yet he made this difficult subject so luminous with his rich stores of biblical learning, that time passed unconsciously to his listening auditors, very many of whom, for want of seats, stood the whole time of the sermon.

This discourse was regarded as very able by those best capable of judging, yet it was valued less on account of its eloquence than for the scriptural light it shed on this most important subject. Instead of the partial views of it taken by many, Mr. Campbell surveyed the whole field. He viewed it not merely as intended to propitiate God, and so to procure favor for man, nor chiefly as a motive to lead man to repentance. He rose above all scholastic philosophies, and treated the sacrifice of our holy Redeemer as having a relation

To God ;

To his government ;

To Sin ;

To the Sinner ; and

To the suffering Savior ;

and discussed all these bearings of the subject in the clear light of the teachings of the Holy Spirit.

The effect of this sermon was immediate and salutary. It presented this vital theme in a breadth and comprehension in which few, perhaps none, had been accustomed to view it ; it asserted clearly and convincingly the death of Christ as a sacrifice, essential to the salvation of sinners ; it vindicated the Holy Scriptures in their teaching on that subject, so often objected to by skeptics ; it delivered the minds of his hearers from limited views, and opened to them the richness and extent of the subject to which they were not accustomed, and greatly exalted Christ and his salvation in the conceptions of the people. It set the pleadings for reformation on a new and solid basis, and greatly enhanced the importance of it as distinguished from the limited creed views of the religious parties. It may well be doubted if Mr. Campbell ever delivered a sermon of greater power, or of more direct and useful purpose. There were twenty-six converts at this meeting.

Three years afterward, September 2, 1842, the great anniversary was again in Bedford. The first tent prepared by the brotherhood for these yearly gatherings was now brought into use. The brethren of Bedford stirred themselves to have it ready for this occasion, and the ample canvas afforded protection from the falling rains. Bentley, W. Hayden, Robison, O'Connor, and A. S. Hayden, resident in the county, were present ; and from other counties,

Henry, of Trumbull; Collins, of Geauga ; Green, of
Summit ; Lanphear, of Medina ; J. H. Jones, of
Wayne ; Arny, of Bethany, Virginia ; besides Moss,
Cooley, and Lillie. This was Bro. Jones' introduction to the Western Reserve. He became immediately identified with all our religious work. At this
meeting the blessed gospel gave abundant proof of
its power to turn the people to the Lord, fifty-four
coming penitently to Jesus Christ. This was the
largest number yet received at any of these meetings.
Brethren Henry and Jones were the Jupiter and
Mercurius of the meeting, and their talents formed a
good combination for public effect. Henry came as
a storm; he spoke with authority, calling to repentance with the fire and zeal of Elijah ; while Jones
flowed in exhortations of persuasive tenderness,
which gained all ears and won many hearts.

He was born June 15, 1813, lived for a time in
Brookfield, Trumbull County, then became resident
with his parents in the county of Wayne, where he
was nourished up in the faith and order of the Baptist churches. At the age of nineteen, he heard the
gifted John Secrest, near Bucyrus, on the waters of
the Whetstone, where he confessed his faith in Christ.
From that day he was the Lord's. He traveled
awhile with Secrest ; immediately and every-where
exhorting sinners to " flee from the wrath to come."
He improved by the ardent and persuasive manner
of that bold and successful preacher, and, like him,
he excelled in touching the heart, and bringing souls
into the kingdom.

But all hearts were warm then, and each one was
ready with a word in season, an exhortation, a

prayer, or a stirring song to sustain the life and animation of the meetings. The memory of those
scenes is inspiring to the heart. They were joyful
with holy enthusiasm, and the new converts were
filled with hope. The hymns—and all sung them—
were, many of them, millennial in sentiment ; and
held to the heart the hope of the coming of the
Lord, and of the glory to be soon revealed. Some
described the day of judgment in such pathos and
power, as to fasten conviction on many souls. So
great was the ardor and zeal, that the gospel in some
of its great themes was the subject of general conversation in private houses, as well as of discourse
in public assemblies.

This congregation has ripened many souls for the
eternal kingdom. Among those deserving a record
is Bro. Charles F. Bartlett, who, immediately on his
conversion in the autumn of 1837, was called by his
brethren to positions of responsibility, first as a
deacon, then as an elder. Possessed of a genial and
affable manner, with a social and warm heart, and
ready in speech, his improvement was so satisfactory that on the 22d of May, 1842, he was called to
the work of the ministry. His influence increased
constantly. He preached in surrounding churches,
every-where respected and beloved. But his life was
cut short in the midst of his days. On the 5th of
February, 1848, he went to his reward. His cheerful, companionable manners and unstinted hospitality, won him many friends. The mourning for him
was deep and general. He sustained himself from
his farm while laboring for the good of others.

Like most of the early preachers, the warfare was mostly at his own charges.

Dr. J. P. Robison, whose accession as a member occurred August 20, 1837, soon became a leader by the concurrent wish of the congregation. His intellectual and social qualities, together with his talent for business management, naturally brought him to the front. Few were the enterprises which rendered this church numerous, which were not either prompted or led on by him. Ready to serve, as well as prompt to direct, with the co-operation of the generous helps in the church who stood with him, Bedford rapidly became a radiating center. Bro. Robison yielded to the unanimous voice of his brethren, and on the 25th of October, 1840, he was appointed and ordained as a preacher of the gospel.

For several years he " gave himself wholly to the work." For it he laid aside an extensive ride as physician, a profession in which he was very successful; and, until driven from the field by scanty support, an experience which he shared in common with others, he preached extensively, and brought many converts into the churches. Throughout the Western Reserve, in Pittsburgh, Bethany, and Cincinnati, he became known by his zeal and success. He labored with all the preachers, but Bro. J. H. Jones and " the Doctor," associated in meetings more than others. During the animating period of the " holy war," from 1840 to 1844, these evangelists proclaimed the glad tidings with unbounded success. Their work was heroic—their dispatches Napoleonic. The following from the Doctor's hand are good specimens of the life and spirit of the times:

"ALLEGHENY, 21*st Feb.*, 1842.

" DEAR BRO. HAYDEN:

" Yours is to hand. I am quite happy to learn that the good cause is still progressing in the land of my friends. We have a great excitement here. Many are inquiring, and many are astonished at the doctrine. Up to this time the converts number fifty-seven,* and the brethren on the other side are waiting with great anxiety for us to come over and help them. They think there never was the like of Bro. Jones, and well may they, for he waxes warmer and bolder in the good cause. All the friends are in health. I may get to see you in Wellsburg. I will, the Lord willing, be at Ohio City the third Lord's day in March. When will you be in Wellsburg, and how long? I hope to go to Bethany. I have said something to them on the prophecies; so has Bro. Jones, who backed me up. My love to all who love the appearing of our blessed Lord.

" Yours in the hope,

" J. P. ROBISON."

"BEDFORD, *October* 6, 1842.

" DEAR BRO. HAYDEN:

" I get joyful news from Euclid. I hear from twenty to thirty are immersed. I have been with you for days in the spirit of the great turning to the Lord. Bro. Collins and myself are to be in Ohio City, the Lord willing, on Friday two weeks. We would be happy to see you there for a few days, or some time during our stay. Please ride up if you can.

" What do you think of the Canada excursion? We ought to let those dear friends know beforehand if we go.

---

* There were one hundred and forty-two converts in the meeting ; thirty of them in Pittsburgh

" I am very busy bringing my business to a close. May the Lord bless you and strengthen you with all strength. I feel for you, and should have been over ere this if I had been more propitiously circumstanced. But those bright ' stars '—heaven alone can reward your exertions.

"Yours in the blessed hope,

"J. P. ROBISON."

The following relates to the planting of the church in Munson, which arose chiefly by the labors of Bro. Robison. It was written the day fixed by Mr. Miller and his friends for the coming of the Lord and the end of the world :

"BEDFORD, 3d April, 1843.

"DEAR BRO. HAYDEN :

"I am just home from Munson where I got seventy-six additions. I am, as you may calculate, nearly exhausted, after speaking almost incessantly for ten days. But the Lord be praised for his goodness, and mercy, and long-suffering, not willing that any should perish.

" Bro. Hayden, I want to see you. If I knew you to be at home, I think I would almost come over. You have heard, no doubt, of the Ohio City thirty. I have got since I returned home from Pittsburgh, one hundred and twelve in all—four Lord's days.

"Yours in the Beloved,

"J. P. ROBISON."

" P. S.   The 3d of April is past, and we are still to ' cleanse the sanctuary ' by preaching the gospel, I suppose.   J. P. R."

"AKRON, February 2, 1844.

"DEAR BRO. HAYDEN :

"I am at Akron—have been here since Wednesday.

Spoke three times, and baptized fifty; among which are Mr. Pickands and family. Speak this evening, and start in the morning for Wooster. Bro. Cook had left some four days before I reached here. Pray for me, Bro. Hayden. I wish you was here. The brethren are happy— Middlebury brethren and all. We have a happy time.

"Yours in the hope of Jesus Christ,

"J. P. ROBISON."

"P. S. My love to Bro. Fitch.

"Spoke this evening—fourteen more. Baptize at eight in the morning, and then start for *Wooster*.

"J. P. R."

The church was sustained by its internal strength, and by aid from abroad in yearly meetings and protracted meetings, till the year 1856, when Bro. J. O. Beardslee was secured to labor in the congregation. He preached till his appointment as a missionary to Jamaica. After him, the church has been served successively by J. H. Jones, E. H. Hawley, Hiram Woods, A. B. Green, and Robt. Moffett.

As overseers, she has had Thomas Marble, Allen Robinett, Enoch Allen, Sidney Smith, J. P. Robison, James Young, C. F. Bartlett, R. S. Benedict, S. F. Lockwood, Augustine Collins, Samuel Barnes, James Egbert, W. B. Hillman, A. T. Hubbell, A. Drake, R. J. Hathaway, Hiram Woods.

For nearly twenty years the Board of managers of the Ohio State Missionary Society was located in Bedford, of which Dr. Robison was the continued chairman; and this enterprising church has always contributed liberally to sustain the missionary work. The number of members rose at one time to nearly five hundred—it is now considerably diminished.

Sketch of our Missionary, J. O. Beardslee.

He was born in Bridgewater, Ct., September 11, 1814. In his fourteenth year he united with the Congregational church, and was sprinkled at the time. He would have preferred immersion, but that church would not immerse him; nor would the Baptists, unless he joined them, which would, by their rules, exclude him from "fellowship" with other Christians. In this dilemma he preferred to him the least objectionable course.

He entered the Western Reserve College in Hudson, in 1833, at the age of nineteen years. His antislavery proclivities took him to Oberlin when presidents Mahan and Finney assumed control there. His class of four was the first that graduated in that institution, in 1837. His studies were all in view of the ministry, and before he left Hudson he had his heart on some foreign mission as his ultimate purpose. While in Oberlin he gathered some converts, one of whom was afterward his co-laborer in Jamaica. In pursuit of better health, he took a voyage to that island, in 1838, just after the emancipation of the 300,000 slaves on the island. Inspired by the congenial climate, and, still more by the necessities of that people, he felt that Providence had selected this as his field of life work. He returned, collected funds in Connecticut and Ohio; was ordained to the ministry in Mt. Vernon, Ohio, and sailed again for Jamaica. For the first seven years his receipts from abroad were only three hundred dollars. He was invited to take charge of the Normal Institution, under the auspices of the British Board of Managers, for fitting native teachers. This post he held seven years, and resigned it to take charge of the Mission church in Kingston, in connection with the London Missionary Society. He lost his companion in 1847; and married again in Kingston, in 1848.

His change of views, and of ecclesiastical position, I can give from his own pen:

"When I left Jamaica in 1855, on account of failing health, I had arrived at the conclusion that the immersion of believers was the only authoritative baptism. After a time, I accepted the charge of a small Congregational church at Rawsonville, (Grafton,) a village comprising representatives of several denominations, no one of them being able to support a preacher. This led me to search for some basis of union. I preached on the subject; and, without knowing the position of the Disciples on that point, I presented what I afterward found to be precisely their views as the only true basis of Christian unity. It was to satisfy the scruples of a young lady on the subject of no creed and infant baptism, that I was led to review the whole matter; and I came to the conclusion that I ought to be immersed forthwith in obedience to the command of Christ. I applied to Elder Nesbitt, a Baptist, who resided in Grafton, to baptize me. He could not attend to it for two weeks, and I went to Wellington to see a Baptist preacher there. But as he would not immerse me except on condition of my uniting with the Baptists, I concluded to wait for Elder Nesbitt. I made known my intentions to the church, and met with no opposition. On the 23d of March, 1856, I was buried with my Lord in baptism. Before leaving the water, I immersed the young lady referred to and another convert. I was then on the eve of a change of location, having accepted a call from the Congregational church in Collamer, with which, and its results you are familiar."

Bro. Beardslee came to enter on his engagement in Collamer, and after his first sermon, which was on a practical theme, he frankly made known his change of sentiments; he was willing to fraternize with them, and they would probably have borne with his baptism, as they were much pleased with him. But on learning, in answer to a

direct question, that he could not conscientiously christen
their children, they reconsidered their call, and, by a
small majority, rescinded it.   Thus, and for this reason,
turned away by that people from their fraternity, he came
that Lord's day evening to hear me, and there commenced our mutual and cordial acquaintance.

Meantime William Hayden had heard of him, and of
his baptism by Elder Nesbitt.   He went to Bro. S. R.
Willard, and urged him to go at once and make known to
him our plea and ground of union.   Bro. Willard was
prompt to visit him, and his message of love was favorably received.   Hayden also went to Bedford, and made
known the case to Dr. Robison, by whose influence the
church extended a call to him to visit them, with a view
to settlement among them.   "On the second Lord's
day," continues Beardslee, "we were mutually prepared
to accept each other as brethren in the common faith.
That was the beginning of a new and blessed era in my
life's history.   Before, I had been as he who saw men
'as trees walking;' now as the same man who saw
'clearly.'"

From this time his heart was set to return to Jamaica.
He longed to reveal to them the light which was so clear
and joyful to him.   Our general missionary society sent
him out, and in January, 1858, he set sail with his family
from New York, for Kingston.   He began his labors in
that city, and on the 1st of May he organized the first
church on the island, on the New Testament basis, with
seven members.   The work went on with great success,
but amidst violent opposition.   In five years there were
nine churches, and about a thousand members.   This was
followed by eighteen months of absence in the United
States.   The work in the hands of the native preachers
was less prosperous.   But Bro. Beardslee returning again
to their aid, two and a half years of unremitting labors
revived the interest, and more than doubled the number

of churches. Bankruptcy in the missionary treasury compelled his surrender of this most promising field. He left Jamaica in 1868, greatly to the disparagement of the mission work, as he was the needed leader of that great work, of which he had been the father and the founder. From that time to the present, his efforts to collect funds to enable him to go to their aid have only resulted in disappointment to him, and to the greater disappointment of the expecting churches of the island.

Among the happy children of this church in Bedford, arose the benignant Harry S. Glasier, a brother, who, in a short time, won to himself the sincerest regards of many friends. He was born in Twinsburg, November 7, 1836, though reared in this church as a nursing mother. He graduated in Bethany, July 4, 1863, and was ordained as a preacher the same day, by Bros. Campbell and Bentley.

His devotion and earnestness in preaching brought many to repentance. He was gifted with a warm, friendly heart, was a good talker, and never failed to improve every opportunity for Christ. He married a companion of equal sincerity, and well adapted to his work—Miss Eliza E. Clapp—and settled with the church in Belair, Ohio. The congregation grew in numbers and religious feeling during the three years of his ministry there. He was naturally a pastor—"naturally caring for the state" of all the members. He became tenderly attached to the people, and they to him; so that when death came and seized him from them, they mourned as for a near kinsman. He went to assist in a meeting in Pittsburgh where he fell, September 8, 1866. He was carried and laid in the cemetery in Bedford. He left his devoted companion and daughter to inherit his virtues and his excellent name.

Bro. Glasier was frank, free-hearted, generous, and unselfish; attentive to all his friends, and of a very sympathetic temperament. He served the people. He served his God, and he took him early.

34

The Congregation in Newburg.

As far back as 1827 and '8, Ebenezer Williams, then an advocate of Restorationism, gathered some converts in Newburg. When the scales of that pernicious speculation fell from his eyes, and he learned the gospel, he sought to undo his work there, and to repair the damage. Some time in the fall of 1828, he appeared among his former admirers, delivered a few addresses, which awakened a marked interest, and left without farther results.

In June, 1832, the first convert was gained. It was under the vigorous appeals of the heroic W. Hayden. Two years before, he had started a church in Aurora. Henry Baldwin, of that place, carried an appointment to Newburg, and urged his sister and her husband, Col. John Wightman, to go and hear this original preacher. A large audience assembled in the town-house. Such preaching took them all by surprise. It was neither Universalism, to which they had been accustomed, nor the doctrine of any of the religious parties. It was only and simply the gospel as taught in the New Testament.

Many saw the truth, but only one man arose to take his lamp to meet the bridegroom. This was John Hopkinson. He was afterward elder of the church, and stands yet,* after an interval of over forty years, on precisely the same ground assumed at the beginning. Hayden and Williams continued their visits, holding the ground, and gaining con-

---

* Bro. Hopkinson has just fallen asleep in the hope of immortality.

verts. September, 1833, Wightman and wife, and
Eliza Everett, and several others, were baptized by
Bro. Williams. Great awakening of the people, and
farther conversions followed. At one of his visits
Williams baptized a young lady of social attractions,
by the name of Julia Parshall. She was gifted with
superior musical powers, and as soon as she was
lifted above the baptismal water, she sang full and
clear:

> "Now my remnant of days
> Will I spend to his praise
> Who has died my poor soul to redeem;
> Whether many or few;
> All my years are his due,
> They shall all be devoted to him."

Williams writes, "There were more than half a dozen
infidels standing within a few feet, who were very
much moved by the scene."

The Disciples were filled with joy and the Holy
Spirit. They studied the Scriptures daily and diligently to learn the truth themselves, and to be able
to teach it to others. They met often for songs, and
prayer, and mutual encouragement, and when a
preacher came, they had many questions to pro-
pound. Thus light rapidly increased, and they became intelligent in the Christian religion. They
were zealous to propagate the gospel which shed so
much light and joy on their own souls. It was
common for the Disciples of Newburg to come to
Euclid, (now Collamer,) to meeting, a distance of
seven miles; and for these in turn to attend at Newburg to help the brethren there. Each was fille
with the joy which inspired all the rest. Happ
times! Will they ever return to gladden our hearts?

Such zeal with our present numbers would in a twelvemonth set the whole land ablaze!

Society in Newburg was full of infidelity. But the gospel never lost a battle. Strong arguments and powerful appeals from such men as Hayden, Hartzel, Green, Allerton, and Moss, laid the foundation of a lasting work, and soon established a church on Bible principles, which has never ceased to meet, nor failed to hold forth the word of life.

The "yearly meeting" for the year 1835 was held in Newburg, on the farm of Colonel Wightman. Collins well said of him, "he was a princely man." With the noblest generosity and breadth of views, he made provision both for the entertainment of the people, and for the best business management of the occasion, that the widest possible benefits might flow from it. It was duly announced in Cleveland. Prominent citizens were especially informed and invited. A grove was selected, seated, and covered with boards. All the other members also came heartily to the work, and there was nothing wanting to make the people welcome. Bro. Wightman lodged a hundred guests, and supplied provisions without numbering the participants of his bounty.

This meeting was historic. The Disciples, now numerous, came·from long distances. Discourses were delivered by Alex. Campbell, Wm. Hayden, A. B. Green, M. S. Clapp, and a few others; and evening meetings were held in neighborhoods around. For four days the meeting, like the manna about Israel, lay round among the people, the subject of thought and conversation by all. A large number of converts were baptized on Monday by Bro. Green.

At 8 o'clock Monday morning, the preachers, at Mr. Campbell's invitation, met him in the rear of the tent, to whom he submitted the proposition to hold meetings for mutual improvement. He spoke of it as a school to be continued, in which there should be sermons delivered, subject to examination in matter and style. It was unanimously approved, and the first one was appointed to be held in New Lisbon in the following December. About fifteen preachers met with him that morning.

The brethren becoming now well established, they assumed the duties and prerogatives of a congregation of the disciples of Jesus Christ. From that period to the present, the candlestick has not been removed.

None of our churches, Warren only perhaps excepted, had preachers or "pastors" settled among them. The casual watch-care and aid given them by the traveling ministers, many of whom were more intent on extending than building up the churches, was insufficient to check dissensions, and to guard the folds from encroaching dangers. Many churches suffered greatly, and some perished. This in Newburg ran low, and its light was nearly extinct. In their extremity they appealed to Bro. Hartzel, who came in April, 1842, and immediately commanded attention by his able statement and defense of the gospel. He lifted it above all mere "church" or partisan religions, and powerfully beat back the forces of infidelity, which had grown strong and defiant. On Lord's day, the twenty-first of that month, he reorganized the church, with twenty old, and fifteen new members. At this time Youngs L.

Morgan and Caleb Morgan came in with their families. The congregation gained such strength that soon after, under the able ministrations of Bro. J. D. Benedict, they built a good house. They have maintained a good testimony, and are now flourishing under the labors of J. H. Jones. For many years their Sunday-school has prospered, and for the last few years especially, by the skillful management of Bro. Browning; and the children are rising up to take the place of their parents in handing down the gospel uncorrupted to generations after them.

INCIDENTS OF THE YEARLY MEETING IN 1835.

On Saturday night some son of Belial thought to break up the meeting by cutting down a large tree, so its immense brushy top might fall directly upon the seated tent. His mischief failed. The tree fell merely along the edge of it, displacing some of the boards, but not otherwise doing any injury. The incident probably added emphasis to many a philippic against sin and sectarianism. Mr. Wightman had no doubt who the malicious man was who perpetrated the deed. He went to him in the morning and said to him: "If it is any satisfaction to you to commit such depredations, you can do it with the assurance that you can never incite me to retaliate. You may depend on my doing you a kindness whenever it is in my power."

Mr. Wightman's hospitality has been mentioned. Tables were carried out in the yard, under the shadowing maples, plentifully loaded with provisions. There was neither stint in the supply nor attempt to number the people who partook thankfully the profusion set before them.   After disposing of his guests one night, Wightman came to Wm. Hayden and said: " Bro. Hayden, the best lodging I can give you is on the floor, for every thing is full."   " I will not sleep on your hard floor," said the witty William. So taking two benches he placed them together and camped down on them, saying " Now I am comfortably fixed for the night."

CHAPTER XX.

Rise of the cause in Euclid—Church formed by T. Campbell—
  Preachers arising, and growing success—The Church in
  Cleveland established—Planting of the congregation in East
  Cleveland.

THE first church in Euclid was Presbyterian. Luther Dille was a member of it. In 1820, Elder Hanks, a Baptist, preached in that town, and Dille, becoming convinced by the New Testament that immersion was the true baptism, united with the Baptists. Having buried his wife, he married, September 7, 1828, Mrs. Clarissa Kent, sister to Benjamin Blish, of Mentor. She was a disciple; her husband and William Hutchinson were the deacons of the Baptist church. Returning from the "Communion" one Sunday, Mrs. Dille asked her husband why she could not commune with them. "I could myself," said he, "but our church could not." "Why not?" "Because you are not of the same faith and order." "That's the creed," she replied; adding, "I can never put my hand to a creed!" He said: "Then we can never be together." She asked him, "If you should see that we are right, would you unite with us?" "I would," was his prompt reply; not thinking, it is presumed, that he would be put to that test. But she was satisfied and comforted by his answer, convinced of his scrupulous honesty and independence of character. Her confidence in these excellent qualities was not misplaced, neither were her expectations of his early change destined to be disappointed.

Soon afterwards, meeting Rigdon in Mentor, she related the conversation to him. He remarked: " I will go up and take their deacons from them." In the autumn of 1829, he came, preached a few days, and baptized Eri M. Dille, Lurilla Dille, Leonard Marsilliott and wife, Mrs. Perry, Mary Ann Perry, Clarissa Perry, Mrs. Cranny, and her daughter Fanny Cranny. These, with Sister Dille, were associated together for meetings. Rigdon, taking Luther Dille's hand, said: " Will you not go with these young converts and take care of them?" " I will." This was his change ; a happy one to him, and blessed to hundreds. He was so full of joy on discovering that salvation is offered to all men in the gospel that he could not sleep. " I always thought," he said, " I was like some whom Paul spoke of, 'ever learning and never able to come to the knowledge of the truth.' The creed and the doctrines of Calvinism I never could see through, but I thought I must accept them, and thought I believed them ; but now the gospel plan of salvation is so plain, it fills my soul with joy unspeakable." " I am tired waiting on the people," said Mrs. Dille ; " you must let me rest." But he could not sleep. He rose, got his hymn-book and sung, then prayed, and so he spent the night— too happy to sleep.

Elder Baily and deacon Beebee came to recover him from the error of his ways. The elder was full of assurance and pomp. " Uncle Luther," new in the faith, was not well prepared for defense. Mrs. Dille wished to help him, but refrained. She stepped

35

across the way and called in A. P. Jones from his school-room, who entered and sat quietly down on a low seat. At a juncture, Baily having quoted Scripture in disproof of the "new" doctrine, Jones spoke: "If you would read the whole of that passage it would make directly against your views." "Modesty becomes a young man," said Baily, in contempt. "And wisdom becomes age," quickly replied the young teacher, and then quoted the language. "It does not read so," said the elder. "We shall see," said Jones; and taking out his testament, he read out the exact words he had quoted. Mr. Baily was discomfitted. He was persuaded with difficulty to remain till after dinner. He returned to deacon Hutchinson's, who asked, What have you done with deacon Dille? "O, he has fallen asleep in the lap of Delilah!"

In April, 1830, Elder Thomas Campbell came and organized the church in scriptural order, setting apart, by imposition of hands, Luther Dille as elder, and Leonard Marsilliott and Eri M. Dille as deacons.

Bro. William Collins came about the same time, laboring with great acceptance, and adding to their numbers. Lanson O'Connor heard him, and said to him: "You are the first man I ever heard preach the gospel." He obeyed it, and plead it zealously till his death. To Bro. J. J. Moss also the church was, and ever will be, greatly indebted for his zealous labors in teaching the people, and defending the principles of the gospel. Rigdon's fall staggered many, but Mormonism never made a convert in Euclid. This is much owing to the presence of Moss. He debated with one of their elders, and so routed him that he fled from the community. Bro. Washington O'Connor rose up in the church and became very useful in keeping the members together, and adding to their numbers. This young brother was soon on the wing, encouraged by the church, and became very useful as a proclaimer of the gospel. He traveled extensively in Lorain, Huron, Erie, Wayne, and Holmes counties, bringing many souls to Christ. He married Miss Elizabeth Dille, and after a few years he settled in Mishawaka, Ind., where his useful life terminated May 12, 1859, aged fifty-one years.

Damon O'Connor, also, was many years a prominent member; and Armon O'Connor, one of the first to embrace the faith, baptized by A. P. Jones, October, 1832, was chosen associate in the eldership with Luther Dille, a position he held with credit for many years, and till he removed to another church.

William Hayden was one of the first to sow the seed of the kingdom in this community. A meeting held by him and Bro. Moss in Shumway's barn made a great impression, and is talked of yet, after nearly forty years, as a notable occasion.

The first of the great yearly meetings in Euclid was in September, 1837, and was a memorable occasion. The attendance was by thousands. Mr. Campbell's former visits to the county, and especially his signal triumph over the Anakims of skepticism the year before, in the city of Cleveland, freshly and favorably remembered, called crowds to hear him. His discourse on Lord's day was one of his most masterly efforts. It was founded on Gen. iii: 15; and showed the nature and design of positive institutions as tests of obedience. It was a powerful argument against infidelity. Assisting in the meeting, were Butler, of Indiana, Hayden, Green, Bentley, Clapp, Moody, Williams, Allerton, Collins, Moss, Veits, O'Connor, Atwater, Brown, and A. S. Hayden. The immediate result was nineteen conversions. This meeting formed an epoch in the history of this church and of the cause of primitive Christianity in all that region. The plea was lifted high into public notice, and many, from this hearing, afterward became obedient to the faith.

In October, the following year, a successful meeting was conducted in Euclid by A. P. Jones, Moody, and Robison. Eight additions.

A few months after, February, 1839, John Henry came for eight days. The brethren not having a meeting-house, they rented a vacant store-room in the village. This, for nearly three years, was their meeting place. It was crowded nightly to hear this invincible champion of the truth. There were ten added to the number, seven of them conversions. Among these last was an old sea captain, Jephtha G. Nickerson, from New Bedford, Mass. In command of a vessel, he had made most of the commercial ports of the world—had visited Malta, the island where Paul was cast ashore. He had been ship-wrecked on the Mediterranean; and now, spending a quiet winter in the secluded village of Collamer, he turned in to hear the stranger. Henry's manner, bold, decided, energetic, exactly suited the captain, whose own nature was a compacted tempest. He understood the preacher. For the first time he heard something plain, tangible, and common sense on the subject of conversion, and well backed up with Scripture. He obeyed, and his soul was as tender as the

mourning-dove. Sleep left him, but "songs in the
night" came to him. He learned the hymns, and his
mouth was opened with a " new song."

He said to Bro. Henry: "I have a brother David.
I 'll have him here next winter. You must come
back and convert him." So spoke the earnest sailor.
Henry made a promise, and he never forgot one, that
a year hence he would return.

Intervening, June, 1839, J. J. Moss and A. S. Hayden held a two days' meeting in the same store-room,
resulting in nine conversions. The next February,
at Bro. Henry's arrival, both the captains were at
home. The younger one discovered in the teachings
of the gifted preacher what had never been suggested
or hinted in all the preaching to which he had listened; that in the gospel God has made known the
way of salvation through faith, repentance and baptism, into the Father, Son, and Holy Spirit; that
this, his established order, is open to all men to the
end of time. His soul was kindled as he saw the
way so plain that " the wayfaring man could not err
therein;" and he also turned to the Lord. Several
others also were added.

The yearly meetings this year, 1840, one of which
was in this church, were marked with peculiar interest. Bro. Campbell says of them:

"We attended the yearly meetings in Warren, and in
Euclid, Ohio, held annually in the last week in August and
the first week in September. Both meetings were well attended with public laborers. Present at Warren, were
brethren C. Bosworth, J. Hartzel, J. Henry, S. Church,
E. Williams, A. Allerton, M. S. Clapp, Dr. Robison,
A. S. Hayden, S. Ryder, W. Collins, M. Martin, C. Mc-

Neely, Z. Rudolph, H. Brockett, W. Beaumont, C. E. Vanvoorhis, Abijah Sturdevant and Dr. A. W. Campbell.
Besides a number of these, there were at the Euclid meeting, Elder A. Bentley, W. Hayden, J. J. Moss, and
others.

" . . . . . From a number of detailed statements we
concluded that the number of disciples on the Reserve
has nearly, or altogether, doubled during the last year.
The churches also are in the very best order; the laborers
have been more industrious, more engaged, and, consequently, more successful during the present season. Bro.
William Beaumont has immersed 75 in New Lisbon; Bro.
Henry, 140 since the beginning of the year; Bro. Wesley
Lanphear and J. H. Jones have baptized many; and,
indeed, all the laborers have reason to bless the Lord and
to renew their courage in the glorious work of saving men."

There were 43 immersed at the meeting in Warren, and ten in Euclid. On Monday, Bro. Moss made
a stirring appeal for greater liberality in support of
the gospel, asserting strongly the need of a brother
to be sent out among the churches to arouse them to
this duty. William Hayden was his man. He offered
to be one of four who would give him the sum of
three hundred dollars for a year's labor to this end.
"Who will be the other three?" Samuel Miller, late
of Willoughby, was quick on his feet. "Who next?"
Casper Hendershot, of Euclid. "Now the third?"
holding firmly to his point. Bro. Webster, of Mentor,
completed the quaternion, and William Hayden accepted the mission.

There was a great ingathering here in October,
1842. A. S. Hayden began the meeting in the audience room of the meeting-house, which was yet un-
finished. The work of conversion began with the

meeting. After several days, and the baptism of twenty-eight, the laborer dispatched a note to Bro. Robison, of Bedford, who was in his carriage in thirty minutes after receiving it, and in ninety minutes more was on the ground, a distance of twelve miles, ready for work. He remained five days. Forty souls were brought into the kingdom.

In March, of 1847, Bro. Isaac Errett labored a week, gathering in twenty; and in 1851, the church was increased by the addition of twenty more by Calvin Smith and B. F. Perky. After this, W. A. Belding and J. H. Jones held very successful meetings at different times. The new meeting-house was erected in 1862-3.

Elder Luther Dille, having served as bishop of the church over thirty years, with great efficiency and universal esteem, fell asleep, April 18, 1863, aged 79 years. The other churches closed their meetings at an earlier hour than usual, that the people might come and mourn together over a man whose Christian character won the respect of all who knew him. That day the church lost its first elder, who, in all his administration, had been a model of firmness, integrity, impartiality and philanthropy.

THE CHURCH ESTABLISHED IN CLEVELAND.

The first discourse in this city, on the "ancient gospel" as plead by the disciples, was delivered by the pioneer, William Hayden. It occurred under the following circumstances: Coming to Armon O'Connor's, a new convert from Euclid, then living in Brooklyn, two miles west of the Cuyahoga River, Bro O'Connor asked him to preach in the village, down near the river. This was before even "Ohio City" was known or named. Hayden replied that he would do so, if an audience could be obtained at 10 o'clock on a certain Monday morning which he mentioned. O'Connor agreed to these terms. About 8 o'clock of the appointed morning, Bro. O'Connor started and canvassed the entire community, visiting every house. One hour and a half accomplished the patrol. Every family was invited, and nearly every one came. The preacher took up the subject of "election," much discussed those times, and in a full and vigorous argument he stated and replied to the leading proofs relied on in support of the foreordination of a select few to eternal life; and in contrast with this unscriptural hypothesis, he opened a free salvation through faith and obedience to Jesus Christ. The sermon was listened to with marked attention, as well for the boldness and novelty of the preacher's manner, as for the freshness and power of the scriptural views he presented. This was in October, 1833. The ground thus gained was never lost. He introduced Bro. Moss and Bro. Green, who astonished the people by their knowledge of the Bible and power in teaching it. Among the first converts were Mrs. Armon O'Connor, baptized by Bro. Moss; and W. B. Storer and his wife, who were baptized by Hayden at the yearly meeting in Richfield, September, 1834. Bro. Hayden preached in the old academy in Cleveland to full assemblies. Some of the converts recently gathered into the church are the fruits of those sermons delivered thirty years before.

At the conclusion of the meeting held on Mr. Wightman's farm, in 1835, it was arranged for Mr.

Campbell to preach in the court-house on Monday
afternoon at 4 o'clock.   It was the old court-house
which stood on the south-west corner of the public
square.   There were only two hours to circulate the
word.   No time for hand-bills.   This appointment
was at the solicitation of Thomas Hawley, an intelligent disciple, who not long before had moved from
Shrewsbury, England, and was then a resident in
Cleveland.   At his suggestion, his son Joseph and
Armon O'Connor went through all the principal
streets, and in clear ringing tones announced in stores,
shops, and private houses, that Alexander Campbell
would preach in the court-house at 4 o'clock.   These
messengers were young and active.   The whole city
heard, and the court-room was overflowing before
the hour arrived, all anxious to hear him.

Sheriff Wightman's influence was great with the
officials, and with the people, by whom he was much
respected.   Through him the court-house was opened
several times for William Hayden, whose discourses
were listened to by full audiences.   His brother held
a two days' meeting in it.   Discourses were delivered
there by Moss, Williams, and Collins.   These sermons,
like the leaven in the meal, were doing their work.
They opened the way for the harvest which ere long
was reaped in the city.   But it was in June, 1836,
the greatest advance was made in Cleveland.   On a
trip to New England, Mr. Campbell stopped in the
city and delivered some discourses in favor of the
Bible.   These sermons aroused the skeptics in the
city, and Irad Kelley volunteered as the defender of
infidelity.   A few speeches and rejoinders were made,
when Mr. Campbell urged the infidel junto, for it

appears they had no defined organization, to put forth their champion, as the discomfiture of any other would not be acknowledged by them as the overthrow of their cause. Skepticism in the city of Cleveland was then delivered into the hands of the intrepid Dr. Underhill, to make for it the best defense in his power. As court was to open the next day, the first Presbyterian church, of which the venerable Dr. Aiken was pastor, was freely granted for the continuance of the discussion.

The conclusion of this debate of four days, which attracted the attention of the whole city, is thus declared by Mr. Campbell:

"After hearing some other reiterations from Taylor, and some explanations from Mr. Kelley, and some very flattering compliments from my friend Underhill, with the greatest urbanity and good nature we came to a close—I recapitulating the whole, and showing that now, after so long and so patient a session, we had heard these leaders of the skeptics of Cleveland display, if not all they had, certainly the best and the strongest allegations they had to offer. It could not be difficult to see the nakedness of the land of infidelity, the poverty of its soul, when such an assiduous cultivator as my opponent had raised so poor a crop after the toils of so many moons. We contrasted the bearings, the prospects, and the ultimate termination of the two hopes—that of immortality, and that of eternal sleep; the present pleasures of religion and the pains of skepticism; and after a word of friendly exhortation to my antagonists, I bade them adieu.

"Thus, after enjoying, with many others, the very kind hospitalities of our benevolent brother Hawley and his amiable family for several days, and various demonstrations of respect and good will from all parties, we retired in the evening of that day to our good but afflicted brother Wightman's, in the country; and, after spending a pleasant evening with himself and family, on the next morning we embarked on Lake Erie for the State of New York.

"We had the pleasure," Mr. Campbell adds, "in the midst of our discussions, to be called to the river to hear the confession of six converts who were immersed into Christ by our brother Adamson Bentley."

This, it is presumed, is the first instance of baptism by our brethren in the city of Cleveland. The occasion is memorable. The administrator was as venerable as a patriarch; and the converts were trophies of a signal victory achieved over the allied forces of infidelity in the city.

The gentlemen who presided, at different times over this discussion, were Elder Bentley, Thomas Hawley, and Tolbert Fanning, of Nashville, Tenn., one of Mr. Campbell's companions in travel.

It is eminently worthy of special attention, that all the participants in that scene are now dwellers among the countless tenants of the grave. Campbell, Bentley, Fanning, Hawley, Wightman; M. S. Clapp also, and William Hayden. Bro. Clapp made two speeches in the discussion, in consequence of Mr. Campbell's hoarseness. All these have wheeled into the ranks of that long procession of immortal spirits who are awaiting their crowns. Dr. Underhill sleeps. And now, within a few days, Irad Kelley, Esq., the lone survivor of that group of historic names, is brought from the seaboard where he died, to rest among his kindred dead.

From that day the cause of infidelity withered. It was the blasting of the fruitless fig-tree. Long afterward in a public assembly of the citizens, Rev. Mr. Aiken declared that to Mr. Campbell was to be credited the downfall of infidelity in the city of Cleveland. In this opinion he only expressed the concurring judgment of other intelligent citizens, some of whom, legal gentlemen of reputation, have so said to me.

The cherished purpose of planting the ancient gospel in Cleveland seemed to be delayed by the death of Col. Wightman. This warm-hearted Christian was no less active than influential. On January 12, 1837, he fell asleep in good hope, after a long and painful illness. The removal of Bro. Hawley and family to Detroit, about this time, was also a blow to hope. It was not long, however, before a door of faith was opened, and in the following manner:

Capt. J. G. Nickerson and his brother, having moved to Cleveland, they importuned Henry to come and preach in the city. This panoplied chieftain opened the siege Friday, the 11th of February, 1842. In three days the meeting was all ablaze. Great numbers were not able to gain admittance. The overpowering mastery of that matchless man held his audiences for an hour and a half to two hours as under a charm. Gentlemen, and sometimes ladies, stood during the sermon unconscious of the time. During the ten days of his meeting there were twenty-six conversions. Three others united, and on Lord's day, the 20th of February, 1842, the church was constituted and left under the general oversight of Dr. J. P. Robison and A. S. Hayden. D. P. Nickerson and Geo. B. Tibbitts were the elders. The next Lord's day, Robison preached and baptized six more. Bro. Jones, whose prowess scents the battle from afar, was quickly on the ground, and made many accessions to the infant church. Soon after, the amiable and gifted Collins, with Robison, held a meeting which resulted in thirty conversions.

On the 10th of December, 1843, the church removed to Apollo Hall, east side of the river. In this and in Empire Hall it met about two years—Dr. Robison and A. S. Hayden alternating in preaching; then, in 1846, the congregation re-established itself in Ohio City. Soon after this, Bro. L. Cooley, who had been an early member here, became their preacher. He was succeeded, in 1852, by Bro. Green, following whom, Bro. Cooley was again employed. In 1860, Bro. C. C. Foot became the pastor; then brethren B. A. Hinsdale, James Canon, and S. E. Shephard served the church successively; the present incumbent is Bro. A. Wilcox.

THE CHURCH IN. EAST CLEVELAND PLANTED.

This church originated as a branch of the church in Euclid. A number of the members residing at this place, known as Doane's Corners, prepared the way for a meeting the 4th of July, 1843. It was held under a tent, and was attended by brethren Hartzel, Clapp, Collins, Robison, Benjamin and A. S. Hayden. All assisted, but the chief preaching was by Hartzel. There were over thirty additions; among them was Dr. N. H. Finney, who afterward attained considerable eminence as a preacher, and who died in the faith a few years after. Thus encouraged and increased, the brethren at the "Corners" presented a petition to the church of Euclid, dated August 7, 1843, signed by seventeen names, asking to be set off to form a separate church. The request being granted, the members met September 4th, at the dwelling of Col. Gardner, nominated their officers, and soon after entered on the exercise of their duties as a church of Jesus Christ.

Their first officers were W. P. Hudson and Theodore Stafford. This band of disciples held their position with great perseverance, having to contend much of the time with sharp opposition. Besides the help which they received from the parent church, Bro. M. S. Clapp was procured for regular visits. Few churches had pastors, or elders, those days, who gave themselves wholly to the care of them. They had "meetings" by Bros. Green, Robison, J. H. Jones, and others. William Hayden was a chief dependence, both for preaching and counsel. Among the last discourses he delivered was to this church, which he loved, and the importance of whose position he fully appreciated, in view of the prospective increase of the city of Cleveland. After meeting for a time in the old stone school-house, the church erected a plain, commodious edifice, which continued to serve them till the erection of their present large and attractive house of worship. In this excellent building, which is a rich credit to the architect, as well as to the liberality and enlightened impulses of the brotherhood, and a monument to the generosity of Dr. W. S. Streator, the church entered on a new and wider career of usefulness. Bro. J. H. Jones was called to the charge of the church. After him Bro. C. C. Foot was their help. Bro. J. B. Johnston, from Illinois, was their minister for a year, greatly beloved. His declining health compelled his resignation. The church has enjoyed the labors also of Isaac Errett and of Dr. L. L. Pinkerton. It is now widening its influence and enlarging its activities under the pastoral charge of Bro. Jabez Hall.

CHAPTER XXI.

The Church in Royalton planted—William Moody and the Church in LaFayette—The Cause in Brunswick—J. W. Lanphear— The Gospel brought into Granger and Ghent.—M. L. Wilcox.

WHEREVER the gospel was proclaimed it found men tired of sects, and possessed of qualities of character which would stamp them as extraordinary men in any enterprise. Noted among such men, was John Baker Stewart, of Royalton. He was born in Bristol, Vermont, May 10, 1791. He emigrated to Cayuga County, New York, where he united with the Baptists. He returned to the place of his nativity, and in 1817, he started with an ox-team for the Connecticut Western Reserve. Forty-two days steady traveling brought him to Royalton. The primitive forest reigned undisturbed. Not a road was laid out in the township. He selected his land on which he has resided ever since. Of education and solid sense above mediocrity he has held a prominent position in the county.

Henry Hudson, a Baptist preacher and a physician, established a church in Royalton. In 1828, through internal broils, it ceased to meet. Before they dissolved, Stewart, for himself and wife, obtained letters of honorable dismission. About this time Edward Scofield came in from Bazetta. He was abreast with the reformatory movement in Trumbull County, and though scarcely equal to Stewart in the stern qualities of leadership, he was a man of culture and independence. From Connecticut, where he was born in 1779, he came to the territory of Ohio in 1797. He assisted in surveying the lot lines in many of the townships. He was the first settler in Bazetta, the nearest neighbor being five miles distant. He built the first mills in that region. Every body was hospitable then—Scofield notably so. In 1817 he was elected to the State Legislature, which position he filled with honor. He took membership with the Baptists in Warren, and soon rose to usefulness. He preached the gospel for many years, and was one of the "charter members" of the church of Bazetta.

In 1822, Ezra Leonard came into Royalton. He and Stewart, and Almon Eastman, were accustomed to meet and compare the doctrines of their creed with the teaching of the Scriptures. Light began to shine. When the "Christian Baptist" started, David Hays, of Canfield, who was father-in-law to both Stewart and Leonard, became a subscriber. His daughter, Mrs. Ruth Leonard, a woman of very remarkable knowledge of the Scriptures, obtained that work, and put it into the hands of Stewart. The first piece he read in it was Mr. Campbell's essay on the call to the ministry. Taught from childhood in the belief that preachers are immediately and divinely called as Moses was, this sharp and sifting analysis of the subject, though entirely successful in correcting his early teaching in regard to it, was very distasteful, as it produced the humiliating conviction that he had imbibed pernicious error. After a few days, he said: "Well, 'honesty is the best policy.' I will be honest, and let the truth have

36

its full effect on my heart." This was his emancipation, and it opened to him a new era and a new career.

So stood matters till late in the fall of 1829, at which time Leonard, being in Canfield, invited William Hayden to Royalton. What were fifty miles, or the sleety storms of coming winter, to him? "I'll go," and Leonard gave notice in Richfield, at Bangs' Corners, that a preacher from Trumbull County would come and preach the *everlasting gospel*. Hayden's limping, white-faced horse, sharing the high enthusiasm of his martial rider, brought the bearer of glad tidings in prompt time. Curiosity to hear the advocate of a new religion, as the everlasting gospel without shadings and trimmings was supposed to be, filled the school-house. The candles were without candlesticks. Setting them here and there into pools of melted tallow, the meeting was opened. The preaching created great excitement. The place was full of skeptics. One night, when the sermon was ended, a man cried out: "Mr. Hayden, how long do you think a man will have to stay in hell?" Answered as quick as asked—"I don't know; I don't expect to go there to see!" For awhile the cause trembled in the balances. Sectarian prejudice joining with infidel opposition, the school-house was locked. Not knowing it, he and the audience convened, and finding the house closed, a gentleman offered the use of his new blacksmith shop. Preacher and people went to work, it was seated, and the crowd filling it, he struck his best key, and for two hours the dark and withering systems of infidelity passed under rigid review in con-

trast with the true rights of man, the high civiliza-
tion and exalted happiness which would follow the
adoption of the Christian religion. From this, he
turned toward the more willing inhabitants of Royalton. Supported by such men as Stewart, Scovill,
and Leonard, the gospel was firmly planted, though
fierce opposition attended every step of its progress.
Dr. Hudson left no artifice unemployed. But the
truth is mighty, and it won at every encounter.
Converts came, and professors of various name saw
the gospel ground of union and co-operation, that,
in coming to Christ, they came to one another.
Among others the manly Dougald McDougall and
family, who had been with the "Bible Christians,"
the excellent and energetic Jewett N. Frost also,
who, though they have gone to their "long sought
rest," left witness behind them in their zealous labors
for the gospel.

Others came in to help on the good begun work.
Bro. Green and Bro. Moody rendered efficient and
timely aid. The church was constituted in the fall
of 1829. The record contains the following names
as the beginning of the church:

Edward Scofield, Mary Scofield, Rufus Scofield,
Roxana Scofield, John B. Stewart, Huldah Stewart,
Jewett N. Frost, Dougald McDougall, Lucia Mc-
Dougall, Adin Pike and wife, Wm. Hatch, Lydia
Hatch, David Wallace, Adaline Wallace, Almon
Eastman, Spencer W. Paine, Miranda Paine, White
Paine and wife, Ebenezer Robinson, Oliver N. Paine,
Renetta Paine, Henry L. Bangs, Almira Bangs,
Elisha N. Bangs, Abigail Bangs, Chauncey A. Stew-
art, Jerry Meach, Lucinda Meach, Sylvia M. O'Brian,

Marcia Whitney, Samuel Verney, Damaris Verney, Hannah Verney, Catharine Fuller, Decius Barnes.

Edward Scofield, J. B. Stewart, and J. N. Frost, were the bishops ; Adin Pike and Dougald McDougall, deacons. Bro. Stewart, whose memory retains its wonderfully retentive power at eighty-three, writes:

" From this time forward Bro. William Hayden looked after, and took very great interest in the welfare of the church. And when we take into account the small amount of compensation he received for his many trips, over bad roads and through storms, the church hold him in grateful remembrance to this day. Most of the preaching was done by him, by Bro. Scofield, Bro. Green, and Bro. Moody. All these brethren are held in high esteem by the older brethren.

" In the year 1835, Bro. Scofield removed to Indiana. Falling sick, he was brought back all the way on a bed. He lived about two weeks after his return, when he went joyfully to meet his Lord."

The subject of unconditional personal election, the staple of many sermons in those days, was always a hard doctrine, and difficult to the studious mind of Stewart. He was relieved in the following manner: Hayden, in one of his sermons, declared: "Put election on character, not on person, and the subject is clear. God has always respected character. He has always blessed those who obey him, and punished the disobedient ; this is the true election. It rests on character, not on person." This threw a flood of light into his mind, and he walked out of the entanglements of a subject which has bewildered thousands.

Conversing with a lady on the claims of the gospel, she said with deep emotion, " Oh, I would give all the world if my heart were changed so I could believe on Jesus." " What would you give," said Hayden, " to believe on Mohammed ?" " Oh, nothing at all," she said. " Why ? " " Because I believe him to be an impostor." " But why do you wish to believe on Jesus ? " " Because I believe him to be the Son of God." " Then you do believe on him, do you not ? " " Oh, yes, with all my heart ! " " Then," continued the preacher, " if your heart were changed, you would disbelieve him, and be an infidel." She saw her mistake : with a heart already penitent and in love with Christ, she was vainly waiting for some miraculous change. She arose, and was baptized, and went on her way rejoicing.

That remarkable man waged a heroic battle for Jesus Christ. Stewart testifies, "A great war spirit was aroused by his preaching." He laid claim to the people as belonging to Jesus Christ, whom Satan has ruined in sin, stupefied in ignorance, and for whom the salves of sectarianism bring no healing. He "gave no quarter to sin, ignorance, nor the devil." In Richfield he preached in a ball-room. At one time he delivered a discourse sitting on horseback. A correspondent writes the first time she heard him was in a saw-mill. Like Paul, whom above all men he admired, and whom he somewhat resembled, he would go to the market, the theater, or the forum, if an audience could there be found to whom he might declare the great salvation.

While the public mind, like the sea, was greatly agitated, a great impetus was imparted to the cause by the yearly meeting held near Bangs' Corners,

September, 1834. It was a large, orderly meeting, and made a favorable and enduring impression. It carried the force of a great public demonstration. In attendance were J. Hartzel, W. Hayden, E. B. Hubbard, A. Allerton, W. F. Pool, A. B. Green, Wm. Moody, and A. S. Hayden. Many converts crowned the meeting with success. Great harmony prevailed, and through acquaintance the hearts of the brotherhood were knit together. This is veritable Christian unity, which was uniting in the same kindred tie the brotherhood now widening and extending in all directions.

The church of Christ in Royalton still flourishes, and is fulfilling its mission. McDougall became an elder, and died in the faith, honored of all. After a little, Bro. Wm. Tousley came in, was chosen an overseer, and for many years was a pillar. The ministry, who, from time to time have labored among them, have been zealous and faithful. Besides those already named, they have had Scott, Campbell, Burnett, Shephard, Buckbee, Robison, Jones, Cooley, Moffett, Hinsdale, and others on incidental occasions. They now have Bro. H. N. Allen for their minister.

WILLIAM MOODY, born in New Hampshire, August 29, 1810, was descended from English and Scotch ancestors. His twenty-third year found him in Ohio. After spending some time in Wadsworth, he settled in Chatham, Medina County.

At the age of nineteen he became a Baptist, in Franklin County, New York. Persuaded that he had a " call " to the ministry, he began preaching. But his *call*, as he felt and related it, was, that he loved God and loved men, and rejoicing in " the liberty wherewith Christ had made him free," he felt a strong impulse to speak of his saving goodness to others. After coming to Wadsworth, he heard Bro. Green on the subject of faith, in which the preacher asserted that "faith comes by hearing;" (Rom. x: 17,) that it is the result of evidence intelligently apprehended by the mind. Moody determined to attack him and expose this false and pernicious position. It denied his notion of the infusion of faith, as a spiritual grace, by a direct act of the Holy Ghost. He thought to panoply himself for the onset by a fresh study and array of his proofs; but he found his strength was weakness. After that sermon his proof-texts did not read to him as before. He was disarmed. The encounter never took place.

Having engaged in service with Bro. Newcomb, the youngest daughter of the venerable elder took up the argument two hours an evening for five nights, chiefly on the work of the Holy Spirit and the design of baptism. He contended earnestly for the tradition of the fathers; but the young and heroic daughter of the covenant was too shrewd for him, well taught as he confessedly was in the general language of Scripture. He fell in the debate, and yielding up the ghost of tradition, he found new life and new joy in the clearer and more scriptural knowledge of the gospel.

From that hour his voice was raised more earnestly in the advocacy of the truth. Though working still as need required, he gave much time to the proclamation of the Word. In the fall of 1837, he stuck the pioneer stake in the town of LaFayette, Medina County. For two nights the people listened attentively, but would not sing. The third night, on approaching the meeting, his heart was gladdened by the sound of songs of praise. "Thank God," he exclaimed, "the waters are moving!" He continued three months, visiting, reading the Scriptures— privately and publicly—preaching the gospel, and exhort- ing the people. He brought into the covenant forty-nine by baptism, recovered others, and founded a church of sixty persons. He instituted meetings for the new converts, in one of which, forty at a single meeting took a part in prayer and exhortation. Discovering that much feeling pervaded the assembly, he offered an opportunity for confessing the Lord. Seven arose, one after another, confessed their sins, and declared their desire for obedience to the merciful Saviour. They were baptized the next morning. This church has stood firm ever since. Bro. Earl Moulton has long stood as a leader and support to them. Bro. Moody has preached a fourth of his time there for thirty-five years, while his labors in surrounding regions has contributed much to sustain the churches in Sullivan, Wadsworth, Brunswick, Weymouth, Granger, Royalton, Birmingham, and many other places.

THE CHURCH IN POMPEY STREET, BRUNSWICK.

Early in the year 1835, five families came to Brunswick from Pompey, Onondaga County, New York. Settling together, their street was called "Pompey Street." They were, John Harris, Darius Wilson, Warren Wilson, —— Chase, —— Garrett, all, with their wives, members of the church in Pompey. Moss and Hayden soon found them. Great was the joy of these disciples to see again those zealous men who had imparted to them so much light in the east. These two brethren—Bro. Green also, and, after a little, Bro. Wilcox—built them up and increased their numbers. Dr. John Clarke, a gentleman of weight and respectability, a member of the Presbyterian church, and a practicing physician, gave a candid hearing, and obeyed the gospel.

A reorganization of the congregation was made in December, 1839. Dr. John Clarke, Samuel Clarke, and Darius Wilson were elected overseers, and Dan A. Moulton and Geo. W. Comstock, deacons.

In this church a Barnabas arose, who in many an Antioch has taught many. This was

J. W. LANPHEAR.

He was born in the State of New York, in 1814. Coming to Medina County in 1834, he soon came in contact with the disciples. William Hayden's original manner and point in argument won the attention and enlightened the judgment of young Lanphear. He was, while in New York, converted among the Methodists, his father being of that order, and a preacher of considerable abilities. The Campbell and Owen Debate fell into his hands. He read it, absorbed it, "devoured it." By it he was thoroughly aroused. He next obtained and studied the new translation of the New Testament, then lately published by Mr. Campbell. The Christian religion became intelligible to him, and was invested in his mind with an indescribable interest. He grasped it, and it won every faculty of his soul. He embraced it, being baptized by William Hayden in the yearly meeting at "Bangs' Corners," in September, 1834.

When the Pompey brethren came and established their meetings in Brunswick, Bro. Lanphear associated with them. He began to exhort; and being possessed of good natural endowments, ardent in his nature, and very studious, he was soon encouraged to assume the more responsible position of a teacher. About fifteen months after his conversion he started forth, with the sanction of the church, as a preacher of the gospel. He attended the first "school of the preachers," in New Lisbon, in December, 1835, and proceeded to Pennsylvania, where he spent the winter. He went into Maryland in the spring, where falling in with Bro. James Darsie, the young preach-

37

ers were a great help to each other. The church of Somerset, Pa., which contained many able and influential members, took him under her care and pupilage for a time, receiving blessings from his labors, and imparting of her benefits in return. He assiduously improved every opportunity to fit himself for his chosen calling. His acute penetration of mind, delicate fancy, well stored understanding and agreeableness of manners, won him a welcome every-where. His path to public favor and usefulness was now open, and the history of the cause of reformation in western Pennsylvania, and north-eastern Ohio, and in other States, has, for thirty-five years, been closely intertwined with that of this useful preacher of righteousness.

The church in Brunswick passed through the variable vicissitudes which mark the history of most communities, till, by the removals and death of its members, it became nearly extinct. The cause has been revived, and a new church formed at Hamilton's Corners, in the south part of the township.

THE GOSPEL BROUGHT INTO WEYMOUTH, GRANGER,
AND GHENT.

In one of his excursions into Medina County, in the year 1830, Hayden delivered several discourses in Weymouth, where a hospitable family by the name of Stiles received him, and heard him gladly. Geo. W. Comstock, also a citizen of influence, became a convert. Harris Reed, from Granger, a candid and intelligent gentleman, was so delighted with these intelligible and consistent views of the gospel, he resolved his fellow-townsmen should have the opportunity of hearing. He was a Methodist, and had not a doubt the Methodist church would be freely opened. The adventurous pioneer, never waiting for more than half an invitation, promptly consented to go.

The Methodist church was refused, and Reed was sharply censured for bringing in a man to preach the doctrine of devils. Mr. Reed cowered not, nor sheltered himself from the gathering storm. He declared openly he had invited him, and that he would see him courteously treated. Prejudice sought to bar the school-house also, but the liberal minded ones prevailing, Hayden gave his first discourse in it amidst much excitement. He loved to walk on the edge of high waves. He saw in the keen attention of the people the augury of good, and announced another appointment. This was a signal for marshaling the troops for battle. He kept up his appointments, and the gospel won friends. The first of the conversions was Mrs. Ellery Lowe, who came forward, singing:

"This is the way I long have sought,
    And mourned because I found it not."

Soon after, Mr. Reed declared for the ancient gospel, the original ground of union and salvation. He was followed by others, and in the spring of 1832, the church was constituted.

It was composed of the following persons: Harris Reed and Sally Reed, Rebecca Lowe, George McCloud and wife, Samuel Crosby, Morris Miller and ―― Miller, Martin Miller and wife, and Conrad Turner and wife. Morris Miller was chosen elder, and Harris Reed and Samuel Crosby, deacons.

This church was never very strong, and after a few years it became so weak that the members

ceased to hold meetings.   About this time, Bro. Wilcox preached with great success in Ghent, a village
only a few miles distant, and founded a church there,
in which the remaining members in Granger united.

THE CHURCH IN GHENT

Was organized on the 10th of April, 1843, with
sixty-two members.   Morris Miller, Thomas Pierson,
and Alexander Martin were chosen elders; and
Thomas Carnaby, Seymour Ganyard, and E. W.
Heaton, deacons.   Bro. Philander Green writes,
(April 3, 1875,) "Only five of the original members
remain in the church now."

This church has had the labors of Wilcox, who established it, Moss, Newcomb, Green, Cooley, John
Encell, Southmayd, and Holland Brown; but longest and chiefly, of Bro. Philander Green.   This
brother began to preach there regularly in 1850, and
for eighteen years he preached stately at intervals
of two or four weeks.   In 1853 he moved his family
there.   Bro. F. M. Green, who has since become
prominent in the work, especially in the cause of
Sunday-schools, was then in his father's family.

From the year 1853 to 1868, the period of Bro.
Green's closest labors there, there were one hundred
and seventy-five additions; at which time the church,
after all the drains upon it, numbered one hundred
and fifty-two souls.   The last seven years Bro. Green
has labored in the church in Lordstown, Trumbull
County.

MARSHALL LOUNDSBURY WILCOX was a man of high order and talent.   Gifted with a happy combination of argument and eloquence, a style well suited to the forum,

united with a pleasing manner, he was one of the most attractive and efficient of the public advocates of Christianity. He was bold and positive, and loved to grapple with strong opposition, especially with the lurking and sinuous infidelity which, at the period of his ministry, had spread much over the Western Reserve. In contending for the faith he rendered excellent service. He was equally vigilant in maintaining the purity of the gospel, as was shown in several discussions, in which he successfully defended the apostles' doctrine against learned and shrewd opposition.

He was a native of the State of New York. He was an exhorter among the Methodists when he first heard the Disciples, and with characteristic frankness he embraced it, and in the defense of it spent the best portion of his life. He preached extensively on the Western Reserve, and died in Centralia, Illinois.

Early in his ministry he received a contusion in his head from the kick of a horse, from which he often suffered severely. It rendered him sometimes fitful and melancholy. He was therefore not always reliable in discourse. The tinge of sadness in his temperament won sympathy. Admired for his eloquence, and loved for his fidelity and friendship, he gained the esteem and confidence of the people wherever he went.

CHAPTER XXII.

Churches founded in Chagrin Falls—In North Eaton—And in
Youngstown.

CHAGRIN FALLS.

IN the winter of 1831–2, A. Bentley moved from
Warren to the vicinity of the Falls. The pri-
meval forest reigned on every side. He began to
collect the people in the log school-house near by,
and to teach them the gospel. It was not long before thirty persons agreed to unite as a church of
Jesus Christ. Bentley was the natural leader and
overseer, and for one year no other was selected.
Then Gamaliel Kent was appointed to assist. The
first deacons were Zadoc Bowell and Ralph Russell,
both of them disciples before coming to that community.

The church met in different places a few years,
mostly in the Griffith school-house. One day a citizen
of the Falls said to Elijah Hill, "Why do not some of
your men come and preach here at the Falls?" Hill
replied, "We have a man who will preach from your
hay-scales, and pay you as much for the use of them
as the weighing would come to while he occupies
them." This brought Wm. Hayden with the gospel
into Chagrin Falls. The news of the singular appointment spread rapidly. There were no reserved
seats in that place of assembling. The day came,

and with it the audience and the preacher. He went in as a standard-bearer; and it was not long before the meetings were located permanently at the Falls.

It must not be supposed this occupancy was a peaceable possession. Asbury Seminary, in charge of the Methodist Conference, located there, was flourishing, with Prof. Williams at its head, and its spirit was bold and aggressive. No marvel that the leaders of that church looked with jealousy on this effort of the disciples to plant there the church of Christ, as an intrusion on their grounds. A correspondence grew up between Dr. Halleck of the M. E. Church, and Elder Bentley, which passed over into the hands of J. Hartzel, of Warren, and resulted in a discussion between Elder J. J. Stedman and Rev. John Locock, of the Methodist church, and Jonas Hartzel and A. S. Hayden, on the part of the disciples. It began November 14, 1843, on the following questions:

"1. Do the Scriptures teach that to a believing penitent, baptism is a condition of the remission of sins?

"2. Do the Scriptures teach that immersion is the mode of baptism?

"3. Do the Scriptures teach that infants are subjects of baptism?"

Revs. Stedman and Locock denied the first two, and affirmed the last. Hartzel and Hayden brought evidence in affirmation of the first two, and against the last. Three days and nights were spent on the first proposition; two days and nights on the second. At this stage of the interview, Messrs. Stedman and Locock plead to be released from the discussion of the remaining proposition; but this not being acceded to by the disciples, they consented to spend one day and night on it, which was done, and the debate closed.

By this discussion all the religious elements of the town were stirred to their profoundest depths. The relative preponderance of the two people most directly concerned in it was soon greatly changed. Asbury Seminary was seized with the symptoms of decay; ere long it was abandoned, and the ample edifice became the High School building of the town. Still it must be owned that many causes often concur to affect mutations, and to bring on the ruin of human enterprises.

There was no lack of home effort by the whole church to hold every foot of ground which the cause of the union of Christians on Bible grounds was gaining. The system of evangelizing, which then prevailed—or rather the custom, for system there was none—brought occasional help from abroad. Bentley was still among and over them. Wm. Hayden frequently threw in appointments, though he was chiefly on the wing abroad. Considerable ability to teach and exhort by the Kents, Pulsifers, Hubbells, and Collins, sustained the interest of the meetings. The cause gained much credit and respect by a prepared course of lectures on the evidences of Christianity, delivered in a large hall in 1849, by Isaac Errett with his known ability. This course had become necessary to meet the sophistries of a subtle infidelity, which had grown defiant in the village. These lectures planted the defense of the Bible on principles which distinguish the Christianity of revelation from all traditions and appendages to it, and they were a direct auxiliary to the aim of the church—to restore Bible Christianity to the world.

For several years skepticism brooded over this town, and blighted every thing. It became belicose, and the traveling emissaries of no faith, no soul, and no God, were encouraged there by the men who scoffed at the faith of Christ and the hopes of immortality. About this time Prof. J. A. Garfield, of the Eclectic Institute, was preaching in this church. Mr. Denton, from Boston, a man of marked ability and a practiced debater, was lecturing at Newton Falls, and was soon to march with threatening portent on Chagrin Falls. A discussion was agreed upon between him and Garfield. The power in debate, and the familiar knowledge of the whole field of religious learning involved in this discussion, displayed by Garfield, was a surprise to every one except his most intimate friends. His complete mastery of his opponent was acknowledged; and all the religious bodies of the town rejoiced in the victory. This was in December, 1858.

Many times the great tent meetings of the county of Cuyahoga have been held with this church, both exhibiting and cultivating a hospitality worthy of great praise. By them the reformatory principles urged by the disciples won a favorable hearing by great multitudes. The first one was held there in September, 1847; again in 1856, attended by Mr. Campbell, J. O. Beardslee, and the preachers generally. Again in 1864, attended by Prof. Loos; also in 1870.

The strength of this church, as every other, has

ever been the home staff. Her overseers were appointed in the following order : Adamson Bentley, in 1831 ; Gamaliel Kent, 1832 ; Fuller Pulsifer, 1842 ; Jedidiah Hubbell, 1845 ; William Hayden, 1848 ; King Collins, 1860 ; J. G. Coleman, 1863 ; A. Burns, 1869. The following brethren have served as deacons: Zadoc Bowell, Ralph Russell, Amos Boynton, Jedidiah Hubbell, Dr. W. S. Hamlin, Lewis Perkins, King Collins, L. B. McFarland, William Collins, Wallace Collins, Hiram Polly, George King, and Ransom Bliss. Sisters Jennie Burns, Louisa Tucker, and Calista McClintock, are deaconesses of the church.

The following brethren have labored in the congregation either as pastors, or as stated supplies : Adamson Bentley, William Hayden, Dr. W. S. Hamlin, W. T. Horner, J. A. Garfield, J. H. Rhodes, B. A. Hinsdale, Sterling McBride, R. G. White, W. S. Hayden, J. G. Coleman, and A. Burns.

As transient preachers : A. B. Green, J. H. Jones, B. F. Perky, J. Hartzel, Benj. Franklin, F. M. Green, R. Moffett, and C. J. Bartholomew.

Present number of members, one hundred and twenty-five ; the highest number at any one time. The whole number from 1831 to 1875, about four hundred and fifty.

This church has a saintly record. Under the "green, turfy grave-yard," repose the remains of Bro. and Sister Bentley, of many gracious and godly memories ; of the untiring Wm. Hayden, and five of his children ; of both King and Wallace Collins, and, lately, of the manly Kent, and a large number resides, who have joined the worshiping host on high.

EATON.

In North Eaton, as in Philippi, the cause sprang into existence through the piety of a devoted woman. This was Mrs. Chloe Tucker, who moved from Windham to Eaton in 1837. Visiting in Windham in 1840, she strongly entreated Bro. M. J. Streator, a young preacher of that church, to come to Eaton and unfurl there the standard of the cross. He was soon in those new settlements. He writes:

"I went to North Eaton in October, 1840, and found the welcome I expected from Mr. Tucker and his family. Hot tears crowd to my eyes while I remember their earnest hospitality. And when I last was at their old home they had gone from 'this low ground where sorrows grow.' Meetings had been announced at the brick school-house. Many came from various motives; but few, I think, expected to hear or learn their duty. The meeting resulted in the conversion of two sons of Mrs. Tucker. Reuben F. Tucker was the first in Eaton to obey the gospel upon apostolic conditions. The pious mother's prayers were now partially answered; but the work did not end with these."

In March of 1841, he was again on the ground. This effort was attended with farther success. The following incident which I give in the words of the persevering preacher, will show the dainty fingered heroes of modern warfare the tack and toil of those hardy times: "A slough of eighty rods in width lay between the settlement in which the Tuckers resided and the place of meeting. The vigorous crossed this bed of mud in the dark and on foot as best they could. But Bro. R. F. Tucker, desiring that the rest should hear, placed them in a strong wagon.

and with two yokes of oxen for a locomotive, plunged in, and finding stations once in every two rods, he brought them through! I never saw a brighter example of the 'pursuit of knowledge under difficulties!'"

Chester Cooley came into Eaton from Shalersville in 1837. His parents and some of the family followed. At Bro. Streator's second visit, he made an appointment at the center of the town, then scarcely inhabited, and calling at Mrs. Cooley's, invited her son Lathrop, then a youth, to go with him to meeting. He did so, and yielding to the claims of the gospel, he was introduced by baptism into the kingdom. His subsequent career of public life is well known in north-eastern Ohio. Immediately on his conversion, his heart was opened to speak for the Master. He entered Bethany College, but baffled by the want of funds in his desires for a training in college, he fell back on his own resources. He erected for himself a neat cabin in the grove, where he instituted his own college—himself the pupil and the professor. "There," said his brother Chester, thirty years afterward, "when I retired at night his light was still burning, and in the morning at first rising, his lamp was already lighted." By such diligence in study, his "profiting" became manifest. The church which heard him for his encouragement, soon heard him for their profit. After a time, William Hayden discovering his gifts, took him in company in his travels. He received great advantage from the counsel and experience of the older workman. He has traveled extensively in preaching the glad tidings, and has been equally useful as pastor of the churches in North Royalton, Cleveland, Painesville, and Akron.

Bro. Streator came again in October, 1842, and gathered the disciples, numbering twenty-five, into church relations. J. D. Swift was appointed the overseer, and J. A. Ferguson deacon. From that day the church has never ceased its meetings. The zeal of the new converts was tempered into prudence by some older members, among whom stands brother Ferguson, of age and experience in the gospel. The brethren there cherish the memory of the wise and faithful labors of Bro. M. J. Streator with warm gratitude. A brother writes: " Bro. Streator continued his visits, laboring with a zeal and earnestness rarely equaled. This dear brother must ever live in sweet recollection in the memory of this band, the greater part of whom remain to this present time, but some are fallen asleep in Jesus."

The truth rose here to victory and power amid an ocean of opposition. "Orthodoxy," enshrined in sacred temples, hurled its anathemas against it. But its assaults rebounded against itself with destructive recoil. At one time, immediately after a vigorous sermon, before a large audience attempting to refute the alleged heresy, a young man solicited baptism at the hands of Bro. Streator. Jordan flowing by, they repaired to its banks, and after some instructive remarks, the holy institution was administered in the presence of all the people so becomingly and scripturally, that no other reply was needed to the abusive harangue they had just heard. The foe most difficult to dislodge was the ignorance of the people. As the preacher brought strange things to

their ears, naturally enough they cried out: "These
people have a new Bible." "Mr. Campbell has altered the Bible just to suit his views." Not a few
gave credit to this slander. One man found indubitable proof that the Bible used by the disciples differed from his, for on examination he found a book
in it called *Philemon*—no such book, he averred,
being in his Bible. On one occasion an "Elder" of
the "Latter-day Saints" came, and in a long discourse
presented the claims of Mormonism. Bro. Streator
proposed a reply. The two "Elders" refused him
the opportunity; but the proprietor of the house
consenting, and the people all wishing to hear the
response, the youthful defender of the ancient gospel, in a rejoinder of half an hour, so effectually exposed the new delusion that nothing was left to
take root and grow.

The congregation received early and able assistance from brethren Green, Moss, and O'Connor.
Dr. Butler, of Ridgeville, a physician of extensive
practice, who had great weight with the people, met
frequently with them.

In the autumn of 1843, the location of the church
was changed to the center. On this occasion Jared
Patchen was chosen overseer, and Chester Cooley,
deacon.

Bro. J. D. Benedict wrought a good work in a
few visits he made there about the year 1845. In
that year the church erected the house of worship.
He attended the opening of it, and gave some able
discourses. With the voice of a Stentor, and a remarkable talent in music, his singing and sermons
swept like a torrent over the assembly. He was

first a member of the Baptist church, and a lawyer
of acknowledged ability. At this time he held the
position of State's Attorney for Lorain County.
With a frankness and independence of character, as
rare as remarkable, he saw and accepted the principles of reform ; and closing up his legal profession,
like Paul, he gave up his life to the advocacy of the
gospel.

William Hayden was frequently with the brethren ;
and William Moody is also well remembered "as
handling the Universalists without mittens, and
often charging into the battery of Thomas Paine."
Successful meetings were conducted by T. J. Newcomb, B. F. Perky, and the lamented Henry Dixon.
Calvin Smith left there ineffaceable memories of the
blessed results of his earnest and self-denying services.

In 1844, Timothy S. Brewster, of experience in
church affairs, came in from Rockport. He was appointed an elder, and served with efficiency till his
removal to Michigan, in 1849. About this time, the
brethren received new strength by the addition to
their number of Raymond Haven, Sheldon Streator,
and some others from Shalersville. Indeed, the
church in North Eaton grew up as a colony from
the older one in Shalersville ; as she, in turn, became
a mother of the young and vigorous church in Bloomingdale, Michigan. This congregation increased,
till their first meeting-house became too small. A
new edifice was demanded, which was completed and
dedicated in the fall of 1862. Bro. J. H. Jones,
chaplain in the 42d Regiment, Ohio Volunteers,

under Col. Garfield, who was at home on furlough, conducted the dedicatory services.

And what shall I say more? Time would fail to speak of Chas. McDougall, who, while a student in Oberlin, rendered them efficient aid ; of Henry Dixon, whose voice was as refreshing as rain on the mown grass ; of W. A. Belding, whose cheerful manner and zeal for his Master's cause, won many friends ; of John Reed also, lucid in statement of truth, and able in defending it ; of Dana Call, whose worth excels his renown, faithful in Bible study, and candid to a proverb. With Green, J. M. Atwater, the Encells, likewise, S. Fairbanks and others, whose names are dearly remembered.

Three great meetings are marked in the more recent history of this congregation : One in 1860, led by C. C. Foote ; one in 1861, by D. S. Burnett ; the other in 1862, conducted by H. W. Everest.

To the home membership is largely due the credit of the success of the effort to plant and sustain the church in North Eaton. Where there is no faithful, well drilled soldiery to march up to the breastworks to "man the ordnance" and stand the shock of battle, protracted meetings, however useful as helps, will be only skirmishes. Nothing gives permanency like the consolidated, constant labors of a harmonious brotherhood in Christ.

YOUNGSTOWN.

This church was born in the agonies of fierce contention. In no place does the history of the planting of the church on its New Testament basis display a greater virulence of opposition.

In March, 1841, a discussion was held between J. Hartzel and Rev. Waldo, a Congregationalist, which made a profound impression. Conversions followed, and a number of Mr. Waldo's friends were baptized into the Lord Jesus. Along with this result, it stimulated a malignant opposition to the principles of the reformation. The watchmen on the walls of their local Zions were alarmed. The Rev. Dr. Boardman, pastor of the Presbyterian church, sounded the war-trumpet, and rushed full armed into the arena. Elder J. J. Stedman, of the M. E. Church, panting for more laurels than he had won on the martial fields of Newton Falls, Bedford, and Chagrin Falls, encountered Hartzel here in a discussion of two and a half days, on the question; "*Is baptism in any case necessary to the forgiveness of sins?*" All the stars of that firmament in their courses fought against the cause represented by the faithful few who were striving for nothing but the Christianity of the New Testament. The members banded together. The church formed. Brethren Henry and Lanphear seconded these efforts of Hartzel. Conversions followed, and the cause began to rise.

In August of this year, 1842, Mr. Campbell came to the Western Reserve. Touching at Fairfield, where he addressed immense congregations, he passed on to Warren, and addressed the public on Christian union, and on education, after which he proceeded to Youngstown.

He found the people in high excitement by these recent grossly false statements of the views of the Disciples. In company with two of the brethren, Mr. Campbell called on Rev. Mr. Boardman, and

38

asked him to do in his presence what he had attempted when he had no respondent. Mr. Boardman's courage failed him, and he refused. He would
not permit Mr. Campbell to examine his manuscript,
that he might reply fairly to his erroneous charges,
nor to use his church, nor would he attend and hear
him on the same subjects. Mr. Campbell then, in
the house used by the brethren, in the presence of a
very large audience, after briefly rehearsing his interview with Mr. Boardman, gave so able and candid a statement of his true position as to gain the
feelings of a large portion of the uncommitted citizens in their favor.

From that day to the present, the light has never
gone out of the church in Youngstown. Bro. J. W.
Lanphear was first secured as its pastor. In March,
1843, he resigned, and returned to New Lisbon.

The yearly meeting for Trumbull County was held
this year in Youngstown. Great expectations, but
with very different states of feeling, were entertained
in respect to the coming convocation, by the members of the church on the one hand, and by the opposers on the other. Preparations were ample, yet
no one looked for such an avalanche of the brotherhood as assembled on that occasion. Bro. John
Henry was the president of the meeting. His
energy and decision came into full play in the management of so great a multitude. In assigning homes
to the people he told them to knock at a brother's
house, and they would see what sort of people they
are within. "Mr. Hornet," said he, "is a very clever
gentleman abroad; but just knock at his door and

you 'll soon see what a reception you will meet !"   Mr.
Campbell says of this meeting :

ANNUAL MEETINGS IN OHIO, 1843.

The meeting in New Lisbon, Columbiana County, was
well attended.   I had not the pleasure of being present.
Thirty-eight were added by baptism.

The annual meeting of the brethren in Trumbull
County, at Youngstown, was the largest assemblage of
persons ever witnessed by any of the ministering brethren
present.   I have seen very large religious assemblies in
Virginia and Kentucky, but none equal to this one.   It
was variously estimated from six to ten thousand persons.
Had it been a political meeting, the general opinion was
that it would have been put down at ten thousand.   Knowing how wont men are to exaggerate in numbers on such
occasions, I choose rather to regard the minimum of six
or seven thousand persons as more nearly approaching the
actual number in attendance.   The number of disciples
present probably amounted to some two thousand.

The immense audience assembled in one of the most
beautiful and commodious groves in the immediate environs of the village of Youngstown, which was courteously
tendered to the brethren by the proprietor, Mr. Wick.   A
tent provided by the brethren, covered only some two
thousand persons.   The remainder, covered by the umbrageous boughs of a dense grove, enjoyed equal comforts
with those under the tent.

During the whole meeting of three days not a single
accident or unpleasant incident occurred.   The most perfect attention and good order seemed universally to obtain.   During these three days some fifty made the good
confession, and were baptized.   Many ministering brethren, probably some thirty or more, were present, and the
meeting was truly refreshing and peculiarly pleasant to all.

A. CAMPBELL.

On Saturday, before the full assembly, Dr. Eleazer Parmly, of New York, read the following correspondence between himself and Prof. Charles Anthon, of Columbia College, N. Y.   Prof. Anthon, as a classic authority, has no superior in America.   Dr. Parmly then gave the letters to Mr. Campbell in presence of the audience :

"No. 1 BOND STREET, N. Y., *March* 23, 1843.
"PROF. CHARLES ANTHON:

"In conversation with Dr. Spring, last evening, he stated that, in the original the word baptism, which we find in the New Testament, has no definite or distinct meaning; that it means to immerse, sprinkle, pour, and has a variety of other meanings—as much the one as the other, and that every scholar knows it; that it was the only word that could have been selected by our Savior, having such a variety as to suit every one's views and purposes.   May I ask you if your knowledge of the language from which the word was taken has led you to the same conclusion? and may I beg of you to let the deep interest I take in the subject plead my apology.

"I have the honor to be, with great respect, most respectfully yours,   E. PARMLY."

"COLUMBIA COLLEGE, *March* 27, 1843.
"DR. PARMLY :

"*My Dear Sir*—There is no authority whatever for the singular remark made by the Rev. Dr. Spring relative to the force of *baptizo*.   The primary meaning of the word is to dip or immerse, and its secondary meanings, if *ever it had any*, all refer, in some way or other, to the same leading idea.   Sprinkling, etc., are entirely out of the question.   I have delayed answering your letter, in the hope that you would call and favor me with a visit, when

we might talk the matter over at our leisure.   I presume,
however, that what I have written will answer your purpose.   Yours truly,

"CHARLES ANTHON."

From Campbell and Rice's Debate, pp. 171, 172.

The intrinsic weight of authority of this testimony, enforced alike by the noble bearing and earnest manner of Dr. Parmly, gave it great effect with
the audience.   And in the hands of Mr. Campbell, in
the Lexington debate, which followed in about two
months, it was a bolt which evidently staggered the
mailed Mr. Rice.

This church has many years maintained the "unity
of the spirit in the bonds of peace."   W. S. Gray,
W. S. Hayden, while teaching, have also preached
for the congregation.   James Calvin has rendered a
very efficient aid, and Dr. Whitsler also, in keeping
up the meetings.   In the beginning of the congregation, Bro. John Kirk, by his talent for management, dash, and zeal, contributed very much to the
success of the gospel in the hands of Henry, Hartzel, Jones, and Samuel Church.

Under the acceptable pastorate of Bro. C. C.
Smith, the church is rising to greater strength.
They have recently completed a costly and elegant
meeting-house, and are in a position to command
public respect.

CHAPTER XXIII.

LESSONS OF OUR FORTY YEARS' EXPERIENCE.

I. ALL the experience of the past forty years confirms the soundness and strength of our position before the world. This position is embraced in three propositions :

1st, The Bible contains God's only and complete revelation to man.

2d, It is to be interpreted by the ordinary, established rules.

3d, It is to be interpreted by every man for himself.

On these three propositions is founded a broad corollary, viz : The Bible, thus interpreted, will inevitably lead Christendom out of its leopard-like sectarianisms back to the original, divine unity, and restore to the church her lost power for the conversion of the world.

On this bottom we put to sea. Not a leak has yet been found. The vessel has proved herself seaworthy. Her *hull* is as sound as when she was launched. Not a plank has stirred. She has weathered many storms and rode out many tempests. She has been attacked by the war-crafts of nearly all nations, and is proved to be invincible.

Every re-examination of the ground of our faith has only confirmed it. Why should it not? Jesus Christ, our crucified and risen Lord, the reigning Sovereign and Monarch of the whole universe, is the

only object personal of our faith, our love, and our
obedience ; and the whole Bible is the "testimony
of Jesus." This is our plea, and it is invulnerable.
It never can be overthrown. " The gates of hades
shall not prevail against it." It can not be improved. We are not advocates of a reformed religion, but of religion itself. Christ's religion can not
be reformed. He is himself the author and the
finisher of his most holy religion ; and, like himself,
it is perfect. This to proclaim, this to defend, on
this divine basis to re-assemble, and re-incorporate
the divided battalions of the Captain of salvation ;
this is our purpose, our work, and our plea before the
men of this generation.

II. Our forty years' experiences teaches the necessity of a due adjustment of the evangelical and
pastoral work.

Under Walter Scott a new order arose. It was
given to him to blow the trumpet of the gospel. His
work was purely an evangelism. The matters of the
Christian religion are classified under two fundamental departments—the evangelical and the ecclesiastical ; or, the gospel and the church. The gospel
is prior to the church. The evangelist forms and
establishes the church. This work accomplished,
there begins another class of agencies specifically
described in the New Testament : This is the eldership, or pastorate of the church.

In the beginning, the recovery of the ancient gospel, as a lost jewel, so startled and excited all hearts,
and the success attending the preaching of it was so
marvelous that little was thought of but the speedy
and certain capture of the world for Christ. The

"sects" would surrender, or be blown to atoms. Nothing was looked for but the immediate triumph of the gospel over all opposition. Nor must this ardent hope be accounted a mere enthusiasm, or be handed over to the credit of an overestimate of the importance of the views of the gospel just then freshly brought to light. The law of Moses was "weak through the flesh;" so, under the gospel of Christ, there is a human side in the affair. Here is where the failure lies of realizing the high hopes of the most brilliant success.

Thoughtful men predicted this at the beginning. The admirable Osborne saw it, and lamented the absence of a system for holding and training the converts. William Hayden foresaw confusion, and a coming disappointment of the mistaken hopes of the more ardent. They remonstrated with Scott, but that angel of the tempest, beholding victory on all sides, blew louder his silver trumpet of salvation, and replied: "O, convert the people, and give them the Holy Ghost, and they will be safe!" Benajah Austin, a man of sense like a governor, said to Bentley and Henry: "You must stop; the longer you go on the worse it will be. It will come to confusion. If you go on twenty years in this way it will be all the worse, for you will have to stop at last. There must be suitable men appointed to take care of the converts."

No one, not even Scott, consented to a loose, disorganized state of the churches. Far otherwise. The scriptural eldership, the discipline and edification of the converts, were the subjects of early and constant discourse. But it was subordinate. Is it surprising, then, that some converts fell away? that churches languished, and that numbers of them fell into dilapidation and were extinguished? If the due adjustment of these two agencies had been suitably disposed at the beginning, it would have resulted in far greater strength and prosperity. It is a marvel that the churches have stood so well—a proof of the truth and power of the principles of our pleading, rather than of the skill or wisdom of our management.

III. It was a mistake to start so many churches. This error was a result of the exuberance of evangelical zeal already noticed. For this there is much apology in the inexperience attending the beginnings of the enterprise, and still more in the lack of men to maintain the ground conquered by the aggression of the heroic evangelist. These cases of neglected congregations are referred to as examples of failure. They oppose now the most formidable obstacle in the way of lifting up the cause into new life.

There is an old Latin proverb which teaches that "it is right to learn, even of an enemy." Other religious bodies could have taught us wisdom, if we had not spurned every thing that the fingers of "sectarianism" had touched. Perhaps it would have been no less wise to have taken a few hints from their management than it is now for us to gather up the needed lessons from a retrospect of our own. Some twenty-eight years ago Episcopacy set its eye on a community within the limits of my labors. That cause was, in all respects, feeble. The Presbyterian, Congregational, and other forms of belief, cried out: "If a

39

fox go up upon it, he shall even break down their stone wall." The reproach passed unheeded. Every year, not one excepted, the bishop of Ohio has made his parochial visit to this feeble parish. Scarcely has he once failed to "confirm" new members of the body. The interests of that cause have been looked after with a vigilance reflecting credit to that people; and, it now stands as a monument of their undeviating perseverance. Is it an evidence of strength in Episcopacy? would it be a proof of weakness in us to adopt a similar policy? Is it strength there and weakness here? Is it surprising that intelligent, discerning citizens, casting about for a "home," turn from a people where they see evidences of looseness in plan, and weakness in system, and yield themselves up in membership to organized bodies who conduct their enterprises systematically and successfully? Our gospel has won many friends who have been lost to us through feebleness of plan and want of system.

It would be neither wise nor just to heap reproaches, as is the habit of some, upon the fathers and pioneers of our religious work, for the misdirected efforts of the early part of our history. This wisdom to direct could be learned only by experience. And this skillful adjustment of materials could be made only when there were materials to adjust and to manage. But on us, the factors of this age, will justly rest reproach, if with the past as a lesson, we do not see where to improve. Still more, if seeing, we refuse, on account of willfulness or indifference, to rectify our errors and to labor for reform in our methods.

IV. THE WANT OF RECORDS.

In the opening of our plea on the Western Reserve the iconoclast was among us. He wrought for us, though in a far less honorable sense, the work which Goethe said was accomplished by Lord Bacon. "He took a sponge and wiped from the tablet all records of former knowledge."

The cry ran—clear away the rubbish, that the foundations of the Lord's house may be laid. Reformation is one thing, demolition another, and restoration still another. Discrimination did not well rule the hour. No records were kept after 1828. Some of the churches thought it a violation of this reformation to have any records whatever, even a list of the names of the members. There was no authority for it in the word of the Lord. "Where the Scriptures speak, we speak ; where they are silent, we are silent." The noblest of rules ; but, applied to mere prudentials, most egregiously misapplied. So, as the Scriptures gave no instructions about church records the whole matter was ruled out of order, and out of the church.

Alas! what has been lost by this misdirected zeal! The zeal was good, but the wisdom was the essence of folly. What would we not give now for a continuance of the records of the Mahoning Association, which met two years under that name after the records ceased ? Why were there no records of our yearly meetings ? What rich and abundant materials for future history and instruction?

Who can tell us, from historic data, even now correctly, about our debates, and the mighty campaigns which have given us so many communities for Jesus Christ? Who now, from any preserved records, can tell the history of Henry, that swift messenger of the glad tidings? In vain we question records for an account of his conversion, his baptism, and how he came forth from being a driver of oxen and a bugler for regiments, to become a leader in the embattled hosts of the armies of the living God. And Brockett, the blessed; and Smith, the saint; and Collins, the colleague of the honorable!

In these pages, personal knowledge and gathered data have, in part, supplied this lack. But this source of information is, with the passing generation, rapidly going down to the dumb grave; the silent receptacle of all things human.

The scribe was a man of high authority among the Jews, a little vain, and a sweep of his robe somewhat too ample. The horn of oil made the nation jubilant when it was emptied in the consecration of a priest or a king. But the horn of ink has made many nations joyful by its recitals of their deeds, and its transmissions of their jubilees.

Oh, that Scott had kept a diary! that our earlier men had written as well as talked! Thanks to Baxter, whose skill and zeal have evoked from the tomb of the mighty, a history distinguished both for its beauty and its truth. Of what infinite embarrassment would he have been relieved by contemporaneous records!

The historic muse prepared his reed to sing the illustrious deeds of the panoplied pioneers, not in verse, but in plain and humble prose. Yet the prose should fall little below the powers of the loftiest muses, to record in fitting terms the grand anthem of their heroism and their triumph. Shall the next generation find this one as barren of records as we find the past?

V. Once more. All our past history proclaims the necessity of a combination of effort to advance the gospel.

This cause originated in conventional effort. After three years these associational plans were laid aside, and we subsided, on this point, into a state of apostasy. During the last twenty years we have been slowly recovering and steadily returning to our first works. In August, 1827, ministers of the gospel assembled in New Lisbon, selected an evangelist, and sent him into the field. This action gave us Walter Scott. In 1828, the churches were again represented by delegation in Warren. This convention chose and sent out Walter Scott and William Hayden. In 1829, the association repeated its work, sending into the evangelical field four men—Scott, Hayden, Bentley, and Bosworth.

On this concert of action, the following observations deserve particular mention:

1st, These evangelists were selected and sent out by the ministry of the church, acting in their delegated capacity.

2d, This joint action was threefold:

(*a*) They selected ministers, or proclaimers of the gospel;

(*b*) They appointed their fields of labor;

(*c*) They arranged for their compensation.

3d, The churches felt bound by the action of their delegates. They received the evangelists, and by contributions and other material ways they assisted and co-operated in their work.

It should be farther noted, that Bro. Campbell was the prime mover and the active leader in this scheme of associational effort to bring an evangelist into the field. This movement was conducted with the most perfect unanimity, not a dissentient in that body. It was the action of the soundest, wisest, most deliberative, and prudent men.

The twenty years succeeding is the period of our anarchy. During this time we had no concert, regular or irregular, stated or incidental, if we except some ineffectual efforts to bring a better order into existence. The great saving power was the yearly meeting system. This, serving as a bond of union, was a powerful support to the cause. These meetings were the conservation of the churches. They were aggressive, adding multitudes of converts. By diffusing a general, personal acquaintance, they cultivated a strong tie of brotherhood. Yet with all their benefits, which were neither few nor weak, they were not organic. They sent out no missionaries; they called for no reports; they performed no action for the churches, nor for the systematic diffusion of the gospel. They came as a cloud with blessings, poured out their treasure of good, and departed.

During these years many attempts were made to form co-operations. They were failures. The cry of priest-craft, or sectarianism, was alone sufficient to blast the effort for order.

The first fact, or action, which gathered to it a general confidence, was the establishment of the Eclectic Institute. It opened its halls for students in

November, 1850. Slowly at first, amid doubts and opposition, it got under way. It gained rapidly, and won the confidence of all the brotherhood in north-eastern Ohio. The chief glory of that institution has not been told : which was, that it created a most desirable and useful general confidence among us. We united. We joined hands around one good enterprise. The purpose succeeded, and vindicated the most useful sentiment of union in action. May this lesson never be lost. As the noble Eclectic Institute, of many happy memories, has not died, but has succeeded in a still more noble and useful Institution, our beloved Hiram College—long may it prosper—so let this general unity of confidence, to which it gave birth, grow into all that is desirable in the formation of all needful plans to send forth the gospel as at the beginning of our blessed work. This confidence is transferring itself to our missionary work. Around this society let it rally till it shall become a permanent power in the land!

VI. Last, but not Least.

As this blessed cause, so dear to our hearts, has maintained itself in all vicissitudes, has braved all opposition, and still flourishes with little combination among its leaders, will our forty years' experience, if questioned, speak out and tell us the reason? I answer most unequivocally, it will. Its answer is in 2 Tim. 4 : 1, 2. " ——— preach the word!" This is the only solution. This answer is complete.

Ask the blessed dead, they will tell you ; the Applegates, the Altons, the Bosworths, the Bracketts, and the Bentleys ; the Collins, the Clapps ; the Haydens,

the Henrys, and the Smiths ; the Otises, the Waits,
and the Violls. They preached the gospel. They
were no mere essayists. They were not theorizers,
nor speculatists. They preached Christ and him
crucified. In this they were a unit. The same gospel was preached in every town, county, and school
district. They used their Bibles. They read, quoted,
illustrated, and enforced the Holy Scriptures. This
lesson is all important. We must "preach the word,"
not something about the gospel, but the gospel itself.
Some of our preachers should sit at the feet of the
departed veterans, and learn to speak and enforce
Bible themes in Bible words. Let us have more
Scripture, in its exact meaning and import ; more
gospel, more of Jesus, his will, his mission, and his
work. This was their power. It will be ours. Most
of all, and last of all, we impress this lesson : preach
the gospel in season, out of season. Preach it as
Peter preached, as Paul preached it. Be not weak,
nor ashamed of its facts, commands, and promises,
as delivered to us by our fathers ; and to them by the
holy apostles.

CHAPTER XXIV.

AN ABBREVIATED ACCOUNT OF CHURCHES OMITTED, OR RECENTLY ORGANIZED.

ALLIANCE, *Stark Co.*—Organized March, 1857, with thirty members, by P. K. Dibble. Elders; Asa Silvers and Elwood Patterson. Deacons; Mathias Hester, H. H. Hubbard, and Edward Pettit. Preachers succeeding Bro. Dibble; A. B. Way, J. Pinkerton, Isaac Errett, J. H. Jones, F. M. Green, E. L. Frazier. Present number, three hundred and thirty-five. Elders; A. W. Coates, J. W. Phillips. Deacons; M. Hester, Saml. Miller, J. C. Sheets, Wm. Watson, J. C. Sutton, J. M. Fogle, G. W. Thornberg.

AUBURN, *Geauga Co.*—Formed April 10, 1841, with twenty-nine members, by A. S. Hayden. R. Granger, overseer; John Brown and Jonathan Burnet, deacons. This church has been aided by most of the preachers. They have a good house, and continue to meet.

BAZETTA, WEST, *Trumbull Co.*—Organized December 16, 1848, by Calvin Smith, with forty members. Levi Bush and Alden Faunce, overseers; Ellis Pierce, Jas. Sage, and Jacob Dice, deacons. This church has received help from most of the preachers. Present elders; Hiram Wilber, Milo Crawford. Deacons; Jacob Shaffer, John Wier, and Jas. Wier. One hundred and four members.

BIRMINGHAM, *Erie Co.*—Began in 1829, by Clapp and Rigdon, under whose influence Elder Orrin Abbott led the chief part of the Baptist church of Henrietta into the reformation. Hayden, Moss, Green, and Moody, followed up the work. Church was reorganized July, 1841, with Almon Andress and D. B. Turner, elders; and Silas Wood, Abner Hancock, and Wm. Parker, deacons. Other leading helps; John Cyrenius, B. Alton, W. O'Connor, J. Encell, and R. G. White.   Bro. G. W. Mapse, of Illinois, arose in this church.

BROOKFIELD, *Trumbull Co.*—The ground was broken as early as 1828 by Hayden, Henry, and Hartzel.   A church was formed there February 22, 1875, with thirty-three names.   Deacons, Robert S. Hart and Henry Hamilton.   Present number, fifty-eight.   Arnold Taylor, Henry L. Patterson, and Jesse Hoagland, overseers.

BRISTOL, NORTH, *Trumbull Co.*—In 1860, H. Reeves baptized twenty-eight.   In 1868, J. N. Smith added fifty-five, when by him and N. N. Bartlett, the church was organized with ninety-two members.   The elders were Hiram Thayer and A. A. House.   The deacons : Jacob Sager and S. A. Davidson.   A live church with a good house.   Dr. I. A. Thayer and D. P. Thayer, preachers, arose here.   E. Wakefield has been a chief support of the church.

CAMDEN, *Lorain Co.*—Organized May 21, 1842, with five names; John Cyrenius, elder.   Established in Kipton, November 27, 1872, with thirty-eight.   Daniel Kingsbury and R. C. Eastman, elders ; deacons, H. H. Crandall and James Van Dusen.   Present number one hundred and thirty-four.   Officers : James Van Dusen, Wm. Anderson, and Hiram Prentice, elders ; deacons, H. H. Crandall, Chauncey Close, Wm. Douglass, and Frank Danzy.   Pastor, James Vernon.

CHESTER, *Geauga Co.*—At the instance of W. A. Lillie and A. Harper, Bro. Hartzel came in October, 1842, when the meetings began and continued.   Reorganized October, 1852, by C. Smith and A. L. Soule.   Alonzo Matthews, overseer ; Cyrus Millard and A. Scott, deacons.   A. Burns, W. A. Lillie, and J. G. Coleman, efficient helps.   Present officers : C. Millard, A. Harper, and C. H. Welton, elders ; Porter Scott and Albert Phinney, deacons.   About forty members.

DENMARK, *Ashtabula Co.*—Planted January, 1857, by Orrin Gates. It had sixteen members; S. S. Chapman and D. G. White, overseers.   This body dissolved in a few years, but it lives in its representatives.   Four preachers came from it, viz.: S. S. Chapman, and the three brothers H. J. White, D. J. White, and R. G. White.

EDINBURG, *Portage Co.*—In 1865, a church of thirty members was planted here by S. S. Chapman, with Wm. Cowell and Cyrus

Turnbull, elders; and Jesse Rogers and George Stump, deacons. Succeeding helps: E. Wakefield, F. M. Green, B. A. Baker, D. C. Hanselman. Present number sixty-five. Linas Rogers, preacher. Three preachers, brothers, have arisen here, viz.: Edwin Rogers, Linas Rogers, and W. H. Rogers, sons of Jesse Rogers.

ELYRIA, *Lorain Co.*—It began in the tour of Clapp and Rigdon in 1829. Wm. Hayden soon came, followed by Green, Moody, and Jones. Church formed in 1832. It increased till there were forty members. Chief men: Herrick Parker, H. Reddington, Asahel Parmly, Dr. Butler. It expired by removals. J. D. Benedict came into the work here, leaving the bar to plead the gospel, in which he won many converts, and a wide reputation.

FAIRFIELD, NORTH, *Huron Co.*—At the request of Ezra Leonard, A. B. Green came July 4, 1835. In 1836 he returned, accompanied by J. J. Moss, when the church began, with Jonas Leonard and ———— McLain, elders. W. A. Lillie, Dana Call, and Wm. Dowling, continued the work. In 1854 the church was organized in North Fairfield with over thirty members, by the lamented Henry Dixon, whose preaching created a wide and profound interest. Many also united under the preaching of A. Burns. Present elders: Isaiah Cline, D. H. Reed, and Bro. Culbertson.

FOWLER, *Trumbull Co.*—Started January, 1832, with thirty members, by J. Applegate, assisted by A. S. Hayden. Early evangelists; Wm. Hayden, Bosworth, and Allerton. Reorganized March, 1851, by C. Smith and J. T. Phillips, with thirty-five members. Elders, A. W. Porter and Milo Dugan; deacons, J. L. Jones, Menville Tyrrell. Succeeding elders, A Humeston, Chas. Fowler, H. C. Williamson, and David Campbell. Deacons following: Hiram Porter, James McCleery, Alex Campbell, Addison Dawson, Jasper Kingsley. Present officers; A. Dawson, Lewis Alderman, Menville Tyrrell, overseers; N. C. Fisk and S. J. Rand, deacons.

GENEVA, *Ashtabula Co.*—Formed October 17, 1868, with thirty-four members, under the auspices of the Ohio Missionary Society. Present, R. R. Sloan, Isaac Errett, A. S. Hayden; elders, A. S. Turney, Edward Brakeman; deacons, E. D. Gage, F. C. Baur, and H. N. Amidon. Present elders, A. S. Turney and

Frederick Dickinson; deacons, D. Foot and H. Saunders. Number of members, one hundred and fifty-seven.

HAMDEN, *Geauga Co.*—This church originated in the labors of Rigdon and Collins. By the latter it was formed in 1829. Geo. Hale, overseer; John Bartholomew, deacon. Sustained chiefly by Thos. Campbell, Clapp, and Collins. In 1848 there were yet twenty-four members. Sometime after this it ceased to meet.

HUNTSBURG, *Geauga Co.*—It arose in 1829, by the labors of Hayden, Henry, Collins, and Saunders. Brethren Howells, Chapin Moss, Brackett, and Clarke, stood long and firmly on the ground. In 1848 they enrolled still twenty-three members. Lillie, A. P. Jones, Robison, and White, have also rendered important service there. A number of members still hold the house, and represent the church.

HAMILTON'S CORNERS, *Medina Co.*—This congregation arose in the labors of J. Encell. It was organized by A. B. Green, July 23, 1871, with thirty-six members. The overseers are S. T. Adams and Chas. Kenyon; W. H. Floyd and O. Birchard, deacons. Brethren Moody, Gibbs, and I. A. Searles, have been helps. Present number, sixty-three.

HARTSGROVE, *Ashtabula Co.*—Formed November, 1854, by C. Smith and O. Gates. J. Bartholomew a frequent aid. Leading members; A. Watson, N. Hubbard, I. Y. McKinney, and Edward Lee. Present number, sixty-five.

HARTFORD, *Trumbull Co.*—Began in the labors of Hayden and M. Bosworth. Formed May 1, 1830, by Hayden, with twenty-two members. Geo. W. Bushnell, overseer; Elihu Bates, deacon. In 1838, Alex. Spears was chosen elder; and John Bates, deacon. Orris Mason, J. B. Jones, Sam'l Bates, and Abner Banning, have also served as deacons. Present overseers, G. W. Bushnell and James Fowler. Number, fifty.

HINKLEY, *Medina Co.*—Organized February, 1870, with fifty-four members at the close of a successful meeting held by R. Moffett. Dr. G. S. Gillett and Geo. E. Weber, elders; John Mussen, Lewis Finch (now deceased), C. J. Green, and Rich'd Dunham, deacons. H. N. Allen preached four years there; now H. B. Cox. A good church property.

HOWLAND, *Trumbull Co.*—In 1828 there arose a church in Howland, supported mostly by the brothers Drake, a noble family of devoted Christians, and Zephaniah Luce, Lewis Heaton, and other families. It is dear for the faithfulness of its members, and for the labors of all the early preachers; the Campbells, Scott, Bentley, Hayden, Henry, Bosworth, Hartzel, and *many* others. The church holds the ground still for the Lord.

JACKSON, NORTH, *Trumbull Co.*—Planted in the fall of 1852, by C. Smith, with fifty persons. • Reorganized May 23, 1874, by H. D. Carlton, with thirty-four members. Elders, W. B. Dean and Joseph Pierce; deacons, Jas. Russell, Geo. Shively, and Christian Shively. Mary Shively, Mary Anthony, and Belinda Kirkpatrick, are the deaconesses. Present number, forty.

LITTLE MOUNTAIN, *Lake Co.*—Organized by D. Otis, April 6, 1843. Forty-seven members. D. Otis and E. J. Ferris were the overseers; Wm. T. Rexford and Chas. Tuttle, deacons. It survived the death of its founder, the zealous Dexter Otis, a few years. In December, 1857, it ceased to meet, and the members united with contiguous churches.

MIDDLEBURY, *Summit Co.*—Started March 30, 1875, with ninety members, under the labors of R. G. White, aided by H. J. White, who is in charge of the church, with Dr. M. Jewett and Almon Brown, as associate elders, and T. H. Botsford and Geo. F. Kent, deacons.

MONTVILLE, *Geauga Co.*—Dr. Lucius A. Baldwin solicited O. Gates to come, who added fifteen, and organized the church, February 12, 1860, with seventeen. Dr. Baldwin and John Murray, overseers; Steven Case, first deacon. The church prospered. Anson Shaw, superintendent of the Bible-school. Meetings have been held by Gates, Burns, R. G. White, Hanselman, Ingram, Wakefield, and Thayer. N. P. Lawrence is their preacher.

MORGAN, (ROCK CREEK,) *Ashtabula Co.*—Church formed May 4, 1874, with over a hundred members. The elders are M. Bretell, D. S. Bacheldor, and H. Pifer; deacons, J. Knowlton, D. R. Phillips, H. Moses, and V. D. Latimer. They have an active Sunday-school, and a valuable house, for which they owe much to the liberality of Mrs. Randall.

NILES, *Trumbull Co.*—In 1842, H. Brockett and J. Henry built up the church with 90. Joshua Carle and A. J. Luse were the first elders; Lewis Heaton, Abner Fenton, and Jacob Robinson, were deacons. Present officers: Benjamin Leach and L. L. Campbell, overseers. Bro. H. Baldwin served 24 years—recently deceased; deacons, H. J. Mason, Lewis Reel, and Stephen Dunlap. Present membership, one hundred. N. N. Bartlett, pastor.

NORTON, *Medina Co.*—This arose from the church in Wadsworth. It was organized in 1837. It had about twenty members. A. B. Green and Gad Bronson, overseers; John Bunnell and Ananias Derthick, deacons. The Bennetts, E. Spicer, C. Beckwith, S. Tyler, Philander and Calvin Green, were leading members. It continued till 1863. P. Green arose here, and also L. L. Carpenter, of Indiana.

ORANGE, NORTH, *Cuyahoga Co.*—Formed by A. S. Hayden and M. N. Warren, June 28, 1845, with fifteen members. It increased to about seventy. The elders from the first were Wm. T. Hutchinson, Ira Rutherford, Selah Shirtliff, Silas Y. Dean, Wm. Shelden and Allen Tibbitts; deacons, Ira Rutherford, Allen Tibbitts, Wm. Shelden, Marcus Lindsley, Henry Halsted, Luther Battles, Jr., and Addison Hoose. After twenty years of useful history, emigration, the foe of churches, ended its existence.

ORANGE, SOUTH.—Planted March 2, 1845, by Bentley and Wm. Hayden. It had seventeen members. Amos Boynton and Zenas Smith were the overseers; W. A. Lillie, M. N. Warren, and Solyman Hubbell, were useful helps.

RUSSELL, *Geauga Co.*—In 1841, Wm. Hayden began preaching here. In the fall of 1842, W. A. Lillie came. The "first fruits" were reaped by Hayden, June 10, 1843, in four converts. Others were baptized by Lillie. The church was formed with fifteen members, by Chas. F. Bartlett. A. L. Myron, and Benj. Soule, the Robisons, with Lillie, S. Robinson, and Matthews, were chief members. The church was built up, first by Hayden, Bentley, and Lillie; then by C. Smith, I. Errett, and Jones; later by A. Burns and J. G. Coleman. Elder S. R. Willard united here from the Baptists. In this church H. W. Everest, late Prest. of Eureka College,

now of Kentucky University, was ordained by A. Bentley and
Isaac Errett, April 18, 1855. W. B. Hendryx began here his
useful career.

SOUTHINGTON, *Trumbull Co.*—An old, stable church. Most of the
Baptists accepted the principles of reform, when this congregation started in 1828, under T. Campbell,—by whom Sam'l
Haughton was baptized,—and Scott and Applegate. It has
always kept the light burning, and now numbers about one
hundred. Present elders: Wm. Bronson, Wm. Haughton,
and Harvey McCorkle; deacons, Henry A. Haughton, and
Charles Wannemaker, who is clerk.

SOLON, *Cuyahoga Co.*—This church has a rich history. It arose by
the labors of W. Hayden and A. Bentley, when S. Norton, H.
Baldwin, S. D. Kelley, L. S. Bull, C. Jewett, and others
moved in from Aurora. The church was reorganized, November 29, 1841, by M. L. Wilcox. Simon Norton, S. D. Kelley,
elders; Henry Baldwin, C. Jewett, and L. S. Bull, deacons.
In March, 1842, E. Williams held a meeting, when J. M.
Hickox and wife, and many others united. Most of the preachers have held successful meetings here—Jones, Green, Hartzel, and Perky. As regular supplies, Garfield, Everest, Hinsdale, Hill; present pastor, C. M. Hemry. Chief men in later
times, C. B. Lockwood and E. C. Parmlee. Present number, one hundred and fifty.

THOMPSON, *Geauga Co.*—Formed January 1, 1848, by E. J. Benjamin, with thirty names. Jacob Norman and Simon Baur,
elders; Paul Baur and Hiram Stevens, deacons. Bro. O. Gates
was a frequent and efficient help, by whom many were added;
also H. Reeves, E. Wakefield, and J. W. Errett. Later, J. G.
Encell, R. G. White, J. W. James, Bartlett, Ingram and
Cook. Present number, seventy, with Chas. W. Foot and
Simon Baur, elders; and Paul Baur, Lewis Keener, and Henry
Malin, deacons.

TRUMBULL, EAST, *Ashtabula Co.*—October, 1858, Bro. Gates, assisted by J. G. Encell, held a meeting here, ending with
twenty-eight conversions, when the church started with forty-
five names. Wm. Nelson was elder; and Harvey Curtiss, deacon. H. Reeves and J. Bartholomew, were cooperating
preachers.

WARRENSVILLE, *Cuyahoga Co.*—The Mormons having made inroads here, A. Bentley, following them up, rescued several, and baptized Mrs. Louisa Hubbell, in May, 1831. The church was set up by Wm. Hayden and J. J. Moss. Isaac Moore was a leading member. The brethren of Newburg and Cleveland met with them. Soon Solyman Hubbell and A. T. Hubbell were appointed elders. Moses Warren, baptized at the yearly meeting in Newburg, 1835, was a deacon and an elder. In December, 1842, a meeting was held by Collins, Alton, and A. S. Hayden, resulting in forty-nine conversions. In September, 1843, a great yearly meeting was held there by Hartzel, E. A. Smith, of Ky., and eleven other preachers. The church flourished many years, till it was dismembered by death and removals.

WILLOUGHBY, *Lake Co.*—The members on Waite Hill and about Willoughby were congregated as a church in that town, September 28, 1873, under the auspices of the O. S. Miss. Society, R. R. Sloan and A. S. Hayden officiating. Elders, A. B. Green and W. A. Lillie; deacons, H. H. Hall and H. J. Randall. It began with thirty-nine names. Present number, eighty. It has a good Sunday School, and is flourishing under the charge, as preacher, of A. B. Green.

SULLIVAN, *Ashland Co.*—The church in Sullivan was established through the agency of Sylvanus Parmly and his amiable family. He was a gentleman of much intelligence and weight of influence in the county. He and his family learned the gospel in Elyria. In the year 1832, having moved to Sullivan, he opened meetings. At his instance Wm. Hayden came; his singing and sermons won the people, and fourteen were associated as a church. A fiery opposition, cruel in its perversions of truth, assailed the work, but it was nobly defended by the intelligent sisters as well as the brethren. Moss, Green and Moody, heroically seconded their efforts; John Henry held there successful meetings, as did also John Reed and James Porter. In June, 1838, under Bro. Reed's labors, J. P. Mann and Milo Carlton, now of Kansas, with many others, turned to the Lord. Bro. Moody and G. W. Lucy conducted a meeting which resulted in bringing in twenty-seven converts. M. L. Wilcox gave powerful support to the cause. All these brethren and others, especially the first named, watered the seed sown, and on that field many ripe sheaves have been reaped by the Lord of the harvest. Few churches have been more severely tried, yet it still keeps its light burning.

INDEX.

Religion in America
Series II

An Arno Press Collection

Adler, Felix. **Creed and Deed:** A Series of Discourses. New York, 1877.

Alexander, Archibald. **Evidences of the Authenticity, Inspiration, and Canonical Authority of the Holy Scriptures.** Philadelphia, 1836.

Allen, Joseph Henry. **Our Liberal Movement in Theology:** Chiefly as Shown in Recollections of the History of Unitarianism in New England. 3rd edition. Boston, 1892.

American Temperance Society. **Permanent Temperance Documents of the American Temperance Society.** Boston, 1835.

American Tract Society. **The American Tract Society Documents,** 1824-1925. New York, 1972.

Bacon, Leonard. **The Genesis of the New England Churches.** New York, 1874.

Bartlett, S[amuel] C. **Historical Sketches of the Missions of the American Board.** New York, 1972.

Beecher, Lyman. **Lyman Beecher and the Reform of Society:** Four Sermons, 1804-1828. New York, 1972.

[Bishop, Isabella Lucy Bird.] **The Aspects of Religion in the United States of America.** London, 1859.

Bowden, James. **The History of the Society of Friends in America.** London, 1850, 1854. Two volumes in one.

Briggs, Charles Augustus. **Inaugural Address and Defense,** 1891-1893. New York, 1972.

Colwell, Stephen. **The Position of Christianity in the United States,** in Its Relations with Our Political Institutions, and Specially with Reference to Religious Instruction in the Public Schools. Philadelphia, 1854.

Dalcho, Frederick. **An Historical Account of the Protestant Episcopal Church, in South-Carolina,** from the First Settlement of the Province, to the War of the Revolution. Charleston, 1820.

Elliott, Walter. **The Life of Father Hecker.** New York, 1891.

Gibbons, James Cardinal. **A Retrospect of Fifty Years.** Baltimore, 1916. Two volumes in one.

Hammond, L[ily] H[ardy]. **Race and the South:** Two Studies, 1914-1922. New York, 1972.

Hayden, A[mos] S. **Early History of the Disciples in the Western Reserve, Ohio;** With Biographical Sketches of the Principal Agents in their Religious Movement. Cincinnati, 1875.

Hinke, William J., editor. **Life and Letters of the Rev. John Philip Boehm:** Founder of the Reformed Church in Pennsylvania, 1683-1749. Philadelphia, 1916.

Hopkins, Samuel. **A Treatise on the Millennium.** Boston, 1793.

Kallen, Horace M. **Judaism at Bay:** Essays Toward the Adjustment of Judaism to Modernity. New York, 1932.

Kreider, Harry Julius. **Lutheranism in Colonial New York.** New York, 1942.

Loughborough, J. N. **The Great Second Advent Movement:** Its Rise and Progress. Washington, 1905.

M'Clure, David and Elijah Parish. **Memoirs of the Rev. Eleazar Wheelock, D.D.** Newburyport, 1811.

McKinney, Richard I. **Religion in Higher Education Among Negroes.** New Haven, 1945.

Mayhew, Jonathan. **Observations on the Charter and Conduct of the Society for the Propagation of the Gospel in Foreign Parts;** Designed to Shew Their Non-conformity to Each Other. Boston, 1763.

Mott, John R. **The Evangelization of the World in this Generation.** New York, 1900.

Payne, Bishop Daniel A. **Sermons and Addresses,** 1853-1891. New York, 1972.

Phillips, C[harles] H. **The History of the Colored Methodist Episcopal Church in America:** Comprising Its Organization, Subsequent Development, and Present Status. Jackson, Tenn., 1898.

Reverend Elhanan Winchester: Biography and Letters. New York, 1972.

Riggs, Stephen R. **Tah-Koo Wah-Kan; Or, the Gospel Among the Dakotas.** Boston, 1869.

Rogers, Elder John. **The Biography of Eld. Barton Warren Stone, Written by Himself:** With Additions and Reflections. Cincinnati, 1847.

Booth-Tucker, Frederick. **The Salvation Army in America:** Selected Reports, 1899-1903. New York, 1972.

Satolli, Francis Archbishop. **Loyalty to Church and State.** Baltimore, 1895.

Schaff, Philip. **Church and State in the United States** or the American Idea of Religious Liberty and its Practical Effects with Official Documents. New York and London, 1888. (Reprinted from *Papers of the American Historical Association,* Vol. II, No. 4.)

Smith, Horace Wemyss. **Life and Correspondence of the Rev. William Smith, D.D.** Philadelphia, 1879, 1880. Two volumes in one.

Spalding, M[artin] J. **Sketches of the Early Catholic Missions of Kentucky;** From Their Commencement in 1787 to the Jubilee of 1826-7. Louisville, 1844.

Steiner, Bernard C., editor. **Rev. Thomas Bray:** His Life and Selected Works Relating to Maryland. Baltimore, 1901. (Reprinted from *Maryland Historical Society Fund Publication,* No. 37.)

To Win the West: Missionary Viewpoints, 1814-1815. New York, 1972.

Wayland, Francis and H. L. Wayland. **A Memoir of the Life and Labors of Francis Wayland, D.D., LL.D.** New York, 1867. Two volumes in one.

Willard, Frances E. **Woman and Temperance:** Or, the Work and Workers of the Woman's Christian Temperance Union. Hartford, 1883.